THE MYSTERY
OF THE SUPERNATURAL

THE MYSTERY OF THE SUPERNATURAL

Henri de Lubac, S.J.

Translated by Rosemary Sheed

Introduction by David L. Schindler

A Crossroad Herder Book
The Crossroad Publishing Company
New York

The Crossroad Publishing Company
370 Lexington Avenue, New York, NY 10017

Originally published under the title *Le mystère du surnaturel*
© 1965 F. Aubier, Editions Montaigne, Paris
English translation copyright © 1967 by Geoffrey Chapman Ltd.
New materials copyright © 1998 by The Crossroad Publishing Company

Nihil obstat: R. D. Jacobus P. Wroe, D.D., Ph.D., censor deputatus

Imprimatur: H. Gibney, Vicarius Generalis

Datum Southwarci de 8a Maii 1967

Printed in the United States of America

Library of Congress Cataloging-in-Publication Data

Lubac, Henri de, 1896–
    [Mystère du surnaturel. English]
    The mystery of the supernatural / Henri de Lubac ; translated by
Rosemary Sheed ; introduction by David L. Schindler.
       p.   cm.
    "A Crossroad Herder book."
    Includes bibliographical references and index.
    ISBN 0-8245-1699-0 (pbk.)
    1. Supernatural (Theology).   2. Man (Christian theology).
3. Catholic Church—Doctrines. I. Title.
BT745.L813   1998
233—dc21   97-42442
                                        CIP

1   2   3   4   5   6   7   8   9   10   02   01   00   99   98

*This book is dedicated as a token of gratitude to
Father Gerard Smith, S.J., of Marquette University*

Ea quae non videntur, fide quaerimus.

Paschasius Radbertus

Weighed down with the deposits of five centuries, scholasticism suffers most seriously from ignorance of itself. To revive it, let us listen to the advice of history: Return to theology!

Etienne Gilson

. . . From excess of reverence, we should not have ventured to listen, or give utterance to any truths of Divine philosophy, were it not that we are convinced in our mind that such knowledge of Divine Truth as is possible must not be disregarded. This conviction was wrought within us, not only by the natural impulse of our minds, which yearn and strive for such vision of supernatural things as may be attained, but also by the holy ordinance of Divine Law itself, which, while it bids us not to busy ourselves in things beyond us because such things are both beyond our merits and also unattainable, yet earnestly exhorts us to learn all things within our reach, which are granted and allowed us, and also generously to impart these treasures unto others. In obedience to these behests we, ceasing not through weariness or want of courage in such search for Divine Truth as is possible. . . .

Pseudo-Dionysius
On the Divine Names, III, 3.
(translation by C.E. Rolt
[London: S.P.C.K., 1940])

Contents

A Note on the New Edition

This book reproduces the translation of the French text by Rosemary Sheed. In addition, however, unlike the previous English edition, this new edition provides translations of the many Latin quotations by John M. Pepino. As an aid to the scholar, the numbers in the margins indicate the page numbers in the original 1965 French text.

Introduction to
the 1998 Edition

In his first book, *Catholicisme,* Henri de Lubac states: "By revealing the Father and by being revealed by him, Christ completes [*achève*] the revelation of man to himself." If this statement has a familiar ring, it is because it turns up in virtually the same form some twenty-five years later, in the well-known paragraph twenty-two of *Gaudium et spes.*[1] The statement points us toward the unifying concern at the heart of de Lubac's theology, as well as to the nature of his permanent contribution to the Church and culture. De Lubac's work originated in the face of what may be termed the problem of Catholic theology's exile from modern culture and of the secularism resulting from the mutual estrangement of the Church and the world in the modern period. The key to de Lubac's response to this problem lies in the organic relation between theology (Christology) and anthropology affirmed in the statement.

My purpose in this Introduction is to say a word about the nature of de Lubac's contribution to modern theology and culture, especially in light of *The Mystery of the Supernatural* (*Le mystère du surnaturel,* 1965). My comments fall into four sections: the general theological and historical background to de Lubac's earlier *Surnaturel* (1946); his argument regarding nature and the supernatural; criticisms of the argument; and, finally, the enduring significance of the thesis proposed by de Lubac—and indeed of the whole of his life's work—for the current ecclesial-cultural situation.

---

1. *Catholicisme* (Paris: Editions du Cerf, 1938), 264. English translation: *Catholicism* (San Francisco: Ignatius Press, 1988), 339. To my knowledge, Paul McPartlan was the first to call attention to this near-identity: cf. his "Henri de Lubac—Evangeliser" *Priests & People* (August–September, 1992):344.

Theological and Historical Background

Against the backdrop of his fundamental concern with secularism, de Lubac's work in the years leading up to *Surnaturel* (1946) may be summarized in terms of a double purpose. On the one hand, he wished to diagnose accurately what, from the side of the Church, had accounted for her failure to make genuine contact with the culture. What in the Church's theology had blocked an effective presentation to the modern world of the abundant riches contained in the revelation of Jesus Christ, as understood in the Catholic tradition? On the other hand, and providing the larger context inspiring this analysis, de Lubac attempted to show in what these Catholic riches consisted, and how they answered truly and comprehensively the deepest aspirations of (modern) humanity.

Thus *Catholicisme* (1938), written for Yves Congar's ecclesiological series *Unam Sanctam*, was intended to retrieve "the social aspects of dogma."[2] Against a modern tendency to make the faith into a matter of private piety, this book attempted to exhibit the radically inclusive character of Catholicism, showing how its main doctrines could address humanity in all aspects of its existence. The book considered at great length the universal solidarity among human beings in what concerns their salvation, and the significance of time and history.

Corpus Mysticum (1944) attempted to retrieve the link between the Eucharist and the Church in terms of the notion of the mystical body of Christ.[3] The patristic and medieval periods understood that the physical body of Christ raised from the dead, the "mystical" body of Christ in

2. This book was based on a series of talks given from 1932 onwards. The fact that de Lubac's books are frequently made up of articles written earlier, and subsequently edited, makes the publication dates of these books somewhat misleading. Interesting notes on the circumstances surrounding each of de Lubac's books are provided in his *Mémoire sur l'occasion de mes écrits* (Namur: Culture et Verité, 1989). English translation: *At the Service of the Church* (San Francisco: Ignatius Press, 1993). For a bibliography of de Lubac's writings, see K.H. Neufeld and M. Sales, eds., *Bibliographie H. De Lubac 1925–1974* (Einsiedeln: Johannes Verlag, 1974); idem, "Bibliographie H. De Lubac, corrections et suppléments, 1942–1989," in H. de Lubac, *Théologie dans l'histoire*, vol. 2 (Paris: Desclée de Brouwer, 1990), 408–20. Shorter notes from de Lubac regarding each of his books are also provided in the Neufeld-Sales bibliography cited below, 59–61—as well as a detailed history of the composition of *Catholicisme*, 62.

3. *Corpus Mysticum: Eucharistie et l'Eglise au Moyen Age* (Paris: Aubier-Montaigne, 1944). This book was actually written in the late 1930s, but its publication was delayed by the war.

the Eucharist, and the "true body" (*corpus verum*) of Christ that is the Church brought into being through sharing the Eucharistic body were all intrinsically related. Modern theology had shifted emphasis away from the relation between the Eucharistic body and the ecclesial body to the relation between the Eucharistic body and the physical body. The result was an "individualized" Eucharist, a greatly diminished sense of the essentially social implications of Christ's Eucharistic presence. De Lubac's point—contrary to critics who feared otherwise—was not at all to reduce the importance of the real presence but only to prevent one-sided emphasis on this from disintegrating the Church-Eucharist mystery.

The concerns of *Le Drame de l'humanisme athée* (1944)[4] and *De la connaissance de Dieu* (1945)[5] correlated with one another. The former explores the absence of God that lay at the heart of the contemporary cultural crisis, the latter the implicit presence of God in every act of consciousness, as affirmed by all the great Christian theologians in the patristic and medieval periods—including both Augustine and Aquinas. De Lubac was "convinced that, until the advent of the modern age, all humans were, in one way or another, so religious in outlook that the existence of a world and humanity without God, or something godly, was unthinkable."[6] These two studies exposed the theological roots of the modern problem by showing, in "positive" and "negative" ways, why atheism is fundamentally "unreasonable," hence dehumanizing.

Several other articles during these early decades of de Lubac's professional life indicate the range and unity of his primary intuitions: on "Apologetics and Theology" (1930); "The Authority of the Church in Temporal Matters" (1932); "Patriotism and Nationalism" (1933); "Remarks on the History of the Word, 'Supernatural'" (1934). In a 1936 article, "On Christian Philosophy," de Lubac, finding points of departure in Gabriel Marcel, argued that there is indeed a truly Christian

---

4. *Le Drame de l'humanisme athée* (Paris: Spes, 1944). English translation: *The Drama of Atheist Humanism* (San Francisco: Ignatius Press, 1995). The first part of this book, says de Lubac, was made up of "several disparate articles coming principally from semi-clandestine conferences with an anti-Nazi purpose" (*At the Service of the Church*, 40).

5. *De la connaissance de Dieu* (Paris: Témoignage chrétien, 1945). A greatly expanded version of this book appeared later under a different title: *Sur les chemins de Dieu* (Paris: Aubier-Montaigne, 1956). English translation: *The Discovery of God* (Grand Rapids, Mich.: Eerdmans, 1996).

6. Karl H. Neufeld, "De Lubac, Henri," in R. Latourelle and R. Fisichella, eds., *Dictionary of Fundamental Theology* (New York: Crossroad, 1995), 226.

philosophy, that is, in a sense that could accommodate while integrating the positions of Blondel, Gilson, and Maritain. In a long essay, also in 1936, on "Some Aspects of Buddhism,"[7] de Lubac expressed the conviction that, "with the exception of the unique Fact in which we adore the vestige and the very Presence of God, Buddhism is without doubt the greatest spiritual fact in the history of man."[8] The book treats the basic question regarding the relation between selfless love in Buddhism and *caritas* in Christianity. In the early 1940s, de Lubac published articles that would eventually become the book *Le Fondement théologique des missions.*[9] This book pointed out that the Church not only has an obligation to take up the missionary task, but she is missionary of her proper essence.

In an important article written in 1942, during the Nazi occupation of France, de Lubac reflected on "The Internal Causes of the Attenuation and Disappearance of the Sense of the Sacred."[10] De Lubac identifies four such causes. First, in the encounter between science and faith in modern culture, the Christian thinker's science is often much more fully developed than his or her faith, which often remains childish (as distinct from childlike).[11] Second, a review of theological literature in recent centuries reveals that theology has been too preoccupied with the polemical concern of opposing heresies, with the result that it has not drawn sufficient positive nourishment from the mystery of the faith.[12] The third cause is the separation of nature and the supernatural. De Lubac insists that, although this separation was worked out in order to protect against errors such as Baianism, which tended toward a confusion of the two orders, it was nonetheless something entirely modern, something never canonized in the entire tradition from the Fathers through Aquinas.[13] Fourth and finally, there is the rationalist spirit of those theologians who, like museum curators, can inventory, arrange,

---

7. De Lubac wrote three books on Buddhism: *Aspects du bouddhisme* (Paris: Seuil, 1951) (English translation: *Aspects of Buddhism* [New York: Sheed and Ward, 1954]); *Rencontre du bouddhisme et de l'occident* (Paris: Aubier-Montaigne, 1952); and *Amida: Aspects du bouddhisme II* (Paris: Seuil, 1951).

8. *Aspects du bouddhisme,* 18.

9. *Le Fondement théologique des missions* (Paris: Aubier, 1946).

10. "The Internal Causes of the Attenuation and Disappearance of the Sense of the Sacred," in de Lubac, *Theology in History* (San Francisco: Ignatius Press, 1996), 223–40.

11. Ibid., 225.

12. Ibid., 227.

13. Ibid., 230.

and label everything, and who have answers for all objections—but who have, unfortunately, lost sight of the mystery of the Lord.[14]

This brief survey of de Lubac's writings, while hardly exhaustive,[15] helps to exhibit the fundamental élan inspiring his work. De Lubac had drawn that élan from Joseph Maréchal (1878–1944) and especially Maurice Blondel (1861–1949), as well as from Pierre Rousselot (1878–1915)—though he followed none of them exactly—and he was aided by his dialogue with Gaston Fessard (1897–1978), the philosopher, and Henri Bouillard (1908–81), the fundamental theologian. De Lubac's work is "apologetic" in the deepest and truest sense: within the context of a radical openness to all that is human, his theology shows how the fullness of Catholic dogma reaches to the heart of human reason, or again how the supernatural reaches to the heart of nature. Catholicism, in other words, in its "integral" and not reduced version, opens to and comprehends all that is human—even as, in so doing, it first "converts" and indeed transforms all that is human.

As we shall see, de Lubac never loses sight of the paradoxical nature of the claims indicated here. The paradox consisted in the fact that the Church could best—most comprehensively and profoundly—speak to the heart of modern humanity, not by shrinking her message, but by displaying the beauty of her central Fact in all of its fullness.

The Mystery of the Supernatural

We turn now to the "technical" core of the above concerns and intuitions of de Lubac: the relation between nature and the supernatural. At the heart of his simultaneously Catholic and catholic engagement with secular culture lay the conviction of a radical heterogeneity between nature and the supernatural coincident with an intimate relation between them: because "nature is made for the supernatural"[16]—and because God is more interior to me than I am to myself ("*Deus interior intimo meo*"—St. Augustine). Here, then, we approach the problem that occupied *Surnaturel*.

First of all, as de Lubac himself notes in his *Mémoire,* the language of

---

14. Ibid., 233–34.
15. For example, we touch here not at all de Lubac's lifelong interest in scriptural exegesis, inspired by his reading of theologians of the patristic period. His books in this area begin to appear in the 1950s.
16. "The Internal Causes," 231.

nature and the supernatural is too abstract, and today the question would be framed rather in terms of the relation between human nature and the covenant or the mystery of Christ.[17] The problem in any case is that modern theology had tended to separate the orders of nature and grace, a tendency which expressed itself in the development of a tradition of "separated theology," accompanied by a "separated philosophy." This double separation both promoted and confirmed a growing remoteness of the inner realities of faith from the ordinary—"worldly"— concerns of daily life. A rationalistic "apologetics" had eventually come to stand in the forecourt of specifically Christian doctrines (like the Trinity), even as these doctrines, considered "in themselves," now became just so far "arbitrary" or "irrational"—that is, (relatively esoteric) matters of interest only to Christians.

It is essential to keep this problematic in mind when we consider the technical issues involved in de Lubac's explicit argument on the subject of the supernatural. On the one hand, if grace did not somehow— always already—touch the soul of every human being, the Christian fact would remain an essentially "private" matter of urgent concern only to those who were already believers. On the other hand, if the order of grace were not essentially gratuitous—that is, did not really add something to nature that could not be anticipated or claimed by nature itself—then the Christian fact would lose its newness and its proper character as divine gift. In either case, Christianity would lose its essentially missionary and indeed apologetic impetus: in the former case, men and women would have no good—that is, profound—reason for for *becoming* Christian; and, in the latter case, they would—effectively— *already be* Christian.

(1) De Lubac's thematic in *Surnaturel: Etudes historiques,*[18] then, is

---

17. *At the Service of the Church*, 198–99. De Lubac always uses the adjectival form "supernatural," rather than the noun "supernature," to help against the tendency to think of "nature" and the "supernatural" as two "entities" standing over against or merely alongside each other.

18. *Surnaturel: Etudes historiques* (Paris: Desclée de Brouwer, 1991) (this is a new edition of the 1946 text, with a complete translation into French of all Latin and Greek citations, prepared and prefaced by Michel Sales). For a genetic history of the composition of *Surnaturel*, see the Neufeld-Sales *Bibliographie*, 63–65. For a genetic schema of the publications of de Lubac on the supernatural, see Sales's presentation in *Surnaturel*, xiii–xvi. As de Lubac notes in *At the Service of the Church*, this book had its origin in a study group led by Fr. Joseph Huby that met each Sunday for debate on important issues. "Father Huby, following the line of reflection inaugurated for us by Rousselot, had warmly urged me to

how human persons in the natural order can be interiorly directed to the order of grace that fulfills them, without in the least possessing this grace in anticipation, and without being able at all to claim it for themselves. In this light, the book attempts, fundamentally, to show how what de Lubac calls "the system of pure nature" had come to prevail in Catholic theology. Neither the Fathers nor the great scholastics had ever envisioned the possibility of a purely natural end for human persons attainable by their own intrinsic powers of cognition and volition, some natural beatitude of an order inferior to the intuitive vision of God. For these earlier thinkers, there was only one concrete order of history, that in which God had made humanity for himself, and in which human nature had thus been created only for a single destiny, which was supernatural.

This unified vision began to unravel in the thought of theologians such as Denys the Carthusian (1402–71) and, more pertinently, Cajetan (1468–1534). Although Denys argued for a natural end of the human person to which a supernatural end must be "superadded," he nonetheless did so consciously in opposition to the teaching of St. Thomas. Cajetan, on the other hand, somewhat later in the same century, made the argument rather *in terms of the thought of St. Thomas*, as a commentary on the latter. It was chiefly Cajetan, de Lubac says, who therefore introduced the idea of human nature as "a closed and sufficient whole" into Thomism—or, more precisely, "actually into the exegesis of St. Thomas himself, thus conferring upon it a kind usurped authority."[19]

---

verify whether the doctrine of St. Thomas regarding [the idea of a 'pure nature'] was indeed [that] claimed by the Thomist school around the sixteenth century, codified in the seventeenth century and asserted with greater emphasis than ever in the twentieth" (35). De Lubac published several articles in the 1930s which were to make up much of *Surnaturel*, although he says he had eventually put the study aside for his teaching (35). In June, 1940, having to leave in haste to avoid the Germans who were approaching Lyons, de Lubac carried along a bag that included the notebook for *Surnaturel*, on which he worked for several days. In 1943, being hunted by the Gestapo, de Lubac fled, again carrying his notebook, this time to Vals. Being unable to leave Vals or even to engage in correspondence, he used the resources of the Vals library to do further work on the book. Although the book was not published until 1946 due to the difficult cultural circumstances, de Lubac says the book had taken sufficient shape to be submitted for review already in 1941. The *nihil obstat* was granted in February, 1942, and the *Imprimatur* in October, 1945. When the book finally appeared in 1946, the total printing consisted of 700 copies, since paper was lacking.

19. *The Mystery of the Supernatural*, 146.

The idea of a "pure nature" intensified in the wake of the naturalism of Baius (1513–89) and Jansenius (1585–1638): a state of pure nature—a hypothesis according to which human persons might have been created with an end proportionate to their natural powers—was seen as necessary to protect the gratuity of the supernatural. Affirmation of such a state, argued de Lubac, overlooked the decisive difference between the created human spirit and other natures. Still, he acknowledged, this hypothetical system rendered eminent service to orthodoxy: offering more than a mere denial of the error it opposed, the system provided "a positive explanation whose clarity and apparent logic satisfied the rational needs of the period." It also enabled Catholic theologians to defend the essential integrity of fallen human nature against the Protestantism that denied it. Despite this service, however, the system at the same time effected a separation between nature and the supernatural that would prove pernicious—by rendering the latter (seemingly) superfluous. Although the system of "pure nature" was perceived to be a novelty when first developed, it eventually came to be taken for granted, such that, by the twentieth century, rejecting it became synonymous with denying the gratuity of the supernatural.

Surnaturel is broken into four parts, which are pieced together from a number of earlier preparatory historical studies (hence the subtitle of the book). The first part, entitled "Augustinianism and Baianism," examines the interpretation of Augustine by Baius and Jansenius, showing how these latter misconstrue Augustine's true intention. Influenced by a juridical-naturalistic way of thinking foreign to Augustine (and to his disciples, including Thomas Aquinas), Baius and Jansenius, according to de Lubac, had in their different ways denied the gratuity of the gifts made by God to Adam. De Lubac shows how the hypothesis of "purely natural finality" attributed to a "pure spiritual nature" was developed to insure this gratuity.

The second part of the book, "Spirit and Freedom in the Theological Tradition," turns to an examination of one of the essential aspects of the spiritual "nature" (both human and angelic), namely, its freedom of choice with respect to its end. This second part considers the tradition from the Fathers up to the seventeenth century, and provides further evidence for the claim that Aquinas, for example, never envisioned any finality for the created spirit but a supernatural one.

The third part of the book examines the "origins of the word 'supernatural,'" including the problematic epithet *"superadditum"* ("something superadded"), and the confusion of the "supernatural" with the "miraculous" (in the sense of a completely arbitrary addition). De Lubac shows in this section that the term "supernatural" was first used systematically by St. Thomas.

Finally, *Surnaturel*'s fourth part offers six "Historical Notes" on St. Thomas and his followers: "Natural and Supernatural Desire"; "Immediate Natural Vision"; "Supernatural Beatitude According to St. Thomas"; "What Does St. Thomas Wish to Demonstrate by the Natural Desire to See God?"; "Has St. Thomas Chosen Aristotle?"; "Three Exegeses of the *Desiderium Naturale.*"

In the conclusion, "Divine Exigence and Natural Desire," de Lubac indicates why it is unnecessary to have recourse to the hypothetical system of pure nature to protect the gratuity of the beatific vision. He frames the argument in terms of paradox. This term, which, as we have suggested, is characteristic of de Lubac, is here used by him in its most fundamental meaning as the paradox of the created spirit who desires God essentially, but without demanding anything.[20] A main point on which de Lubac rests his concluding argument concerns God's fundamental intention in creation: that is, God wished to communicate himself as absolute love and to inscribe this wish *of his* in the innermost being of the spiritual creature, so that the creature recognizes therein the "call of God to love." The creature, therefore, instead of making demands itself, stands by its very essence under the "demand" of God always already inscribed in its nature. De Lubac summarizes the import of his thesis strikingly by insisting that we are created not only for our own beatitude but for the glorification of the God of grace and love. Hence the paradox of the human person, for whom "beatitude is service, vision is adoration, freedom is dependence, possession is ecstasy. Thus one who defines our supernatural end by possession, freedom, vision, and beatitude defines only one aspect"—which indeed remains *anthropocentric.*[21]

(2) De Lubac's *Le Mystère du surnaturel,* the book here translated, was published in 1965, along with what he calls its twin, *Augustinisme et*

---

20. De Lubac affirms the paradoxical nature of all ideas "that bear upon the reality of our being in relation to God" (*The Mystery of the Supernatural*, xxxiv).
21. *Surnaturel* (1991), 492.

théologie moderne.[22] The two volumes serve primarily to clarify numerous objections to *Surnaturel,* while separating the historical (*Augustinisme*) and the dogmatic (*Mystère*) problematics. The latter book, he says,

> point by point, in the same order, and without changing the least point of doctrine, the article published under that title in *Recherches* [*de science religieuse*] in 1949;[23] in 1960, as all hope of publishing in France still seemed fanciful, my old friend and colleague Gerard Smith of Marquette University . . . , and Dr. [Anton] Pegis, Director of the Institut d'études médiévales in Toronto, had offered to publish it in America: they took charge of everything: translation, printing, publishing; that is why the book is dedicated to Father Smith. The second, *Augustinisme et théologie moderne,* reproduced with similar fidelity the first part of the old *Surnaturel,* enlarging it with new texts."[24]

The 1949 article to which de Lubac refers here, he says, was intended not to repeat *Surnaturel,* but to complement it. Further, the article was meant not to stand alone but to constitute the second part of a little book, the first part of which would contain precise responses to the objections made to *Surnaturel.*[25] The General of the Jesuits warmly approved its publication, and the censors said that it provided "very salutary clarifications for a better understanding of *Surnaturel.*"[26]

(3) In 1980, de Lubac published a final book directly on the problematic of the nature-supernatural relation: *Petite catéchèse sur nature et*

22. *Augustinisme et théologie moderne* (Paris: Aubier-Montaigne, 1965). English translation: *Augustinianism and Modern Theology* (London: Chapman; New York: Herder & Herder, 1969).

23. "Le Mystère du surnaturel," *Recherches de science religieuse* (1949): 80–121; English translation, "The Mystery of the Supernatural," in *Theology in History* (San Francisco: Ignatius Press, 1996), 281–316. See the note by Michel Sales summarizing the circumstances and issues surrounding this article: 281–82.

24. *At the Service of the Church,* 123. De Lubac notes that he sent copies of the books to Etienne Gilson, and that this elicited three letters from the latter containing strong—and vivid—expressions of support. Cf. *Letters of Etienne Gilson to Henri de Lubac* (San Francisco: Ignatius Press, 1988).

25. *At the Service of the Church,* 62. As part of these responses, de Lubac had written, at the request of his superiors, an "Examination of Theological Conscience, March 6, 1947." This striking statement is printed in full in *At the Service of the Church,* 268–71. It should be noted that, although, as we will see, de Lubac denied that Rome (*Humani Generis*) ever meant to condemn the fundamental claim of *Surnaturel,* he himself—as this 1949 article shows—realized that clarifications were needed, and indeed noted some criticisms of the book himself: cf. *At the Service of the Church,* 198–200. Cf. also *The Mystery of the Supernatural,* 50–52, where Lubac expresses gratitude for criticisms of *Surnaturel,* and acknowledges weaknesses in the book.

26. *At the Service of the Church,* 62.

grace.[27] This book had begun as a short note written at the request of Philippe Delhaye, Secretary of the International Theological Commission, to help the Commission in its work. The note, first published as an article in the French *Communio,* was later expanded and published in book form. The goal of the book, says de Lubac was twofold:

> on the one hand, to summarize the doctrine of the supernatural, such as it emerged from my previous historical studies on the subject, in a simple and up-to-date way . . . ; on the other hand, to complete it with an exposition on grace, the liberator from sin.[28]

Various points of immediate historical-cultural importance are treated in several appendices. Among these points is the question of the use of the term "supernatural" in the documents of the Second Vatican Council. De Lubac notes that, although the term is used only fourteen times in these documents—because the Council generally prefers concrete language[29]—the Council nonetheless maintained the distinction between nature and the supernatural,[30] and consequently defended the gratuity of the vocation to divine communion,[31] but without recourse to the hypothesis of "a purely natural order."[32]

Criticisms

The general history of the reactions to *Surnaturel* is well known.[33] The term "new theology," which came to be associated with the argu-

---

27. *Petite catéchèse sur nature et grace* (Paris: Fayard, 1980). English translation: *A Brief Catechesis on Nature and Grace* (San Francisco: Ignatius Press, 1984).

28. *At the Service of the Church,* 154.

29. Ibid., 178.

30. Ibid., 186.

31. Ibid., 189.

32. See *Brief Catechesis,* 177–90. It should be said in this connection that the charge that de Lubac retreated after the Council to a "reactionary" position, opposite from his pre-conciliar stance, is a misconstrual of the facts. The truth of the matter is that de Lubac maintained a remarkable consistency throughout the whole of his life, even if, as in the case of the nature-supernatural problematic, he saw it necessary to highlight different points in response to different cultural situations. Relative to this problematic, for example, de Lubac was convinced that the pre-conciliar dualism of nature and the supernatural had given way to a post-conciliar tendency to "immanentism." The pertinent point, however, is that de Lubac (consistently) understood both tendencies to give (unconscious) support to "naturalism," albeit from opposite directions.

33. For a sampling of some of the first reactions to *Surnaturel* (including favorable responses from Gerard Smith and Dietrich von Hildebrand), see *At the Service of the Church,* 200–203; for a reprinting of several reviews of the book, see ibid., 203–23; for a

ment of de Lubac, was in fact coined by one of the critics of the book, Father Garrigou-Lagrange.[34] In 1950, de Lubac was asked by the General of the Jesuits to stop teaching and to give up working at *Recherches de science religieuse*.[35] The order was given to withdraw three of his books—*Surnaturel, Corpus Mysticum,* and *De la Connaissance de Dieu*—as well as the volume of *Recherches* containing the article on the "Mystère du surnaturel," from Jesuit libraries (and from the trade).[36] This occurred shortly after the appearance of Pope Pius XII's encyclical, *Humani Generis*. This encyclical is often interpreted as having condemned the main argument of *Surnaturel*. French theologian Michel Sales, however, states: "Contrary to a tenacious legend that continues to circulate . . . , [this] encyclical, far from condemning the views set forth here, ratified them by repeating on its own account one key sentence from [de Lubac's 1949 article on the supernatural]."[37] De Lubac himself notes that, in addition to repeating this sentence, the encyclical likewise did not use the term "'pure nature' that a number of highly placed theologians were accusing [him] of misunderstanding and which they wanted to have canonized."[38] Furthermore, when Pius XII learned through de Lubac's Superiors and the mediation of Cardinal Bea of the continuing criticisms of de Lubac, he had Cardinal Bea send a letter to de Lubac "whose every word he dictated," in which he thanked de Lubac "for the work accomplished up until then" and encouraged him

---

listing of reviews and discussions of *Surnaturel*, see the Neufeld-Sales *Bibliographie*, 85–86; for de Lubac's own discussion of the reaction to the book, see *At the Service of the Church*, 60–79—as well as the extensive documentation (including texts of censures, memoranda containing key dates, and so on) that accompanies this discussion, in Appendix IV, 245–309. On the question of *Humani Generis*, cf. *At the Service of the Church*, 308–9, and also the note of Michel Sales attached to "'The Mystery of the Supernatural,'" *Theology in History*, 281–82.

34. *At the Service of the Church*, 60. The irony is to see how often the proponents of "pure nature" in the sixteenth century were themselves described by contemporaries as *moderniores, recentiores, neoterici*, and so on: cf. Joseph Komonchak, "Theology and Culture at Mid-Century: The Example of Henri de Lubac," *Theological Studies* 51 (1990): 585 n. 21. Komonchak's article offers a good overview of de Lubac's theology in its cultural implications.

35. *At the Service of the Church*, 64. De Lubac notes that he had already stopped teaching in 1940, and had in fact taught only one course formally at Fourvière: in the history of religions, from 1935–1940 (Ibid., 67–68)!

36. Ibid., 74.

37. In de Lubac, *Theology in History*, 281.

38. Cited in Sales's note, Ibid.

about continuing such work since it "promised much fruit for the Church."[39]

In any event, the controversy provoked by the book, as already suggested, concerned especially the question whether its argument implied a confusion of the orders of nature and grace, and hence a denial of the gratuity of the supernatural order. To clarify the argument of *Surnaturel* in response to such criticisms, de Lubac, in his 1949 article, lay "more explicit stress on the 'twofold gratuitousness,' the 'twofold initiative,' or the 'twofold gift' of God" (i.e., creation-elevation).[40]

One of the most thorough and thoughtful critiques of *Surnaturel* was that by Karl Rahner.[41] Rahner agreed with de Lubac's thesis, insofar as it rejected the older "extrinsicism" that made grace into a kind of "accidental" appendage to an already constituted nature. Rahner, however, feared that de Lubac's solution risked fusing the gratuity of creation with the gratuity of God's self-revelation, thereby leveling the orders of nature and grace. To avoid this problem, Rahner proposed his well-known theory of a "supernatural existential" planted by God at the heart of our nature from its creation, but (conceptually) distinct from nature. Given the limits here, I record only the heart of de Lubac's response as indicated in *The Mystery of the Supernatural*:

> to the extent that this "existential" is conceived as a kind of "medium" or "linking reality," one may object that this is a useless supposition, whereby the problem of the relationship between nature and the supernatural is not resolved, but only set aside. (132 n. 2)

The issue between Rahner and de Lubac, then, takes the form of a difference regarding the priority of a "supernatural existential," as distinct from "paradox," as the best way to conceive human persons in their concrete-constitutive relation to God. This difference between the two theologians has played itself out further over the years in terms of controversies such as that concerning the existence and meaning of "anonymous Christianity," whether there is a distinctively Christian

---

39. Ibid. See also *At the Service of the Church*, 88–90: the letter is reproduced on 88–89.

40. *The Mystery of the Supernatural*, 51. De Lubac notes that this 1949 article was "published . . . following upon the approval and encouragement I received from Rome itself."

41. "Eine Antwort," *Orientierung* 14 (Zurich, 1950): 141–45.

ethics, the Church-world relation, and the nature of the missionary task of the Church.

Another implication of the charge that de Lubac had confused the orders of nature and grace was that he thereby also denied the integrity of nature or the natural law.[42] The heart of de Lubac's response to this criticism was that the criticism itself confused the *integrity* of nature with a (would-be) *purity* of nature. For the pertinent point is that the legitimate (and, on a Catholic understanding, necessary) integrity of nature is to be found only *within* and *not outside* the existential conditions of the one concrete order of history, hence only as always-already affected by both grace and sin. This response indicates also the principle of de Lubac's reply to the similar charge that emphasis on the single supernatural end of the human person evacuates any penultimate ends of their legitimate integrity.[43]

Another important criticism by Thomists concerned whether de Lubac wrongly attributed an Aristotelian nature to Aquinas: that is, both by construing the Aristotelian nature in a too Averroistic sense—

---

42. Cf., e.g., *The Mystery of the Supernatural*, 31–36.

43. The following statement illuminates de Lubac's fundamental spirit—and indeed his central notion of paradox—pertinent to the claim indicated here: :

The reader may find it helpful . . . to consider a comparison [which I offer with some] reservations. As between the Platonic and Cartesian doctrine which makes the body and spirit two substances, or the Aristotelian and Thomist doctrine which sees man as substantially one being, it is not the first which better assures the true recognition of bodily values and better resists the influence of false spiritualisms, in conformity with revelation itself; it is incontestably the second. (*The Mystery of the Supernatural*, 32–33)

To be sure, de Lubac is aware that this argument needs to be interpreted in terms of analogy: because there are crucial distinctions to be made between the kind of union indicated in the body-soul relation and that indicated in the nature-supernatural relation (hence de Lubac's reference to having reservations). The Lubacian principle enunciated here is only that it is not separation but union that can best differentiate: can differentiate, that is, both cleanly and most truly. Thus de Lubac characteristically prefers to speak of uniting in order to distinguish, rather than of distinguishing in order to unite. Although both ways of speaking are legitimate, the former secures the true integrity of union while maintaining a real distinction; the latter, on the other hand, tends to equate distinction with separation, even as it tends (consequently) to confuse authentic union with what is merely an addition.

In terms of the present case—that of the integrity or "solidity" of nature or the natural law—, the implication is that nature's de facto integration into a divine calling renders nature not less but *more* (i.e., more deeply and truly) natural. Hence, again, the paradox fundamental to de Lubac: recovery of an integrated sense of the supernatural is indispensable for the sake, not only of an adequate notion of the supernatural, but also of the "legitimate autonomy" of nature itself!

i.e., too closed in on itself—and by ascribing such a nature too simply to Aquinas.[44] Furthermore, in construing nature as closed, de Lubac was forced, in order to maintain his thesis, to rest his argument about a single supernatural finality on the human person's exceptional character as spirit—hence, strictly speaking, as not a thing of nature at all. Gerard Smith, however, pointed out that Aquinas's central principle of *esse* in fact entailed a significant transformation of Aristotle. Smith argued that recognition of *esse* would thus enable de Lubac to see more harmony between the Aristotelian and the Patristic views of nature. Presumably, it would also make it less necessary for de Lubac to draw such a sharp dichotomy between "physical" nature and "spiritual" nature: the sharp distinction drawn by de Lubac in *Surnaturel* between the non-human and the human is related also to a later criticism that de Lubac neglects somewhat material creation and hence the cosmological dimension of creation and redemption.[45]

The Present Ecclesial-Cultural Situation

After the years of controversy and debate, has de Lubac's theology of nature and grace been vindicated? What is its significance for the current ecclesial-cultural situation?

In answering this question, it is necessary first of all to distinguish de Lubac's basic thesis and indeed the fundamental élan of his work, from

44. Cf. the helpful articles in Vol. XXIII of the *Proceedings of the American Catholic Philosophical Association* (1949): Gerard Smith, "The Natural End of Man," 47–61; and Anton Pegis, "Nature and Spirit: Some Reflections on the Problem of the End of Man," 62–79. As Smith notes in his introduction, he is playing the role of "devil's advocate" (47). Pegis rightly argues that Aristotle did not know of man's creation or redemption, but that his nature, strictly speaking, was neither (simply) closed nor (simply) open: see 68–69, and *passim*. The key, says Pegis, is that "[n]ature means wholeness, not closedness; and the finality of a nature is as open as that nature is in its constitution" (69). Hence both authors agree that de Lubac could sustain his central thesis that Aquinas affirmed a single—supernatural—end for the human person, while detaching the thesis from (possibly) questionable historical claims—or indeed philosophical claims about closed natures. .

45. Cf. Paul McPartlan, *The Eucharist Makes the Church* (Edinburgh: T&T Clark, 1993), 30, 42, and the Conclusion, 289–305. Cf., for example, *The Mystery of the Supernatural*, 72, where de Lubac asserts that the supernatural finality has no direct relation to the laws of physics or chemistry (although he says this in the context of affirming, with Blondel, the "homogeneity" of the whole order of creation). The criticism here seems to me important. I would nonetheless add that de Lubac's sustained (critical but supportive) engagement with the work of Teilhard de Chardin seems clearly to show a substantial cosmological intention in de Lubac. Cf. especially de Lubac's *The Religion* [more accurately translated: "The Religious Thought"] *of Teilhard de Chardin* (London: Desclée, 1967).

the detailed historical-philosophical and theological claims in terms of which he works out the thesis. Thus, for example, the question of whether de Lubac was entirely accurate in his interpretation of commentators on Aquinas such as Cajetan and Suarez; whether the Aristotelian nature in fact tends toward Averroism; whether a non-spiritual nature is simply closed in upon itself; whether Aquinas himself was entirely successful in integrating the Aristotelian nature with the Patristic sense of the *imago Dei;* whether a "supernatural existential" in the creature is needed to secure the required gratuitousness of the order of grace; the vexed questions regarding *potentia obedientialis* and the distinction between *imago* and *similitudo, datum optimum* and *donum perfectum,* and *datio* and *donatio*—all of these questions are legitimate and hence remain matters concerning which conscientious theologians and philosophers will continue to differ. After all, what is most fundamentally at stake in all of these questions is the *mystery* of God's creation and redemption in Jesus Christ. It is entirely in the spirit of de Lubac himself, therefore, that such questions continue to be asked—so long as they are asked in the context of service to this mystery: in the context, that is, of giving account for the hope that is in us (1 Peter 3:15–16), and not of "dominating" the mystery, through (would-be) exhaustive rationalization.

What is most important in assessing the enduring significance of de Lubac's argument, in other words, is that we not lose sight of the main point of that argument: namely, to secure theologically the truth of creation as understood in the Gospel, which requires a non-divine subject that is nonetheless always-already, in the one order of history, invited to participate in the divine trinitarian *communio* revealed in Jesus Christ. De Lubac sees it necessary to insist on the simultaneity—and hence just so far the paradox—of the two elements of the twin claim implied here: on the one hand, a gratuity of grace distinct from and unanticipated by (but not merely "super-added" to) human nature; on the other hand, a human nature always-already called to a divine vocation in Jesus Christ, and hence just so far imbedded from the outset in a supernatural order. In the careful expression of one of the early reviewers of *Surnaturel,* "[t]he supernatural is not abnormal; it does not point to something adventitious, but it remains gratuitous, even if it is deeply rooted in our nature."[46] Any alternative proposal to de Lubac's "solu-

46. Cited in *At the Service of the Church,* 209.

tion" must show how it can better account for the double burden presented by the Gospel, of an utterly gratuitous gift on God's part coupled with the human person's profound—non-arbitrary—desire for this gift, both of these present being already at the beginning of each creature's existence.

Once we have clarified what is basic to de Lubac's theological "project," we can see that it has been vindicated. Indeed, we need only recall the text from *Gaudium et spes* with which we began this Introduction: "Christ the Lord, Christ the new Adam, in very revelation of the mystery of the Father and of his love, fully reveals man to himself and brings to light his most high calling" (no. 22). As is widely known, nearly every encyclical of Pope John Paul II invokes this text in a prominent way. Indeed, John Paul has stated on several occasions, referring to this text, that an organic relation between "theo-[christo-]centrism and anthropocentrism" is perhaps the most fundamental principle taught at Vatican II.[47] My suggestion is that this is likewise the most fundamental principle in the life-work of Henri de Lubac.

Let it be clear: whether the text from *Gaudium et spes* was consciously taken over from de Lubac's *Catholicisme* is not the main point here. Nor is it necessary to offer a detailed genetic history of de Lubac's influence at the Council.[48] Nor need we ponder the details of Wojtyla's friendship with de Lubac at the Council or Pope John Paul II's later appointment of de Lubac as cardinal.[49] The burden of my suggestion, rather, rests above all on the intrinsic nature of de Lubac's basic theological achievement relative to those of the Council. Here, in addition to de Lubac's and the Council's near-identical affirmation of an organic relation between christology and anthropology, we should also consider: the nature of the Church as mystery and the universality of the call to holiness, and the catholicity of the Church as the sacrament of "com-

47. *Dives in misericordia,* no. 1; cf. *Redemptor hominis,* 1–12. Cf. also John Paul II's *Crossing the Threshold of Hope* (New York: Alfred Knopf, 1994), 48–49; and Cardinal Wojtyla's *Sources of Renewal* (San Francisco: Harper & Row, 1980), 75.

48. For a detailed study of the history of the preparatory periods of the Council, 1959–62, regarding the term "supernatural," and indeed in light of the work of de Lubac and Teilhard de Chardin, cf. Etienne Michelin, *Vatican II et le "Surnaturel"* (Venasque: Editions du Carmel, 1993). Michelin argues that the *centre réel* of the Council lay in its affirmation of the unity of the human vocation, "which is a divine vocation" in Jesus Christ (307).

49. Cf. *At the Service of the Church,* 171–72. For Pope John Paul II's own comments, see *Crossing the Threshold of Hope,* 159.

munion with God and of unity among all men" (*Lumen Gentium*); the
consequent importance of the world and of the vocation of the laity
(*Apostolicam actuositatem*); the nature of divine revelation as the truth
first, not of a (dogmatic) proposition, but of the person of Jesus Christ
(*Dei Verbum*); the urgency of the problem of atheism (*Gaudium et spes*);
the essentially missionary nature of the Church (*Ad Gentes divinitus*);
the importance of dialogue with non-Christians (*Nostra aetate*); and the
fundamentally marian nature of the Church.[50]

This is not at all to suggest that these conciliar themes are unique to
the theology of de Lubac! The point is only that the themes are central
to his life-work—indeed, that most of them embroiled him in controversies throughout the early decades of the century and on into the
Council itself. The bishops and theologians at the Council who were
responsible for the preparation of the Council documents were surely
not ignorant of these controversies and, consequently, the similarities
between de Lubac's theological emphases and those of the Council
were hardly coincidental.

But a further question remains regarding the contemporary significance of *The Mystery of the Supernatural*. Who holds a "pure nature"
hypothesis any longer? And if no one holds this hypothesis, is the book
still what the French call "*actuel*"? De Lubac himself points the way to
an appropriate answer to this question, in his Preface to the book. The
dualist or separatist thesis proposed by theologians, he says, "has finished its course" (xi). Nonetheless, the thesis

> may be only just beginning to bear its bitterest fruit. As fast as profes-
> sional theology moves away from it, it becomes so much more wide-

---

50. The question regarding where to treat mariology in the Conciliar documents—
i.e., in a separate document or within *Lumen Gentium*—was of course controversial at the
Council. Though the majority of Council Fathers clearly wanted mariology included within the constitution on the Church, there was less agreement regarding where it would be
placed within this constitution and, indeed, regarding the precise terms of the desired
integration of mariology and ecclesiology. (Wojtyla, for example, wished to have treatment of Mary placed immediately after the first chapter on the Church as mystery, and de
Lubac agreed with him on this.) At any rate, the presumption in my suggestion here is
twofold: (1) the mariology developed in the pontificate of John Paul II represents an
authentic development of Conciliar teaching: cf. especially in this connection the *Catechism of the Catholic Church*, no. 773, which affirms the priority of the marian over the
petrine dimension of the Church in the order of holiness; (2) affirmation of the basically
marian character of the Church is central to the work of de Lubac: cf., *inter alia*, the last
chapter of *Méditation sur l'Eglise* (Paris: Editions Montaigne, 1953); English translation,
The Splendor of the Church (San Francisco: Ignatius, 1986).

spread in the sphere of practical action. While wishing to protect the supernatural from any contamination, people had in fact exiled it altogether—both from intellectual and social life—leaving the field free to be taken over by secularism. Today that secularism, following its course, is beginning to enter the mind even of Christians (xi–xii).

De Lubac goes on to indicate that this secularist tendency is also fueled today by the "immanentism" that is but the obverse of the modern dualist coin.

De Lubac's observation here seems remarkably prescient. On the one hand, it seems clear that few today would bother themselves over the question of "pure nature" in the technical terms argued in modern theology, let alone defend vigorously anything like a *simply pure* nature (even if only "hypothetically"). At the same time, it seems equally clear that a "softer," or what may be called "methodological," version of the "pure nature" theory remains widespread. How so?

Illustrations may be offered with respect to both the conception of "apologetics" dominant in the social-cultural order, and the "critical methods" characteristic of the academy. Central to the contemporary notion of "apologetics" is the metaphor of "common ground." That is, given a pluralistic society that includes non-believers, non-Christians, and non-Catholic Christians, Catholics, in their engagement with the social-cultural order, must establish a common ground which enables meaningful communication with such persons. Moreover, the establishment of such common ground entails some significant (i.e., "strategic") sense of abstraction from theological differences—from the ultimate or religious end which these various groups conceive differently.

Something analogous happens in the academy: each of its disciplines involves a certain methodical abstraction: "x" must be temporarily bracketed in order to get clear first about "y." This methodical abstraction has probably been most resolutely practiced in the "natural" or "physical" sciences, but the pertinent point is that all the disciplines in some significant sense characteristically bracket Revelation, or the Christian Fact, for critical-methodological purposes.

More generally, we have all frequently heard the suggestion that we should first seek to ascertain what reason alone or the empirical evidence alone has to tell us, before going on to introduce the Christian "perspective."

Now, the first thing to be said about these tendencies is that each contains an essential—ineliminable—truth. Certainly no claim regarding the relation between nature and grace made in the name of de Lubac would permit us to deny that some notion of "common ground" is necessary for communication in a pluralistic society; that some methodical abstraction is necessary for intelligent inquiry; or that some significant sense of appeal to reason and indeed to nature is appropriate and often even necessary "prior" to an (explicit) appeal to Revelation. Nonetheless, the subtle but absolutely crucial point required by de Lubac's theology is that none of these tendencies can any longer be rightly understood as implying *neutrality* with respect to the truth revealed by God in Jesus Christ. Neither any "common ground," nor any "methodical abstraction," nor, finally, any appeal to reason or nature alone is ever, from its first actualization, innocent of implications (positive or negative) relative to this truth.

I am not suggesting, of course, that one cannot legitimately abstract from the order of grace—in the name of common ground, critical method, or reason. The point, and it is fundamental for de Lubac, is that this abstraction must not be taken to imply that the order of grace is to be subsequently (simply) *added* to what has been first abstracted (cf. the idea of the "*superadditum*"). The fact that the "superaddition" occurs now for methodological reasons does not render it any less problematic as a false abstraction, hence as wrongly autonomous,[51] relative to the order of grace.

How, then, do we determine whether abstraction has been made truly in the spirit of de Lubac's theology of nature and grace? The crucial question is whether, in abstracting (in seeking a common ground, in appealing to reason), one remains dynamically open, both in form (in terms of one's interior disposition) and in content (in terms of the object of one's inquiry) to the realities of grace and sin that are always-already operative in the one historical order.[52] The fact that the realities

---

51. Thus an interesting and important question bequeathed to the Church, in light of both *Gaudium et spes* and the work of de Lubac, is how best to integrate the *iusta* or *legitima autonomia* of the created order affirmed in *GS*, nos. 36, 59, with the "trinitarian christocentrism" affirmed in *GS*, no. 22.

52. It should be pointed out that this is why, for de Lubac, the question of whether apologetics should proceed "from above" or "from below" is, strictly speaking, otiose: cf., for example, the discussion in de Lubac's *Athéisme et sens de l'homme* (Paris: Cerf, 1968), 91–96, where he affirms both approaches to be necessary, provided that the approach "from below"—"from the starting point of human reality"—remains dynamically-intrinsically ordered toward the divine end revealed in Jesus Christ.

of grace and sin may sometimes—for legitimate methodological purposes—be left (temporarily) unthematic does not mean that these realities in the meantime cease to operate, both in the inquiring subject and in the object of inquiry!

The crucial test, in a word, is whether one's abstraction remains open *extrinsically* or *intrinsically* to the order of grace. Only an "intrinsically open abstraction" can finally realize the Catholic and catholic truth envisaged by de Lubac.

Spelling out the difference between the two kinds of abstraction indicated here, in each of the various contexts indicated, is of course a delicate and excruciatingly difficult task. It suffices for our purpose only to draw attention to the continuing relevance—indeed urgency—of de Lubac's theology in and for the present ecclesial-cultural situation. As de Lubac himself said, long after the cruder, more explicit version of the "pure nature" hypothesis has died, the hypothesis now seems to be bearing its bitterest fruit. The explicit and resolute atheism of the modern period reinforced—unintentionally, to be sure—by a theoretical "pure nature" has been largely replaced in our social, cultural, and academic milieu by an implicit or methodological atheism, reinforced now by an apologetic-strategic or methodological "pure nature."

Thus it is clear that the issues raised by the work of de Lubac—and in particular by his book *The Mystery of the Supernatural*—are scarcely arcane matters of only historical interest. On the contrary, the issues still go to the heart of the Church in her contemporary engagement with humanity and indeed with all aspects of creation and culture. This new presentation in English of *The Mystery of the Supernatural*, which now for the first time includes translation of the abundant Latin texts, is as timely and important as the original publication in 1965.

Davɪᴅ L. Sᴄʜɪɴᴅʟᴇʀ
*John Paul II Institute for Studies
on Marriage and the Family*

Preface

The purpose of this book is not wholly historical. It is theological as well. Yet it hardly oversteps the bounds of positive theology; the author has made no attempt to transpose, or even extend, the theories of the schoolmen. In his statement of the problems as in his choice of arguments, and even in the vocabulary used, he has closely followed the tradition he would love to see better known by adopting the expressions given to it by the great masters of scholasticism. His work is one among an already long series of "tedious commentaries on the natural but impracticable desire to see God according to St Thomas," a literary form we have good reason to feel that we have had enough of.[1] Though he does not deny that an attempt to go further might be legitimate or in some cases even necessary, the author does not himself want either to open fresh perspectives, or to take fresh material from more up-to-date problems, or to make use of categories not considered previously. He has purposely set himself a more basic and more modest task. Starting from the classic question of the relationship between nature and the supernatural, he has restricted his theological reflections to the sphere of formal ontology where they are normally carried out, without any attempt to make them more concrete;[2] he has not therefore made use

[1] Cf. Georges van Riet, *Revue philosophique de Louvain* 62 (1964): 370. There are few questions in our time which bear out more precisely the observation of St Bonaventure: "About this question philosophers seem opposed to philosophers. Indeed, great and profound scholars who were great seekers of truth have been at variance both in philosophy and in theology" (*In 2 Sent.,* dist. 3, p. 1, art. 1, q. 2: *Opera,* Quaracchi, vol. 2, p. 96).

[2] Cf. Karl Rahner, *Sendung und Gnade* (Vienna-Munich, 1961); Eng. trans. *Mission and Grace,* vol. 1 (London, 1963).

14   either of the "covenant" vocabulary, or of that of the "Christian mystery."[3] He has even forborne to enter the discussion centering upon the
efficaciousness of grace and free will; he has not therefore studied
either the metamorphoses of the "appetite of nature," or the ecstasy of
beatitude. *A fortiori,* then, he has considered neither the mediating role
of the incarnate Word,[4] nor the entry of the adopted creature into the
relations of the Trinity.

All he has tried to demonstrate is contained in a single idea. It is to
establish or illustrate the one idea that all his arguments are directed,
and he would instantly abandon any that turned out in the end to compromise or obscure it. It is a simple idea which, to be accurately
grasped, requires only that one be willing to look with a single gaze on
all the lines of thought which converge upon it. It is a paradoxical idea,
as are all the ideas that bear upon the reality of our being in relation to
God. It is a concrete idea, expressing something which, though essential to human experience, is nevertheless fatally blocked up or misinter-
preted apart from revelation. It is an idea which is in itself independent
of many of the particular theories and arguments into which I propose
not to enter, although I shall mention their underlying motives. It is an
idea which has never been in any way contradicted by the teachings or
warnings of the magisterium, but rather defended or rectified against
all denials or deviations of any kind. It is an idea so fundamental that it
has been proclaimed, often with total unanimity, in all the ages of
Christendom.

At the beginning of our own age it seemed for a time to become
obscured. Some set it aside with the notion that they were simply giving
the autonomy of nature and natural philosophy their due. Others did so
in the name of a purer orthodoxy: rightly wanting to condemn the
excesses which sought to deny something of the Creator's sovereign
freedom and the complete gratuitousness of his gift, they did not realize
that they were in fact falling into the opposite error and watering down
the traditional idea. This misunderstanding showed a certain timorous-
ness, to say the least, in face of the denials of the period; it might be

---

[3] Cf. Henri Bouillard, "L'idée de surnaturel et le Mystère chrétien," in *L'Homme
devant Dieu,* vol. 3 (coll. "Théologie," 58 [1964]), pp. 153–66.
[4] St Thomas, *Tertia,* q. 9, art. 2: "Toward this end of beatitude human beings are led
through the humanity of Christ." H. Urs von Balthasar, *La prière contemplative* (Fr. trans.
p. 59); *La théologie de l'histoire* (1955), p. 169.

taken to be the indirect sign of a wavering faith. For sixty years now, in spite of occasional somewhat compromising deviations, and in spite also of obstinate, and sometimes even violent, opposition from people who misconstrued its meaning, the idea has been gaining ground again. The old tradition, which we are coming to explore more deeply, shows it up with great clarity. However, it is yet again in danger of being eclipsed; fresh assaults are being made upon it, from two directions.

15

On the one hand, though the dualist—or, perhaps better, separatist—thesis has finished its course, it may be only just beginning to bear its bitterest fruit. As fast as professional theology moves away from it, it becomes so much more widespread in the sphere of practical action. While wishing to protect the supernatural from any contamination, people had in fact exiled it altogether—both from intellectual and from social life—leaving the field free to be taken over by secularism. Today that secularism, following its course, is beginning to enter the minds even of Christians. They too seek to find a harmony with all things based upon an idea of nature which might be acceptable to a deist or an atheist: everything that comes from Christ, everything that should lead to him, is pushed so far into the background as to look like disappearing for good. The last word in Christian progress and the entry into adulthood would then appear to consist in a total secularization which would expel God not merely from the life of society, but from culture and even from personal relationships.

On the other hand, however, the teachings which at the beginning of the century were summed up under the generic title of "doctrines of immanence" are also coming to the fore. Under some quite subtle forms, they imperceptibly color the outlook of many Christians whose intelligence and self-awareness are of the more demanding kind. (Man will never cease to want to be enclosed within himself!) It is chiefly a question of a "historical" immanentism, concentrating completely upon history, and envisaging the end of its development as a "universal reconciliation" which, both in itself and in the means needed to achieve it, would exclude everything supernatural. Where it is sometimes deceptive is when this immanentism of our age easily develops a dialectic of transcendence actually within the human being. It becomes all the more attractive as, presenting itself as the heir of Christianity (at last fully understood), far from rejecting it, it claims at last to fulfill perfectly the hopes awakened by Christ in men's hearts; and it is all the more for-

16

midable in being borne along on the most powerful current of thought in the age, and in presenting itself as making the only valid response to the challenge of historicity. I realize that the only way to "refute" it is by absorption, and I am confident that Christian thinking, once again, will be adequate to the task. Our own thinking will draw—and here and there has already begun to do so—new depth from it. But meanwhile, some among us may be in danger of succumbing, while others who should be protecting them are so involved in the controversies of the past as not to recognize this present, and pressing, danger.[5]

Faith must provide the needed answer, and must do so before it is too late to be of help to many. For "it is a question of ourselves and all that we are and have." Through all man's changing cultures, the human condition remains fundamentally the same. Man's relationship with God, who has made us for himself and never ceases to draw us toward him, remains essentially the same. There is always "in primeval nature just as in nature as developed through history, a depth, a living response, a natural desire, a 'force' upon which freely given grace finds something to work. As the Greeks used to say, the incarnate logos gathers the 'seeds' planted by the creating logos. The Latins expressed it in different terms: man, as God's image, is fitted to enter into communion with him, in liberty of mind and initiative of love."[6] This is what we must, if only as a duty to God, continue to clarify with all the means that this age places at our disposal. This is the fundamental truth which we must never allow to be obscured or compromised.

It is in this spirit that I add my modest effort to so many others, not seeking to develop every aspect of this vast truth, nor claiming to explore totally even the single aspect I am considering here. I am of

[5] Cf. the explanations given earlier by Mgr. Gasser in regard to a similar situation, upon the third canon proposed to the Fathers of the First Vatican Council, in the schema of the constitution *De fide catholica*, c. 2 (Collectio Lacensis, vol. 7, col. 148): ". . . The third canon is borne against the progressists (pardon the word) of our day. This particular opinion is the most recent and saddest offspring of pantheism. Progressists, having abandoned the worship of the true and living God, are given over to the worship of plain humanity; or rather, they take humanity itself for true and absolute divinity and hence maintain that it is impossible for man to be raised to any supernatural knowledge of God. Rather, they say that man himself is capable of infinite progress, not even from God, but from himself. And that is why this canon runs thus: If any one should say, that man cannot be raised to supernatural knowledge by God's aid, but in the end can and must by continuous progress [*jugi profectu*] independently attain the possession of all truth and goodness, let him be anathema."

[6] M. D. Chenu, O.P., *L'Evangile dans le temps* (1965), p. 676.

course well aware that the way to salvation does not depend on any speculative science; yet methodical reflection can still have some value in pointing out the way, removing obstacles, and indicating the routes to be avoided. Thus it seems to me at the moment that whatever contributes to exploring tradition, which is the norm of all future speculation, whatever throws light on anything in past theological thought that can help to make believers aware, and explicitly aware, of the sense of their eternal vocation, is more important than ever.[7]

[*Fecisti nos ad te, Deus*]
"You have made us for yourself, O God."

---

[7] Whatever unforeseeable forms our civilization may take in the future, there will never be any "integral humanism" except on condition of recognizing and respecting in man "that image of God" which is called to be like God, in other words, to "see God." Cf. Jacques Maritain, *Humanisme intégral* (1936), p. 104; Eng. trans. *True Humanism* (London, 1938), pp. 86f. For the origins of this book, see below, the final lines of chapter 3. I have not sought to bring up to date the pages written at an earlier time.

CHAPTER 1

Ebb and Flow
in Theology

"Whoever studies older Christian philosophy at its sources cannot
but notice the difference in some concepts and doctrines that separates
the doctors of the older school from those of the modern, and this in
matters of no small moment. This difference generally is easily
explained by the advance in knowledge; in some instances, however, it
appears to warrant a different explanation sought from an exterior principle."[1]

These words were said by Père Elter, forty years ago, on a subject kindred to ours here, his concern being to contrast the old and new schools
on the idea of beatitude. As he shows, one could quote many other
examples of theological theories which were held, or seemed to be held,
almost with unanimity at one time, at least in one part of the Church,
and later faded into the background, or should by rights have done so. I
will mention a few examples that can hardly be contested.

In the normative explanation of the relations between Church and
state, did not the so-called "direct power" theory hold sway, in spite of
strong opposition, for several centuries? Yet what theologian would
want to revive it today? Indeed, it has not simply been abandoned: official papal teaching, which once favored it, has spoken definitively
against it. However, I feel sure that if it were once again to find sup-
porters (like the fiery Abbé Jules Morel in the last century) they would
certainly declare it as having been defined in the bull *Unam sanctam,* or
argue from the fact that St. Robert Bellarmine got into trouble for his

[1] E. Elter, S.J., "De naturali hominis beatitudine ad mentem Scholae antiquioris,"
Gregorianum 9 (1928): 269.

"indirect power" theory which was at that time thought to be danger-
ously minimalist.[2]

In regard to the redemption, Canon Jean Rivière, the author of a
series of excellent historical works, once appealed to the "law of development" to show that while the dogma itself clearly remained
unchanged, "theological reflection worked gradually to translate it into
ever less inadequate concepts."[3] What this meant in the concrete was
that a direct development would, by a sure progression, lead to a conclusion known in advance to the author. Hence, all the traditional elements which that theory could not accommodate must be ultimately
rejected as "incurable archaisms."[4] Now, only a few years later, we are
being asked from all sides—not without reason, though sometimes also
not without inverse partiality—to reverse the process. We must, we are
told, return to the rich and deep sources of Christian antiquity which a
one-sided "development," falsely extending the ideas of St. Anselm, has
wrongly rejected.[5] We must return to the idea of Christ's victory, and in
our studies of the redemption give back to Christ's resurrection the key
position it should never have lost.[6] A stern but true lesson for our modern self-sufficiency![7]

21

As for Christ's human freedom and merit, Abbé Maurice de Baets
declared at the beginning of this century—and his opinion seems to

[2] See my article "Le pouvoir de l'Eglise en matière temporelle," *Revue des sciences religieuses* (1932).

[3] Jean Rivière, *Le dogme de la Rédemption au début du moyen âge* (1934), p. 256; see also p. 252.

[4] *Op. cit.,* p. 4; cf. 'The archaism which still prevailed among the Fathers, whose soteri-ology was in a framework of superficial categories. . . ." And *Le dogme de la rédemption dans la théologie contemporaine* (posthumous, 1948), pp. 130, 222, 235, 249; p. 156: "It is well known that the theology of the redemption was only developed in the middle ages."

[5] This is, however, no reason to give up the advantage of the Anselmian analyses. It has been rightly pointed out that St. Thomas Aquinas did not follow the exclusive line of the extreme Anselmians.

[6] See F. X. Durrwell, *La Résurrection de Jésus, mystère de salut*[7] (1963), p. 11, Eng. trans. *The Resurrection* (London, 1960), p. xxiv: "Not so long ago theologians used to study the Redemption without mentioning the Resurrection at all." Cf. Y. de Montcheuil, *Leçons sur le Christ* (Paris, 1949), chapters 11 and 12.

[7] In a recent study, "Sur la methode de la théologie," Bernhard Welte speaks of "that very naïve faith in progress which it sometimes shows, and which is justifiable only in nat-ural sciences"; see *L'homme devant Dieu* (Théologie, 56–58) (Paris, 1964), 3:314. Back in 1921, Cardinal Louis Billot held this mistake up to ridicule, but with an intemperance more suited to a pamphleteer, speaking of "historical theology which modernizes" and of "ruin of faith" ("A propos d'un livre de théologie historique," *Gregorianum* 2 [1921]: 4–7).

have been ratified by theologians as a whole—that abandoning the authors of the past had been far from being invariably an advance:[8] *"Innovations were not always improvements."* The same must be said, he considered, on a great many questions upon which the old doctrines had been more than once wrongly abandoned. Among these "numerous questions" [*permultae quaestiones*] we can certainly include those so bitterly discussed since the seventeenth century concerning grace and predestination. Certainly, neither the Molinist system of "middle knowledge" [*scientia media*], nor the contrary explanation linked with the name of Báñez, ever had the support of all theologians, but between the two they mustered almost all of them. Yet there are more and more people today coming from both camps who consider it better to hold a view at once simpler, less anthropomorphic, and older than either. Sertillanges, refusing to enter "a nest of arguments,"[9] made a great many converts on this point, not least among them Maurice de la Taille.[10]

De la Taille's name brings to mind his *Mysterium fidei* which might well be described as an essay in the liquidation of the over-complicated systems worked out in modern times, indeed ever since the Council of Trent, about the sacrifice of the Mass. Having declared that the doctrine of sacrifice "is one of the least-developed of all the Church's doctrines," he does not hesitate to state that "the three past centuries have not marked an advance, but a regression" and that "the theologians of the second half of the sixteenth century, from whom the theological teaching of our own day directly descends, . . . falsified the meaning of immolation."[11] One need not agree on all points with his masterly study in order to recognize that in embarking on criticism of this kind de la Taille was doing something most salutary. The immense opposition he aroused is now only a memory,[12] and the essence of what he taught is now commonly accepted.

22

---

[8] M. de Baets, *De libera Christi obedientia* (Louvain, 1905), p. 5. We find a similar lament in the author of the Preface to the *Libellus de libero arbitrio* by Bl. Alger of Liège (*PL*, 180, 969).

[9] A. D. Sertillanges, *Saint Thomas d'Aquin*[3], vol. 1, pp. 259–68; also in the Revue des Jeunes edition of the *Summa theologica, Dieu*, 2:400, on 1 a, q. 14, a. 13: "Article 13 is a nest of disputes into which I do not wish to enter."

[10] "Sur diverses classifications de la science divine," *Recherches de science religieuse* 13 (1922): 7–23.

[11] *Esquisse du Mystère de la Foi* (1924), pp. 51–52; see also p. 18. *Mysterium fidei* (1921; 1924[2]).

[12] See M. de la Taille, *The Mystery of Faith and Human Opinion* (London, 1930).

Finally, not to dwell too long upon examples,[13] we have for the past thirty years been witnessing a similar movement in regard to the whole idea of what theology is. For some centuries—almost exactly the same time during which the systematized notion of "pure nature" was developing and finally coming to hold complete sway—theologians were in general agreed in thinking their discipline was essentially a science of "conclusions"; their work was not so much to penetrate, so to say, the revealed "object" in order to gain some understanding of it, as to start from it as a basis and go on to find more and more consequences which must, of their nature, become more and more remote.[14] Now, despite the considerable differences, even of method, among them, the theologians of our day seem ever more united in rejecting such a conception as a mistaken one, and a more exact knowledge of the teachings of the great scholastics, especially St. Thomas Aquinas, strengthens them in this view.[15] St. Thomas conceived the science of theology "less as something added to scripture than as something contained in it."[16] For him "to study and understand the Bible" remained "an end, and theology a means."[17] Following him, therefore, we are tending to recognize that theology, however elaborate its methods, however much it makes use of "the instruments of reason," however independent of exegesis in its complete "autonomy of technique," never really goes beyond the Word of God which must always measure, impregnate and judge it.[18]

[13] Another example: Père Louis Bouyer has spoken of a "deterioration in our thinking over the theology of confirmation. . . . The vague and weakened idea of it left to us by the end of the middle ages has dragged both the sacrament and him who is given to us in it into the same obscurity" (*Le sens de la vie monastic* [1950], pp. 120–21). See also his "On the Meaning and Importance of Confirmation," *The Eastern Churches Quarterly* 7 (1948). And what are we to say of "episcopal collegiality" and all its varied implications?

[14] Certain indications and references will be found in my study "Le problème du développement du dogme," *Recherches de science religieuse* 35 (1948).

[15] M. D. Chenu, O.P., *Introduction à l'étude de saint Thomas d'Aquin* (1950), pp. 221, 226.

[16] Etienne Gilson, *Le Thomisme*[4], p. 21, note.

[17] P. Mandonnet, "Chronologie des écrits scripturaires de saint Thomas," *Revue thomiste* 2 (1928): 35.

[18] In his introduction to *Symbolik* (Eng. trans. *Symbolism* [New York: Crossroad Herder, 1997]), Moehler made similar reflections on the practice of Protestants. Why, he asks, are Protestants so anxious to attribute to the universal Church the opinions of its individual members, as if this or that doctor had brought it into existence? He states that it would be absurd to confound them with the teaching of the Church, and that it may indeed happen that, for a certain time, this or that system may be generally accepted, but it cannot on that account be considered an integral part of dogma.

What has happened to so many other theories[19] may well happen to the theory of "pure nature" that has been developed, specified and systematized in the West over the course of recent centuries. It has ruled uncontested among theologians, and has been accepted as fact.[20] We may note however that its reign appears short in the context of twenty centuries of Catholic tradition. We may also note that it is a theory that has never penetrated the theology of the East.[21] Nor has its absence ever been seriously considered as an obstacle to unity; even those who, like A. Palmieri, have set out to stress the doctrinal divergence between the two Churches, make not the smallest allusion to this particular point of difference.[22] This is most significant, especially to those who quite rightly consider that a knowledge of eastern doctrine is "indispensable to the healthy Christianity of the Latin West."[23] It is not that we must always sacrifice or even modify our own ways of thinking; but the recognition of this kind of divergence within the unity of faith has a most beneficial effect on our sense of proportion. It saves us from certain exaggerations: it helps us to keep in their proper place theories which, however strongly we hold them, we might be tempted to let intrude into the sphere of divine truth.

The fact that "pure nature" in the modern sense of the word is something not considered at all in eastern theology is explained by the fact that early Greek tradition contained no such idea. (I do not say that it therefore denies it.) Nor, I believe, was it contained in Latin tradition till a very late date.

24

---

[19] In the practical order the same is true. Every change, however generalized, and however fully justified by circumstances, is not necessarily pure and simple progress. See Dom Pierre Salmon, *L'Office divin* (1959), p. 65: "Every individual Church had its liturgy, its Pontiff, and consequently its liturgical books. Though the unification brought about by St. Pius V for the Roman liturgy, and the return to it in the nineteenth century, were a necessity, it was not pure gain. By stressing union with Rome, the significance and the celebration of the individual Church was lost. One may wonder whether the private office, recited from the Roman Breviary at everyone's personal convenience, is an adequate expression of the great reality of the prayer officially and publicly celebrated at the same time in all the churches in a diocese, and in every diocese, as was the case for ten centuries."

[20] This is apart from the Augustinian school and certain other isolated instances.

[21] V. Lossky, *Essai sur la théologie mystique de l'Eglise d'Orient* (Paris, 1949), pp. 96–97, Eng. trans. *The Mystical Theology of the Eastern Church* (London, 1957), pp. 101–2.

[22] *Theologia dogmatica orthodoxa ad lumen catholicae doctrinae examinata et discussa*, vol. 2, *Prolegomena* (Florence, 1913), reacts against those writers who minimize the divergence (pp. 174–80).

[23] M. D. Chenu, *op. cit.*, p. 212.

Certainly the building up of the new theory had varying repercussions on the interpretation given to older texts. One can see this even among the major authors, for instance St. Thomas dealing with a double beatitude[24] or man's supernatural destiny.[25] "The clear opinion of the Angelic Doctor has been obscured and drawn to alien meanings."[26] So ingrained has the habit become, that it calls for much time, and sometimes the most painstaking effort of analysis, for us to learn again how to read these texts, even when in themselves they are perfectly clear. Yet the phenomenon is a natural one. Then too, many people are already coming to abandon the former arbitrary harmonizing of Augustinian and Thomist doctrines, with the result that many—but not all— have no hesitation in rejecting St. Augustine, or at least admitting that he is less explicit, or less "distinct." Generally speaking, they somewhat reluctantly recognize that "some ancient authors speak obscurely and ambiguously on this matter."[27] But there are some who still believe their theory to be supported by St. Thomas Aquinas—though there are signs that they are becoming less certain of this. Thus, Père Pedro Descoqs, seeing that St. Thomas's opinion was being interpreted in every way, recently declared that it should be "left out of the argument." "We will leave it to the professional historians," he said, "to resolve the debate, if

[24] See my article "Duplex hominis beatitudo," *Recherches de science religieuse* 35 (1948): 290–99.

[25] Thus, in the analysis in 1a, q. 1, a. 1, St. Thomas, writes Père M. J. Congar (art. "Théologie" in D.T.C., 15, col. 379), "establishes that it is necessary (the necessity is hypothetical, but absolute) that, once raised to the supernatural order, man should receive communication" etc. Now St. Thomas says simply: ". . . Since man is ordered by God to a given end that exceeds the understanding of reason . . . ," with nothing to suggest any "hypothetical" necessity. See too the prologue of the *Summa Contra Gentiles,* book 4, where there is no longer a question of any "elevation" hypothesis: ". . . Lest so noble a creature should seem to exist altogether in vain, or incapable of attaining its proper end, man is given a certain way by which he can rise to the knowledge of God. . . ." There is a more sober commentary in Gilson's *Le Thomisme*[4], p. 30, Eng. trans. *The Christian Philosophy of St. Thomas Aquinas* (London, 1957), p. 17. And Toletus, for instance, simply said: "Hence [St. Thomas] proves that necessary knowledge has been revealed to man, since his end is supernatural" (*Enarratio,* vol. 1, 1869, p. 17). And F. de Vitoria: "He proves [the necessity of revelation] because man is ordered to God as to a final end. But in this way God, to the extent that He is a final end, exceeds human reason" (Bricio Torres, p. 33); and, in the same work, ". . . nor can man, by his natural lights, know God as the object and end of the human creature."

[26] Victor Doucet, O.F.M., "De naturali seu innato supernaturalis beatitudinis desiderio juxta theologos a saeculo XIII usque ad XX," *Antonianum* 4 (1929): 189.

[27] Thus V. Cathrein, S.J., "De naturali hominis beatitudine," *Gregorianum* (1940): 408.

they can ever do so."[28] And many of the wisest historians have prudently sidestepped the issue.[29]

The turning-point in the history of Thomistic thought is marked
chiefly by the work of Cajetan (1468–1534), though this was of course
laid on ground already prepared, and was accompanied, and then continued and to some extent transformed, by the work of others. The six-
teenth-century theologians took note of it. Suarez, for instance, while
following Cajetan on essentials, recognized the innovations in the latter's position, though he looked for some solid traditional support for
Cajetan's eclecticism.[30] There were some who judged the matter in
stronger terms. Francis Toletus, the Jesuit, for example, fought most
conscientiously to re-establish the true thought of St. Thomas against
what he considered the innovations of Cajetan;[31] Dominic Soto, the
Dominican, considered that Cajetan's "gloss" on the text of the *Summa*
"destroys the text" [*destruit textum*];[32] later, Macedo the Franciscan bitterly criticized the arbitrariness of Cajetan's commentaries;[33] and there
were many more, some of whom I shall have occasion to quote further on.

These statements and protests seem then to have been quite forgot-   27
ten. But for some time similar voices have been heard again. "One wonders," wrote Canon Balthazar in 1928, "how Cajetan could have arrived
at his interpretation, and how it could have really been taken seriously
for so long."[34] In 1933, in the *Bulletin thomiste*, Père A. E. Motte wrote:
"Basically Cajetan's exegesis . . . misconstrues the whole direction of St.

[28] *Praelectiones theologiae naturalis*, vol. 2, 1932, pp. 431, 239, on the Thomist doctrine
of "natural desire."

[29] See Juan Alfaro, S.J., *Lo Natural y lo Sobrenatural, estudio historico desde santo Tomas
hasta Cayetano, 1274–1534* (Madrid, 1952), p. 15, on "natural desire": "I am not attempting to investigate whether Cajetan faithfully interpreted St. Thomas on this point" ("No
tratamos de investigar si Cayetano interpretó fielmente en este punto a S Tomas"), etc. A
justified prudence, following a serious study. This work in a remarkable new edition has
cast great light on the theological tradition concerning our subject.

[30] This affirmation of Suarez was pointed out by John O. Riedl in *Jesuit Thinkers of the
Renaissance*, ed. Gerard Smith (Milwaukee, 1939), p. 215.

[31] Toletus, *In Primam*, q. 1, a. 1; q. 12, a. 1.

[32] *De sacra doctrina, In Primam Partem*, q. 1 (ed. Candido Pozo, S.J., *Archivo teologico
Granadino* 21 [1958]: 218).

[33] *Collationes*, vol. 2, pp. 396–400. Similarly Johannes Prudentius, *Opera theologica
posthuma* (1960), p. 46.

[34] In *Criterion* 4 (1928): 473. See earlier Père Martin, O.P., *Ephemerides theologicae
lovanienses* 1 (1924): 352–54.

Thomas's work"; the interpreters who came after him "softened" the "crystalline texts of both Summas"; they misunderstood the "point of view of the schoolmen" and "erred in their interpretation."[35] In 1934, in *Angelicum,* Father Vallaro, though not discovering St. Thomas's thought fully, also showed the gulf between the *Summa* and its major interpreter.[36] In 1936, again in the *Bulletin thomiste,* Père Motte was able to rejoice to see the growth in the number of "theologians who are breaking with the tradition of Báñez and Cajetan"[37] and carried on by the Salmanticenses, Gonet, Gotti and Billuart. Father A. Raineri echoed this in *Divus Thomas.*[38] A few protests, like that of Father Angelo M. Pirotta complaining of this "audacity"[39] and trying to prove that Cajetan with perfect coherence "always and everywhere published and taught the true and solid teaching of St. Thomas on the question at hand," failed to arrest the movement. In 1952, though still somewhat timidly, Father Juan Alfaro, S.J., added his protest.[40] And then, in 1957, in the first fascicule of his review *Divinitas,* Mgr. Antonio Piolanti declared that the great cardinal "separates" the two orders, natural and supernatural, in a way that completely differentiates him from St. Thomas.[41] It is in fact quite clear that in denying the created intellect any natural desire to see God[42]—whereas St. Thomas said and repeated: "Every intellect by nature desires the vision of the divine sub-

[35] Vol. 3, 1933, pp. 660, 665, 674.

[36] Vol. 11, pp. 141–42.

[37] Vol. 4, 1936, pp. 547, 580.

[38] "De possibilitate videndi Deum per essentiam," in *Divus Thomas* (Plac.) vol. 39 and 40 (1936, 1937), especially vol. 39, pp. 422–44.

[39] "Escatologiae seu Eudaemonologiae creaturae intellectualis lineamenta iuxta Caietani doctrinam" in *Il Cardinale Tomaso di Vio Gaetano nel 4° Centenario della sua morte* (*Riv. di filosofia neo-scol.* 27 [March 1935]): 73: "Nor should one believe that Cajetan's teaching strays from the intention of St. Thomas, as some (e.g. Vallaro, O.P.) dare to write" etc. Father Pirotta sees the whole difference as lying in the fact that St. Thomas was speaking to theologians, whereas Cajetan was speaking to the gentiles: "thus Cajetan's interpretation is deeper and truer." But to say that the interpretation is "truer" than the text is surely to admit a real difference in the thought.

[40] See *infra,* chapter 8. It is useful also to study the Rome thesis of Father Lorenzo M. Berardini, O.F.M.Conv., *La nozione del soprannaturale nell' antica Scuola Francescana* (1943); on Cajetan, p. 28.

[41] "Vecchie Discussioni e Conclusioni recenti nel Soprannaturale nel Pensiero di S. Tommaso," *Divinitas* 1 (1957): 93–117. See *infra,* p. 154 n. 72.

[42] *In Primam,* q. 12, art. 1: "It does not seem true that the created intellect desires by nature to behold God"; and, if possible, even clearer still in *De potentia neutra et de natura potentiae receptivae.* See *infra,* pp. 156–57.

stance" (*Omnis intellectus naturaliter desiderat divinae substantiae visionem*)[43]—Cajetan was in no sense "clarifying" or "developing" Thomist teaching on the matter; far from "pushing it to its ultimate conclusion," or bringing it to its goal, as has been suggested in a praiseworthy attempt to achieve harmony, he was profoundly altering its whole meaning.[44] Etienne Gilson has pointed this out more than once in relation to other articles of the *Summa Theologica:* whether interpreting St. Thomas or Aristotle, Cajetan never brought to bear "any disinterested historical curiosity"; several times "Cajetan's commentary is not what St. Thomas says, and we can observe in him a kind of failure to enter into the fundamental ideas" of his author; "the distinctions he introduces so skillfully are not directed to making St. Thomas's thought clearer, but to substituting his own"; by the end of his commentary "as much remained of the article as remains of a watch when the spring has been taken out."[45] Father S. Dockx, O.P., confirms this in regard to the subject we are considering here: Cajetan, he said, "deciding that he cannot accept that man, as God's image, should be ordered to the beatific vision as his end, alters the reasoning" and even "the text of St. Thomas." Instead of basing his argument on "the nature of man as made in God's image," he regards that nature simply as "elevated by grace."[46]

29

As long ago as 1908, in his distinguished but largely misunderstood thesis, Père Pierre Rousselot demonstrated this. To counter Cajetan's interpretations, he said, it is enough "to quote the development of the theory in the *Summa contra Gentiles*. In it the same proofs are taken as conclusive, both for man and for separated substances: through what experience has one perceived in them that desire, if it be not natural but contingent? . . . St. Thomas thus sees the need for beatitude as some-

---

[43] *Summa contra Gentiles,* book 3, chap. 57.

[44] See *infra,* chapter 8. Père Vincent Bainvel having written, in *Nature et surnaturel* (1903), p. 130, that progress had been achieved in Thomist language and thought by the introduction of the idea of "historical nature," Canon Pierre Tiberghien replied, in his duplicated study, *La question des rapports du natural et du surnaturel,* p. 17: "If we decide that St. Thomas's thought needs to be *clarified,* must we not seek to carry it further in the same direction in which he has begun it?"

[45] "Cajetan et l'humanisme théologique," *Archives d'histoire doctrinale et littéraire du moyen âge* 22 (1955–56): 133, 118, note 1. "Cajetan et l'existence," *Tijdschrift voor Philosophie* 15 (1953): 268, 271.

[46] "Du désir naturel de voir l'essence divine d'après saint Thomas," *Archives de philosophie* (1964): 79–80.

thing anterior to concrete, redeemed man as we observe him. The first
and most general [of his arguments] clearly and of set purpose applies
both to angels and men. . . . It is in the nature of intellect as such that he
places a certain attraction, a certain longing to see God as he is."[47]
Apart from the word "need," which belongs to the vocabulary of modern controversy, and is not a good translation for St. Thomas's idea, I
cannot see how one could deny what Rousselot says. At the same date,
another theologian, H. Ligeard, a Sulpician, recognized somewhat
euphemistically that Cajetan's teaching is "rather on the fringe of his
master."[48] A disciple of Rousselot, Père Guy de Broglie, was later to
speak of Cajetan's "subterfuges"[49] and to regret how many modern
Thomists had "stumbled into" them. "Cajetan leading the way" [*prae-*
eunte Caietano], Père Victorin Doucet added soon afterwards.[50] And
Père E. Brisbois described the whole interpretation as "governess-like,"
"restrictive and minimizing."[51] Père T. Deman, O.P., coming to define
the famous Salmanticenses' doctrine on "the natural desire to see the
divine essence" said that they "placed themselves in the Thomist tradition of their time which was likely to be less faithful to what we today
tend to think of as St. Thomas's authentic thought."[52] Most people, in
other words, whatever may be their personal view, have given up making St. Thomas responsible for the dualist theory which would deny all
natural desire to see God—a theory which used commonly to be
fathered upon him, owing to quite untenable interpretations.[53] In 1905,
Père Vincent Bainvel had practically abandoned them, considering that
St. Thomas's answer to the problem "is made rather to surprise than to
instruct us," and admitting later that his formulations seemed "rather
disconcerting."[54] In the same way, Père Pedro Descoqs, returning to

---

[47] *L'intellectualisme de saint Thomas*, p. 192 (1936[3], pp. 183–84).

[48] *La théologie scolastique et la transcendance du surnaturel*, p. 42.

[49] *Recherches de science religieuse* 14 (1924): 203.

[50] *Loc. cit.*, p. 177.

[51] "Le désir de voir Dieu et la métaphysique du vouloir selon saint Thomas," *Nouv. revue théol.* 63 (1936): 983–84.

[52] T. Deman, O.P., "Salamanque (Théologiens de)" in the *Dictionnaire de théologie catholique* 14 (1937), col. 1025.

[53] The analyses in the *Bulletin thomiste*, and still more those in the *Bulletin de théologie ancienne et médiévale*, have done much in recent years to lead to a better understanding of Thomist thought.

[54] *Nature et surnaturel* (1905), p. 129. Also *Revue pratique d'apologétique* 1 (August 1908): 650, note 1.

the subject in 1938, declared St. Thomas's texts on the natural desire to be "really antithetical," and his thought "carried into two exclusive and irreconcilable streams"; he then looked upon Cajetan not as a faithful commentator, but as "a metaphysician and theologian of the first rank" giving a "reasonable" explanation to account for his master's apparent inconsistency.[55]

In these circumstances, still to persist in seeing St. Thomas as the source of our modern dualism, by arguing that "any concession on the point" must turn St. Thomas into "an Augustinian,"[56] is not a real argument at all, but an admission of defeat. Few of those who really read and compare the texts would now give unqualified support to the idea that Cajetan "did not innovate," or that the dissertations of John of St. Thomas on the subject constitute "a veritable summit of that powerful and traditional effort which had been going on for several centuries."[57] Few would be satisfied to settle the debate by referring to the "capital distinctions" established by the great commentators.[58] Few, if any, now faced with perfectly clear texts would think it enough to observe that "one cannot follow St. Thomas by falling into a material literalism"[59] and continue to say without closer examination that "the traditional positions of the Thomist school are perfectly in accord with those of its founder.[60] It is understandable that some have taken time to accept the idea that "our great commentators" might not always have been

31

---

[55] *Le mystère de notre élévation surnaturelle,* pp. 128–33.

[56] L. Jugnet, *Pour connaître la pensée de saint Thomas d'Aquin* (1949), p. 23.

[57] Dom G. Frénaud, "Esprit et grâce sanctificante, notes d'histoire doctrinale sur les premiers théologiens de l'Ecole thomiste," in *La Pensée catholique,* vol. 6 (1948), pp. 33, 45. These reflections are surprising in a study which is aiming in addition at correcting historical errors. Clearly Cajetan did not invent his thesis; he and some of his contemporaries made innovations on a thesis taken from St. Thomas. See John of St. Thomas, *Cursus theologicus,* dissertatio 12, art. 2,3 (Solesmes ed., vol. 2 [1934], pp. 130–45).

[58] See Gombault, "Le problème apologétique"; after some faltering explanations of the text, he goes on: "For the rest, the commentators of St. Thomas bring to bear . . . several major distinctions": *La science catholique* (1903), pp. 196–97. This method has since had many disciples.

[59] Père Garrigou-Lagrange, *Revue thomiste* (1936): 124, note 20; and *Angelicum* (1935): 218: "Is it true that since Cajetan's time the majority of the commentators of St. Thomas misunderstood his teaching on natural desire?" He returns several times to the point, but without ever seriously trying to refute from the texts those historians whose statements he rejects. Père Motte could sum up his position on one major point thus: "It is a waste of time reading the texts. St. Thomas cannot have claimed to prove it" (*Bulletin thomiste* 4, p. 574).

[60] *Angelicum* (1948): 298.

absolutely faithful mirrors,[61] or that they might not always have been content, as the Carmelites of Salamanca put it, to "guard the deposit faithfully."[62] None the less, a rightful anxiety for historical accuracy now
32   replaces "that rather dubious exclusivism," as Père H. D. Gardeil, O.P., delicately but effectively put it, "which sometimes ended in masking, to some extent, the master's own thought by that of his commentators."[63] A few lazy minds will soon be left alone in defending what they continue, despite all the evidence, to call "the common interpretation."[64]

Indeed there are many theologians who would go much further, and now declare that they can find no explicit affirmation in St. Thomas of the concrete possibility of a purely natural order—remembering always that this means a complete order, bearing within it its own final end, in the modern sense of the expression.[65] They now expect, rightly, to find only that he lays the ground, though obscurely and in a somewhat roundabout way, for a theory which they can themselves see no way to reject or modify. This is what Père M. J. Le Guillou expressed in carefully chosen terms in 1950,[66] and the Rev. Edward J. Montano said something similar in 1955.[67] "Medieval theologians were not concerned with the question of pure nature," as Père Jacques de Blic points out.[68] And Père Guy de Broglie set out to investigate "why it was only in the
33   sixteenth century that the theory of pure nature was first explicitly stated." Others, like Père Kors,[69] or Père Congar, make it clear that in

---

[61] See R. Mulard, *Revue des sc. philos. et théol.* 14 (1925): 5.

[62] Salmanticenses, *Cursus theologicus*, vol. 10, Dedicatio.

[63] *L'œuvre théologique du P. Ambroise Gardeil* (1954), p. 171.

[64] Here I find especially applicable the reflections of Père G. Dejaifve S.J., *Vision de Dieu et Agapè, Pour une histoire de la notion thomiste de béatitude*: "Though too few people have so far set out to undertake an exegetical and historical study of the Thomist synthesis, it is regrettable that most of the recent interpreters of St. Thomas's text are satisfied with the easier path of studying the classic commentators of scholasticism." The author adds: "This is particularly the case with the commentary recently published by Père Garrigou-Lagrange, 1951 . . ." (From a duplicated thesis, Paris, pp. 308, 309).

[65] Père Théodore de Régnon, among others, recognized this quite some time ago.

[66] "Surnaturel," *Revue des sciences philosophiques et théologiques* (1950): 235, 238: "St. Thomas did not consider the question explicitly"; in his writings, however, the "modern distinction between natural and supernatural begins to develop. . . ."

[67] *The Sin of the Angels, Some Aspects of the Teaching of St. Thomas* (Catholic University of America, Studies on Sacred Theology, series 2, no. 89 [Washington, 1955]), p. 335: ". . . a facet of the problem which did not occupy the Angelic Doctor himself." See also p. 113.

[68] *Mélanges de science religieuse* (1947): 100. The author considers however that it is because it "was not seen as a problem in the common theological thought at that time."

[69] *La justice originelle . . .* (1922), pp. 119–20.

St. Thomas's language a "state of pure nature" would be self-contradic-
tory, since to him "pure nature" is nature "considered in itself," in other
words independent of all reference to God, in its constitutive principles,
"in its *quid,* independent of the *status* in which it is to be found."[70] Some
good historians are even more decidedly and radically negative. One,
for instance, tells us that the thirteenth-century scholastics considered
the problems of nature and grace without ever reverting to "the idea of
a natural order within creation characterized by a transcendent natural
end."[71] The same is said more precisely of St. Thomas by Edgar de
Bruyne,[72] Dom A. Stolz,[73] and, with a more detailed analysis, by Père
Henri Bouillard.[74] It seems to me that the view of these historians cannot fail to become the accepted one, with the proliferation of painstaking and disinterested studies on the subject. As Père Henri Rondet has
said, "sooner or later, agreement is bound to be reached."[75] But it is not
with this last point that we are chiefly concerned here.

If we look more closely at the question, it is hardly surprising that the   34
resistance should have been so strong. A number of theologians, continuing to maintain *en bloc* the "natura pura" theory which has always
been the framework in which they have seen the whole doctrine of the
supernatural, refuse to examine its origins and foundations. Others,
however, influenced by the change effected in the historians' positions,

[70] Congar, "Théologie" in D.T.C., vol. 15, col. 386–87: For St. Thomas "things have
their proper nature, which does not consist in their reference or ordering to God"; hence
the distinction between *principia naturae* and *status.* See *In 2 Sent.,* dist. 20, q. 1, a. 1;
Prima Secundae, q. 85, a. 1 and 2.

[71] Père René Charles Dhont, O.F.M., *Le problème de la préparation à la grâce, débuts de
l'Ecole franciscaine* (1946), p. 211, note 70.

[72] *Saint Thomas d'Aquin* (1928), p. 97. The author, basing himself on the presuppositions of modern times, sees this nevertheless as a "blot" in St. Thomas's work.

[73] *Theologie der Mystik* (Salzburg, 1938), French trans. *Théologie de la mystique* (1939),
pp. 156–62.

[74] *Conversion et grâce chez saint Thomas d'Aquin* (1944), pp. 77–82. See also Dom M.
Cappuyns in *Bulletin de théol. anc. et médiévale* 5 (1947): 152. Aimé Forest, *Saint Thomas
d'Aquin* (1923), pp. 133–35, etc.

[75] "Nature et surnaturel dans la théologie de saint Thomas d'Aquin," *Rech. de sc. rel.* 33
(1947): 485; see also pp. 56–97. As long ago as 1913, M. Blondel, who had acquired a real
familiarity with the work of Aristotle as well as with parts of that of St. Thomas, pointed
out "the positive error of attributing to either of them the idea of determining, of codify-
ing 'pure nature' as against supernature": Bernard de Sailly, *Comment réaliser l'Apologétique
intégrale,* p. 180, note. In *Archives d'hist. doctr. et lit. du m. âge* (1965): 67-88, Gilson published a study "Sur la problématique thomiste de la vision béatifique" which is indispensable reading.

are ready to make that critical examination. They no longer then see this question of "pure nature" as a "troublesome question" whose theological solution presupposes "the demonstration of its philosophical bases," and which can be left aside in order to come to an agreement.[76] Some are even more definite in considering that "this hypothesis is of more embarrassment than use to theology."

To give up using such a hypothesis systematically and exclusively, to consider the way it has developed not as a central blossoming of theological thought, but rather an excrescence, does not necessarily mean that we reject it totally in itself. Nor does it mean that we abandon those aspects of truth which, for a time, it was able to preserve. Nor, certainly, does it mean that we derive the precisely opposite conclusion from the same presuppositions. It does not, therefore, mean that we align ourselves necessarily with those who for one reason or another deny its possibility. Indeed it may even be the best service we can render to the demands of its warmest supporters. What it must mean, as in several of the cases I mentioned earlier, is that we return at once, at least to some extent, to simplicity and to antiquity.

Returning to simplicity. Complication does not always indicate progress in thought—far from it. "Indeed multiplication does not always mean fruitfulness."[77] Obviously one must not, in theology or any other discipline, systematically reject every analysis, every distinction, every new precision which results from the need to avoid errors or from the spontaneous activity of the mind. But it must be admitted that often the force and even the depth of a doctrine are more diminished than increased by over-enthusiasm. The tendency to "curious" questionings is not always the tendency to genuine thought; Gerson said as much in speaking to the theologians of his day.[78] The indefinite proliferation of concepts or accumulation of hypotheses is not always without its dangers. In theology as in philosophy, it may from time to time be indispensable to go on that "slimming diet" which Léon Brunschvicg once recommended.

Returning at the same time, in some sense, to antiquity. This does not

[76] A. Michel, in *L'Ami du clergé*, 21 July 1949, pp. 462–63.

[77] St. Augustine, *In psalmum 4*, n. 9.

[78] See Gerson, *Prima lectio contra vanam curiositatem*: "Just as curiosity deceived the ancient philosophers, so too should we beware lest the very same curiosity should deceive the theologians of today" (*Opera*, vol. 1, 91 B).

mean returning to a "rudimentary" or "undifferentiated" state of doctrine. It is naïve to picture the movement of ideas through the ages, above all in theology, as never being anything but a long elaboration, a long process of passing from the implicit to the explicit, the confused to the distinct, the virtual to the actual, until that marvelous time when this evolution will have reached its final point—unless perhaps we see the road as one that remains for ever open. After all, while from the point of view of a later age he might appear less distinct, an author might in fact be far more so in relation to the problems of his own time.[79] Then too, by stressing some values, human weakness, from which theologians are not exempt, inevitably leads them to neglect others, and theology is not miraculously preserved from periods of decadence. Such ideas are in fact—in a science whose nature should have preserved it better from such encroachments—echoes, though of course unconscious ones, of the facile doctrines of progress in which an earlier age delighted. But we cannot take as models either the middle classes under Louis-Philippe, who thought they had brought the era of revolution to an end, or the intellectuals at the beginning of this century who gazed with delight at perspectives of unending progress opened to them by Condorcet.

36

This we know: the Church, guardian of revealed truth, assures for us in every age the unfailing preservation of faith, pure and complete. Every age contributes more or less felicitously its effort to express the meaning of that sacred deposit, with explanations adopted by the magisterium, and sometimes actually solemnly ratified by it.[80] Not everything that results from all this theological labor is, however, destined for such ratification. Not everything can be canonized. Nor is everything equally sure, equally permanent. "In the development of dogma, acquisitions and exclusions are permanent; in theology there is room for a

---

[79] Gilson is reacting against a similar illusion when, at the beginning of his book *La Philosophie de saint Bonaventure*, Eng. trans. *The Philosophy of St. Bonaventure* (London, 1938), he refuses to see Bonaventure as "a potential and incomplete St. Thomas" (p. 11, Eng. trans. p. 11) and his teaching as "a hesitant Thomism." Those who make this interpretation, Gilson says, do not see to what precise problems Bonaventure's teaching provides an answer, which is why they imagine it to be providing an imprecise answer to problems which it was not in fact considering because it was not then necessary to do so (pp. 16–17, Eng. trans. pp. 10ff.).

[80] On the part played by theologians in the development of dogma I put forward some ideas in the study referred to earlier, *Le problème du développement du dogme*.

mass of hypotheses, probabilities, controversies"[81]—of stumblings and recoveries. "Extravagant branches"[82] sometimes grow upon the tree. History is always there, sometimes of quite recent date, to remind us of this. I cannot therefore share the superstition to which some theologians seem so subject that praises "modernity" as such—whatever their precise definition of the term may be. I do not think we can cast off doctrines that have a long tradition behind them, and which no competent authority has disclaimed, simply by labelling them "archaic concepts," or "outworn theories," and giving no reason for doing so.[83] I do not consider that an attitude of scorn towards the past disposes us well for preserving its heritage, even the best elements in it. Nor do I think that some happy fate destines us to think of everything in a less "inadequate" manner simply because we have been born more recently; we cannot authorize every new theory as a "development"[84] without discriminating; we can add nothing to our admiration of God by praising "the splendidly modern character of his creative personality"![85] I do not deny progress, even in theology; I do not even say that no progress is surer or more permanent than that element in theological progress which advances in the development of dogma and ultimately becomes part of it; I realize that apart from this element there is another of great value, and I am far from the spirit of angry grief felt by the writers of Port Royal who constantly complained of "new inventions being fabricated," as they said, "every day before us" and passed off "as the ancient faith of the Church";[86] for that ancient faith, we know, is alive, and life must of its nature be fruitful.[87] What I believe is simply this: that theological progress is never total, never without false steps, and that not everything should be accepted always on principle, without examination and thought.

37

[81] L. de Grandmaison, "Le développement du dogme chrétien," *Revue pratique d'apologétique* 15 (January 1908): 527.

[82] The expression, in a different context, comes from Karl Barth, *Church Dogmatics*.

[83] Jean Rivière, *op. cit.* Cf. *supra*, p. 2.

[84] Of certain recent extreme cases, Père Louis Bouyer has spoken of "bewildering" theories of development.

[85] See Blaise Romeyer, S.J., *La philosophie chrétienne jusqu'à Descartes*, vol. 2 (1936), p. 65.

[86] See Pascal, 3e *Provinciale*. See my own *Méditation sur l'Eglise*[2] (Paris, 1953), chapter 1, Eng. trans. *The Splendour of the Church* (London, 1956).

[87] See M. Blondel, *Exigences philosophiques du christianisme*, p. 31: "Tradition . . . is the voice of eternity actually in time; . . . it is a perpetual renewer, because it draws the truth it transmits from a spring that never dries up."

In the case we are concerned with here, the doctrine of the supernatural, are we, as some people think, returning to Augustinianism? Yes
and no. Yes in one sense, for it is certainly true that Augustine's work
offers us one of the most profound expressions of that "fundamental
paradox which is man's relationship to God."[88] But, first of all, the
essence of this "Augustinianism" applies as much to the great scholastics of the thirteenth century as to Augustine himself, and one would
not wish to lose the advantage of any of their clarifications. It applies
also, as I have said, to the Greek tradition; it is not linked exclusively
with the thought of Augustine, and the greater example of Thomas
Aquinas shows that it can be well integrated with an Aristotelianism
transformed by the principles that underlie all Christian philosophy.[89]
"The vision of God itself is essentially the final end and beatitude of the
human soul": an Augustinian teaching, certainly, but the text is from St.
Thomas.[90] Secondly, St. Augustine himself and many of his disciples
generally lumped together two problems which we have long since
learned to separate—and which in fact the Greek doctors who came
after Irenaeus separated—the problem of the final end, and that of
man's initial equipment for the journey to salvation.[91] Misunderstandings have continued for fifteen centuries as a result of that confusion,
and it is of major importance for us to clarify it.[92]

38

[88] Gilson, *Philosophie et incarnation selon saint Augustin* (Montreal, 1947), p. 9.

[89] Do we ourselves tend to "exaggerate the doctrinal agreement between St. Augustine
and St. Thomas," to "harmonize too much," to be insufficiently aware of their differences
in phrasing and ideas because we do not fully appreciate their meaning? To this question,
asked by Dom M. Cappuyns in no carping spirit (*Bulletin de théologie ancienne et médiévale*
5 [1947]: 253), I would reply that I view all "concordism" with the greatest suspicion; but
the more marked the differences in concept and system, the more clearly can we see certain fundamental ideas whereby, even beyond the strict unity of faith, a certain unity of
Christian thought has been preserved throughout tradition.

[90] *In 4 Sent.*, dist., 49, a. 2. See *infra*, various other texts.

[91] In the Baianist and Jansenist double controversy, it is clear that, underlying the problem of sin and of its consequences, it is the second of these questions which was directly
at issue, the first entering only indirectly into the discussion.

[92] There was in this matter a valuable point, that could have been noted, in St. Thomas,
De veritate, q. 18, a. 1, ad 5am, 6am and 7am: "Man had been made for the purpose of
seeing God not at the beginning but at the end of his perfection" etc. See *Prima Secundae*,
q. 5, a. 7: "It is proper to God alone not to be moved to beatitude through any prior operation . . .; cf. *In 2 Sent.*, q. 1, a. 1. Similarly in St. Bonaventure, *In 2 Sent.*, d. 3, p. 2, a. 1,
q. 1: "It is necessary that all that God has made be perfect or perfectible"; d. 29, a. 1, q. 2,
ad 3am: "To the objection that the works of God are perfect, one must answer that it is
perfection so far as concerns primary being, and it is perfection so far as concerns secondary being . . ."; and a. 2, q. 2, ratio 3ª (vol. 2, pp. 114, 703). See Robert of Melun, *Sen-*

39   Lastly, returning to the essence of an older position can never be purely and simply a return. Archaism—I use the word advisedly--of this kind is always deceptive. It is as illusory, in the reverse sense, as the idea of inevitable progress. "Those who wrote before us are not our masters, but our leaders" [*non domini nostri sed duces fuerunt*].[93] To refer to the ancients, said Cassiodorus, enables us to escape from all kinds of objections and difficulties.[94] And there are some "difficulties" that face us from which we ought not and cannot escape. The passing of time has brought to light deviations and errors, sometimes of the greatest subtlety, which we must meet with an equal subtlety and exactness. Furthermore, neither St. Augustine, nor St. Thomas, nor many others, could consider all the problems which arise and will always arise in the human mind as it studies the datum of dogma, in the same terms as we must, without unthinkingly adding any personal factors, consider them today. In this sense it is true to say that we never retrace our steps. We never return to the past. Our faith is not old, is not something of the past: it is eternal, and always new.

Although, as it seems to me, no change need be made in the general economy of past teaching, and although we can still adopt the idea our
40   fathers have left us of our fundamental relationship with our supernatural end, there is still much to be done in accordance both with our actual intellectual requirements and with the present state of theology, and in view of the difficulties which the development of thought has produced or accentuated there is a need to show more clearly how this key idea remains completely in harmony with the demands of faith.[95]

---

tentiae, book 1, p. 1, c. 20: "I flatly deny their contention that it is improper for divine providence to have made something imperfect, and for its wisdom to have made something without form. Indeed I assert the contrary statements without a doubt, namely that it is proper for divine providence to have made something imperfect, and for its wisdom to have made something without form . . ." (ed. Martin, p. 219).

[93] Guibert de Tournai, "De modo addiscendi," *Revue néo-scolastique* (1922): 226.

[94] *Institutiones divinarum et saecularium litterarum* (*PL,* 70, 1107 A 1108 A, B). Cassiodorus is speaking chiefly of the suspicion of boasting and presumption which falls on the innovator.

[95] I must add that if, in the course of this effort, I should have occasion to disagree with explanations that differ from my own, I am far from intending to impugn the good will or orthodoxy of their authors.

CHAPTER 2

An Inadequate Hypothesis

In a new situation we are called upon to make a new effort of think- 41
ing, which should, perhaps, in regard to Augustinianism, consist chiefly
in a stronger affirmation of the real value of the natural order in all its
degrees, in a clearer distinction between that natural order in itself and
the order that results from sin, and, further, in seeing in our analyses the
difference between the problems of destiny and of origins.

"The will of so great a Creator is the nature of each created thing":[1]
this is a definite and basic truth, but an incomplete one. It was necessary to stress it, as Augustine did, in order to break away completely
from the naturalism of the ancient world, and whatever one's philosophical method, one must never forget it. Malebranche thought the
idea of nature a pagan one because he still understood it to mean what
it meant in antiquity, something self-subsistent and living by its own
power. But the dogma of creation has profoundly and permanently
transformed the idea philosophers must have, whether of individual
natures or of the totality of the universe.[2] Creation is not simply some- 42
thing that happened to every "being in the past, a cause or precondition
for existence it is something that affects it totally and at every moment;

---

[1] De Civitate Dei, book 21, ch. 8, n. 2 (Bibliothèque augustinienne 37 [1960], p. 412).
[2] Etienne Gilson, L'esprit de la philosophie médiévale² (Paris, 1944), pp. 345–53: "The
profound transformation imposed upon the Greek nature by the doctrine of creation and
of providence. . . ." See Jules Lachelier, Vocabulaire philosophique by A. Lalande, p. 650:
"the fundamental sense" of nature in Aristotle "is the idea of an existence which produces
or at least determines itself . . . without needing any cause outside itself." Malebranche
did not allow for this radical transformation which was effected more or less consciously
by Christian thought.

19

it confers on things both a contingency and a dignity undreamt of in pagan antiquity. God is never absent from his work: "He did not create and leave." In brief, the ancients' nature has become creation in a Christian context;[3] and no one has shown this better than Augustine.[4] No one has demonstrated its consequences better, both in the cosmic and the intellectual spheres.[5] But in order to avoid falling into the trap of an amorphous supernaturalism, one must go on to recognize the other aspect of things.

Despite all that has been said to the contrary, we must certainly maintain that "St. Augustine taught as clearly as possible the ontological value of the distinction between nature and grace"; "he clearly affirmed that distinction even for the state of innocence."[6] The definitely and intrinsically supernatural character of divine adoption is one of the fundamental elements in his teaching; it is expressed there so clearly, and so insistently, that we should be astonished to find that it has not always been recognized. Augustine's thinking is by no means as totally dominated by the "postlapsarian" outlook as has been said. When he wants to establish that the divine adoption of man is an incomparable, unimaginable grace, he proves it not by alluding to our present sinful state, but on the basis of that universal reason—acceptable according to every hypothesis—that God has but one Son begotten of his substance, that by creation we have received human nature, and that adoption in the only-begotten Son makes us share in a marvellous fashion in the nature of God.[7] "Before being sons of God," he says,

43

[3] On the Augustinian idea of nature, see J. Gonsette, *S. Pierre Damien et la culture profane* (1956), pp. 50–51. See also William A. Christian, "Augustine on the Creation of the World," *Harvard Theological Review* 46 (1953): 1–25; André Blanchet, "Claudel à Notre-Dame," in *La Littérature et le spirituel,* vol. 1 (1959), pp. 314–20.

[4] St. Bonaventure, *Epistola de tribus quaestionibus,* n. 12: "No one better than Augustine describes the nature of time and of matter . . . , no one better the outcome of the forms and the dissemination of things [*exitus formarum et propaginem rerum*] . . ., no one better the nature of the creation of the world. . . ."

[5] Etienne Borne, "Pour une doctrine de l'intériorité et vie spirituelle" (1954), p. 24: "In Augustinianism, because it does not find its illumination in itself, because it is known within a truth which supports and surpasses it, and makes it something that spirit can shine through, nature is neither an empty appearance, nor a divine absolute, nor a blind opacity, but becomes real and intelligible, open at last both to the poetry and the science of the modern world."

[6] Jacques Maritain, *Les degrés du savoir* (Paris, 1932), p. 602, Eng. trans. *The Degrees of Knowledge,* newly translated (London, 1959), pp. 303–4.

[7] *Contra Faustum,* book 3, ch. 3: "God has an only son whom he begat of his own sub-

for instance, "we were already something, and we then received the grace that enabled us to become what we were not. Grace made us what we were not, that is to say sons of God, but we were something even before that, and that something was vastly inferior: we were sons of men."[8] Our "deification" is an incredible marvel, and we can believe it only because of that even greater marvel in which it originated—the Son of God becoming a son of man. "Acknowledging therefore our condition, even though we are sons through grace, we are nevertheless slaves on account of our being created, since every creature is a slave to God."[9]

If there is a lack in Augustine's teaching, it does not consist in an insufficient stress on "deification,"[10] nor in any confusion between natural and supernatural orders. Both in Augustine himself, and in many of his disciples who represent "pre-Thomist Augustinianism," people have frequently exaggerated what is called the tendency to "efface the barriers between the order of nature and the order of grace."[11] Gilson, in recalling Augustine's doctrine of God as "originator of natures" [*naturarum auctor*], is not straining to find an artificial harmony when he says that upon this major point there is a deep bond between Augustinianism and Thomism, deeper than all their technical divergences."[12] Yet

44

---

stance. . . . He did not, however, beget us of His own substance, for we are a creature which He did not beget, but made. And so in order to make us the brothers of Christ in his own manner, He adopted us. Accordingly, this manner by which God begat us to be his sons by his word and his grace, although we had already been not born of him but made and established, is called adoption. Hence John says: He gave them the power to be made sons of God. . . . It is he Whom we have as God, Lord, and Father: God, for we were . . . made by him; Lord, for we are subject to him; Father, for we were born again by his adoption" (*PL*, 42, 215–16).

[8] Letter 140, *Ad Honoratum*, ch. 4, n. 10: "We were indeed something before being sons of God, and we received the divine favor to become what we were not. . . . Through His grace we became what we were not, namely sons of God; still, we were something, and this was something far inferior, that is, sons of men" (*PL*, 33, 541, 542); and nn. 11–12 (col. 542).

[9] *In psalm. 122*, n. 5 (*PL*, 37, 1634). See *Sermo* 166, n. 4 (38, 909); s. 342, n. 5 (39, 1534). *In psalm. 49*, n. 2: "By justification they were made gods, for they shall be called sons of God" (35, 565); etc.

[10] This is shown clearly by Father Vittorino Capanaga, O.E.S.A., "La deificación en la soteriologia agostiniana" in *Augustinus magister* (1954), vol. 2, pp. 745–54, with references to numerous texts.

[11] See F. Van Steenberghen, in *L'Histoire de l'Eglise* (ed. Martin et Fliche), vol. 13, 1951, p. 205.

[12] "Moyen âge et renaissance" in *Héloïse et Abélard* (1938), pp. 216–17. Similarly, Père Garrigou-Lagrange: "Saint Augustine . . . rightly . . . showed the real distinction between

Albertus Magnus had some justification in saying of Augustine: "He did not know natures well."[13] It was not a matter of Augustine failing to affirm natures in an emphatic way, even in the spiritual sphere; on the contrary, his own words were: "the soul is without a doubt nature."[14] Nor did he think it necessary, as is sometimes said of him, to abstract from the causality of the creature in order the better to exalt the Creator's activity.[15] In fact he had a clear concept of an "order of natures" [*ordo naturarum*].[16] While closely relating the idea of "nature" to that of origin or birth,[17] he could recognize in the diverse natures, distinct, and differing in degree, of which the world is composed,[18] an intelligibility, a consistency, an activity governed by its own special laws—in short, as we would say today, a fixed "structure."[19] It was simply that all this hardly interested him. He almost always moved on immediately either to their first origin or to their final End. It is this that St. Thomas was pointing out when he said: "Augustine speaks of nature not with respect to natural being, but as ordered towards beatitude."[20] In other words, for him the "theological" point of view outweighed the purely "philosophical" one—the terms are ours today but were already used here by St. Thomas; for, as he himself says, "the study of creatures is proper to theologians and philosophers, but in different ways; for philosophers consider creatures as they are in their own nature, where-

45

---

nature and supernatural things," and in these general terms the statement is true. "De natura creata per respectum ad supernaturalia secundum s. Augustinum" in *Acta hebdomadae augustinianae-thomisticae* (1931), p. 226.

[13] *In Physic.* (ed. Borgnet, vol. 3, p. 312).

[14] *Contra Julianum opus imperf.*, book 5, c. 40: "What is the motion of the soul but the motion of nature? The soul truly is without a doubt nature; therefore the will is the motion of nature, for it is the motion of the soul" (*PL*, 45, 1476).

[15] *De civitate Dei*, book 7, c. 30: "He governs all that He created, so that He permits them even to exercise and conduct their own motions." See also book 12, c. 26. (Bibl. august., 34, p. 210; 35, pp. 236–38).

[16] *De civitate Dei*, book 12, c. 8: "[The will's] deficiency is not towards evil things, but is itself evil; in other words it is not towards evil natures, but is evil itself because contrary to the order of natures it goes from the superior to the inferior" (Bibl. august., 35, p. 172).

[17] See, among other texts, *Retract.*, book 1, c. 13, n. 6, in regard to the *De duabus animabus* (Bibl. august., 12, p. 370).

[18] Ibid., c. 2: "[God] ordered natures by degrees of essences" (35, p. 154).

[19] *De Genesi ad litteram*, book 9, n. 32 (*PL*, 34, 406). *De moribus Ecclesiae catholicae*, book 2, n. 2: "Nature is nothing other than what something is understood to be in its kind" (*PL*, 32, 1346). On the idea of nature in St. Augustine, see F.J.T.'s note in *Augustin, Cité de Dieu*, Bibliothèque augustinienne, vol. 35, pp. 513–15.

[20] *De spiritualibus creaturis*, a. 8, ad primum.

as the theologian considers them as coming from their first principle and ordered to their last end, which is God."[21] For a full and balanced understanding, neither of these two points of view must eclipse the other. I shall therefore, without intending any criticism of Augustine, fully adopt this view which is directly inspired by St. Thomas: "Respect for natural values in their own structure is the best measure of our respect for the supernatural in its absolute originality."[22]

We have to make an analogous effort in regard to Thomism. This will consist chiefly in showing more explicitly that the "close accord" and the kind of "continuity"[23] summed up in the axiom (stated of old by William of Auxerre and William of Auvergne) "grace perfects nature"[24] or "grace is proportionate to nature as perfection is to the perfectible,"[25] or again "nature is anterior to grace"[26] by no means preclude, from another aspect, the total transcendence of the supernatural gift, its perfect spontaneity, and its difference in kind from "nature."[27]

46

---

[21] *In 2 Sent.*, prol. Also *Summa contra Gentiles*, book 2, c. 4: "For the philosopher considers creation in one way and the theologian in another." See Etienne Borne, *op. cit.*, p. 25: in Augustinism, "man is then more assured of his spiritual vocation than of his human condition."

[22] M. J. Le Guillou, O.P., "Surnaturel," *Revue des sciences philosophiques et théologiques* (1950): 238 (on St. Thomas's teaching on the natural perfection of angels). See *Summa contra Gentiles*, book 3, c. 69: "To take away from the perfection of creatures is to take away from the the perfection of divine virtue," etc. *De Potentia*, q. 3, a. 7. St. Thomas is concerned to show that even within the embrace of beatitude nature remains secure: "Nature must always be preserved in beatitude." See Aimé Forest, *La structure métaphysique du concret selon saint Thomas d'Aquin* (1931), pp. 5–10. L. B. Geiger, O.P., *La Participation*[2] (1953), p. 305.

[23] Gilson, *Le Thomisme*[5] (1945), pp. 495–96: "There is an intimate accord, indeed almost a continuity of order between the earthly beatitude accessible here below and the heavenly beatitude to which we are called." "Thus," concludes Gilson, "Thomism continues nature into supernature." Louis Roy, S.J., "Le désir naturel de voir Dieu," *Sciences ecclésiastiques* 1 (1948) (Montreal): 112. L. Cognet, in *Dévotion moderne et spiritualité française* (1958), p. 41, speaks of the "wonderful glimpses so dear to Flemings and Rhinelanders on the continuity of the spiritual nature which unites the soul to God." See also on *Canfeld*, p. 53.

[24] *De veritate*, q. 27, a. 6 ad primum; *Prima*, q. 1, 8, ad 2um. *Prima Secundae*, q. 3, a. 8. See the formula quoted by Gratry in *De la connaissance de Dieu*[2], vol. 2 (1854), p. 190: "reason perfected by supernatural understanding."

[25] *De veritate*, q. 27, a. 5, obj. 17.

[26] *In Boetium de Trinitate*, q. 2, a. 3; ibid.: "The gifts of graces are added to nature in such a way that they do not raise it but rather perfect it."

[27] See J. B. Beumer, S.J., "Gratia supponit naturam, Zur Geschichte eines theologischen Prinzips," *Gregorianum* 20 (1939): 381–406. Erik Przywara, S.J., "Der Grundsatz

St. Thomas no more misunderstood the nature of the supernatural order than St. Augustine did that of the natural. He explained most clearly that grace, "in so far as it is given freely, excludes the notion of debt," and expressly excludes all possibility of "debt" [*debitum*], either because of anything in nature, or because of any merit or personal action: "supernatural gifts are void of either debt"; grace and the infused virtues, he says again, "do not have absolute necessity, but only have necessity derived from the supposition of a divine order."[28] It is true, however, that his teaching on this is marked by a certain stress which can be explained to some extent by his own temperament, and even more so by the circumstances of his time. Between nature and grace, he "admits a close parallelism and union."[29] He is especially careful to show grace as "a perfection given to nature in the same direction towards which its own tendencies are working."[30] The first of the three "modes" of man's likeness to God, he explains, consists in his having "a natural aptitude for understanding and loving God, and that aptitude itself consists in the very nature of spirit, which is shared by all men"; so much so, he concludes, that simply by the fact of our created condition, "the light of Thy countenance, O Lord, is signed upon us."[31] Far from being any kind of selfishness, our first natural love is for him almost a beginning of charity: charity, he says, comes "not to destroy, but to fulfill it."[32] He was not satisfied with establishing his first point, that Greek

47

'Gratia non destruit sed supponit et perficit naturam,'" *Scholastik* 2 (1942): 178–86. Dom Bernhard Stoeckle's study "Gratia supponit naturam, Geschichte und Analyse eines theologischen Axioms," *Studia anselmiana* 49 (1962) covers a much wider field, and enters that area of renewed doctrinal interpretations to which I wish all success though I am not myself entering it (see the Preface to this book).

[28] *Prima Secundae*, q. 111, art. 1, ad 2um; *In 4 Sent.*, dist. 17, q. 1, a. 2, q. 3, s. 3. See also *In Boetium de Trinitate* (see *infra*, p. 26 n. 40). It may be noted however that St. Thomas is not as explicit as this when speaking of finality.

[29] A. Lemonnyer, O.P., in *Saint Thomas, La vie humaine, ses formes, ses états* (*Secunda secundae*, q. 179–89), p. 500 (Revue des Jeunes ed., 1926).

[30] Guy de Broglie, S.J., "Autour de la notion thomiste de la béatitude," *Archives de philosophie* 3 (1925): 222, note. See *In 4 Sent.*, d. 17, q. 1, a. 5, sol. 1: "The natural order is within the soul for it to follow the rectitude of justice." *Prima secundae*, q. 57, a. 4, ad 3um, etc.

[31] *Prima*, q. 93, art. 4. This text is finely commented on in an article by Charles J. O'Neil, "St. Thomas and the Nature of Man" in *Proceedings of the American Catholic Philosophical Association* (1951).

[32] *Prima*, q. 60, a. 5: "If [man or angel] by nature loved himself more than he does God, it would follow that natural love be perverse and that it be not perfected by charity but destroyed." One can recognize an offshoot of this Thomist spirit in an article on *Caro* by

man could, in the strictest sense, adapt himself to Christianity; he wanted to prove positively that "Christianity was necessary for him" because "only it could fully guarantee his ideal and let him fully realize it."[33] The fact that his modern disciples often want to prove the opposite—because their needs, or at least their circumstances, are different from his—should not mislead us. And although he never speaks of a demand on the part of created nature, St. Thomas does say things which anyone reading him today might well see as paving the way for such a statement. While setting aside all heterodox interpretations of the texts he quotes, Père Pierre Rousselot thinks that one can discern in Thomist teaching "a mysterious demand for the supernatural life springing from the very nature of spirit."[34]

It is certainly quite legitimate to note, as does Père S. Dockx, O.P., that the desire to see the divine essence spoken of by St. Thomas "results from intelligence as nature (ut natura), and not from intelligence as an operative power," and that therefore, in his eyes, "from the fact that he makes man tend towards a good which he cannot reach by his own powers, [he] has no necessary connection with that good, and makes no demand upon it; it is simply the sure sign that God intends actually to satisfy this longing which he has himself implanted in rational nature"; for God's *debitum,* even to himself, is based only upon the actuality of the creature, either according to its being, or to its action, which is not the case here: so much so that the life of grace remains always and in every individual "the object of divine election." One can further note, with the same commentator, that St. Thomas finds no "incompatibility" between the restricting precision of his argument and the mysterious nature which he himself ascribes to the beatific vision, since a truth of faith "of its nature transcends all rational proofs."[35] One cannot therefore, if one enters deeply into his statement of the problem, reproach St. Thomas either for explaining away the mystery, or for diminishing the gratuitousness of the gift.

48

J. Lachelier (1864): "Thought and love already shine, as through a veil, in the instinctive wisdom of nature and the spontaneous tendency of beings towards their end."

[33] Gilson, *Saint Thomas d'Aquin* (Paris, 1925), p. 5, Eng. trans. *Moral Values and the Moral Life* (London, 1931), p. 5; quoted by Dom A. Stolz, *op. cit.,* French trans. *Théologie de la mystique* (Paris, 1939), p. 156.

[34] *L'intellectualisme de saint Thomas*[3] (1936), p. 185.

[35] "Du désir naturel de voir l'essence divine d'après saint Thomas," *Archives de philosophie* (1964), pp. 63, 90–91, 93–96.

49   There are other less important points of a historical nature to be considered. Père Joseph Maréchal has rightly pointed out that "in the context of his time" St. Thomas had above all "to defend the possibility of the [beatific] vision." He had to defend it—whatever Cajetan may later have said—against the objections of the "philosophers," which were at that time a very real and urgent threat. He had also to defend it against the excesses of one traditional line of thought which tended in a similar direction. There were several people at the time who proclaimed the invisibility of the supreme essence,[36] which according to them could only be contemplated "in some brilliant reflection [*refulgentia*] of His splendor."[37] Such an opinion, he declared, is "false and heretical on three counts."[38] Faced with these converging errors—to which we shall be returning later—it was thus essential first of all to explain how the *ordo gratiae* (order of grace) contains and perfects the *ordo naturae* (order of nature). And, while it is true that St. Thomas did not therefore fail to be "attentive to the mystery of divine liberty,"[39] and to show elsewhere "the absolute gratuitousness and superabundant generosity of the gift God makes to his creature,"[40] it is also true—as one of the finest historians of his thought points out—that "the dogmatic disputes since the Reformation have made us more aware of all the difficulties" of this aspect of things.[41] They have put us more on our guard against one-sided formulas which, though harmless in the past, can be fraught with danger today. Anyone who wants to work on this purely as a historian

50 should at this point follow to the letter the advice given by Père Rousselot:

[36] Joseph Maréchal, S.J., *Etudes sur la psychologie des mystiques*, vol. 2 (1937), pp. 195–96: "Throughout his works, from the commentary on the Sentences on, St. Thomas defends–against objections largely based on the erroneous interpretation of certain patristic or scriptural texts–the *possibility* of a direct intuition of the divine essence by the created intelligence; and he shows that possibility at least partially *realized* in heaven."

[37] *In 2 Sent.*, d. 23, q. 2, a. 1: "Certain writers err who posit that God is never seen in His essence, neither in heaven nor on earth. . . ." *Expositio in Matthaeum evangelistam*, c. 5: "Some have posited that God is never seen in His essence, but in a sort of brilliant reflection of His splendor; the Gloss, however, disproves this" etc.

[38] *Lectura in evangelium secundum Ioannem*, c. 1, lectio 2: "There were some who said that the divine essence would never be visible to any created intellect, and that it is invisible to angels and the blessed. This position, however, is shown to be false and heretical on three counts. . . ."

[39] M. J. Le Guillou, *loc. cit.*

[40] L. B. Geiger, *op. cit.*, p. 102, note.

[41] R. A. Motte, O.P., in *Bulletin thomiste* 3 (1933): 674.

"One must not read St. Thomas in the light of the heresies that have come after him, but of the philosophies that went before. One must give no more thought to Pascal or Baius than he did himself";[42] nor to Leibniz, wondering at "the pre-established harmony" which "results in things leading us to grace by the ways of nature itself";[43] nor to Wolff, nor to many others. Anachronisms may be as misleading in the history of ideas as in that of institutions and events. But from the theological standpoint the question presents itself differently. Certainly St. Thomas was no more an early Baianist than the Greek Fathers were Pelagians. "He was speaking unencumbered" [*securus loquebatur*]. Nor was his language, as has been said, possibly in a wish to escape the full implications of his teaching, "obscure and ambiguous."[44] At least, it was not so for his contemporaries. However, in some cases, despite all the nuances and precisions which anyone who studies him closely will discover, he has sometimes become so for us, and the explanations he uses will not always stand today without amplification. "After various errors have arisen," we may say using his words,[45] we are forced to speak "more carefully and precisely" [*cautius et elimatius*].

There are times when he helps us, as when he prevents us from taking the axiom "grace perfects nature"[46] too straightforwardly—but not always. The fact is that in modern times many of his disciples have been frightened—some thinking they could not follow him on this or that major point,[47] while others could not bring themselves to believe that they understood him aright, fearing that it might be "in a sense opposed to the Church's definitions."[48] To demonstrate the fundamental ortho-

51

[42] *L'Intellectualisme de saint Thomas*³, p. 182.

[43] *Monadology*, n. 88. *Les principes de la nature et de la grâce fondée en raison*, p. 15: ". . . The harmony pre-established from all time between the kingdoms of nature and of grace . . . are such that nature leads to grace, and grace perfects nature while making use of it" (André Robinet ed., 1954, pp. 57, 125).

[44] J. V. Bainvel, *Nature et surnaturel*, p. 130. Cajetan said the same; see also Báñez, *In Primam secundae*, q. 3, a. 8 (vol. 1, Madrid, 1942, p. 122).

[45] *Contra errores Graecorum*, prooemium.

[46] *In Boetium de Trinitate*, q. 3, a. 1, ad 2um: The perfection of nature "consists in that man has all the things that are due to his nature; but after the debt of nature are straight away added to the human race some perfections from divine grace alone, among which is faith. . . ." Nothing could be less Baianist! In chapter 5, *infra*, I shall propose an equivalent distinction.

[47] Thus Count Domet de Vorges, *Congrès scientifique international des catholiques* in Brussels, 1894; vol. 3 of the proceedings, 1895, p. 320.

[48] Ibid., p. 321, Abbé Gayraud.

doxy of his thought it is not enough simply to say as Rousselot does that the demand he mentions, or supposes, is "mysterious," and that for him the beatific vision is only demanded "in some sense" by the nature of the intellect. "I think," writes Rousselot, "that he would not have had to alter a line in order to be able to reply perfectly to the questions his method raises"—and which are also raised by some of his theses and formulas.[49] But the fact remains that he himself has not given these answers; the clarifications which he could easily have given never had occasion to be given. Nor did his contemporaries give them. The task devolves therefore on anyone who wants to do serious theological work—and I believe in fact that one can and must achieve such work while remaining substantially faithful to Thomism, more faithful than many modern Thomists have dared to be. Fidelity to the great masters of Catholic tradition can never, in any case, be content with merely historical exactitude, with merely sticking to the letter alone.[50]

Perhaps indeed this indispensable effort offers scope for trying to show more clearly how supernatural reality "only crowns and completes human efforts because it first of all turns them upside down."[51] Perhaps it is also the occasion for showing more clearly that not only does our perfection "come to us from one other than ourselves," but that that perfection is not simply the straightforward and normal completion of tendencies which only needed supernatural help in order to reach their final goal: it is a "transforming union," and therefore one cannot see how, under any circumstances, it could be attained without some kind of intrusion into nature to effect a "passive purification." This would lead us to discern in finite beings two opposing tendencies, both equally natural and basic, so that the passage to the supernatural order, even for an innocent and healthy nature, could never take place without some kind of death.[52] For God's infinite is not a "composite infinite," a false

52

---

[49] *Loc. cit.*

[50] See Maréchal, *Revue des questions scientifiques* (1913): 632–34 (the text published in *Mélanges Joseph Maréchal* 1 [1950]: 44–46). The author was speaking of philosophy; but, suitably transposed, his reflections apply perfectly here.

[51] Hans Urs von Balthasar, *Théologie de l'histoire* (Paris, 1955), p. 167 (French trans. of *Theologie Der Geschichte*[1]).

[52] We must in this case distinguish between death as the necessary gate of entry to Life, and the form of death we know which is the consequence of sin. This is the purpose of G. Martelet's analyses in *Victoire sur la mort, éléments d'anthropologie chrétienne* (Editions de la Chronique sociale de France, 1962), which distinguishes death as a biological end from death as existential suffering; see especially pp. 90–114.

infinite that could be reached simply by an extension of the finite. It is not a matter of the finite being's simply consenting to having a cubit added to his stature. He must consent to a more total sacrifice. Thus his natural tendency is to shrink into his own finitude, to "entrench himself," as Claudel says, "behind his essential difference." For is it not this difference that makes him what he is? Are not his limitations also the protection of his autonomy? The approach of the living God therefore leads him to draw back: "by pride we wish to rest in our own sphere, leaving divine things to God"—so Cajetan explained the temptation that caused Lucifer to fall.[53] In his impatience with limitations, and his wish to "be as a god," he hates being dependent on the God without whom his impatience and longing are meaningless. It was not only the awareness of sin, therefore, that made Augustine say (and we must say it with him) whenever he felt that approach: "I both shudder and flare up [*et inhorresco et inardesco*]."[54] It is not only of dying to sin that we can say with him: "Love has made in us a sort of death."[55] And certainly, when Maurice Blondel wrote in *L'Action:* "Man, by his deliberate intention, can only rise to the heights of his spontaneous aspiration by annihilating his self-will and establishing within himself the opposite will, the will to mortification"; and, again, "No man can see God without dying. Nothing can touch God and not be raised up again; for no will is good unless it has come out of itself to leave room for a total invasion by

[53] *In Primam*, q 63, a 3, n. 13: "The sin of the angel is more reasonably placed in his impulse to rest in a natural beatitude than in an impulse to desire the supernatural [*beatitude*] separately from mercy; besides this impulse is natural to the angel and nature impels the proud rather to the former than to the latter, as our own experience reveals, when by pride we wish to rest in our own sphere, leaving divine things to God." See Billuart, *De angelis*, disp. 5, a. 3. I have shown in my *Le Surnaturel*, part 2, how this could not apply as it stands to the case of angels, as Cajetan believed. My demonstration was described by Rev. Edward J. Montano as "very much to the point," in *The Sin of the Angels, Some Aspects of the Teaching of St. Thomas* (Washington, 1955), p. 113, note 90.

[54] *Confessions*, book 11, c. 9, n. 11: "I shudder at how unlike Her [divine Wisdom] I am, I flare up at how like Her I am." Book 12, c. 14, n. 17: ". . . the shudder of honor and the quaking of love." See also *In Joannem*, tract. 21, n. 12: "so that we should not tremble at the Eminent, but should arrive at the Humble" (*CCL*, 36, 219). In the article referred to, Le Guillou also recalls "to what extent in primitive religions man is both drawn and repelled by the mystery of God, which appears at once "fascinosum" and "tremendum.". . . See Gen. 28:17.

[55] *In psalm 121*, n. 12: "The fortitude of charity could not have been expressed more wondrously than when it was said: mighty love is like death. Who indeed resists death, brethren? . . . And since charity itself kills what we were, so that we be what we were not, love has made in us a sort of death" (*PL*, 37, 1628).

God's will,"[56] he was not dealing with the same problem as St. Thomas or the scholastic tradition, but was reflecting upon human nature as marked by sin; but this does not mean that he remained the prisoner of empirical observation in the matter, any more than St. Augustine was. The twofold, simultaneous experience which such writings reveal certainly carries us beyond all moral systems, all changing psychology, perhaps even beyond the "wound" of man's first sin, to the depths of our original nature:

> Saisi d'horreur, voici de nouveau que j'entends
> L'inexorable appel de la voix merveilleuse. . . .[57]

54   In short, if we refuse to follow St. Thomas by interpreting him according to hypotheses which he never formulated, we are in no sense weakening the idea of the supernatural, we are not so to say making it "less supernatural," or less completely a free gift in relation to nature, also itself freely given. Quite the reverse, as I hope will become clear further on. One's ideas on this subject are often not very precise. The realities which are most separable materially are not necessarily those which appear most distinct: the very act of separating them, of setting them side by side or one above the other, indicates a certain identity of character between them. Union and differentiation are more like two things that grow side by side. "Distinguish to unite" is a phrase we sometimes hear. Certainly, and at the moment it is the operation most needed. But it can sometimes be useful to recall its converse: unite in order to distinguish the better.[58] If I may be permitted a comparison—

[56] *L'Action* (1893), pp. 383, 384. See also *Lettre sur les exigences . . .* (1896), p. 83: "The natural order is not sufficient to our nature, which yet rejects the supernatural." On the differing points of view of Blondel and St. Thomas, see Henri Bouillard, *Blondel et le christianisme* (1961), pp. 129–31. See Manuel Ossa, *La "nouvelle naissance" d'après Maurice Blondel* (typewritten thesis, 1964), pp. 98–99.

[57] "Gripped with horror, once again I hear the inexorable call of the wonderful voice . . . ," Paul Claudel, *Vers d'exil*. The same idea is suggested in a remarkable page by Fr. Martin D'Arcy in *The Mind and Heart of Love* (London, 1945). It can also be found in Robert Hamel, "Humanisme et christianisme," *Revue pratique d'Apologétique* 50 (1930): 641–42. See also Friedrich von Hügel, Letter to M. Blondel, 26 May, 1896: "From childhood I have had a most lively conviction, and one which has often enough troubled me, along the middle course we always steer, that this middle course *un-crowns* Christianity by taking away its impressive crown of thorns. It takes away all its power . . . even for an instant to picture the relations between nature and grace as a peaceful accord, a practical and basically uninteresting arrangement."

[58] I have analyzed this in *Catholicisme,* chapter 11 (4th ed., 1948, pp. 286–90; Eng. trans. *Catholicism* [London, 1950]).

and it only applies to this point—scholasticism admits that matter has no existence independent of form;[59] does this mean that matter in itself has some resemblance to form, that it is, so to say, cut out of the same cloth, or that one should consider it as already being an "inchoate form"? As everyone knows, precisely the opposite is true. Similarly, when certain Fathers, and certain medievals all the more so, said that "the image" which is in us is made in the "likeness" of God,[60] and that therefore we have to pass from the "dignity of the image" received at the "first creation" to the "perfection of the likeness" which is "reserved for the consummation of all things," they were in no sense intending to affirm by this that this "likeness" was of the same nature as the "image," that it had nothing specific to add to it, or that it was not superior in kind, and the object of a further totally free gift.

This brings us back again to our subject. The fact that the nature of spiritual being, as it actually exists, is not conceived as an order destined to close in finally upon itself, but in a sense open to an inevitably supernatural end, does not mean that it already has in itself, or as part of its basis, the smallest positively supernatural element. It does not mean that this nature, "as nature, and by nature," is elevated.[61] "Without the presence of a certain salt in the mouth, no one would want to drink";[62] yet it is quite clear that the salt which makes us thirsty is not the water which quenches our thirst. Thus this fact does not mean that God is in the smallest degree bound. Nor does it mean that that nature does not have its own proper stability and its own definite structure. Nor does it involve any disregard, either from the metaphysi-

[59] Hence the terms analogous to those it uses for our subject. See St. Bonaventure, *In 2 Sent.,* d. 12, a. 1, q. 3: "Since formless matter had an impulse and inclination towards many forms. . . ." The comparison, of course, has no more point once one considers that matter can have no existence without form.

[60] Thus Irenaeus, Clement, Origen, etc. Origen, *Periarchon,* book 3, c. 6, n. 1: "Man has received the dignity of image from the first creation, but the perfection of likeness has been reserved for him at the consummation of the world." There are many similar texts. Thus Rupert of Deutz, *In Genesim,* book 2, c. 3 (*PL,* 167, 249 B); *De Spiritu sancto,* book 1, c. 11 (167, 1581); *De divinis officiis,* book 7, c. 4 (170, 148 C).

[61] Which seems to me, I need hardly say, as being both contradictory and unacceptable in good theology. To be already "raised up" and to be destined to be "raised up" are two different things. Tendency and finality are neither a deposit nor a seed. See *infra,* chapter 5, pp. 84–88. See also Charles Boyer, "Nature et surnaturel . . . ," *Gregorianum* 27 (1947): 387.

[62] Friedrich von Hügel, "Du Christ éternel et de nos christologies successives" in *La Quinzaine* (1904), p. 288.

56 cal or the moral point of view, of what St. Thomas called the *ordo naturalis*.[63] Once again, this time in the words of Père Blaise Romeyer:
"Only by taking care not to disregard the relative specific consistency of
our nature, and by taking it as a genuine substratum for grace, can we
fulfill the requirements either of belief or of thought."[64] But in order to
avoid the danger indicated here, it is not indispensable to conceive of
man as having a twofold final end, with all the inextricable complications this involves.[65] Indeed I think—for reasons which I will give—that
it is better not to do so. In other words, it is not the ancient concept of
natura pura, but the system which has grown up around it in modern
theology and profoundly changed its meaning, which it seems to me
could be set aside without any loss. As it has developed, with its denial
of any organic connection, this system, unknown to the great scholastics, seems to me to be neither the only nor the best means of assuring
the stability and dignity of human nature or the transcendence and
freedom of the supernatural.

"Grace must be acknowledged, but nature must not be ignored."[66] I
would wish to assert both terms of this precept to the full.

The reader may find it helpful towards a greater awareness of this to
consider a comparison similar to the one I offered earlier, and with the
same reservations. As between the Platonic and Cartesian doctrine
57 which makes the body and spirit two substances, or the Aristotelian and
Thomist doctrine which sees man as substantially one being, it is not
the first which better assures the true recognition of bodily values and
better resists the influence of false spiritualisms, in conformity with rev-

[63] See, for instance, *De Malo*, q. 16, a. 3.

[64] "La théorie suarézienne d'un état de nature pure," *Archives de philosophie*, 18, p. 52.

[65] See *infra*, chapter 4. It has been said that I want to do away with the concept of
nature (*Greg.* [1947], pp. 392, 393). But the only proof offered is a single sentence, so
shortened and altered, that though a few words have survived unchanged, it no longer has
anything in common as to meaning with what I wrote. In its original form this sentence
said nothing different from the following—which I quote from Maréchal (*Le point de
départ de la métaphysique*, vol. 5 [1926], p. 180): "Our mind, it is true, has an unhappy tendency to set up created objects, once they have come into existence, as so many little
absolutes, subsisting in themselves; in reality, however, their ontological poverty and their
need of a principle of being are as basic once they exist as before." See St. Thomas, *Prima*,
q. 104, a. 1. See *infra*, chapter 6, pp. 102–3.

[66] St. Ambrose, *In Lucam*, book 8, n. 32. By these words, however, Ambrose does not
mean to exalt nature but, by distinguishing the two orders of reality carefully, to remind
man of his natural condition of servanthood.

elation itself; it is incontestably the second.[67] The example of St. Thomas Aquinas would seem to be sufficient proof of this. No one has ever accused him of failing to recognize the stability of natures; no one would deny his having given "solidity to the abstract consideration of human nature and metaphysical essences."[68] Now, "he acknowledges and maintains a 'natural law,' but there is no suggestion whatever (and that fact alone is significant) that its observance leads man to any natural beatitude, or constitutes any 'order' other than purely social and 'mundane': he expressly denies that it suffices to guide man to his final destiny."[69] This, which I quote from Victor White, O.P., is decisive. "Since man is ordered to an end of eternal beatitude that exceeds the limits of natural human faculty, it was therefore necessary that, besides natural and human law, man actually be directed to his end by a law given by God."[70] For St. Thomas then—which is all I want at the moment to demonstrate—neither the objectivity of laws nor that of natural essences is prejudicial to the supernatural quality of man's final end, nor is the supernatural goal of the subject prejudicial to the solidity of the laws of his physical or moral nature, considered objectively.

58

Nature has its own consistency, and is different in kind from the supernatural: we must not be too quick to take these two things as established, because we have formed the satisfactory hypothesis of a really possible universe in which created nature can develop fully and reach its "proportionate" end, without ever being elevated above itself

[67] From the opposite point of view, Maxime Chastaing produces similar conclusions: "Just as we imagine the supernatural as *another* nature, when we succumb to the temptation to separate it from nature, and just as so-called primitive minds think of the soul as a shadow of the body, almost a second body, because they separate soul and body, so the philosopher who sets out to separate spirit from matter will treat both spirit and matter as parts of a complex that is essentially made up of detachable parts. The natural light which shows us that space is substantially different from our thinking about space consequently shows us that the two cannot be taken apart. To dissociate spirit from flesh is to confuse the two; to distinguish between them is to unite them" ("Descartes, Fauste de Riez et le problème de la connaissance d'autrui" in *Etienne Gilson, philosophe de la chrétienté*, pp. 203–4).

[68] M. D. Chenu, *Introduction à l'étude de saint Thomas*, p. 47.

[69] "The Supernatural," *Dominican Studies* (Jan. 1949): 70. This is the point which was missed by a theologian who complains that I (and indeed St. Thomas) deny any objective order of natural morality: "Morale et surnaturel," *Gregorianum* 29 (1948): 536–43. I cannot see in these pages anything other than a complete misunderstanding both of my thinking and of that of St. Thomas.

[70] *Prima secundae*, q. 91, a. 4.

as far as *theōsis*. Such a preliminary thesis would be no more than a beginning; we cannot let ourselves off so lightly. Is it not rather the same in this matter as in that of certain doctrines of so-called "tolerance" or "neutrality"? There exists, as we know, an attitude which consists in setting one's mind at rest by beginning with the affirmation of an absolutely intransigent "thesis," and then going on in practice to yield to every weakening and abandonment of it under the guise of a "hypothesis." It looks as though the structure is maintained intact, and even exaggerated in theory, yet in effect everything is compromised. Now similarly, it is possible to lay great stress on the idea of a wholly ideal order of "pure nature," and then at once, in the actual order of reality, to crush that poor nature, as it actually exists, within the grip of an ill-conceived supernatural.[71] The status one appears to give it in theory is

59   thus destroyed in practice.[72] Yet ultimately, all that interests us is what exists in fact, the reality of our nature as it is, acting at this moment, in God's creation as it is.

In the old teaching, which remains for us the traditional one, the argument was based on no such duality of ends. The supernatural, which always represented God's will for the final end of his creatures, put no obstacle in the way of the normal development or activity of nature in its own order; in other words, it fully assures the distinction between nature and grace. Philippe Delhaye showed this not long ago, in relation to Geoffrey of Saint Victor's *Microcosmus*.[73] St. Thomas, as

---

[71] Bouyer rightly praises Thomist theology, and then the spirit of humanist Christianity, for permitting the "coordination . . . of a whole order of secondary ends to a supreme, but not exclusive end," for not always setting forward at once "finalities which are properly and directly sacred," for not "absorbing" into the final end "other more immediate ends" (*Autour d'Erasme*, pp. 15–16, Eng. trans. *Erasmus and the Humanist Experiment* [London, 1959]). This praise is well merited. But neither in fact nor in theory is this connected, as some seem to think, with the modern speculation on another kind of supreme and final ends—a speculation which, though it may be quite legitimate, does not in itself avoid all risk of exclusivism and absorption.

[72] As the result of a similar confusion, it is sometimes thought that if the democratic theory of the state were true, it should be applied equally to the Church, and the divine right of the Church's pastors is established on the basis of a refutation of Rousseau's *Contrat social*.

[73] *Revue du moyen âge latin* 3 (1947): 243, "Nature et grâce chez Geoffroy de Saint-Victor": "One must stress how forcefully Geoffrey establishes the distinction between nature and grace. It is not for him an unimportant thesis; it is the basis of his whole work.

we have recalled, allowed for a complete order of natural morality. From his teaching as a whole, as Père Jacques de Blic has said, there emerges "an admirable Christian humanism";[74] or, perhaps Père Bouyer would like it better if we call it an admirable humanist Christianity. Later on, the theologians who remained completely faithful to that teaching could also, and without any contradiction, become champions of humanism. Dominic Soto, for one, wrote his *De natura et gratia* against the pessimism of Luther and the extreme theses of Gregory of Rimini.[75] Or again, Toletus who, commenting on St. Thomas's *Summa,* preserved the old tradition right up to the threshold of the seventeenth century,[76] though he was open to the generous tendencies so forcefully emanating at the time from the theologians, missionaries, educators and spiritual writers of the Society of Jesus.[77] Then, too, there were the Capuchin humanists of the seventeenth century, who have been restored to honor in modern times through the writings of Père Julian Eymard d'Angers.[78]

60

If we begin by dissociating the two orders completely, in order to establish the existence of a natural order that could be fully and finally self-sufficient, we are all too likely to end up by seeing not so much a distinction as a complete divorce.[79] And we may risk also losing the profound sense of their "infinite qualitative difference." Indeed it is extremely hard—as experience has shown—to pursue this idea of "pure nature" and make it anything other than a great "X" for which we have no precise intellectual meaning, and which cannot therefore help our

---

. . . We see here how foreign is this essential distinction to the hypothesis of pure nature with which it is so often linked."

[74] *Mélanges de science religieuse* (1947): 104.

[75] *De nat. et gratia* (Antwerp, 1550), book 1, c. 3, pp. 7–8; c. 20, pp. 68–70.

[76] As we know, his commentary on the *Summa,* the fruit of repeated teaching, was rewritten by him at least twice if not three times, and he continued to work on it up to the very end of his life, in 1596. It seems that this was his favorite work, and the one he was most anxious to see published among those which remained to be published. Cf. Franciscus Toletus, *In Summam theologiae S. Thomae Aquinatis Enarratio ex autographo in Bibliotheca collegii romani asservato,* vol. 1 (Rome, 1869), p. xxvi (*Prolegomena,* by Père Paria).

[77] Cf. *In Secundam Secundae,* q. 26, a. 3 (vol. 2, pp. 180–82). To prepare a field for the unfolding of a natural order, Toletus liked to base himself, like Soto, on the Thomist thesis of the inclination of created nature to love God more than itself.

[78] In *Antonianum, Etudes franciscaines,* and *Mélanges de science religieuse,* from 1950 on.

thinking along very much,[80] without our ending up by gradually attributing to it more and more of the qualities and privileges which attach to our present human nature in relation to God. Thus the supernatural order loses its unique splendor; and, as we shall see, by a logic whose headlong course we cannot halt, often ends by becoming no more than a kind of shadow of that supposed natural order.

---

[79] Cf. Henri Rondet, *Rech. de science relig.* (1948): 493.

[80] On the essential point of our relationship to God as our last end. Naturally, we

CHAPTER 3

The Two Tendencies of the Hypothesis

There can be no doubt that this is the direction in which a large seg- ment of modern theology is tending, for given its point of departure, it cannot logically do otherwise. It sees nature and supernature as in some sense juxtaposed, and in spite of every intention to the contrary, as contained in the same genus, of which they form as it were two species. The two were like two complete organisms; too perfectly separated to be really differentiated, they have unfolded parallel to each other, fatally similar in kind. Under such circumstances, the supernatural is no longer properly speaking another order, something unprecedented, overwhelming and transfiguring: it is no more than a "super-nature," as we have fallen into the habit of calling it, contrary to all theological tradition; a "supernature" which reproduces, to what is called a "superior" degree, all the features which characterize nature itself.

Take, then, the great traditional texts, from Augustine, say, and Thomas, dealing with man's final end and beatitude: they will be systematically brought down to a natural plane and their whole meaning thus perverted. They will no longer be taken to be anything but affirmations of a purely natural philosophy. The "perfection" of human nature spoken of in these texts, a perfection which was recognized as meaning its supernatural consummation, will thus become a completely natural perfection which can be adequately defined by pure philosophy. "All the doctors of the Church," it will be said, "hold it to be a philosophical truth that man's happiness can be found only in possessing God." But it does not stop here. The theory goes on to describe—against the evidence of the texts upon which it is based—that "possession of God," that supreme good which makes man "perfect" and "wholly satisfies the appetite of the will," as the crowning point of a purely philosophical ethic. It declares this to be the ultimate end of human effort, without any suggestion of help from the supernatural properly so called, without the slightest allusion to any divine initiative, any divine gift.[1] Final end, beatitude, perfection, these three concepts taken from St. Thomas are used to designate not merely the same thing, but a thing wholly contained within the limits of the natural order.[2]

To be obliged to misconstrue so profoundly one of the essential elements in the teaching of the great masters is in itself somewhat astonishing. When St. Augustine uttered his famous declaration "You have made us for yourself, O God . . . ," he never anticipated that one day in the twentieth century this would be taken in a purely natural sense. When St. Thomas Aquinas said "Grace perfects nature," he did not foresee that what he said about the completion or perfecting of nature would be retained, while the grace which effects that completion would be left aside. When Scotus Erigena gloried in "the pure and direct contemplation of the divine essence" it never occurred to him that people would ever see in it anything other than the happiness "promised to the saints," the happiness spoken of by St. Paul and St. John, the inspired writers of revelation.[3] When Albert the Great explained the contemplation of "the face of God" by describing a "presence of God shown and presented without mediation," he thought thereby to be describing quite clearly and unmistakably the "beatific vision" and nothing else.[4]

63

---

[1] Thus C. Boyer, S.J., *Cursus philosophiae, Ethica generalis, q. prima, De fine moralitatis,* art. 5, "Utrum Deus sit beatitudo hominis": "All Christian doctors hold as a philosophical truth that the beatitude of man is found only in the possession of God. . . . Thesis: the beatitude of man is God alone, who is to be possessed by acts of the intellect and of the will" (p. 453). "God is the beatitude of man. (1) Beatitude is the final end of man; furthermore the final end of man is God . . . , therefore . . . (2) Beatitude is the good that totally quells the appetite of the will; furthermore, etc. And this is confirmed by experience: [Augustine says:] 'You have made us for yourself . . .'" (p. 454).

[2] Ibid.: "Corollary, on the perfection of human nature. . . . The following three terms, which are different in concept, nevertheless signify the same thing, namely: the final end of man, the beatitude of man, the perfection of man" (pp. 455–56).

[3] *De divisione naturae,* bk. 1, c. 8: "What then shall we say of that future felicity, which is promised to the saints, which we believe to be nothing other than the pure and immediate contemplation of the divine essence itself, as say John and Paul . . . ?" (*PL,* 122, 447, AB).

[4] *Summa theol., Prima,* tract. 3, q. 13, membr. 4, sol.: "It is most fitting that the face of God be called essential, the presence of God shown and revealed immediately, in the way in which it reveals itself to the blessed."

When St. Thomas further said: "This immediate vision of God is guaranteed to us in Scripture,"[5] he could not have supposed that one day people would attribute to him the idea of another vision of God, equally "direct," which could be obtained without reference to anything promised in scripture. When he spoke of the "contemplation of Heaven, in which supernatural Truth is seen in its essence,"[6] he did not imagine that later "disciples" would come to divide that contemplation into two kinds, of which the first while remaining "by essence" [*per essentiam*] would none the less be "purely natural." Nor could he have imagined that those "disciples" would do the same for the "spiritual union [*societas spiritualis*] with God," the "rational union of the mind with God" [*societas rationalis mentis ad Deum*], the "gratuitous love" [*amor gratuitus*], the "love of charity" [*dilectio caritatis*], and so on.[7]

But beyond this, the consequences of making this kind of division and providing this kind of option are quick to follow. Henceforward all the values of the supernatural order, all those which characterize the present relationship between man and God in our economy of grace, will be gradually reabsorbed into that "purely natural" order that has been imagined (and I say "imagined" advisedly). In that order as in the other we will find faith, prayer,[8] the perfect virtues, the remission of sins by infused charity,[9] grace,[10] divine friendship,[11] spiritual union with

64

---

[5] *Summa contra Gentiles*, bk. 3, c. 51.

[6] *Secunda Secundae*, q. 5, a. 1, ad 1um.

[7] Cf. the texts quoted by André Hayen, S.J., "Théologie de l'amour divin et métaphysique de l'acte d'être" in *Teoresi* 9 (1954): 144–45.

[8] St. Thomas said (*Secunda Secundae*, q. 83, a 10, ad 1um): "To pray is proper to the rational creature," and at the same time: "to pray belongs to him that accepts it through grace." Cf. *In Boetium de Trin.*, q. 3, a 2. St. Augustine, *De perfectione iustitiae*, n. 21 and 40 (*PL* 44, 313, and 314); sermo 115, n. 1 (*PL*, 38, 655).

[9] Thus Medina, *In Primam Secundae*, q. 113, a. 2; Salmanticenses, *De iustificatione*, disput. 2, dub. 7, n. 256; etc.

[10] Suarez, *De fine ultimo*, Disput. 13, sect. 2, n. 11: "It is probable that God was going to give to man in this state some genus of providence, by which he might turn himself towards God in a natural love beyond all . . ." (vol. 4, p. 149); *De gratia*, bk. 1, c. 28, n. 4 (vol. 7, p. 522), etc. Cf. de Rubeis, *De peccato originali* (1757), c. 52, which recounts a certain number of different opinions, and itself supports that of Thomas of Lemos (1857 ed., pp. 302–9).

[11] Cajetan, *In Primam Secundae*, q. 99, a. 9, n. 3: "Man's friendship for God can be understood under two headings: first, simply, through grace and charity; second, relatively [*secundum quid*], that is to say, it can exist between man in pure nature and God to the exclusion of grace"; note that Cajetan still makes it "relatively [*secundum quid*]": cf. *Theologia Wiceburgensis*, *De peccato originali* (1880 ed., vol. 7, p. 129, n. 138): "Every knowledge, even also natural love, of God is not sufficient for natural beatitude; but God

God, disinterested love,[12] and a docile abandonment to "personal Love."[13] In short, nothing is lacking. Nothing—for there is even a revelation which, while supernatural in origin and mode, has none the less, owing to its object, always been "entitatively natural."[14] One may say, indeed, that the substitution is complete—but I prefer myself to say that the disguise is complete. Everything that now comes to us by the grace of God is thus withdrawn from the "supernatural" properly so called of our present economy, and "naturalized"—at the risk of being attributed afresh to some special intervention by God according to a different "mode." No difficulty is found in speaking of "natural graces," "natural contrition,"[15] of friendship with God "to the exclusion of grace" [*seclusa gratia*] or "purely naturally" [*in puris naturalibus*]; there seems no obstacle in conceiving of a disinterested love of God, a love that is "most excellent" [*excellentissimus*] and "above all things" [*super omnia*], directed towards "the author of nature," and existing as a fruit of "pure nature." Henceforth, everything, from the first beginnings, from the very appetite for happiness, is thus seen in a kind of double way: "The beatitude of man is twofold: one is natural, in whose acquisition the natural appetite rests. . . . The other is supernatural, in whose acquisition the supernatural appetite rests. . . ."[16] This applies to everything, up to the final point, the "perfect beatitude," the "direct vision" and—this has recently been said—the "possession" of God.

65

What remains peculiar to the supernatural order, except the word? Neither Pedro Descoqs, with his "direct natural vision of God,"[17] nor

---

must be known as a friend, so that hence may arise a friendly love, which supposes a mutual friendship" (H. Kilber).

[12] Lessius, *De summo bono*, bk. 2, c. 23, n. 190: "By some excellent natural love" (Hurter ed., p. 375). A. Moraines, *Anti-Jansenius* (1652), p. 201: "I answer, that it is not impossible for there to be any purely natural love of God *propter se*." Fénelon did not fall into this confusion: cf. *Responsio D. Camerensis ad Epistolam D. Parisiensis* (*Oeuvres*, Paris ed., vol. 2; pp. 553–54); *3ᵉ Lettre en réponse à celle de Mgr L'évêque de Meaux* (ibid., p. 654), etc.

[13] Blaise Romeyer, S.J., "La théorie suarézienne d'un état de nature pure," *loc. cit.*, p. 57.

[14] Cf. F. Teresius a S. Agnete, O.C.D., "De natura fidei theologicae secundum Salmanticenses," *Ephemerides Carmeliticae* 1 (1947): 287.

[15] F. B. Franzelin, *De Traditione et Scriptura* (1870), p. 556.

[16] Medina, *In Primam Secundae*, q. 3, a. 8 (Venice, 1590), pp. 45–47.

[17] *Le mystère de notre élévation surnaturelle*, chap. 7 (1938). See also V. Cathrein, *art. cit.*, *Gregorianum* (1930): 402–7.

Père Peillaube,[18] nor Charles Boyer with his "natural possession" of God,[19] has stood out from the chorus, so to say, to produce any really personal idea requiring individual consideration. But they have borne a single stream of thought along to its goal; and long ago others had preceded them in this. Ignatius Neubauer, for instance, or Henri Kilber, Sylvester Maurus;[20] or Gotti. The idea of "natural possession" was indeed put forward in the sixteenth century. Suarez, however, felt obliged to refute it[21]—without realizing that he was thereby attacking the logic of his own position. That logic was to triumph among a large proportion of theologians, to such a point that they came in the end to conceive the state of pure nature in all its detail as "a transfer of the concrete, existing order."[22] In the complete system, the two series— pure nature and supernaturalized nature, or nature called to the super- natural—flowed along parallel channels in complete harmony. But the only intelligible difference, if difference it be, between the two consists in the epithet applied to each respectively. Without anything apparently to distinguish them, one is called "natural," the other "supernatural."[23] In both there is seen a "perfect possession of the highest good," the two being to all appearances identical, though we are told that one is attained "through acts of the natural order" and the other "through most excellent [*praestantissimos*] acts."

Then again, we find on one side the "natural desire" for God which man would have felt in a state of pure nature, and on the other the

66

---

[18] *La destinée humaine* (1930), p. 56.

[19] *Loc. cit.*, p. 453.

[20] *Opus theologicum*, bk. 6, tract. 7, q. 47.

[21] *De ultimo fine hominis*, Disput. 16, sect. 1, n. 5 (*Opera*, vol. 4, p. 152; cf. p. 145). Cf. St. Augustine, *De Trinitate*, bk. 15, c. 7, n. 11: "Nothing pertains to the nature of God that does not pertain to the Trinity" (*PL*, 42, 1065).

[22] Henri Rondet, S.J., "Le problème de la nature pure et la théologie du XVIᵉ siècle," *Rech. de sc. religieuse* (1948): 518 (on Suarez).

[23] Thus *Theologia Wiceburgensis, De beatitudine*, c. 1, a. 1. The author of this treatise, Ignatius Neubauer, distinguishes natural happiness, "which is the perfect possession of the highest good through acts of the natural order," and supernatural happiness, "which is the perfect possession of the highest good through pre-eminent acts, going beyond what is due, the strengths and exigencies of created nature" (3d ed., vol. 5, 1880, p. 3). Scheeben, in *Nature and Grace* (London, 1954), remarks on "what theologians call 'grace of the natural order'"; cf. however, in the same *Theol. Wiceb*, in the treatise *De gratia*, ed. H. Kilber, c. 1, a. 2: "perfect possession of the natural order" is a "vision that is abstractive and natural"; one may however wonder what an "abstractive vision [*visio abstractiva*]" is (vol. 8, p. 144).

supernatural hope of the Christian: the object, Suarez tells us, is in both cases "God as the highest good lovable by the love of concupiscence, i.e. to the advantage of the one loving"; only, whereas natural desire envisages God as "natural good of man," supernatural hope sees him as "supernatural good."[24] What illumination do we get from this? The kindred distinction Kilber makes between chaste love and rightful love which presupposes grace when it is supernatural, but does not need it when it is natural, does not really tell us much more.[25] Any means we might have had to apply a different content to each has been taken from us in advance by our being given a concrete definition which applies equally to both. These examples further demonstrate that if, in such a system, the state of pure nature becomes a "transfer of the existing order," it may also happen in reverse that the existing, supernatural order may become the transfer of a wholly "natural" order: how can one see in this the fulfillment of supernatural hope, or supernatural love? But whichever way we look at it, are we not bound to be forced into a complete nominalism, or even a mere parroting of words? For, having constructed a complete, imaginary "natural" universe, with supernatural treasures which seem no longer to have anything of wonder attached to them, one is then obliged to postulate beyond that universe another, designated as "supernatural" and declared "more excellent," "more perfect," or rather perfect in a different way, but of which there remains nothing else that can be said.[26]

67

---

[24] *De spe,* disput. 1, sect. 3, n. 4.

[25] H. Kilber, *De gratia,* c. 1, n. 4: "A pure, right and supernatural love . . . cannot be had without grace properly so-called, I concede; a natural [love], I deny" (vol. 7), p. 160. Cf. Bartholomew Durandus, *Clypeus scoticae theologiae,* vol. 2 (3d ed., Venice, 1709), p. 307. To these distinctions Macedo replies: "What, I ask, is to love God above all the goods of nature, if not to love him supernaturally and indeed with a supernatural love" (*Collationes* 2 [1673]: 399). A distinction like that of Simonnet is perhaps less purely verbal, but makes only a difference of degree between the two orders: "Man placed in the state of pure nature can love God on his own [*propter se*], with a holy and pure love, though less perfect, less constant, less appreciative than that love to which man is raised up by the supernatural habit of charity" (*Institutiones theologicae,* vol. 4, *de Gratia* [Nancy, 1723], pp. 89–90).

[26] It is hardly illuminating when one has spoken of a "natural possession" of God, to add that there may be obtained through grace "another more perfect possession." Cf. Sylvester Maurus, *Opus theologicum,* bk. 6, tract. 7, q. 47: "The natural desire of the rational creature is quenched when the rational creature irrevocably possesses the highest good in a possession that is appropriate and proportionate to it, and known as such, even though it does not possess it in another more perfect possession, which either is altogether impossible for it, or is not in fact appropriate and proportionate to it."

I may add that it seems hardly fitting—to put it mildly—to the reverence which religion, even the "natural" kind, inspires in us for God, for his majesty and his independence, to bestow so readily upon man as something taken for granted and as a "purely natural end," more than many people would once have dared to declare bestowed upon him by the liberality of God himself. In the eyes of those believers of old, the essence of the Godhead was an inviolable mystery, so profoundly hidden that, even in a universe ruled by grace, no creature could ever see it direct. God, they thought, would only be found, even in the light of eternal beatitude, by being forever sought. As we know, several of the Greek fathers tended to this theory; we find it especially in the works of Gregory of Nyssa. Denys, Maximus the Confessor and John of Damascus handed it on to the West. Scotus Erigena was one of those who proclaimed it.[27] Did not scripture tell us that God "dwells in unapproachable light" (1 Tim. 6:16)? How, then, can we contemplate him except by means of "theophanies"?[28] 68

This doctrine of "the impenetrability of the divine secret" seems to have "caused some thirteenth-century theologians to pause for a moment,"[29] as we see from the first proposition condemned in 1241 by William of Auvergne, Bishop of Paris, at the instigation of the professors of the university: "Divine essence in itself [*in se*] will be perceived neither by man nor by angel."[30] It did not, then, appear possible to

[27] *De divisione naturae*, bk. 5, c. 23, 27 and 38 (*PL*, 122, 905 C, 919 C, 998 BC, 1000 BC); bk. 1, c. 8 and 10 (440 BC, 450 CD); bk. 2, c. 23 (576 A); etc.

[28] Cf V. Lossky, "Le problème de la 'vision face à face' et la Tradition patristique de Byzance," *Studia Patristica* 2 (1957): 512–37; *La Vision de Dieu* (Paris, 1962), Eng. trans. *The Vision of God* (London, 1963). M. Lot-Borodine "La Béatitude dans l'Orient chrétien," *Dieu Vivant* 15 (1950): 85–115. Henry of Ghent, *Quodl.* 3, q. 1: "Some say that God is not seen by the created intellect except in certain sublime reflections of him and in theophanies; this is patently heretical" (J. M Rovira Belloso, *La Vision de Dios segùn Enrique de Gante* [1960], p. 42).

[29] H. F. Dondaine, O.P., "Hugues de Saint-Cher et la condamnation de 1241," *Revue des sciences philos. et théol.* (1949): 170–74; *L'objet et le médium de la vision béatifique chez les théologiens du XIIIe siècle* (1953); cf. *Archives d'hist. doctrinale et litt. du moyen âge* 18 (1951): 249, 280. M. J. Le Guillou, *loc. cit.* Joseph Maréchal, *Etudes sur la psychologie des mystiques*, vol. 2 (1937), p. 140. Cf. my own *Le Surnaturel*, p. 447, note 5; and *supra*, chap. 2. Cf. Maximus, *Scholia to the heavenly hierarchy*, IV, 3: "Denys affirms no one has ever seen or will ever see the inner reality of God, in other words his essence" (*PG*, 4, 55).

[30] *Chartularium Universitatis Parisiensis* 1 (1889): n. 178. Père Chenu, in *La Théologie au XIIe siècle* (1957), p. 334, has given a good account of the opposition between the Greek and Latin perspectives. He concludes thus: "The intervention of the Paris *magistri* in 1241 was to remain, though to the advantage of orthodoxy, affected by a Latinism with little

these theologians to admit of more than a certain "unsatisfied longing which for ever binds the blessed spirit to the invisible cause." Hugh of Saint-Cher, in his commentary on St. John's gospel, denied that God could ever be seen "in his essence."[31] Alexander of Hales resisted this line of thought, but Albert the Great remained "very impressed" by it;[32] dealing on several occasions with this "then burning" subject, he allowed that the saints in heaven, like the angels, have a certain though obscure sight of God "as he is" [*ut est*], but no vision of "what he is [*quid est*]."[33] St. Bonaventure still felt obliged to combat the error of those who said that one could not see God "in his essence" but only "in his brightness" (others said "in his glory"[34]). These over-cautious theologians were certainly wrong. Their hesitations and reservations perhaps resulted from an imperfect understanding of the Greek fathers, for they do not seem to have fully grasped the distinction between *phusis* and *prosōpon*;[35] and in some of them, their doubts were reinforced by the influence of Avicenna.[36] But the tendency was an old one, though not for that reason running any less counter to the authentic tradition always preserved in the stream of Augustinianism. Ambrose Autpert[37]

---

understanding of the problems and inspirations of the most important doctors of the East."

[31] A later author corrected his text: "God will be seen in heaven . . . according to his essence" (Dondaine, 1949, p. 173).

[32] H. F. Dondaine, "Cognoscere de Deo 'quid est,'" *Recherches de théologie ancienne et médiévale* 22 (1955): 74.

[33] *De resurrectione:* "One must distinguish that it is one thing to see God as he is [*ut est*], and another to see who God is [*quis est*]. . . . The most perfect knowledge of God is the vision of his very being with the recognition of the impossibility of attaining his essence [*quid est*]." *In Epist. quintam Dionysii,* dubium 1: "He will be seen of himself neither on earth nor in heaven except "because" [*quia*] confused, though God himself be seen more clearly or less clearly according to the diverse modes of seeing and of those seeing." *In caelestem Hierarchiam,* c. 4, n. 5, 8um: "God can be seen essentially [*quid est*] by no one in such a way that the terms of his essence are grasped, neither by man nor by angel." Cf. Dondaine, 1949.

[34] *Utrum sancti in patria videant Deum per essentiam* (Glorieux ed., 1950, p. 56).

[35] Cf. Losski, *loc. cit.;* M. D. Chenu, *La théologie au XIIᵉ siècle,* p. 334; H. Urs von Balthasar, *Dieu et l'homme d'aujourd'hui,* pp. 226–28, Eng. trans. *Science, Religion and Christianity* (London, 1958).

[36] Cf. P. M. de Contenson, O.P., "Avicennisme latin et vision de Dieu au début du XIIIᵉ siècle," *Archives d'hist. doctrinale et litt. du moyen âge* 26 (1960): 29–97.

[37] *In Apoc.,* bk. 10, commenting on 1 Cor. 13: "What we should know is that there were many to say that, in the region of beatitude, God is in fact seen in his distinctness [*claritas*], but that in his nature he is seen not at all. I certainly marvel that the subtlety of the inquiry deceived them, for the distinctness of his simple and immutable essence is not

and Hugh of St. Victor[38] gave it a battering. Hugh of Rouen did the   70
same.[39] Like Alexander of Hales and St. Bonaventure, St. Thomas had
to combat it and justified his position, without sacrifice of God's incom-
prehensibility, by the distinction he made in imitation of St. Augustine
between "seeing what is" [*videre quid est*] or "seeing by essence" [*videre
per essentiam*] and "understanding" [*comprehendere*].[40] Finally, the
authority of the Church, in an irrevocable decision, removed the last
scruples which prevented belief in the ultimate consequence of God's
unimaginable love.[41] The fullest meaning could be given to St. Paul's
words: "Then I shall understand fully, even as I have been fully understood":[42] thus, in an instant, there were drawn back the "seventy thousand curtains of light, shadow and fire" which an Islamic tradition sets
between the angels and the glory of God. But one must not forget that
the same authority was obliged in the following century, under Clement
V, to take another decision against the opposite excess, and to condemn
at the Council of Vienna the proposition that "The soul does not lack
the light of glory that elevates it to the vision and blessed contemplation
[*fruendum*] of God." And one would like to see, in these theologians
who are so sure of themselves and of their natural faculty for seeing the
divine essence, something to give even some faint suggestion of the
restraint of the Greek fathers, or the scruples of those who took their
inspiration from them: one would like to see in these theologians a similar sense of God's transcendence.

one thing and his nature another, but his very nature is his distinctness, his very distinctness is his nature" (*Max. Bibl. Vet. Patrum*, vol. 13, p. 647 F). Similarly, Julian of Toledo,
Prognosticon, bk. 2, c. 36; bk. 3, c. 62 (*PL*, 96, 496 A, 524BD).

[38] *Expositio in cael. Hierarchiam S. Dionysii*, bk. 2, on these "theophanies": "They place
them [theophanies] between rational creatures and God, just as intermediary images of
the hidden divinity. . . . But in fact these images are their own, the phantoms of vanity. . . .
Let them take away their phantasies, by which they strive to overshadow the light of our
minds . . . ! I say that, just as a thing cannot satisfy beyond itself, so also can it not stand
before itself [*usque ad ipsum*]" (*PL*, 175, 954–55).

[39] *Contra Haereticos*, bk. 3, c. 9 (*PL*, 192, 1297 D). Similarly Peter Lombard and Innocent III (*Sermo* 31, *PL*, 217, 593 A).

[40] *In 4 Sent.*, d. 49, q. 2, a. 3: "The saints will see what God is [*quid est*], but will not
comprehend him." Cf. a. 1, ad 1um and ad 2um. *De Veritate*, q. 8, a. 1: "Whoever knows
something through its essence [*per essentiam*], knows of it what it is [*quid est*]"; cf. ad 8um.

[41] Cf. 1 John 4:16.

[42] 1 Cor. 13:12. But it must not be forgotten that in the following century, under
Clement V, the Church had to make a decision in the opposite direction, with the condemnation of the proposition that "The soul does not lack the light of glory that elevates
it to the vision and blessed contemplation [*fruendum*] of God."

71   There are however some, apparently aware of both the intellectual difficulty and spiritual inadequacy which I have indicated, who seek a way out by means of a distinction that aims to provide a more precise meaning, and therefore a more acceptable doctrine. "Is it absurd," asks Pedro Descoqs, for example, "to conceive of a real vision of God, the author of nature, which would not reveal him according to his inmost perfections which are of the transcendent supernatural order, but, while remaining in some sense proportionate to our nature, would still be intuitive and go beyond the scope of abstract concepts or infused species?"[43] Expressed thus, the hypothesis is very like the opinion put forward by Sylvester of Ferrara in his commentary on the *Summa contra Gentiles:* he considers that there is in human nature a genuine desire to see God, but to see him "as cause."[44] But St. Bernard gave the answer to them both long ago, when he said that only someone who does not yet see can think in terms of such distinctions: "many are the words, many the paths, but only One is signified by them, only One is sought."[45] And Vasquez, speaking of Sylvester, made no bones about calling them "frivolous": "For, since the clear vision of God is one, single and indivisible and the blessed cannot by it distinguish in God diverse attributes and predicates, the whole supernatural vision will consist precisely in its clarity, and from a supernatural principle, without a doubt proceeding from the light of glory."[46]

There has been no lack of theologians to object to these explanations for their vague and extended use of the terms "nature" and even "pure nature," to include supernatural, or at least preternatural, elements. But, though these others are thus aware of the fatal current into which some of the rest are drawn, and themselves resist it, they sometimes only go on to let themselves be drawn along by a contrary logic whose

72   conclusions seem no better. For they are just as ready to give a precise form to their concept of a purely natural "economy"; and while that form is certainly more coherent, "more simple and rational," may it not

---

[43] *Op. cit.,* p. 126.

[44] In bk. 3, c. 51: "We naturally desire the vision of God inasmuch as it is the vision of the first cause, not however inasmuch as it is the highest good. . . ."

[45] *De consideratione,* bk. 5, c. 3, n. 27.

[46] *In Primam Secundae,* disp. 22, c. 2 (vol. 1, Compluti, 1599, p. 216). Cf. *In Primam,* disp. 118, c. 2 (vol. 1, Ingolstadt, 1609, p. 62), quoting St. Bernard: "By these words he so intelligently expressed the whole matter, that nothing could be said or desired [to be said] more clearly by anyone who studies Scholastic Theology."

also be perhaps even more dangerous? In that economy, as they present it, all of man's moral life would depend exclusively on his own innate powers, exercised in full autonomy, "almost as understood by Aristotle."[47] Is not this likely to end in the idea of an order of things whereby man would be cut off from the "superior part of his soul," his "highest faculty," that which makes him *mens,* a mind marked with the image of the Trinity?[48] Does it not lead us to suppose a being similar to that so often presented by rationalist philosophies—both ancient and modern: a being sufficient to himself, and wishing to be so; a being who does not pray, who expects no graces, who relies on no Providence; a being who, depending on one's point of view, either wants only to continue as he is, or seeks to transcend himself, but in either case stands boldly before God—if he does not actually divinize himself—in a proud and jealous determination to be happy in himself and by his own powers? It seems to me that this line of thinking leads to a natural morality pure and simple, which must tend to be a morality without religion—or at least with only a natural religion "which is itself only one natural moral virtue among others."[49]

Such fears are not an invention of my own. A century ago Franzelin demonstrated the dangers in such a conception. The theologians who adopt it, he said, "without a doubt are mistaken."[50] Nor is it any more acceptable with the correction made by Baius. It may indeed happen that this "purely natural" man becomes aware that he cannot completely eliminate God's action if he is to perfect himself; he then dena-

73

---

[47] Guy de Broglie, S.J., "De gratuitate ordinis supernaturalis ad quem homo elevatus est," *Gregorianum* 29 (1948): 463, final note: "Many scholastics understand the economy of 'pure nature' as the order of things in which our moral life is to be conducted only through the innate and properly autonomous powers of man (almost as understood in Aristotle). This conception clearly is more simple and rational than any other, it seems."

[48] Cf. St. Thomas, *De veritate,* q. 10, a. 1 and a. 7, etc. St. Augustine, *De Trinitate,* bk. 7, c. 6, n. 12 (Bibl. august., 15, 1955, pp. 550–52) etc. Cf. *infra.*

[49] Etienne Gilson, *Le Thomisme*[4], p. 469ff., Eng. trans. *The Christian Philosophy of St. Thomas Aquinas* (London, 1957), pp. 338ff. How very different is the "natural religion," as set out by Newman, within our order of Providence!

[50] *De traditione et Scriptura*[3], p. 642. Cf. de Broglie, *Conférences sur la vie surnaturelle,* vol. 2, 5th lecture, also stating that "pure nature," if conceived as being without help from God, is an abstraction which can never be realized. Franzelin, *loc. cit.:* "They are without a doubt mistaken who so compare the present order of providence with the state of pure nature that they consider the present state to be void of all supernatural assistance, and with none other to substitute for it than natural aids; then indeed they persuade themselves that such is the state of pure nature."

tures it; for he demands of his Creator a happiness "required in justice," and which can only be attained by helps similarly required—whether they be "general" or "special," "permanent" or "transitory." Hence, though not identified with what is "constitutively natural," the supernatural becomes something "natural by requirement."[51] The final result is Pelagianism, or Baianism: in either case we arrive at a hypothetical creature who has no kind of relationship of love with God; at a "beatitude" which the creature requires and which God owes him. In the "purely natural world" where this creature lives, all idea of God's free gift is lost. How can one say that such a picture, in either possible form, is in harmony with any idea we could have (no matter whether from reason or revelation) of the one true God? Is there any justification for formulating as possible a hypothesis by whose terms God must in justice assure man of any beatitude, however "natural"?[52] Is there any justification for proposing in this way a possible order in which God would, in the strict and proper sense of the word, owe man something? Is there any real difference between such a hypothesis and the ideal of "rational sufficiency" against which, when it first reared its head clearly in a Christian society, about the beginning of the thirteenth century, "the Christian soul felt an immediate shock of horror, as faced with the concupiscence of the mind which was the completion of original sin"?[53]

74

The two kinds of theory we have been looking at in turn do not merely differ in a few details. It is not simply a question of degree. It would be a euphemism to say of those who have followed them that they "are far from having arrived at complete agreement," and it may be asking the impossible of a theologian to tell him, in face of these mutually contradictory explanations, that he "has no right to treat them as illegitimate or illusory."[54] For if he in fact tends towards accepting one, he can hardly help to that extent rejecting the other. They diverge from the start, and seem totally opposed in spirit. These two "purely natural" universes, whose respective protagonists seem, in addition, quite

[51] F. X. Le Bachelet, "Baius" in *Dict. de théol. cath.*, vol 2, col. 69.

[52] One theologian wrote to me: "If, in the system of pure nature, it must be allowed that man has rights over God and that his end is *owed* to him, that seems to me reason enough to reject the system." And there are other theologians who would agree. Cf. V. Cathrein, S.J., "De naturali hominis beatitudine," *Gregorianum* (1930): 402, 403, 407, stating that man could require his natural happiness of God.

[53] M. D. Chenu, *op. cit.*, p. 31.

[54] L. Malevez, in *Nouvelle revue théologique* (1953): 689.

unaware of one another, and which are each presented to us in turn as representing almost the whole of theological thought—for one will be put forward as being the opinion "of most of the scholastics" while the other claims to be the only opinion accepted by "the theologians"[55]— can only be seen as being in almost every way the antithesis of each other. No doubt I shall be accused from both sides of taking an extreme view; and I would certainly agree. I would not claim that any given theologian is so totally committed intellectually to either—although some of the texts I have quoted are in themselves rather disturbing. But my wish here is to draw attention to difficulties which seem to me quite real. As soon as one begins actually to put into words the idea one has been vaguely forming of this "pure nature" with a purely natural destiny, it becomes hard not to fall into one or the other of these two opposing excesses. Otherwise, as I have said, one is left with only a formal hypothesis, quite legitimate, perhaps, but almost empty of meaning, and quite incapable of becoming the basis for any kind of system: it presents a human nature of which we can only say. with Père E. Brisbois, that it is "materially" different from the nature known to us,[56] and the absence of any perceptible link between that hypothetical nature and our concrete humanity in regard to the point at issue makes the hypothesis an unusable one.

75

In these circumstances, it is surely "more simple and reasonable" to return, as I propose, to the earlier position which is hampered by no such hypothesis. Without dogmatically denying that there may be other

[55] It does not, in fact, seem that the conception sketched here is that "of the majority of scholastics" (Cf. *supra*, p. 47 n. 47). In any case, in regard to this state of pure nature "in which man depends on his own wisdom and is left with only his own powers, in which he must develop and perfect himself unaided," a theologian wrote with equal certainty only the previous year (and in the same *Gregorianum*—28 [1947]: 387): "The state of pure nature known to theologians is very different." What are we to understand by "theologians" here? Do these "theologians" of the one writer and the "scholastics" of the other constitute too utterly different and completely separate worlds? Which of the two should we choose? And whichever we do choose, how are we to avoid the anathemas hurled at us from the other?

[56] Cf. E. Brisbois, S.J., "Le désir de voir Dieu et la métaphysique du vouloir selon saint Thomas," *Nouvelle revue théologique* 63 (1936): 1105: "Prior to any exterior call, the divine call echoes in the depths of human nature and inspires in it a new will which has not been the subject of deliberation. . . . Thus man's call to supernatural perfection materially modifies human nature. . . ." That profound need which characterizes him thenceforth "would never have existed in the will left to its natural conditions." And again, pp. 1109–10: "The psychology of human desire is completely changed."

possibilities, without rejecting any abstract hypothesis which might be a good way of making certain truths more vivid to us, it is surely "more simple and reasonable," when working out a theological doctrine, not to try to get away from reality as we know it. That is, of course, provided that we show—as we must in any case, though without claiming to give a complete elucidation where the mystery is concerned—how one may try to think of the utter gratuitousness of God's gift, that supreme gift which is none other than himself; provided also that we show intelligibly how God can never be under any obligation, any sort of requirement, to give himself to the being he has made, as is clear from the most elementary and basic Christian teaching, recalled in our own day in Pius XII's encyclical *Humani Generis*.[57]

76

This is what I tried to do first in a quick sketch at the end of my historical study, *Le Surnaturel*. Written in haste at the request of various people, the sketch was in fact too rapid. It was not intended to treat of the whole problem of the supernatural, and indeed only touched on the major lines of it. On the one question it was concerned with, more than one theologian found it convincing,[58] and a great many declared their positive agreement with me.[59] I received some detailed objections to things I actually said in it, and have taken careful account of these, for which I should like here to thank their authors. The misunderstandings and misconstructions—some of them truly astonishing—which have been put upon it have been sufficiently dealt with by others,[60] and I

---

[57] "Others corrupt the 'gratuity' of the supernatural order, when they assert that God cannot create beings endowed with intellect without ordaining and calling them to the beatific vision."

[58] One may indicate, for instance, the important account by Dom M. Cappuyns, in the *Bulletin de théologie ancienne et médiévale* 924 (Oct. 1947): 251–54; he essentially approves my historical positions, especially the interpretations I put forward of Thomist teaching. See also G. Philips, in *Erasmus,* I, n. 5 (March 1947), p. 263: "Père de Lubac's demonstration is sound and illuminating. . . . He in no way compromises the gratuitousness of grace . . . , etc. Cf. Antoine Chavasse, *Revue du moyen âge latin* (1946), pp. 352–54; P. Kreling, in *Jaarboek,* 1949; etc.

[59] In a profound study, Anton C. Pegis, President of the Pontifical Institute of Medieval Studies in Toronto, declared his agreement with me, and Gerard Smith, S.J., concluded with only one objection: that I have not affirmed strongly enough the fact that my conclusions are completely based on the premises of St. Thomas (*Proceedings of the American Catholic Philosophical Association* 23 [Boston, 19-20 April, 1949]); *Philosophy and Finality* (Washington, 1949): G. Smith, "The Natural End of Man," pp. 47–61; A. C. Pegis, "Some Reflections on the Problem of the End of Man," pp. 62–79.

[60] See in particular the critical study by Victor White, O.P., "The Supernatural," *Dominican Studies* 2 (Jan. 1949): 62, n. 1: "Quite a number of the more vigorous attacks

hope that they will be obvious enough to the attentive reader to make it   77
unnecessary to recall them all. I shall do so only in so far as it is indispensable if further misunderstandings are to be prevented.[61] A few
pages of conclusion, however, could not possibly illuminate every
aspect of so major and complex a question. They require not merely
revision, but completion. That is why, without repeating what had
already been said, I presented some further reflections, laying more
explicit stress on the "twofold gratuitousness," the "twofold initiative,"
or the "twofold gift" of God, in an article in *Recherches de science
religieuse* published in 1949, following upon the approval and encouragement I received from Rome itself. People whose opinion is worth
having have considered the article a useful and illuminating one.   78

---

have been directed against opinions which seem to have been conjured up by the attackers, and will be sought in vain in the book itself"; and again: "It is noteworthy that his
thesis seems to have a sympathetic echo particularly among those who approach the subject from his own fields of specialized studies. . ."; and p. 70: "I think his case is far
stronger than his critics recognize. He has himself forestalled a number of criticisms in a
quite satisfactory manner, and others totally miss the target they are aiming at."

[61] I must however point out one later misunderstanding which touches the essence of
the matter. In 1957, in the review *Divinitas*, Mgr. Antonio Piolanti wrote: "Il desiderio
naturale non importa per sè l'esigenza dell'appagamento? C'è in questi ultimi tempi chi
ha riposto assolutamente in modo positivo: qualunque desiderio naturale dello spirito
importa un'esigenza di soddisfazione, in modo che il desiderio naturale di Dio è un'esigenza della divina visione: 'Désir naturel, exigence divine' (cf. H. de Lubac, *Le Surnaturel*
[Paris, 1947], pp. 105–6). Una simile affermazione è in netta antitesi con la dottrina di S.
Tommaso. . . ." As presented here by Mgr. Piolanti, such a statement is not merely contrary to the teaching of St. Thomas: it is a formal contradiction of the teaching of the magisterium. But it is equally contrary to my ideas, and indeed to my explicit statements.
"*Exigence divine*" in French has never meant "demand for the vision of God," nor "something required of God." I could never have foreseen quite such a radical misinterpretation. The author's excuse is no doubt to be found in the difficulty of catching the nuances
of a foreign language. But he could find enough explanations in the whole context, and
there is plenty to undeceive him in the formulas I use there; for instance, p. 486: "It would
be contradictory to express such desire by the word 'exigence'; or, p. 428: "The supernatural . . . infinitely surpasses the demands of any kind of nature," or again, in "Le mystère
du Surnaturel" (*Recherches de sc. religieuse* [1949]: 120): "Nothing limits the sovereign
independence of God who gives himself; no demand from any order can be imposed
upon him"; and so on. Everyone has a right to criticize, but not to begin by attributing to
me an idea "assolutamente" the opposite of mine.

I would like also to indicate, in the same volume of *Divinitas*, p. 17, some words of Pius
XII, recalled most opportunely by Cardinal Ottaviani in his speech in February 1957 to
the Congress of Literary Critics. If one turns to a critic for a judgment about a book, the
Pope observed, it is primarily because one trusts him "to describe its content"; this is
therefore his responsibility.

Others, though equally friendly, have asked for still further elucidation. I therefore decided, in answer to a great many requests, to reformulate and develop the argument in this book. Without the ambition, which I also did not have then, to say the last word on the subject, or even to cover every aspect of it, I will therefore attempt by means of a "calm disputation" [*serena disputatio*],[62] and as the ancients said, *gumnastikōs,*[63] to take my study somewhat further. I believe that it is possible to do so, as St. Augustine says, "in catholic peace by a peaceful zeal."[64] And it is to this end that I shall start by asking the theologians who base everything on the modern hypothesis of "pure nature," those who, so to say, place their trust in that and that alone, this simple question: Do you think that this hypothesis, as you present it, even were it basically sound, is really useful here? And again: Do you above all think that it is completely adequate, for any even remotely exacting mind, to achieve the end which all of us who profess the same faith agree in proposing to ourselves?

[62] St. Augustine, *De duabus animabus*, c. 2, n. 2 (Bibl. aug., 17, p. 54).

[63] Cf. Clement of Alexandria, *Stromata,* 5, c. 1, 11, n. 1 and 4: "Casting aside all party spirit, all jealousy and argumentativeness . . . faith must go forward, not in laziness, but with every effort to discover the truth."

[64] St. Augustine, *De Trinitate,* bk. 2, c. 9, n. 16 (Bibl. aug., 15, p. 222).

CHAPTER 4

Towards a Real Gratuitousness

The question is thus a circumscribed one, but none the less impor-   79
tant for that. In effect, one of the chief motives that have led modern
theology to develop its hypothesis of "pure nature" to such an extent
that it has become the basis of all speculation about man's last end has
been the anxiety to establish (as against the apparent deviations of
Augustinianism) the supernatural as being a totally free gift.[1] In practice it has succeeded. One may wonder, however, whether a more rigorous reflection would not fault the theory from this point of view. It
would not be the only example in the history of theology of a theory
which, though achieving its immediate goal in practice, did not succeed
in satisfying the mind from every aspect. Since, then, our way of looking
at things today cannot be the same at all points as that of the sixteenth-
and seventeenth-century theologians, one may ask whether the theory
elaborated by some of them can be adequate as a permanent safeguard
for the dogma of the complete gratuitousness of the supernatural. Is it
sufficient? Does it not require at least some modification? Without
being a slave to philosophical fashion, without servilely accepting every
new system of thought, one cannot prevent time from doing its work.
One cannot, if one is to act intelligently—and theology requires that we
should—refuse to answer real problems in the form in which they are
presented. It is not this or that individual who dictates these changes in   80
the formulation of problems; it is not something we ourselves do. They
are imposed upon us as upon everyone else. To recognize them does not
involve any conniving with the spirit of the age, nor any relativism in

[1] Henri Rondet, "L'idée de nature pure au XVIᵉ siècle," *Recherches de science religieuse*
35 (1948): 481–521.

regard to doctrine; without recognizing them one is unlikely to be able to say anything relevant at all.[2] As will be seen, we can in fact return through them to the most traditional lines of thought. Let us then put the question.

It is said that a universe might have existed in which man, though without necessarily excluding any other desire, would have his rational ambitions limited to some lower, purely human, beatitude. Certainly I do not deny it. But having said that, one is obliged to admit—indeed one is automatically affirming—that in our world as it is this is not the case: in fact the "ambitions" of man as he is cannot be limited in this way. Further, the word "ambitions" is no longer the right one, nor, as one must see even more clearly, is the word "limits." In me, a real and personal human being, in my concrete nature—that nature I have in common with all real men, to judge by what my faith teaches me, and regardless of what is or is not revealed to me either by reflective analysis or by reasoning—the "desire to see God" cannot be permanently frustrated without an essential suffering. To deny this is to undermine my entire Credo. For is not this, in effect, the definition of the "pain of the damned"? And consequently—at least in appearance—a good and just God could hardly frustrate me, unless I, through my own fault, turn away from him by choice. The infinite importance of the desire implanted in me by my Creator is what constitutes the infinite importance of the drama of human existence. It matters little that, in the actual circumstances of that existence, immersed as I am in material things, and unaware of myself, this desire is not objectively recognized in its full reality and force: It will inevitably be so the day I at last see my nature as what it fundamentally is—if it is ever to appear to me in this way. "Certainly it is not now that reason dissimulates truth, or that the soul declines the view of reason, disconnected from corporeal limbs and drawn into itself."[3] For this desire is not some "accident" in me. It does not result from some peculiarity, possibly alterable, of my individual being, or from some historical contingency whose effects are more or

81

---

[2] There is no need for me to stress the fact that to do so is, on the contrary, the result of our dedication to timeless, absolute truth. But as for knowing whether we, in our human theorizing and with the help of our human reasoning, attain to that truth more closely in every way than our ancestors or our successors, that is another matter. To doubt it deserves not so much the title of relativism, as of modesty. It is up to each of us to examine himself. Who could in all sincerity claim that he has been totally able to "get rid of his shadow," or the shadow of his age?

[3] St. Bernard, *De consideratione*, bk. 5, c. 12, n. 26 (Leclercq ed., vol. 3, 1964, p. 489).

less transitory. *A fortiori* it does not in any sense depend upon my deliberate will. It is in me as a result of my belonging to humanity as it is, that humanity which is, as we say, "called." For God's call is constitutive. My finality, which is expressed by this desire, is inscribed upon my very being as it has been put into this universe by God. And, by God's will, I now have no other genuine end, no end really assigned to my nature or presented for my free acceptance under any guise, except that of "seeing God."

It remains necessary therefore to show how the supernatural is a free gift not only in relation to a given hypothetical human nature, or in relation to a given hypothetical state of human nature, or even in relation to human nature in general as it may be abstracted from the observation of its concrete realization; but how it is so precisely in relation to the concrete human beings we are, in relation to all those who make up mankind as it is, mankind created by God to see him, or, as we sometimes say, "historic nature." It remains to be shown that the supernatural is absolutely freely given *to me,* in my condition now. Otherwise nothing at all has been said. For my situation in relation to my final end is no longer exactly the same as the situation of nature from which we first reasoned (whatever may be the link or absence of link which we thought we saw between that nature and its supernatural end). For instance when St. Irenaeus declared: "God makes himself seen by men when he wishes, to whom he wishes, and how he wishes," we can only understand his words (which are the expression of his faith) if we apply them directly to the human beings we are now, to all the people in the world, and first of all to our first father, in the concrete. In other words, the real problem, if problem it is, involves the being whose finality is "already," if one can say so, wholly supernatural—for such is the case with us. It involves the creature whose "vision of God" marks not only a possible, or futurable, or "most fitting" end, but the end which, as far as it can be humanly judged, seems to have to be—since it is, by hypothesis, the end God assigns to that creature. As soon as I exist, in fact, all indetermination vanishes, and whatever might have been the case "before," or whatever might have been in any other existence, no other finality now seems possible for me than that which is now really inscribed in the depths of my nature;[4] there is only one end, and

82

---

[4] This was seen very clearly by Père Brisbois in the article quoted *supra,* p. 10 n. 51. It is what Karl Rahner today calls "an abiding supernatural existential foreordained to grace"

therefore I bear within me, consciously or otherwise, a "natural desire" for it.

Whatever may be said of desire being "elicited" by, or following upon, a knowledge of the object, however indeterminate that object in fact remains, this "natural desire" is not only just as "necessary," but just as "determinate" as its correlative end. "To each thing a single end is naturally appropriate, which it seeks by a natural necessity, for nature always tends to one thing," says St. Thomas, and he says further: "the natural appetite is determined to one thing." He is definitely concerned here with the end and the desire of a rational being, possessing free will, whose acts are not "determined to one thing" in the same way as those of "things lacking cognition."[5] In terms reminiscent of the Scotists, Gregory of Valencia gives a similar explanation:

83

> To seek in this way [=naturally] beatitude in general and in particular is nothing other than to have some measure of, and capacity to, nature. This objectively truly limits the common concept of beatitude, and even the particular [concept of beatitude] to the enjoyment of God, which is known to be true beatitude. But it is placed in the freedom of no man to have or not to have this capacity of nature, since all men naturally, and to this extent necessarily, have it. Therefore naturally and necessarily all men seek beatitude in general and in particular by an appetite that is natural and not elicited.[6]

And it is this same fundamental reason that makes St. Thomas conclude so certainly, regardless of the contradictory evidence that common experience seems to suggest: "*Every* intellect naturally desires the vision of divine substance."[7]

("Relationship between Nature and Grace" in *Theological Investigations*, vol. 1, p. 312, n. 1).

[5] *De Malo*, q. 16, art. 5; *De Veritate*, q. 22, art. 3, ad 5um. Cf. Peter of Tarantaise, *In 4 Sent.*, dist. 49, q. 1, art. 2 (Doucet, *loc. cit.*, p. 184).

[6] *Commentaria theologica*, vol. 2 (3d ed., Lyon, 1963), col. 99 B.

[7] *Summa Contra Gentiles*, bk. 3, c. 57, etc. I wonder whether it is enough to speak of an "indeterminate disposition," or "indeterminate tendency," which the author of an *Essai sur le problème de la destinée* (1933) considers "essential to the natural desire of the mind." It is an idea similar to that found in John of St. Thomas, *Cursus theologicus*, Disp. 12, n. 23: "Man, by reason of his own nature, does not have a final end determined materially and in particular, but only vaguely and in general, and according to the reason of beatitude, i.e. the good" (Solesmes ed., vol. 2, p. 145). Cf. Dom Georges Frénaud, who speaks of a certain natural capacity "open in itself to a whole gamut of possible finalities, with no strictly determined orientation to any one of them" ("La gratuité des dons surnaturels,"

That is why, if I fail to achieve this which is my end, it may be said that I have failed in everything; if I lose it, I am "damned"; and to be aware of such a situation is for me the "pain of damnation." This *poena damni,* as I have said, can be explained in no other way: for, as Karl Rahner observes, "the loss of a good which is possible but not the object of an ontological ordination prior to free endeavor (*voluntas ut res*), can only be felt as a painful evil when the loser wills it *freely.*"[8] Hence the statement of the Venerable Mary of the Incarnation: "I contemplated the court of heaven itself, that abode of the blessed, with all the happiness that scripture tells us is felt there; and all that happiness without God seemed to me nothing but misery and grief of heart."[9] This is what Augustine expressed so magnificently in the *Confessions:* "This only I know, that I am wretched apart from you, not only without, but also within myself, and all plenty that is not God is indigence."[10]

This is the human situation resulting from the free will of God, as Christian tradition has expressed it over and over again. Bérulle, as magnificent as he is severe, wrote:

> Let us bless God who has given us being, and a being which has a relationship and a movement towards him. That movement is impressed by the Creator's power in the depths of his creature, deep within it from the very moment of its creation. And it is a movement so deep and so powerful that the will cannot affect it except to fight against it, that no sin we commit can hold it back, that hell itself cannot obliterate it. That move-

---

La Pensée catholique 6 [1948]: 40). The element of truth that we can recognize here is that in fact the nature of a spiritual, intelligent and free being is not "determined towards one thing [*determinata ad unum*]" as is that of "natural beings" (see *infra,* chapter 7). Further, that the last end actually assigned to human nature is only known naturally "vaguely and in common [*vage et in communi*]," this I understand and would allow (*infra,* chapter 9); but that it is in itself, in man as he actually exists, as God wills, envisages and sees it, "vague and common [*vaga et communis*]," this I find harder to understand. Cf. P. Trigosus, "An in nobis sit naturale desiderium . . ." (in J. Eymard d'Angers, *Antonianum* [1957]: 9).

[8] *Loc. cit.*

[9] *Relations d'oraison,* first relation, 2, n. 2 (Jamet ed., vol. 2, p. 30). Cf. St. Catherine of Genoa, *Vita e dottrina,* chapter 7: "She said: A soul which truly loves God, if it is drawn to the perfection of love, as it sees itself imprisoned in the world and the body, if God does not support it by his providence, then bodily life will be a hell for it, because it prevents it from attaining the end for which it has been created" (ed. Pierre Debongnie, *Sainte Catherine de Gênes,* Etudes carmélitaines, 1960, p. 30).

[10] St. Augustine, *Confessions,* bk. 13, c. 8, n. 9 (Bibl. aug., 14, p. 438). *De Civitate Dei,* bk. 12, c. 1, n. 2: "the creature is blessed in possessing that which, by its absence, leaves it miserable" (Bibl. aug., 35, p. 150).

85

ment will last as long as the creature itself, and is inseparable from it. And the struggle that will take place in hell between the movement naturally imprinted upon the creature by the Creator, and the movement of will whereby the creature turns away from him, will be one of the chief and everlasting torments of the damned. That inclination, which is natural to the soul, is hidden in this life, just as the soul is hidden from itself as long as it is buried within the body. It sees neither its own being, nor what lies at the depths of its being. When it leaves the body, it will see itself and will then also feel the powerful weight of that inclination, but without the power or freedom to make any good use of it.[11]

Such a being, then, has more than simply a "natural desire" [*desiderium naturale*] to see God, a desire which might be interpreted vaguely and widely, which might, as a later commentator on St. Thomas has said, simply be "a desire conform to nature," or as another says, "in proportion to nature" [*juxta naturam*].[12] St. Thomas is most clear that such is not the case. The desire to see God is, for him, a "desire of nature" in man; better, it is "the desire of his nature," *naturae desiderium:*[13] this expression, which he uses on several occasions, should be enough in itself to do away with any tendency to fancy interpretation. It therefore remains necessary to show how, even for a being animated with such a desire, there still is not and cannot be any question of such an end being "owed"—in the same sense in which the word rightly gives offense. It remains to show how it is always by grace—even apart from the additional question of sin and its forgiveness—that God "shows himself to him."[14] Whether or not

[11] *Opuscules de piété*, 27, on man's obligation, in nature and in grace, to refer himself wholly to God, n. 10 (ed. G. Rotureau, 1943, p. 134).

[12] T. Richard, O.P., "A propos d'une célèbre controverse," *Revue thomiste* (1936): 229: "The true formula is this: I would like to see. The desire is neither so urgent nor so universal as some writers seem to think."

[13] "Natural desire" [*desiderium naturale*] can be translated in various senses, but "desire of nature" [*desiderium naturae*]" has only one, far more pregnant, meaning. *Prima*, q. 12, a. 1: "the desire of nature will remain vain [*remanebit inane naturae desiderium*]." *Summa contra Gentiles*, bk. 3, c. 48: "It is impossible for natural desire [*naturale desiderium*] to be vain . . . the desire of nature [*naturae desiderium*] would be vain, if it could never be fulfilled." These texts can be compared with *De Malo*, q. 5, a. 2. My intention here does not include any deeper study of this "desire," either in itself, or in Thomist thinking. Yet I do wonder how anyone could believe, as Père A. Gardeil has recently claimed (*op. cit.*, vol. 1, pp. 305–6), that the desire St. Thomas speaks of is no more than a desire of mere "complacence," solely stimulated from without, and free, optional and uncertain in its exercise. Cf. S. Dockx, O.P., "Du désir naturel de voir l'essence divine d'après saint Thomas," *Archives de philosophie* (1964): 49–96.

[14] Cf. St. Thomas, *Summa contra Gentiles*, bk. 3, c. 52, quoting John 14:21.

the hypothesis of a purely natural universe, involving a "purely natural   86
end," and the various conclusions that may be drawn from such a
hypothesis, do in fact date from a much earlier age, we certainly cannot
dispense ourselves from envisaging this new aspect of the problem now.
Whatever suppositions we may accumulate, this aspect will constantly
reappear, "demanding" to be envisaged. We may re-echo the words of a
great Thomist who died in 1351:

> No created intellect, human or angelic, is able by its natural powers to
> attain the vision of the divine essence in which perfect beatitude con-
> sists; [it is able to] out of divine grace. . . . God cannot be seen in his
> essence unless by the grace of God. . . . No one arrives to it of himself
> but one to whom it is given from the gift of God. It is not in our power
> to see God, but in his power to appear . . . , to be seen is in his will: the
> will of God is to be seen. For if he wills it, he is seen; if he does not will
> it, he is not seen. Now he appeared to Abraham, because he willed to; to
> others he did not appear: because he did not will to.[15]

For in effect, to maintain the gratuitousness of the supernatural
simply by referring to another possible end, it is not enough to say, as
we have just seen, that the same human nature might, in a different
order of things, have been constituted with that other finality. This does
not bring us sufficiently to grips with the question. One would have to
be able further to affirm it of the same humanity, of the same human
being, and ultimately of myself as I am. And this, if one considers it,
makes no sense. For by putting forward the hypothesis of another order
of things, one cannot help by that very fact supposing another humanity, a different human being, and thus a different "me." In this "purely
natural" universe which some have imagined, or have at least declared
to be possible, "my nature," they say, would be included. We may perhaps agree—though it cannot be as certain as they think, except in the
most abstract sense, since it must be said at the same time that this   87
nature would be "materially" different. But even then it would not be

---

[15] Raynerius de Pisis, *Pantheologia, Beatitudo,* c. 11 (Brescia, 1580), vol. 2, 1, p. 242.
And the nominalist Gabriel Biel, *Collectorium,* bk. 1, dist. 17, q. 1, F: "Whenever God
beatifies, he does so merely contingently, freely and mercifully, from his grace. . . . No
form is needed for eternal life, not even a supernatural one; but, just as he pours out grace
from his goodness freely and contingently, so also, granted whatever form, does he grant
eternal life freely and mercifully from his grace, and always would be able not to confer it
[without injustice to himself]."

the same "me." You may put into this hypothetical world a man as like me as you can, but you cannot put me into it. Between that man who, by hypothesis, is not destined to see God, and the man I am in fact, between that futurable and this existing being, there remains only a theoretical, abstract identity, without the one really becoming the other at all. For the difference between them is not merely one of individuation, but one of nature itself. What can possibly be learnt from the situation of the first, the hypothetical man, in regard to the gratuitousness of the gift given to the second, the man that I am in reality? I can only repeat that ultimately it is solely in relation to me, in relation to us all, to our nature as it is, this actual mankind to which we belong, that this question of gratuitousness can be asked and answered.[16]

In other words, put in terms which, though not those used by St. Thomas, express his ideas faithfully, if it is true that "the power to see the divine essence is the specific obediential power (*potentia obedientialis*) of man as an intellectual creature,"[17] it is important to demon-

---

[16] The objection will have particular force against the thesis that denies all "natural desire" properly so called in the state of pure nature. If, indeed, the vision of God in himself does not inspire "any curiosity" in created spirit, then either an effective ordering to that vision, supervening upon another state, is not felt by it as a blessing (and it reacts as does a man who is not hungry to even the finest of meals); or, in order that hunger may come with that ordering, the spirit in question will have to be very profoundly transformed. And if so (apart from the dangerous empiricism which such a conception of spirit must suppose), if it was already clear that there was no identity of subject between one and the other, it now becomes clear that there is no identity of "nature" either. How can the hypothesis of "pure nature" help to resolve the problem in these circumstances?

[17] A. Raineri, O.P., "De possibilitate videndi Deum per essentiam" in *Divus Thomas* (1937), p. 4: "The power to see the divine essence is the specific obediential power of man as an intellectual creature [*potentia visionis divinae essentiae est potentia obedientialis specifica hominis, prout est creatura intellectualis ut sic*]." P. 113: "Only in the actuation of its specific obediential power, or only in the vision of the divine essence according as it is in itself [*in se*], does the perfect beatitude of man consist, which however by no means establishes its own natural or due end." "Despite the contrary opinion of certain theologians, the texts of St. Thomas show that he considers the desire for the vision as distinct from the obediential power": B. Fraigneau-Julian, P.S.S., in the French edition of Scheeben's *Natur und Gnade* (French trans. 1957, p. 74, note); and ibid., p. 34: According to St. Thomas, natural desire "is distinguished from mere obediential power by four characteristics: by its particular object, which is the vision of God, and not the infinite mass of actuations of which a creature can be the object; by its subject: only the intellectual creature is capable of that desire, and this is one of its proper characteristics; by him who brings it about: it belongs only to God to actuate that power, not as creator, but as directly superior agent; finally, by its nature: it brings to the intellectual creature not some random achievement, but its own final perfection, in other words its perfect happiness."

strate that in the world as it actually is, this power still remains in that 88
sense wholly "obediential."

Put in yet another way, if I should be able to declare unequivocally
that God gives himself to me, and makes himself to be seen by me
freely, and quite independently, then that supernatural gift must be
clearly seen to be free not merely in relation to some generic nature,
abstract and theoretical, but actually in relation to the concrete nature
in which I, here and now, share. Just as "it is the gratuitousness of God's
plan *now* and not of some hypothetical plan, that we need to know," so
too it is "God's plan now that is the theologian's true object of contemplation."[18] We must be grateful to Père Le Guillou for reminding us of
this; it was thus that the great scholastics understood it. One may point
out that they did not deny the hypotheses of the moderns; nor would I
dream of doing so. But it remains true that they did not put them forward, and when they spoke of the gratuitousness of the supernatural
they did not mean it in terms of some abstract human nature as envisaged in those hypotheses. They would have found such an approach
most unsatisfactory. St. Thomas, for instance, says: "That God wishes to
give to someone [*alicui*] grace and glory proceeds from his sheer generosity." *Alicui*: to someone, to some person at whom we can point.[19] To
someone, to you, to me, this very day. God can be no more bound by
our nature as it is than by the nature of some humanity that might have
been. I do not believe that it keeps the truth of the dogma intact to sug- 89
gest, as Palmieri (among others) does in his great *Tractatus de ordine
supernaturali,* that human desire can *claim* the vision of God from the
moment of its being no longer the desire of "pure nature," but of nature
"raised up" or "called."[20] This would hardly allow for the liberty of God

[18] M. J. Le Guillou, O.P., *art. cit.,* 1950, p. 242.

[19] *De Veritate,* q. 6, a. 2. Similarly, when speaking of knowledge, St. Thomas says:
"Here the individual man understands." I would say here: "Here the individual man has a
gratuitous end."

[20] 2d ed., 1910, p. 109: "The desire of which Augustine speaks . . . is the elicited
desire, but of raised up nature, which consequently demands the acquisition of the vision
of God through supernatural powers." Such a requirement seems to me as unacceptable
in itself as it is contrary to the teaching of, for instance, St. Augustine, or of St. Thomas as
set out perfectly clearly in *De Veritate,* q. 6, a. 2. Similarly, Brisbois, *art. cit.,* p. 1104:
"There must then be, in human nature as called to supernatural beatitude, a new subjective disposition, a new demand, prior to any deliberate choice of the will, prior even to
faith and sanctifying grace which directs human nature to its supernatural destiny in the
guise of a necessary, unreflecting need for the final absolute good." That same word

in distributing his gifts; it would make supernatural beatitude no longer "truly a grace," but, as Fénelon pointed out, "a debt given the title of grace."[21]

Then there is the hypothesis that seeks to posit a "purely natural" universe, in which man could claim "natural" happiness from God. Now, alongside this another universe is imagined—our own in fact—in which man still requires happiness from God, this time "supernatural." Whether we add the two together or set them up against each other, we can hardly hope to find in them the gratuitousness we are looking for.

It is always within the real world, within a world whose supernatural finality is not hypothetical but a fact, and not by following any supposition that takes us out of the world, that we must seek an explanation of the gratuitousness of the supernatural—in so far as the human mind can do so. But this is precisely what the modern hypothesis we are concerned with fails to do. I do not say that it is false, but I do say that it is insufficient. For it completely fails to show, as people seem to think and as by the logic of the theory it should, that I could have had another, more humble, wholly "natural" destiny. It only demonstrates— presuming it to be well-founded—that in another universe a being other than myself, with a nature similar to mine, could have been given this humbler destiny. But, I repeat, what has this other being really to do with me? What have I to do with him? To convince me that I might really have had this humbler destiny—humbler, but note, also less onerous— you need only show it to me, even momentarily, as something really imprinted upon me, in my nature as it is. Most people would agree that this is precisely what is, by hypothesis, impossible. My destiny is something ontological, and not something I can change as anything else changes its destination. We must therefore seek along some other path for a more real certainty of the gratuitousness we need to find.

90

"demand" (*exigence*) occurs again in a note. When Fr. Philip Donnelly wrote in "The Gratuity of the Beatific Vision and the Possibility of a Natural Destiny" (*Theological Studies* 11 [1950]: 392): "God cannot refuse to fulfill this supernatural destiny which is inscribed in the very nature of finite spirits," he intended it as a formulation of my position, but was in fact stating the precise opposite of what I have clearly said. But that is what Palmieri seems to think, and with him many others; and it is that which in fact fits in with the logic of one theory of "pure nature," at least when being used as an ultimate explanation.

[21] Cf. Fénelon, *Réponse à la Relation sur le Quiétisme*, foreword. Cf. id., *Première lettre à M. de Chartres* (*Oeuvres*, vol. 3, pp. 128–29). Also *Troisième lettre en réponse à celle de Mgr l'évêque de Meaux* (vol. 2, pp. 654, 664).

There may be those who fear that reasoning of this kind is dictated by a nominalism or an empiricism which allows no specific reality to nature but wants only to see the individual in the concrete. This would be a misunderstanding. There is no question of making human nature a mere abstraction. I must recognize that I, as an individual, participate in the same nature as Socrates, for instance, or any "simple native," or every other man who exists or ever will exist in this world. Mankind is a reality. Human nature is, in its way, a reality. But the fact that we all share in it is precisely, at least in part, because we all have the same essential finality. If someone then tells me of another nature that might exist, with another finality, in another universe—and this is in fact what is being done by those who speak of the "futurable" of "pure nature"—I can feel only the most abstract link with it, however much they may describe it as being like ours. Such an abstract link cannot possibly lead to the consequence we are seeking. The great scholastics, with their absolute realism, proposed no such thing. 91

This inability of the modern theory to carry through to the end the part for which it was conceived appears more and more clearly as, under the influence of Christian thought, we come to a better idea of what a person is, and to an ontology of a more concrete kind. But we must not make the mistake of thinking that this is, in essence, a new view. Rather it is a return to the point of view of past tradition, which was far more "personalist" and far more "existential" (though not existentialist!) than its language always leads one to suspect. Excessive naturalism and essentialism belong much more to a stream of modern philosophy—which has to some extent invaded the manuals of scholasticism,[22] but in doing so has perverted the traditional teaching it was intended to transmit.[23]

[22] Cf. Etienne Gilson, *L'être et l'essence* (1948), p. 176, note: "The influence of Wolff on modern scholasticism" sometimes affects "even the actual philosophical exegesis of Thomism," and if one then speaks of "traditional philosophy," one is really speaking "of what has become so since the time of Leibniz and Wolff, but which is in direct contradiction to that of St. Thomas Aquinas."

[23] One sees this clearly, for instance, in the chapter on creation. According to St. Thomas, *Prima*, q. 45, a. 6, "to create belongs to God according as he exists, which is his essence, which is common to the three Persons" (Gilson, *Le Thomisme*[4], p. 174). The relationship of creation with the divine persons is not then for him simply appropriation, but a real ontological relationship; by appropriation we attribute the act of creation to the Father, but the three persons come together indivisibly in it. In art. 7 ad 3um St. Thomas says: "Even the processions of the persons are the cause and reason of creation in any

92   On the other hand, in the Fathers, and especially in Augustine, we do not find this clear-cut opposition between an abstract "essential" order, a *de iure* order, and a concrete "historical" order which is merely *de facto,* an opposition which fills a large part of certain modern treatises. For them the created essence is itself "historical" and history in that sense is essential. The Fathers certainly never dreamt of reasoning from the basis of a pure abstraction unconnected with the concrete natures that actually exist in our universe; they spoke without doubt, as St. Maximus says, of "the nature of the humble human being that we are,"[24] they never sought to understand the economy of salvation revealed in Christ by envisaging "other, merely possible economies": but it would, I think, be wrong to conclude that they were therefore lacking in any genuinely metaphysical thought. It is a conclusion that is sometimes drawn.[25] But it does not, for instance, do justice to St. Augustine's thought to declare—not entirely without exaggeration—that for him the term "nature" "is not to be understood in at all the same sense as it came to have later in scholastic theology," and to add that this term designates "only a type of particular, historical and concrete

93   man."[26] Nor does it do him justice to say further that the root of the

---

way"; and *In 1 Sent.*, prol.: "Just as a byway is derived from a stream, so also the temporal process of creatures [is derived] from the eternal procession of the persons." Now all this, while not perhaps being formally denied, is at least left in the shade by the thesis in certain modern works of scholasticism that "God creating is God as nature" [*Deus creans est Deus ut natura*]. They seem not to be aware that in this case God would create—if the word is still appropriate at all—of necessity. Père Théodore de Régnon pointed out a similar error in his *Etudes sur le dogme de la Trinité*, vol. 1, pp. 329–30. On the "manifold links between creation and the Trinity" in St. Thomas, see the work by F. P. Slader, O.E.S.A., analyzed by F. V. in *Bulletin de théologie ancienne et médiévale*, vol. 4, p. 295 (no. 1573–74).

[24] *Ambigua (PG,* 91, 1361 A–B).

[25] Cf. Guy de Broglie, S.J., "De gratuitate ordinis supernaturalis ad quem homo elevatus est," *Gregorianum* 29 (1948): 44: "The fathers do not usually indulge in those abstract considerations which the scholastics later investigated, nor do they ever show themselves concerned with expounding and deducing distinctly what could have come to be by reason of different, merely possible, economies." Without denying that there is a certain truth in such explanations, I am convinced that they cannot be automatically invoked in all cases, and that one must never misuse them in order to deny the "Fathers" all metaphysical value. One might by the same token be led to deny equally the evidence of the great medieval theologians, or great mystics like Ruysbroeck.

[26] Ibid., in *Augustinus Magister* (1954), vol. 3, pp. 328–29. These exaggerated oppositions are sometimes found, in addition, to support a kind of concordism, against which Gilson has wisely protested: "Note conjointe à l'étude de saint Augustin," *L'année théologique* 5 (1944): 326.

problem "was bound to escape his scriptural realism and the concrete nature of his genius," or that his method and turn of mind made him incapable of a certain indispensable kind of abstraction, or that his thought, wholly immersed in the order of actual existence, was powerless to see through to the eternal order of essences. It does not do him justice to see in his analyses of the human mind and soul no more than the workings of his extraordinary gifts as a psychologist; nor (when not actually denouncing it as romanticism) to allow only an empirical value to the famous sentence from the *Confessions:* "You have made us for yourself, O God, and our hearts are restless until they rest in you."[27] Medieval theologians saw it very differently. It is certainly true that St. Augustine's thought always appeared "engaged in the reality of lived experience,"[28] but that does not mean that he never got beyond empiricism. To claim, as has even been done, that he only treats the problems relative to man's last end "within the hypothesis of an elevated nature,"[29] or to say with Báñez "He speaks of fact,"[30] or with Bernard de Rubeis "from the laws present in Divine Providence and manifest in the revelation of the Scriptures,"[31] is altogether too superficial. As Gilson rather wryly says of these attempts to explain away his ideas, "Whatever they may say, Augustine was not wholly unworthy to be called a philoso-   94

---

[27] *Confessions,* bk. 1, c. 1. Antoine Guillaumont observes more accurately that "for St. Augustine the word *cor* is a poetic equivalent of the word *anima,*" and that it spontaneously appears whenever he substitutes a poetic and biblical style for the language of philosophy; he quotes the parallel text, *Confessions,* bk. 10, c. 10, n. 65: "Nor in these things, which I go over consulting you, do I find a safe place for my heart but in you." For the sense of the names for the heart in antiquity, see "Le coeur," *Etudes carmélitaines* (1950): 73. Yet another text from the *Confessions* (bk. 13, c. 8, n. 9) indicates an even clearer metaphysical intention: "For even in that very wretched restlessness of the spirits who pass away and exhibit their darkness unveiled as it is by the clothing of your light, you sufficiently show how great you have made the rational creature, for whom anything less than you is in no way sufficient unto blessed rest, and so it is not [sufficient] for itself." Cf. *De natura boni,* c. 7; *De civitate Dei,* bk. 11, c. 13, n.

[28] H. I. Marrou, *Saint Augustin et l'augustinisme* (1955), p. 72.

[29] Thus D. Palmieri, *Tractatus de ordine supernaturalis*[2] (1910), p. 100: "The response of the Catholic theologians is that Augustine is speaking within the hypothesis of raised up nature"; cf. *supra,* p. 61.

[30] *In Primam,* q. 12, a. 1 (1584 ed., p. 452).

[31] *De peccato originali,* 1757, preface; ibid.: "from hypothesis [*ex hypothesi*]." Or J. Navarro, S.J., *Cursus theologicus* 2 (1766): 152: "Augustine speaks about men according as they are ordered to happiness above; we know this ordering by faith." We shall see further on in what sense we are to accept this.

pher."[32] More recently, Père C. Couturier has shown that, "contrary to a somewhat widespread opinion, St. Augustine possesses a very definite metaphysic of the world," that his principles, once established, "highlight in a startling way many texts which are often seen only as more or less approximate concrete descriptions," and that he analyses the "metaphysical structure of created being" very profoundly.[33] St. Bonaventure spoke long ago of "Augustine . . . , who was the loftiest of metaphysicians."[34]

As for the great scholastics, though their thought is undeniably of a much more abstract nature, and their curiosities often subtler, their approach is basically the same. When St. Thomas, in particular, takes up the problems of our last end, he does it always both by analyzing created spirit in its essence and at the same time remaining within our universe, that universe whose goal, as he constantly says, is a supernatural one. Hence the difficulty some commentators find when faced with those passages where this is made particularly clear—a difficulty they try to avoid in a way similar to the one we have seen used in connection with the Fathers. According to the scholastics, St. Thomas too would only have spoken in this way while placing himself in the hypothesis of the "historical order." For instance, when he says in the *Summa contra Gentiles* that the angels do not rest content with their natural knowledge of God, it is, they say, because "he is speaking of fact [*de facto*] since they were created with the faith of a supernatural beatitude."[35] This is the view of Báñez. In our own day, Père Blaise Romeyer has made this comment more general. If St. Thomas, he says, did not explicitly speak of the idea of a nature without any supernatural finality, it was because he was content "to reply to the immediate demands of the dogma he was studying"; one should therefore recognize that "his weakness lay in not setting out from the start to build a metaphysical totality on a central intuition."[36]

Such comments leave one thoughtful. At least they admit, without

95

[32] *L'esprit de la philosophie médiévale*[2], 1944, p. 434.
[33] "Structure métaphysique de l'être créé d'après saint Augustin," *Recherches de philosophie* 1 (1955): 83: "Let us add that a genuine exegesis of Augustinian thought, especially in regard to the nature of man, can only be established on the basis of its proper context. . . ."
[34] *In 2 Sent.*, d. 3, p. 1, a. 1, q. 2. Cf. *Sermones selecti*, sermo 4, n. 19.
[35] Báñez, *In Primam Secundae*, q. 3, a. 8, dubium, in regard to the *Summa contra Gentiles*, bk. 3, c. 2: "Because the divine Thomas says that the angels do not rest in natural cognition, he is speaking of fact . . ." (p. 131).
[36] *La philosophie chrétienne jusqu'à Descartes* vol. 3 (1937), p. 144.

feeling the need to refer to the idea beloved of so many moderns, that St. Thomas succeeded in "replying to the immediate demands of dogma." The difficulty they express confirms me in my conviction: St. Thomas "deals only with real man" and in this he is "closer to modern thinking" than many of today's Thomists.[37] We do not find in him, any more than in the Fathers, that radical separation between abstract essence and the existing world which characterizes certain present-day scholastic speculation. He does not reason from a "disexistentialized" human essence.[38] When he writes, for instance: "Since the soul has been made by God immediately, it will therefore not be able to be happy unless it sees God immediately,"[39] whatever weight we attach to his argument, whatever its exact significance, how could anyone maintain that for him, in a "purely natural universe," the human soul would not have been directly created by God? St. Thomas does not deal with a certain number of difficulties in regard to this matter which were only raised later on, and which we have to take into account nowadays; thus he does not treat in all its details the problem of gratuitousness: the philosophers or the heretics with whom he was arguing set him, as we have seen, a different task.[40] It remains none the less true that, when he does deal with it, he never brings the finality itself into question.[41] It seems likely, then, that had he ever had the problem put more immediately before him, he would have considered any solution dependent on the hypothesis of a "purely natural order," in other words the hypothesis of a different man placed in a different world, to be verbal and irrelevant.[42] No system entirely constructed on such a foundation-stone could legitimately base itself on him.

96

---

[37] Jacques Leclercq, *La philosophie morale de saint Thomas devant la pensée contemporaine* (1955), p. 283 (chapter 8, "Du désir naturel de voir Dieu").

[38] One may see a certain sign of this fact in the continuity of sense that he notes between the various meanings of the word "natura," ranging from "birth" to "essence": *De unione Verbi incarnati,* a. 1.

[39] *Quodl.* 10, art. 17.   [40] Cf. *supra,* chapter 2.

[41] Cf. Dom M. Cappuyns, *loc. cit.,* p. 252: For St. Thomas, the end of created spirit "in every hypothesis is God himself, in other words the supernatural."

[42] It may not be merely chance coincidence that, during this same period when we have shown the invasion of the system of "pure nature" into theology, there developed in philosophy the process which was to result in what Gilson calls a disexistentialized essence, from which developed those scholastics of Wolffian inspiration so far removed from genuine Thomism. Cf. Etienne Gilson, *L'être et l'essence,* p. 176, note: If Wolff "claims the right to make use of the medieval scholastics' terminology, modern scholastics have not been slow to make use of his. The influence of Wolff on modern scholasticism continues to grow . . ." etc.

Sought along this path of a different finality, the solution to the problem of the gratuitousness of the supernatural could only really be found in the following way. It would have to be possible to note in the actual course of every real and personal existence—or, at least, if one envisages not so much individuals in themselves as the humanity of which they are a part and which unites them by the assignation of a single destiny, in the actual course of our race's concrete, historic existence—a definite moment when God intervenes either to assign an end which till then had been in doubt, or to change the end previously assigned to me. Either hypothesis would be absurd, if one considers it. In either case, one would be supposing a radical extrinsicism which must destroy either the idea of nature or that of finality, or possibly both. Neither the epic of the universe, nor the acting out of my personal destiny could include such a second start. Such a supposition is in any case—at least apparently and in principle—excluded by the axiom, which everyone admits, that the so-called state of "pure nature" can only be posited as a "futurable," as something which has never actually existed, even for a moment. However, it becomes impossible to escape from it once one has produced the theory that an end cannot be given freely for a definite being, existing here and now, unless there had first of all been a different end for him that was objectively, concretely realizable—in other words, once one has made "pure nature" in the modern sense the indispensable and sole guarantee of the gratuitousness of the supernatural.

97

In fact, this modern theory of a spiritual nature—whether angelic or human—with a "purely natural" finality, was born and developed in the intellectual context of a watered-down idea of what finality is. What it assumed at its beginnings, though not always very explicitly, was something very different from what most of those who hold it today would assume. This was that every man, in our world as it is, before having received the grace of baptism or any other enabling grace, was in that state of "pure nature" (at least if one excludes original sin and its consequences).[43] Finality was therefore considered as something fairly extrinsic: not a destiny inscribed in a man's very nature, directing him

---

[43] Though this restriction does not apply to the teaching of all of them. "Suarez considered temerarious and to be mistrusted the opinion of those who dared to affirm that, in the state of fallen nature, man as he actually is is intrinsically wounded, weakened or unbalanced" (Blaise Romeyer, "La théorie suarézienne d'un état de nature pure," *Archives de philosophie*, vol. 18, pp. 44–45).

from within, and which he could not ontologically escape, but a mere destination given him from outside when he was already in existence.[44] This is certainly what Suarez supposes, for example; for him, the punishment of Adam's sin was essentially the withdrawal of the supernatural finality which God had bestowed upon human nature as one gift, among others, added over and above nature.[45] According to this idea— put forward again in so many words in modern times by Fr. Philip Donnelly[46]—if God had not then envisaged and determined upon the plan of redemption, Adam and all his descendants, all those people whose names and histories we know, all existing mankind to which we ourselves belong, all these people, *ipsissimi,* would have had to merit, in a nature left essentially intact by sin, by the use of a free will left to itself but keeping all its original strength, "a certain state of happiness in its own order and level" [*in suo ordine et gradu*], or as some express it, a certain "natural possession" of God, as the only end to which they were called by anything actually inscribed within them.[47] "Had God not redeemed us," comments Blaise Romeyer, "we should be born *viatores* journeying towards a possession to be won by the right use of our free will."[48] In short, fallen man, brought back by this fall to his natural state, was no longer "called." In the framework of ideas which this theory presupposes, there would be no obstacle to a "supernatural" beatitude reaching a stage where, at any given moment, by God's decision, it is given in addition to the essential, wholly natural, happiness that is desired, postulated, required, and won by nature. This seems indeed a most simple and satisfactory explanation of the whole thing.

This theory had begun to take shape well before Suarez. Cajetan was not properly speaking its inventor, for it was not produced all of a piece

---

[44] And even that was only made possible, it seems, because of an initial ambiguity: the expression "pura natura" (or earlier such similar expressions as "pura naturalia") having for a long time meant no more than a certain state of nature as yet unprovided with supernatural gifts, without reference to its finality or later history. One can see thus how the transition took place between the older teaching and the new.

[45] See also, in regard to the supernatural gifts bestowed on the first man, gifts which he compares to that of eternal beatitude, his naïve way of saying: "The question needs to be enlarged to all time. . . . More, or less, does not change its form" (*De gratia,* prolog. 4, c. 1, n. 5: *Opera omnia,* vol. 7 [1857], p. 180).

[46] "The Gratuity of the beatific Vision," *Theological Studies* 11 (1950): 401–3. It is rare for anyone today to take up Suarez's teaching as literally as this.

[47] Suarez, *De Gratia* (Vivès ed., vol. 7, pp. 206ff., 216–21).

[48] "La théorie suarézienne d'un état de nature pure," *loc. cit.* One may note in passing this "conquest" of the possession of God.

99   in a day, but he was one of its chief initiators.[49] He certainly would seem
to have been the first to claim the patronage of St. Thomas for it, in his
commentary on the *Summa Theologica*. As I noted earlier, it is usual now
to speak in this context of "historic nature." Now, we must not forget
that this "historic nature," with the desire to see God which goes with it
and marks it out in contrast with "pure nature," involves according to
Cajetan both positive revelation and the objective knowledge of certain
supernatural effects observed in the world.[50] It was far from being that
nature first established in another state, and belonging to all those who
make up the human race now. It could only be taken to be so if the
theory of "pure nature" were explicitly stated, and in Cajetan's day that
had not yet been done. In other words, according to this notion, which
Père Gardeil rightly judges to be "singular,"[51] and which is the earliest
notion to be formulated of "historic nature," there is no room for what
Maurice Blondel was to call "the transnatural state."[52]

[49] Cf. Suarez, *De Gratia,* prolog. 4, c. 1, n. 2: "Cajetan, and more recent theologians,
considered a third state, which they called purely natural . . ." (Vivès, vol. 7, p. 179). See
infra, chapter 8; also my *Augustinisme et théologie moderne* (Paris, 1965), chapter 5, Eng.
trans., *Augustinianism and Modern Theology* (London: Chapman; New York: Herder &
Herder, 1969); Juan Alfaro, S.J., *op. cit.* (1952), is very instructive on the antecedents of
Cajetan's teaching.

[50] *In Primam,* q. 12, a. 1: "He knew certain effects, say of grace and glory, whose cause
is God as God is in himself absolutely [*ut Deus est in se absolute*], not as a universal agent.
Now since the effects are known, it is natural for the individual intellect to desire acquain-
tance with the cause. Therefore the desire for the divine vision, although it is not natural
to the intellect absolutely created, is nevertheless natural to it granted the revelation of
such effects"—what a contrast with the simple and pregnant "desire of nature [*desiderium
naturae*]" of St. Thomas! In *Secundam Secundae,* q. 3, a. 8: "The author deals with man as
a theologian. . . . And so, although there is no such natural desire in man in the absolute,
it is nevertheless natural to man ordered to heaven by Divine Providence . . . , for it has
been naturally evidenced that, once the effect has been seen, we desire to know what is
the cause, whatever it be." Cf. John of St. Thomas, *Cursus theologicus,* Disput. 12, a. 3, n.
6: "Cajetan explains this concerning man with some knowledge of faith or of supernatural
things being granted, not considering him from a strictly natural point of view" (vol. 2,
p. 140).

[51] *La structure de l'âme et l'expérience mystique*[2] (1927), vol. 1, p. 183: "it is clear that St.
Thomas envisaged no such restriction" which takes away from his effort "all real interest."

[52] When Père Rousselot, *op. cit.,* 2d ed., p. 183, Eng. trans. *The Intellectualism of St.
Thomas* (London, 1935), p. 179, wrote of "those who see man's whole orientation towards
the Beatific Vision as due to some secret transformation of man brought about historically by grace. It was in this sense that Cajetan interpreted the view of St. Thomas," the
interpretation which he himself put forward of Cajetan was, to say the least, incomplete;

Since then, various theologians have taken up this "singular opinion." They still understand "historic nature" in Cajetan's sense—which is also that of Suarez. Even among those who appear nowadays to give it the greatest depth and consistency, there are a certain number who, basically, mean nothing else by it. When they say with the rest that the state of "pure nature" has not in fact ever existed, or that "historic man" has been in fact created in a supernatural order, it becomes clear in what an attenuated, or perhaps rather extenuated, transformed sense, one must understand their statement. For them, the ultimate destination of the universe has been changed in the course of time, without this fact making any change in the structure of that universe or the essence of the beings who constitute it; supposing that God had not willed to make himself seen, or even that to see him were utterly impossible, everything that goes to make up the universe and man would still be exactly the same.

This paradox has been upheld by various commentators of St. Thomas, for instance Billuart[53] and Gotti. Yet one informed historian of Thomist thought, Père A. Motte, has written: "One could dream of no more categorical reverse inflicted by commentators on the idea of the Master."[54] We know how firmly St. Thomas held that finality is something intrinsic, affecting the depths of the being. We know too what reality he attached to what he called the "order of the universe" [*ordo universi*] or "order of the parts of the universe in relation to each other"[55]—so much so that for him a single change in the natures making up the universe would be enough to mean that one was really dealing with a different universe.[56] Duns Scotus here joins with St. Thomas in a general reproof of those who, by distending the organic bonds of reality too much, "make the substance of the universe discontinuous

100

101

---

it was indeed incorrect too, if what it was saying was that the "inner transformation" was to be understood as affecting the nature of every man coming into this world.

[53] "[The intuitive vision of God] has no connection with natural cause or effect from the understanding of which the mind may ascend to its investigation or demonstration. As a result, if this vision did not exist or were impossible, all natural things would nevertheless have the same existence as that which they have now" (Quoted with approval by Père Garrigou-Lagrange, *Le sens du mystère*, part 2, chapter 2, pp. 191, 192).

[54] A. Motte, O.P., in *Bulletin thomiste*, vol. 4, p. 577.

[55] *Summa contra Gentiles*, bk. 1, c. 78. *De Potentia*, q. 3, a. 16, ad 1um; etc.

[56] *Prima*, q. 25, a. 6, ad 3um: ". . . God however could make things differently, or add others to those things already made, *and there would be a different* better *universe*."

[*inconnexam*]."[57] To both these men, "everything in the real world is linked together."[58] "Creation is homogeneous."[59]

Here I will rest content for the moment with pointing out that, if the conception inherited from Cajetan and completed by Suarez is all that really follows from the premises I have been criticizing, in itself it appears to have little meaning. One can of course readily admit that the supernatural finality of our universe has no direct relationship with, for instance, the laws of physics or chemistry; and that therefore if *per impossibile* this universe should be suddenly deprived of any supernatural finality, those laws would remain unchanged. But can anyone reasonably say that the same would be true of man, of the foundations of his intellectual and moral life? And even supposing such a radical change had no repercussion on the material universe or the knowledge man can have of it, would it not be change enough that man himself was not exactly the same?[60] And finally, on the other hand, how could one allow that the Creator would so recast his work? What possible acceptable meaning could there be in such "repetitions of the creative act"?[61] If God really destines man to see him, one can understand his not actually admitting him to that vision from the first, but there can be no under-

102

[57] *In 2 Sent.*, d. 1, 4, 11: following Aristotle, *XII Metaph.* A general principle recalled in regard to those who deny "that relation is a thing outside of the act of the intellect [*relationem esse rem extra actum intellectus*]."

[58] Testis (= Maurice Blondel), *La semaine sociale de Bordeaux* (1910): "The lower degrees, though not ceasing to be lower and to be powerless of themselves to initiate any ascent, are none the less degrees, in other words stepping-stones, springboards. . . . The higher degrees are really the final cause of this world, which is not just a patchwork of coinciding episodes, but an order filled with the unity of the divine plan. . . . Through the condescending action of the higher, the lower is, as it were, pregnant with a higher cooperation."

[59] Cf. Paul Claudel, "La théologie du coeur" in "Le coeur," *Etudes carmélitaines* (1950): 396: "If we firmly accept this idea that God created all things together (Ecclus. 18:1), that creation is homogeneous. . . ." People will argue similarly (and indeed some have done so) in relation to sin; this was expressed naïvely by Alexander Neckam, *De naturis rerum*, bk. 2, c. 156: "Bear in mind that because of the sin of original prevarication, the brilliance of planets and stars was diminished . . ." (ed. T. Wright, 1863, p. 251).

[60] Then too, if I can thus be given a new finality at will, we must allow that the arbitrary is the rule, and give up any consistent idea of nature or of reason.

[61] Cf. A. Gardeil, O.P., "Le désir naturel de voir Dieu," *Revue thomiste* 9 (1926): 409–10: ". . . the existence in rational nature of a capacity for the divine vision, of the same order as the capacity of every being dependent upon God to be subject to renewals of his creative action, in any way that does not contradict what has gone before."

standing the idea that he only destines him to it from a given moment of his life or of world history.

Either the idea of "pure nature" must be conceived as being actually in our world now, as its protagonists see it; in that case, if we are not to be led into absurdity, we must return to its earlier significance which never questioned the supernatural character of the last end, but only described "the structure proper to created spirit in our world."[62] Or this idea of "pure nature" must be related to a different universe, since a purely natural order has never in fact existed, as the great majority of theologians would hold nowadays;[63] in that case, being quite abstract, though there is nothing to criticize in it of itself, it does not appear wholly suitable for the service expected of it. However, whether one adopts or rejects it, if one succeeds in making clear—as at all costs we must—that the supernatural end can *in no case* be the object of any requirement or debt, even by a being who here and now has no other end, then there will no longer be any need to refer to this indirect consideration of an order that is purely natural even as to its finality. We have seen that it is not an adequate consideration. Perhaps we may now go so far as to admit that it is not a necessary one either.[64] By trying, without seeking any fiction to take us beyond the limits of our world as God has made it, the only world we know, to show that the gift God offers of himself is and can only be totally free, and that one could never imagine any loftier or purer gratuitousness, I think we are embarking upon a really effective way, a way along which others may happily advance further. It seems to me, too, that this is the chief way opened to

103

[62] When, for instance, Père Le Guillou writes (*loc. cit.,* p. 242): "Pure nature is not a nature wholly foreign to us . . . ; it indicates the structure proper to created spirit in our world," I find myself in complete agreement with him provided always that he is concerned, as is St. Thomas himself, with our world and the structure of our being, and is not tacitly introducing a different kind of finality from that spoken of by St. Thomas.

[63] Cf. F. Taymans, S.J., "L'encyclique Humani generis et la théologie," *Nouvelle revue théologique* (1951): 17: "It is thus the common opinion of the weightiest doctors that the purely natural order has never in fact existed." See also E. Brisbois, O.P., "Le désir de voir Dieu et la métaphysique du vouloir selon saint Thomas," *Nouvelle revue théologique* (1936): 1103–5.

[64] It was right to allow for it at first, in order to avoid any conception of "nature" which did not fully preserve the gratuitousness of the supernatural. But it would not be legitimate; it would be reversing the roles, and taking the means for the end, to think only of avoiding every conception which would not appeal exclusively to "pure nature," for one would in that case be treating it as an absolute.

us by tradition. If I succeed in this, without totally rejecting or obliging anyone else to reject every idea of "pure nature," then I shall have reinforced this all too fragile rampart of a fortress which defends for us all a truth older and loftier than all our reasonings and theories,[65] a Truth which the Church's magisterium has recalled to us many times in the most explicit terms,[66] and reiterated quite recently, without ever having allowed any one explanatory theory to become tied to it. And if there are those who feel that it is impossible to preserve that divine truth except by reference to the system of "pure nature," I would be the first to tell them that not merely have they every right to maintain it, but that they would be wrong to reject it.

[65] Cf. J. Lebreton, in *Revue pratique d'apologétique* 4 (1907): 197: "The revealed dogmas are not to be treated as theorems to be inserted into the working-out of our human systems; they are the facts which must govern them."

[66] See *supra,* chapter 3, and *infra,* chapter 6.

CHAPTER 5

The "Donum Perfectum"

"That is all very well," it may be said, "but we do not take those last 105 words as simply a concession for some people. We take them as the admission of a necessity which, whatever you may say, is imposed upon everyone. For despite all your arguments, it remains true that if the end to which God is leading our universe now is a totally free gift on his part, it must be true that another universe might have existed, created by him, which not merely would not have been led to that end, but would have had no connection with it. How can one see the matter otherwise? There can be no free gift unless the giver could withhold it. When, of old, the clergy of France used to vote their 'free gift' to the king, which they were bound by force of custom to do, they were well aware that the description was a false one. When I give a present to someone, if it were not honestly possible for me to withhold it, then it would not really be a present, and to the extent that I am bound by convention to make the gift it becomes a present only in an improper sense. Nothing can destroy the common sense of this view. And that is why if one is to explain the supernatural gift, it will always be necessary to make use of a hypothesis of 'pure nature,' as understood for the past few hundred years."

A common sense view, yes. And again, at its own level, I would not dream of gainsaying it, nor do I think anyone would who understands the meaning of the Catholic faith. I wholly agree with it. But ultimately, it must be admitted, this is a rather superficial analogy for the unique 106 and mysterious reality we are considering. God's gift to his creature, that gift which is himself, is not really comparable to a present given by

one man to another. We can subject the analogy to a few moments' criticism without having to get involved in any dangerous subtleties or minimalist exegesis. I shall take as starting-point a different analogy: that of
the first gift God gave us by giving us being. For there is, as we shall see,
a genuine parallelism between that first gift of creation and the second,
wholly distinct, wholly super-eminent gift—the ontological call to deification which will make of man, if he responds to it, a "new creature."

To describe these two fundamental blessings God gives me, blessings both of which logically precede any offer of grace to my free will,
any action of providence within me, I naturally proceed along the lines
of the analogy of a gift given by one man to another. I must, of course,
represent myself first of all as existing already, make of myself the subject of attribution—or rather of reception—for these two successive
gifts. Thus I first declare: "God has given me being"; then, the second
blessing: "Upon this being he has given me, God has imprinted a supernatural finality; he has made to be heard within my nature a call to see
him." In this way I must, fatally, appear to precede my actual being, and
my being in turn appears to precede its own finality. It is a process of
dissociation, a spontaneous and inevitable process of dissociating and
holding apart which the distinguishing intellect [*intellectus dividens*]
always performs, at least provisionally. If I wish, therefore, to form a
correct idea, however inadequate it may be, of the initial twofold gift I
have from God, it is impossible not to do this. The first idea, that "God
has given me being," does in its way express total contingence; it
expresses the basic difference between my essence and my existence.
Similarly, the second, that "God has imprinted upon my being a supernatural finality," expresses in its way that the supernatural gift is totally
gratuitous, and in no way bound to the gift of being; it expresses the
basic difference between my natural being and my supernatural finality,
in other words, between my creatureliness and my divine sonship. Here
we are on firm ground, and no explanation or later critical reflection
which ends up by denying or even placing in doubt the truth it has
sought to interpret can be valid.

However, though one cannot avoid proceeding in this way, neither
can one rest at that. In the first place, it is clear that I did not already
exist before my creation in order to be given then a being somehow
handed from God to me, like a present given to a child by its parents. If
our first phrase were taken literally, univocally, it would be meaningless.

It would be a contradiction in terms, for in creation it is my being itself that I receive: "the whole substance of a thing is produced in its being."[1] "He gave so that you might be what you had not been before."[2] But, above all—and this is the point which most concerns us—it would not really or adequately express, in all its force, the radical gift of being which God has given me (inevitably we fall back into this language) by creating me. For it is a gift totally interior to me; nothing is left out of it, and nothing of myself is without it. It is incomparably more a gift than any outward, additional gifts which may later be given me by men. There is no proportion between them; as an analogy they are infinitely inadequate. If I want to remedy the weakness of my language slightly without attempting the impossible task of radically changing it, I will be led into saying, in that traditional formula so dear to Bérulle, that by   108 creation God has given me, or rather continues constantly to give me, to myself:[3] for "each one of us is in a position to recognize that his own essence is a *gift,* that it is not a *datum;* that he himself is a gift, and that in the last analysis he has no existence at all through himself." These words of Gabriel Marcel can be linked to Fénelon's: "All is a gift. He who receives the gifts is himself the first gift he receives."[4] And both echo the statements of Augustine: "All these things are gifts of my God, —and they are good—and all these things, am I":[5]

> There was nothing in me that preceded all his gifts, nothing able to receive them. The first of his gifts on which all the others rest, is what I call myself; he gave me that self: I owe him not only all that I have, but

---

[1] St. Thomas, *Summa contra Gentiles,* bk. 2, c. 17. Cf. Etienne Gilson, *Le Thomisme⁴,* p. 173: "To say that creation is the gift of being is still a misleading formula, for how can anything be given to something that does not exist? To say that it is a reception of being is scarcely better, for how can what is nothing receive anything? Let us say, then, if you like, that it is a kind of reception of existence, without thinking that we are explaining it." And Gilson quotes *In 2 Sent.,* d. 1, q. 1 ad 2um: "Creation is not a making [*factio*] that is a change [*mutatio*] properly speaking, but is a certain receiving [*quaedam acceptio*] of being." Note "quaedam," a word frequently used by St. Thomas.

[2] St. Bernard, *In ps. Qui habitat,* sermo 14, n. 2 (*PL,* 182, 239 B). Cf. Robert Grosseteste, *Commentary on Mystical Theology,* c. 1, n. 3: "In every created thing, its non-being is before its being" (Uld. Gamba ed., 1942, p. 30).

[3] Cf. Romano Guardini, *Prayers from Theology* (London, 1959), p. 16: "Always I receive myself from your hand."

[4] G. Marcel, *The Mystery of Being,* vol. 2, *Faith and Reality* (London, 1951), p. 173. Fénelon, *Lettres sur divers sujets de métaphysique et de religion,* 1, Paris, vol. 1, 2, p. 96; cf. p. 120.

[5] *Confessions,* bk. 1, c. 20, n. 31.

also all that I am. O incomprehensible gift, which our poor language expresses in a moment, but which the human mind will never arrive at understanding in all its depth! This God who made me has given me myself to myself; the self I love so much is simply a present of his goodness. . . . Without him I would not be myself; without him I should have neither the self to love, nor the love wherewith I love that self, nor the will that loves it, nor the mind that knows it. All is a gift: he who receives the gift is himself the first gift he receives.[6]

109   And the same remarks can be made validly, *mutatis mutandis,* in regard to the second statement about our supernatural finality. It too is phrased in a way that supposes the imperfect analogy of a human gift, as though God, though infinitely better and more powerful, stood in the same relation to me as another man; as though his situation were completely exterior to me, so that he could only give me a present, a completely exterior gift. As with the first statement, if we want to hold fast to the whole truth suggested by the analogy, we cannot rest there. The analogy of human gifts can certainly help us to understand God's gift; but it is obviously not enough by itself. It is no more sufficient than is, for instance, the analogy of human evidence in explaining divine faith. It is a necessary springboard, and there is no question of retreating from it, but its only justification is the jump we can make from it to leave it behind at once. For it lacks that element of inwardness—which we also call transcendence—which belongs to the creating God who "is more interior to me than I am myself," "Deus interior intimo meo." This fundamental criticism of the analogy does not, as I must again stress, mean any doubt or even cheapening of the value of the idea of gift—or the idea of witness. Quite the reverse. The witness of God is incomparably higher than any human witness, and similarly his gift. This does not mean simply that his witness is stronger, more incontestable, or that

---

[6] Fénelon, *Lettres . . . ,* 1, c. 4, n. 1 (*Oeuvres spirituelles,* vol. 1, 1810, p. 174; *Oeuvres,* Paris, vol. 1, 2, p. 96; Versailles ed., vol. 1, pp. 306–7). Cf. Pierre Teilhard de Chardin, *Le Milieu Divin,* p. 76, Eng. trans. London, 1960: "I receive myself far more than I make myself." I could have used yet another example to work from. When St. Robert Bellarmine said, in one of his sermons: "Below the moon there is nothing but what is mortal and fleeting, except the souls given to mankind by gift of God" (*Conciones de quatuor novissimis,* 4; *Opera,* vol. 9, p. 447), he spoke like everyone else, and no believer will contest the truth of his statement. It remains none the less true that the human race did not exist first, and could not exist first—even for a purely logical instant—in order then to receive spirit as a gift from the hands of God.

his gift is freer or more magnificent. Though it is not wrong to say this, it is inadequate; it leaves us still within the human order. The human analogy would not yet be really faulted. It means that his witness is more really a witness, his gift more really a gift, in a higher sense. The formal idea of gift, like that of witness, is verified in God in his relationship to us in a higher way—especially if one recalls that God's gift is God himself—than is accessible to our experience in human relations. Hence the unique certainty of faith, the unique gratuitousness of the supernatural.

In short, as soon as I say "I," I exist and I have being; and once I exist and have my being, I have a finality. It is impossible to dissociate in reality these three elements by spreading them out over three instants in time with gaps between. Strictly speaking, the statements "God has gratuitously given me being" and "God has impressed a supernatural finality upon my being," are therefore quite inadequate. Having naturally and necessarily stated them, we must immediately object to them. One thing, however, is to be noted. Our objection does not make us retreat; we do not in any way reject the truth which led us to state them. We in no sense set them aside as false in order to affirm something opposite. Nor do we even want to water them down. What we must show is that one can only say them at all by inventing a fictitious subject—something rather different. Such a subject disappears as soon as it is looked at closely. This can hardly be denied. Thus, far from rejecting or even diminishing the reality that the two statements affirm, I am merely showing up the fictitious presupposition that underlies them. In neither case is there anything fictitious about the gratuitousness of God's gift. The opposite is true. And thus analyzing our language we should be able at least to glimpse in his gift a twofold marvel of gratuitousness which no analogy drawn from human gifts could possibly show us so well.

Thus our phase of negation, following on the earlier phase of affirmation, is in fact negative or reductive in appearance only. In reality it is no more so than "negative theology" is a negation of God. On the contrary, if "negative theology" is actually the extreme opposite of atheism, then our negation will be in the same way the extreme opposite of naturalism. We may still continue to say, just as we did before, and indeed we must say without reservation, that God could, if he had wished, not have created us at all; and then, in addition, that he need not have called this being, which he has given us, to see him. God was not or is not in any way obliged to destine us for that "true and perfect beatitude"[7] which is only realized in seeing him. No kind of constraint or necessity, whether internal or external, "moral" or "natural"—or in the terms of a modern theologian "juridical" or "ontological"—forces the divine will to either of these two initiatives.

Not merely do we continue to say this, but we can now say it with a greater depth of understanding. We can now see more fully how wrong it would be to say "God cannot create," and the further mistake there would be in saying "God cannot create beings endowed with intellect without ordering and calling them to the beatific vision."[8] For while the formulas I have been criticizing are undoubtedly inadequate, their inadequacy certainly does not lie in failing to recognize God's sovereign liberty, either in the act of creation, or in his calling those he has created to see him. For the reason I have just given, those formulas must be criticized—as indeed we must criticize everything we say of God and the things of God in human language, though we must continue saying it[9]—but they none the less express (imperfectly, though in the only way possible) a most important truth, whereas the contrary statements, which would in any case be inadequate in precisely the same way, must be completely rejected as expressing a double error. We know this on two counts: what we know of God, and what we know of creatures. God could never have been constrained or required by anything or anyone, either outside or inside himself, to give me being. Nor could he be constrained or required by anything or anyone to imprint on my being a supernatural finality; therefore my nature cannot possess any claim upon it. If, by a legitimate and indeed necessary process of analysis, we

111

112

---

[7] St. Thomas, *Prima Secundae,* q. 3, a. 6; q. 5, a. 3.

[8] Pius XII, *Humani generis.* Cf. my earlier article, "Le mystère du surnaturel," *Recherches de science religieuse* (1949): 104.

[9] In a similar way we must criticize, though we cannot always avoid making use of them, certain ways of speaking of the act of creation. Père Sertillanges explained this in his work, *L'Idée de la création et ses retentissements en philosophie,* p. 140: "In our theory of creation, the supposition of a direct operation working upon creatures as a whole throughout time in order to 'make' them does not really make sense. There is no creative act, as we have seen, except in eternity. Again this is a completely human way of speaking, whereas it is an act of God alone. In any case there is nothing in time by way of divine action, creative divine intervention; it is only a manner of speaking which we have recognized as legitimate and indeed inevitable in common usage, but which is formally incorrect, and which must always be rectified when it occurs, as St. Thomas never fails to do."

distinguish these three things even more clearly, by staggering them, so to say, in time—the fact of the creation of a spiritual being, the supernatural finality imprinted upon that being's nature, and finally the offer presented to his free choice to share in the divine life—we shall have to recognize that the first thing does not necessarily imply the second, nor the second the third, in any sense that would inhibit God's utter independence. There cannot be the faintest question of that; it remains only to try to understand more fully what they mean.

It is true that in God all attributes become one, in a perfect simplicity, since in him everything is absolute, necessary and unchanging.[10] God "decreed all that exists in the indivisibility of a single act of his sovereign liberty; the distinctions which may be introduced into that divine act by the imperfection of our understanding can only be justified by the created connection that exists between created things and that divine decree."[11] Such distinctions, however, are not merely justifiable: they are indispensable. As St. Francis of Sales tells us: "God then has no need of several acts, since a single act of his almighty will suffices to produce all the variety of his works, because of his infinite perfection: but we mortals need to consider them with the manner of understanding that our little minds can reach."[12] For us simplicity can come only at the end. If, for instance, we say with St. Thomas: "Nothing can be called a miracle in comparison with divine power,"[13] we in no way deny the possibility and concrete realization of miracle in our world, nor are we thereby in any way justified in suppressing the distinction between the two sorts of divine causality which we define by their respective effects—that which is exercised in the ordinary course of nature, and that which is exercised in miracle. It is the same with our present subject: we must be careful to distinguish two instances of gratuitousness, two divine gifts, and consequently—if it is legitimate to speak in this way, designating it not in itself but in its twofold goal, its twofold object—a twofold divine freedom.[14] It is as though there were two lev-

113

---

[10] Cf. T. de Régnon, S.J., *Etudes de théologie positive sur la Sainte Trinité,* 3d series, 1 (1898), p. 345.

[11] Juan Alfaro, S.J., "Marie sauvée par le Christ," *Maria* 6 (1959): 469.

[12] *Traité de l'Amour de Dieu,* bk. 2, ch. 1 (Annecy ed., p. 87).

[13] *Prima,* q. 105, a. 8.

[14] Here I would not unreservedly subscribe to the formula whereby Blaise Romeyer distinguishes "specifically elevating gratuitousness" from "merely creative gratuitousness" (*Archives de philosophie,* vol. 17, c. 2, biographical supplement, p. 5); but I would be as

els, two floors with no connection between them. For the two orders are incommensurable. There is a double ontological movement, doubly impossible to the creature without the double initiative that brings him into being and calls him; in effect this brings him into being in order to call him. "Gratuitous being is of a genus different from natural being."[15] One can imagine no kind of metaphysical necessity which the creation of spirit would impose upon God. Just as creation itself is no kind of necessary consequence of something which "preceded" it within God, so the gift—and also therefore the offer of the gift—of the supernatural is no mere consequence of creation [*sequela creationis*]. If creation itself can in a real sense be called a "grace," then the call to see God is another one: "Although it is rightly called a certain grace by which we were created, . . . it is by another that we . . . are called. . . ."[16] If the first grace is contingent, then we may say that the second is "supercontingent."[17]

114   To borrow from a sermon by Eckhart, one might put it that, if the two graces could be compared to rivers, the source "from which creatures emanate from God is as far from that whence grace comes as heaven from earth."[18]

"This exaltation of the rational creature is above natural achievement."[19] Two simple comparisons may help us to understand this. Even were one to admit that the whole evolution of the universe is to culminate, in God's plan, in the appearance of man, would one feel bound therefore to conclude that his appearance was a mere consequence of universal creation [*sequela creationis universi*]? Or again, if it is true that the whole history of Israel ultimately only receives its meaning from the coming of Christ for which it was a preparation and to which it was directed, should we see this as a reason to deny that, even in relation to Israel, that coming was something totally new and gratuitous?[20]

---

anxious as he is to distinguish absolutely the gratuitousness of elevation from the gratuitousness of creation. It seems to me that this more objective language is more exact. But in either case the idea is the same.

[15] St. Bonaventure, *In 2 Sent.*, dist. 29, art. 2, q. 2. Cf. dist. 3, p. 2, art. 2, q. 2: "Divine light, because of its eminence, is inaccessible to all the powers of created nature, and therefore it lets itself be known through a certain kind condescension . . ." (Quaracchi, vol. 2, pp. 123, 703). On the other hand, one cannot seriously maintain that St. Bonaventure leaves any room for the modern idea of "pure nature."

[16] St. Augustine, *Epist.*, 177, n. 7 (*PL*, 33, 767–68); cf. n. 2 (765).

[17] The term is Père Chenu's, *op. cit.*, pp. 157–58, referring to the incarnation.

[18] Meister Eckhart, *Sermon on accomplishment*.

[19] *Summa* of Alexander of Hales, bk. 2, p. 1 . . . (n. 509; vol. 2, p. 743).

[20] Cf. Heb. 3:6; John 1:17.

But further, just as the coming of Christ, though fulfilling the history of Israel and giving it meaning, marks the passing into a new order, which wholly transcended the order that preceded it—"He brought all that is new" [*omnem novitatem attulit*]—so it is with our supernatural finality. Between nature as it exists and the supernatural for which God destines it, the distance is as great, the difference as radical, as that between non-being and being: for to pass from one to the other is not merely to pass into "more being," but to pass to a different type of being. It is a crossing, by grace, of an impassable barrier. One does not merely need extra strength, such as an actual grace would give: one needs a new principle, that principle of divine life which we call "sanctifying grace." The "affinity" which exists, as William of St. Thierry tells us,[21] between the soul and "eternal and divine blessings"—"a certain natural affinity" [*naturalis quaedam affinitas*]—is an affinity not of essence, but of vocation. For those blessings form no part of *natural* or *substantive properties of the soul* [*naturalia, substantiva animae*].[22]

None of this has anything in common with any of the apparently   115
varied, but basically very similar, doctrines that express a naturalist mysticism. For the Buddhist of the "Greater Vehicle," for instance, every individual nature is "an embryo of Tathagata," and is therefore destined to become a buddha; "there is a buddha-nature in every being"; "it shines right in its depths, immense, infinite, only covered over, like a lamp whose light is hidden in a jar, by the black cloud of false thoughts and passions."[23] The "Pseudo-Gnostics" of the first centuries A.D.—who have their counterparts in our own day—also professed what Didymus the Blind called "the myth of natures," whether they only accorded the same sublime destiny to a certain category of higher beings, or thought that everyone would eventually attain to it.[24] Christians have no belief of this kind. We say with Clement of Alexandria: "We shall become like the Master, but with all the difference between *thesei* and *phusei*."[25] We

---

[21] *Speculum fidei* (PL, 180, 386 BC).

[22] Tertullian, *De anima*, 20, 1: "[I conclude that] all the natural properties of the soul, as its substantive properties, are inherent to it and both grow and develop with it." Cf. 22, 1.

[23] Cf. the texts quoted by Paul Demiéville, *Le concile de Lhasa,* 1, 1952, p. 95, note 1; and many others.

[24] Didymus, *In primam epist. Petri* (Zoepfl, p. 10: cf. p. 22). And Origen, *Periarchon,* bk. 3, 1, 23 (Koetschau, p. 240).

[25] *Stromata,* 2, 77, 4 (1, 153; Mondésert ed., Sources chrétiennes, 38, p. 95).

say with Origen: "Is it not extremely impious to hold that those who adore God in spirit are of the same essence as his unbegotten and blessed nature?"[26] He says with St. Augustine: "This is of grace adopting, not of nature generating";[27] or again, with St. Cyril of Alexandria: "It is by the illumination of the Holy Spirit that we are gods and sons of Gods; . . . we only become light, sons of God, through grace";[28] and so on.

In other words, "in man himself, the real gift of sanctifying grace is, not only formally but also materially, something quite different from his spiritual openness to the absolute with all the energy that may arise from it, although that 'quite different' thing does adapt itself precisely to that openness."[29] In short, for Christians created nature is no kind of divine seed. The "depths" of the spiritual soul, that "mirror" where the image of God is reflected secretly, is indeed, as Tauler says, the "birthplace" of our supernatural being: but it is not its seed or embryo. It is indeed our "capacity" for it—to take a word used by Origen, St. Bernard, St. Thomas, and many others—but that does not make it a participation in it, even initially or distantly,[30] "which needs but to be developed and enriched."[31] It is not even the promise of it, so long at least as the objective promise has not been heard there.[32] The longing that surges from this "depth" of the soul is a longing "born of a lack," and not arising from "the beginnings of possession."[33]

If we want to keep to the strictest sense normally given to the words in the Thomistic vocabulary—which is virtually also the same sense they would have for Bonaventure, Duns Scotus, and many others—it is not

---

[26] *In Ioannem,* 13,25 (Preuschen, p. 249): man is not of the same substance as God [*homoousios theō*], as the *"pneumatikos"* of Heracleon claims; "What sacrileges and impieties would not follow such ideas about God! It is dangerous even to think of it!" And again: "We are not sons of God either in nature [*phusei*], or according to essence [*kata tēn ousian*] or according to substance [*kata tēn kataskeuēn*]" (20); and so on.

[27] *In psalm. 49,* n. 2.

[28] *Commentary on St. John,* 1, 8–9 (PG, 73, 116–17; cf. 128–29 and 153).

[29] E. Schillebeeckx, O.P., "L'instinct de la foi selon saint Thomas d'Aquin," *Revue des sc. philos. et théol.* 48 (1964): 400.

[30] St. Augustine, *De Trinitate,* bk. 14, c. 8, n. 11: "The mind must be considered in itself before it is a partaker of God and before his image is to be discovered in it" (*PL,* 42, 1044). St. Thomas, *De veritate,* q. 22, a. 2, obj. 5.

[31] Cf. M. Blondel, who warns against the danger of this mistaken thesis: *La Philosophie et l'esprit chrétien,* vol. 1, p. 261.

[32] Cf. *infra,* chapter 9.

[33] Cf. Gratry, *De la connaissance de Dieu,* vol. 2. (2d ed., 1854), pp. 310–11.

even possible to say that such a longing is the preparation for supernatural being, nor a "disposition" for it. Scotus would even say that man is "indispositus" to his end, though explaining that this end is natural to him in spite of not being naturally accessible to him; he would say that man needs to be "gradually disposed" to it, especially through the revelation of a certain, still imperfect, supernatural knowledge.[34] This work is completed by sanctifying grace, "grace that renders pleasing" [to God] [*gratia gratum faciens*], of which St. Thomas tells us that "it disposes the soul to the possession of the divine person."[35] And that natural "capacity," to which the natural "longing" corresponds, is not a "faculty"; it is no more than an "passive aptitude" [*aptitudo passiva*], and though the being who desires to see God is certainly "capable of this blessed cognition,"[36] it does not follow that his nature is of itself "efficacious to seeing God [*efficax ad videndum Deum*]." The desire itself is by no means a "perfect appetite."[37] It does not constitute as yet even the slightest positive "ordering" to the supernatural. Again, it is sanctifying grace, with its train of theological virtues, which must order the subject to his last end; at least, it alone can order him "sufficiently" or "perfectly," or "directly."[38] This grace is a certain "form," a certain "supernatural perfection" which must be "added over and above human nature" in order that man "may be ordered appropriately to his end."[39] St. Bonaventure, for instance, says not that the rational creature "is

117

[34] *Ordinatio*, prol., 1: "Man is ordered to a supernatural end, for which he is of himself indisposed; he falls short, then, of being disposed to possessing that end. This happens through some imperfect supernatural cognition . . ." (*Opera omnia*, 1, 1950, p. 30; cf. p. 19).

[35] *Prima*, q. 12, art. 5; q. 43, art. 3, ad 2um; *Prima Secundae*, q. 122, art. 2 and 4; q. 113, art 7; *Summa contra Gentiles*, bk. 3, c. 53; *In 4 Sent.*, dist. 49, q. 2, art. 6 and 7; etc. Macedo, *Collationes*, vol. 1, p. 17: "This inclination is not merit, it is not disposition, and it does not in any way oblige God." Johannes Prudentius, *Opera theologica posthuma in Primam Partem D. Thomae* (Lyon, 1690), p. 52: "Take note, that this inclination to the vision in human nature does not render a vision that is itself owed to the nature."

[36] *Tertia*, q. 9, art. 2, etc. Johannes Tinctor (in Alfaro, *op. cit.*, p. 236).

[37] St. Thomas, *In 4 Sent.*, dist. 49, q. 1, art. 3, q. 3 ad 3um; and art. 3, sol. 3.

[38] *Prima Secundae*, q. 62, art. 1 and 3; q. 111, art. 5; *Summa contra Gentiles*, bk. 3, c. 147, n. 1; *In Boetium de Trinitate*, q. 6, art. 4, ad 5um. Cf. *In 4 Sent.*, dist. 49, q. 1, art. 3, q. 4, ad 4um (the twofold meaning.of the phrase "to be ordered through desire" [*ordinari per desiderium*]). Harphius, *Theologia mystica*, bk. 1, part 2, C. 86: "Let us say, following Thomas . . . that man is perfected by virtue to the acts by which he is ordered to beatitude" (Cologne, 1611, p. 382).

[39] *Summa contra Gentiles*, c. 150. *Prima*, q. 12, art. 2. Cf. the *Summa* of Alexander of Hales, n. 509 (Quaracchi, vol. 2, p. 743a).

ordered" [*ordinatur*], but that "he is born to be ordered to God immediately."[40] If therefore the desire is truly a "natural inclination," it is not by that fact a "sufficient" or "proportionate" inclination;[41] it does not desire its object "sufficiently"; or, in other words, as in the case of free will left to itself, so this desire is unable to strive "suitably" or "efficaciously"; to put it yet another way, it is not the source of any "sufficient activity" which would make it, however minimally, of itself "a certain inchoative possession."[42] In this order, any "inchoatio" comes by grace. However profound, however lofty it may be, created spiritual nature is in no way "proportionate"—except "as the effect to the cause, or the potency to the act"—to what infinitely surpasses it.[43] Nor can we say that it is naturally "raised up": it is an infused grace that raises up the essence of the soul to some divine *esse,* making it truly fitted (*idonea*) for divine activities;[44] it is the "light of glory" which strengthens the intellect and thus raises it up to a vision of the divine essence.[45]

We have here a vocabulary which, despite certain slight variations of overtones as between one author and another, or even in the same author, is coherent. We may quote a few more examples to fix it in our mind. The first will be from the Franciscan Eudes Rigaud, an example

---

[40] *In 2 Sent.,* dist. 16, art. 1, q. 1 (vol. 2, p. 395). Compare Cajetan, *In Primam,* q. 82, art. 1, n. 7: "In fact, God ordered the rational creature to an ulterior end."

[41] *De spe,* a. 1, ad 8um; *Summa contra Gentiles,* bk. 3, c. 44; *In 3 Sent.,* dist. 23, q. 1, art. 4; cf. q. 4, art. 3. Scotus, *Lectura in 1 Sent.* (*Opera,* vol. 16, 1960, p. 21); *Opus oxon.,* 4, dist. 49, q. 11, n. 9 (vol. 21, p. 417). John Dominici, O.P., *Lucula Noctis,* c. 38: "It remains to be clarified just how the highest part of the human genus, whose author is God, created for unspeakable happiness, sufficiently disposed here on earth can at length attain [this happiness]" (R. Coulon, 1908, p. 336). F. de Vitoria, *In Primam,* q. 1, art. 1, etc.

[42] St. Thomas, *Prima Secundae,* q. 62, art. 1, ad 3um.

[43] *Compendium theologiae,* c. 114 and 107. St. Bonaventure, *Utrum sancti in patria videant Deum per essentiam* (Glorieux ed., 1950), p. 57: "There is no commensurate proportion . . . , but rather a proportion of order, because the intellect, thus raised up through the gift of glory, is ordered to see the divine essence immediately . . ."; p. 59: "The glorified intellect is ordered immediately to seeing the divine essence." *Breviloquium,* P. 5, c. 1 (vol. 5, p. 252). St. Thomas, *Prima,* q. 12, art. 1, ad 4um.

[44] St. Thomas, *De veritate,* q. 13, art. 3; *Summa contra Gentiles,* bk. 3, c. 53, 57, 59; *In 2 Sent.,* dist. 26, q. 1, art. 3. Bonaventure, *Itinerarium,* c. 1, n. 1 (vol. 5, p. 296b). Later theology was to speak of "elevation to a supernatural end" and introduce a tractatus "de Deo elevante"; but that is not the terminology of the great scholastics. Cf. Henri Rondet, S.J., *Recherches de Sc. rel.* (1946): 63.

[45] Bernard of Trilia (d. 1292), quoted by L. B. Gillon, *Revue thomiste* 47 (1947): 307. Cf. John of Paris (ibid., p. 305).

of the early Augustinian school; the second again from St. Thomas. This will have the added advantage of showing once again the essential harmony, not merely in doctrine—which goes without saying on so fundamental a point of faith—but even in the use of words.

Eudes Rigaud wrote, in his commentary on the second book of the *Sentences,* composed around 1241 to 1245:

> The highest good infinitely exceeds human desire [*affectus*]. Our desire therefore cannot by itself be raised up to the highest good by love to the extent fitting to it, unless something intervening, which would in fact have to be above our desire, raises it up. But this disposition that thus raises up our desire is that which we call grace. . . . Likewise, glory is above all created nature. . . .
>
> [It is necessary] to posit a created grace, which disposes the soul itself, and elevates and unites it to God. . . . For the soul never attains to supernatural glory unless it elevates itself through some means.[46]

Let us now return to St. Thomas:

> No rational creature can have a motion of the will [*motus voluntatis*] ordered toward this beatitude, unless it is moved by a supernatural agent.
>
> All that is raised up to something that exceeds its own nature is properly disposed by some disposition that is above its nature.
>
> No created nature is a sufficient principle of an act meritorious of eternal life, unless some supernatural gift is added, which is called grace.[47]
>
> Through created charity the soul is raised up above nature, so that it is more perfectly ordered toward the end that the faculty of nature has.
>
> Through [grace] man is sufficiently ordered into eternal life.
>
> It is fitting that in addition to man's ordering to the good of eternal life, there be some beginning [*inchoatio*] of it in the person to whom it is promised.[48]

There they are: disposition, proportion, "sufficient" inclination, "immediate" ordering, or ordering "in due fashion" [*debito modo*],[49]

---

[46] *In 2 Sent.,* dist. 26, m. 1, q. 1 (J. Bouvy, *Rech. de théol. anc. et méd.* 27 [1960]: 306, 308). Q. 1 *de libero arbitrio:* "It has a natural, but not sufficient, appetite" (Auer, p. 48).

[47] *Prima,* q. 62, art. 2; q. 12, art 5. *Prima Secundae,* q. 114, art 2.

[48] *De caritate,* art. 1, ad 16um. *De veritate,* q. 14, art. 2; q. 27, art. 5; et ad 1um.

[49] *Prima Secundae,* q. 4, art. 4 et ad 3um. *De virt. in comm.,* art. 10, art. 12 ad 16um. For "sufficiens" see M. D. Chenu, *Revue des sc. phil. et théol.* 22 (1933): 251–59.

120   inchoativeness, raising up . . . : all these words, unlike "receptive potency" [*potentia receptiva*], "capacity" [*capacitas*], "ability" [*habilitas*] or
"aptitude" [*aptitudo*],[50] are generally used to designate a kind of reality
which belongs not to the order or finality of nature, but in varying
degrees, at varying stages, and from varying perspectives, to the supernatural order: the order of grace, free will and merit,[51] the order of the
theological virtues,[52] and finally, the order of glory and of vision.[53]

There can be no question here of any kind of *debitum naturae*, anything owed to nature, no suggestion of anything resembling a demand.
Man's longing for God is in a category of its own; we cannot apply univocally to it any of the patterns of thought which we generally use to try
to define relationships between beings in this world.[54] "The total gratuitousness of our adoption as sons by God the Father transcends without
absorbing it the utter gratuitousness of the fundamental gift of
creation."[55] It is, as Harphius said, "a most particular grace" [*gratia spe-
cialissima*].[56] Even had there been no sin, the *imago recreationis* could
never have been simply the consequence, the natural development, or
the "logical complement" of the image of creation [*imago creationis*].[57]
We could still have said as we still must: "O God, Who established the
nature of man in wondrous dignity, and still more admirably restored

121   it. . . ." "In effect what we have been given in order to exist is one thing,
what we have been given in order to become saints is another"—in
other words, the spirit of man is one thing, the Spirit of God another,

---

[50] St. Thomas, *In 2 Sent.*, dist. 30, q. 1, art. 1, ad 5um. Eudes Rigaud, *In 2 Sent.*, dist. 28, m. 1, q. 1, ad 1um (*loc. cit.*, 28, 1961, p. 72). "Gratuitorum habilitas": Alan of Lille, *De virtutibus*.

[51] Again *Prima Secundae*, q. 114, art. 1; q. 109, art. 5. *In 1 Sent.*, dist. 14, q. 3. *De veritate*, q. 27, art. 1.

[52] John of Paris again, quoted in O. Lottin, *Psychologie et morale aux XII*e *et XIII*e *siècles*, vol. 3, 2, p. 476; etc. Cf. Petrus Trigosus (*loc. cit.*, p. 10).

[53] *Prima Secundae*, q. 63, art. 3, ad 2um. *In 1 Sent.*, dist. 14, q. 3. Similarly St. Bonaventure, *In 2 Sent.*, dist. 19, art. 3, q. 1: "Insofar as the beatifiable conveys aptitude, so also is it in man through nature; for man has from his nature the aptitude for beatitude. But insofar as it conveys sufficient disposition, through which one attains to beatitude, or sufficient ordering for acting, so also is it in man not through nature, but through grace, through which he is sufficiently disposed to glory. . . ."

[54] Cf. J. Sestili, *loc. cit.*, pp. 955–57. See *infra*, chapter 9.

[55] Blaise Romeyer, *loc. cit.*, p. 56, note.

[56] *Theologia mystica*, bk. 1, p. 2, c. 17 (Cologne ed., 1611, p. 160).

[57] Cf. St. Thomas, *Prima*, q. 93, a. 4, who finds these traditional expressions in the *Glossa ordinaria*.

although once given, the latter becomes equally and literally "our spirit."[58] In different terms again, the gifts of grace and of glory *[dona gratiae et gloriae]* could never be confused with the gifts of nature *[dona naturae]*: "At the same time creating their nature and bestowing grace upon them," St. Augustine said of the angels, deliberately contrasting the two.[59] This soundly based and carefully thought-out distinction is familiar to a number of writers in the past who certainly never had the slightest notion of any state of "pure nature" in the modern sense, but of whom it cannot possibly be said that they did not fully realize the distinction between the natural and supernatural orders. One may instance Florus of Lyons,[60] Pseudo-William of St. Thierry,[61] Hugh[62] and Richard of St. Victor.[63] It was this same distinction that St. Thomas was making when he declared: "the end is awaited from another's giving it,"[64] and when he said of sanctifying grace: "men are created according to it, that is, they are established in a new being out of nothing *[ex nihilo]*."[65] It is this that the Church teaches us from generation to generation. In our day she lays stress on it which is amply explained and justified by the dangers of naturalism and immanentism which surround us, but she will never dictate any one system of explanations to account for it; as for instance when she tells us that the supernatural constitutes a perfection "that is higher than the natural" *[quae naturalem superet]*,[66] or again, as I recalled a few pages back, that its special gratuitousness would be destroyed by the claim that God could not create intelligent beings without calling them to see him.[67]

122

Two traditional terms, taken from St. James' Epistle, express the same doctrine. Those two terms, quoted by Pseudo-Denys in the *Hierarchia caelestis*, are commented on by the western commentators along the same lines as Scotus Erigena: the "greatest gift" *[datum optimum]* St.

[58] St. Augustine, *De Trinitate*, bk. 5, c. 14, n. 15: "But what we have received in order to be is one thing; it is another thing that we received in order to be holy . . ." (Bibl. aug., 15, p. 458).

[59] *De civitate Dei*, bk. 12, c. 9, n. 2.

[60] *Liber adversus Ioannem Scotum*, c. 7 (*PL*, 121, 145 AC).

[61] *Disputatio altera adversus Abaelardum*, bk. 3 (*PL*, 180, 323 BC).

[62] *Expositio in Hierarchiam caelestem S. Dionysii*, bk. 2, c. 1 (*PL*, 175; 936–37).

[63] *Adnotatio in psalmum 2* (*PL*, 196, 269–70).

[64] *Prima*, q. 62, a. 4: "perfect beatitude is perfect only to God."

[65] *Prima Secundae*, q. 110, a. 2, ad 3um.

[66] First Vatican Council, canon 3 *De revelatione* (Denz. 1868).

[67] *Humani generis*. Cf. *supra*, p. 80, and *infra*, chapter 7, p. 130.

James speaks of is nature; the "perfect gift" [*donum perfectum*] is grace: the two are different ways of sharing in God's goodness.[68] This explanation was general in the twelfth century: we find it in Hugh of St. Victor,[69] Geoffrey of St. Victor,[70] Gilbert of Hoyt,[71] Otto of Freising.[72] It passed into the works of such great scholastics as Alexander of Hales[73] and St. Bonaventure.[74] Some writers, notably Gilbert of Hoyt and

123

---

[68] Scotus Erigena, *Super Hierarchiam caelestem S. Dionysii*, c. 1, n. 1: "This apostolic declaration distinguishes, in an admirable differentiation, the divine gift [*dationem*] from the divine endowment [*donationem*], assigning the best gift [*dationem*] of every creature to substitution, and on the other hand the perfect endowment [*donationem*] of divine grace to liberality; for all that exists participates in divine goodness in two ways: the first is in the condition of nature, the second is perceived in the distribution of grace." However, the second concept remained very wide for Scotus Erigena, who adds: "Certainly there is nothing in every creature that lacks these two; for everything that is exists, and participates in divine grace according to the analogy fitting to it" (*PL*, 122, 127 BC). Certain precisions follow (127–28, 130 B). Cf. c. 15, n. 3: "where it is given to be understood, free will is to be reckoned among the givens of nature [*data naturae*], not among the gifts of grace [*dona gratiae*]" (259 A).

[69] *In Hier. cael.*, bk. 2, c. 1: "Indeed the rational creature, which alone was made in the image of the maker, receives the given and the gift [*data et dona*]" (*PL*, 175, 936 D).

[70] *Microcosmus*, c. 43 (ed. P. Delhaye, 1951, p. 63). This distinction suggested to Geoffrey the plan for his *Fons philosophiae*; cf. Philippe Delhaye, *Le Microcosmus de Godefroy de Saint-Victor, étude théologique* (1951), pp. 80–81.

[71] *Tractatus ascetici*, tract. 5, *In Jac.*, 1, 17, nn. 2–3: "What does he want for himself that is placed, given and gift, best and perfect [*positum est, datum et donum, optimum et perfectum*]? This distinction is signaled by certain nouns. . . . In the first place, the following distinction seems to be tenable between the given [*datum*] and the gift [*donum*]. The given [*datum*] is what one does not have of himself; the gift [*donum*] is what is not from merit. There is a given [*datum*], when one receives; a gift [*donum*], when one merits it thereafter. A given [*datum*], when one has it for use; a gift [*donum*], when one possesses it for enjoyment" (*PL*, 184, 271 D, 272 A).

[72] *Gesta Friderici imperatoris*, bk. 1, c. 60: "Whatever is called a good in nature [*in naturalibus*] is so either simply or relatively [*secundum quid*]. If it is simple, then it is called a given of nature [*datum naturae*], just as a gift of grace is conceded, according to the expression: 'Every gift is good [*Omne datum optimum*]' etc." (*MGH, Scriptores*, vol. 20, p. 386; ed. Roger Wilmans).

[73] *Summa theologica*, 1, no. 431: "Good being [*bene esse*] is a gift [*donum*] of divine goodness. . . . And it is neither contained within the confines of created nature, nor does it function according to natural virtue, but it accomplishes its effects superessentially and beyond all created natural senses. . . . Nature is a given [*datum*], but grace is a gift [*donum*] . . ." (col. 904–5).

[74] *In 1 Sent.*, d. 18, q. 3: "Although both 'given' and 'gift' [*et datum et donum*] are said with reference to the divine, nevertheless it is more convenient to say 'gift' [*donum*]. The reason for this is twofold. First, because 'given,' since it is either a participle or a verbal noun, concerns time; and 'gift' [*donum*], on the other hand, is outside of time, and since all that is divine is above time, it is more convenient to say 'gift' than 'given.' Second, because 'gift' adds to the meaning of 'given' the condition of generosity, which is a condi-

Bonaventure, tried to base the use of the words upon reasons of a semantic nature which are not of great importance to us here. Honorius linked it with a terminology inherited in part from the Greek Fathers and in part from St. Anselm, distinguishing being [*esse*] from good being [*bene esse*], and the will to beatitude [*voluntas beatitudinis*] from the will to justice [*voluntas justitiae*].[75] Similarly St. Thomas carefully distinguishes between *datio* and *donatio* to indicate the difference between the gift given out of love and the gift that is love itself.[76] Denys the Carthusian, who is one of the earliest witnesses to the modern theories, reproduces it faithfully.[77] All these writers explain that the *donum perfectum* is quite different from, and infinitely more than, the continuation or intensification of the *datum optimum*. Completely "descending from the Father of Lights," it is, as Pascal was to say, "of a different, supernatural, order." It is a whole "new world" to which one can only attain "by a new principle": for just as in giving us natural life God "gives us this world and ourselves," so, "giving us Jesus Christ for our life, he gives us a new world, that is, himself, who is a new world"[78]—so wrote Bérulle, maintaining simple fidelity to scripture and common tradition, without any recourse to the distinctions of later scholasticism. St. John has told us: we only obtain this "new being" by means of an adoption which is genuinely a "new birth."[79] And St. Paul says the same thing: in this new creation, which is incommensurable with the earlier creation,

124

---

tion of great nobility, and therefore strives for divinity the most; this is why 'gift' is appropriate for free gifts, and not only for the Holy Spirit, who is the principle of free gifts" (vol. 1, p. 327).

[75] *De libero arbitrio libellus,* c. 6: "Man therefore has two wills, one to beatitude and the other to justice. The will to beatitude is called nature, and the will to justice is called grace. The former is called a 'given' [*datum*], the latter 'gift' [*donum*]. Certainly being is given [*datur*] to man; but good being [*bene esse*] is given as a gift [*donatur*]" (*PL,* 172, 1225–26). A text like this would be interesting to study in detail.

[76] *In 1 Sent.,* d. 18, q. 1, a. 2 and 3, ad 4um. Cf. *In 2 Cor.,* 5, lect. 2, which contrasts Gen. 2:7 and 2 Cor. 5:5.

[77] *Opera omnia,* vol. 15, p. 13: "Every best gift [*donum*], that is, every truly good and celestial gift [*munus*] in the genus of natural gifts [*donorum*], as they are intellectual powers and habits in which the image of the Holy Trinity is first considered in every man; and every perfect gift [*donum*], that is every supernatural gift [*munus*] of grace, and also every gift [*donum*] of glory."

[78] Bérulle, *Opuscules de piété,* 128, 1 and 138 (ed. G. Rotureau, pp. 381, 415–16). Cf. op. 151, 3 (p. 441).

[79] John 3:3–7. Cf. St. Augustine, *Contra Maximum,* bk. 3, c. 15. Bérulle, *op. cit.,* 27, 11 (p. 134), etc. On Bérulle's teaching, see Jean Orcibal, *Le cardinal de Bérulle* (1965), p. 40, etc.

we become "a new creature in Christ Jesus."[80] The teaching is a fundamental one, and St. Bonaventure comments on it thus:

> Creation is twofold: one in the being of nature and the other in the being of grace. The first creation gives being to nature; the second gives being to grace. Of the first, Ecclesiasticus says (17:1): "God created man of the earth," that is to say, so that he might be; of the second creation, Psalm (103:30): "Thou shalt send forth thy spirit, and they shall be created," that is to say, in the being of grace, so that they might be good.[81]

Again, Bérulle says, in his small book *De la double création de l'homme:*

> We have another emanation from God, one which obliges us far more to sanctify ourselves, that of Jesus; Jesus is its principle, and we are born of him: *I have given you the power to be made sons of God.* By the first we are God's servants; by the second we are God's children. In the first, God made us in his image; in the second God makes himself in our image and likeness. In the first we receive nature; in the second, we receive grace. In the first we enter this world; in the second we enter Jesus. St. Paul calls us the created in Jesus Christ, *creati in Christo Jesu.* A magnificent phrase which teaches us much that we did not know about our condition. It teaches us that we are created in this new birth, just as we were the first time; and that there is in us no principle or subject of grace; just as there has not been in nature: *Creati in Christo Jesu.* It teaches us that we are created in Jesus Christ, and that as God living is the principle of our existence in nature, so God mortal and dying is the principle of our existence in grace: *Creati in Christo Jesu.* It teaches us that as we come from God in two ways, and have two different beings, we also have two entries into two very different worlds and for two very different ends. For in the first creation, we enter this world that we see, and in the second creation we enter a world that we adore; in other words we enter, we

125

---

[80] 2 Cor. 5:17. Cf. Gal. 6:15; Eph. 2:10. These texts are commented on by St. Augustine in numerous passages, especially *In Galat.* (PL, 37, 1388); *Enchiridion,* c. 31, n. 9 (40, 247); *Contra Faustum,* bk. 3, c. 3 (42, 215–16); *Epist.* 140, n. 81 (33, 575), etc. Cf. St. Thomas, *Prima Secundae,* q. 110, a. 2, ad 3um.

[81] *De S. Patre nostro Francisco, sermo 3* (*Opera,* Quaracchi, vol. 9, p. 583). There may even be a first expression of this teaching in the prologue of St. John, if it is true that John 1:3 is speaking of the creative work of the Word, and John 1:4–5 of his saving work: the first creation thus being done by the Word, the second in him. Cf. M. F. Lacan, O.S.B., "L'œuvre du Verbe incarné, le Don de la Vie," *Recherches de science religieuse* 45 (1957): 61–78.

live, we act in Jesus: *Creati in Christo Jesu.* And as he is our principle, he is our universe too, he is our world and we live in him.[82]

Without being drawn into any dualist theory of last ends, no one who reads scripture without bias can miss so fundamental a duality. The whole of Catholic tradition proclaims and explains it: the texts we have just recalled are only a few samples of this. It can be misunderstood only by someone who, like Michael Baius in the sixteenth century, begins from a misconception of the intrinsic character of the "perfect gift." Baius failed to recognize that this "perfect gift" of the supernatural, which is completed in the vision of God, constitutes for created nature, however high we rate that nature, a real sublimation, a real exaltation above itself, in short a real deification: "a human exaltation, from which man participates excellently in the things that are God's."[83] In his eyes this gift in no sense constituted a "new spiritual creation"; it did not gain entry into God "beyond all natural dignity";[84] It still belonged to that divine decree "whose effect is the production of natural divine works."[85] Thus for this theologian the whole order of grace was no more   126 than a means placed at the service of human nature and its activity; it was "a necessary logical complement of the creation of spirit, not a privileged condition raising spirit above its natural state."[86] Baius had lost the understanding of those "most great and precious promises" spoken of in 2 Peter by which we are to be made "partakers of the divine nature."[87] This is very clear from his own statements against the wording of several propositions condemned by St. Pius V,[88] as well as from the explanations he gave twenty years later in a theological discourse.

---

[82] *Op. cit.,* 125, 2 (p. 377). Cf. 128, 2 (p. 382). Compare Gregory of Nyssa (H. Urs von Balthasar, *Présence et Pensée* [Paris, 1942], pp. 104–5).

[83] St. Bonaventure, *In 2 Sent.,* d. 27, a. 1, q. 3: "By this indwelling man is elevated [*sublimatur*] and rises to greatness [*ad magna*]." Dist. 29, a. 1, q. 1: "It cannot but be gratuitous, on the one hand on account of the gratuitous condescension of God, on the other hand on account of the exaltation of the creature above the terms or states of nature," etc.

[84] Scotus Erigena, *De divisione naturae,* bk. 5, c. 38 (*PL,* 122, 1001 B; cf. 902–5).

[85] I borrow these terms from Père François-Xavier Jansen's *Baius et le Baianisme, étude théologique* (Museum Lessianum, 1927), p. 128.

[86] Père Jacques de Blic, "Bulletin de morale," *Mélanges de science religieuse* (1947): 111.

[87] 2 Peter 1:4.

[88] I show this in greater detail in *Augustinisme et théologie moderne* (Paris, 1965), chapter 1, Eng. trans. *Augustinianism and Modern Theology* (London: Chapman; New York: Herder & Herder, 1969).

"When Baius in his minor writings upheld the thesis of grace owed to innocent nature [*naturae innocenti debita*], the fundamental idea he was thus expressing was certainly not so much that of humanity aspiring to divine union or any connaturality of spirit with the divine, as of the first man's needing—in order to realize his righteousness—the 'charity of God poured [in the heart] through the Holy Spirit. . . .' It was that which, for Baius, made necessary, and therefore something owed to the creature as a whole, the logical complement which was grace."[89] According to him, man was made to act well, as birds to fly, and the help of the Spirit which he was given before the fall was no more than wings are to a bird. . . .[90] With the best intentions, this doctor's perspective was too narrowly moralizing, and one can almost hear Jesus saying to him: "If you would know the gift of God. . . ."

127   But once one has really perceived what this gift is in reality, it becomes impossible ever to fall into such an error. How could one take the supernatural gift to be an element which would simply complete nature—"pertaining to its integrity"[91]—when it actually comes in fact to perfect it (*gratia perficit naturam*)?[92] How could one include it "in the rational order of essences," or consider it as "necessary to the essential structure of the world created by God"?[93] How could nature require it? By what title? It does not need it for its natural completion. No obligation can arise in it in regard to a reality which is absolutely beyond it. The supernatural is not owed to nature; it is nature which, if it is to obey God's plan, owes itself to the supernatural if that supernatural is offered to it.

---

[89] J. de Blic, *loc. cit.,* p. 101.

[90] *Narratio brevis eorum verborum, quae Lovanii in scholis theologorum intersesserunt inter magistrum nostrum Michaelem de Bay et Cornelium Gaudanum, die 12 novembris anni 1580:* "Man was created to perform good works, just as the bird was manifestly made to fly. . . . Just as the bird with broken wings cannot fly, so too man deprived of the Holy Spirit cannot perform well." Miguel Roca, *Documentos ineditos en torno a Miguel Bayo (Anthologica annua* [Rome, 1953], p. 475).

[91] Baius, *De justitia primi hominis,* c. 6 and 11.

[92] The difference between these two verbs, to complete and to perfect, indicates the whole, radical difference between Baius and St. Thomas. For the latter, all the goods of grace "are superior to the order of nature [*ordinem naturae excedunt*]": *Compendium theologiae,* c. 214. Cf. earlier William of Auvergne, *De anima,* c. 6, n. 20: "Neither grace nor glory destroy or damage nature, for they *incomprehensibly* adorn, decorate, and *perfect* it [*exornat, decorat ac perficit*]."

[93] Edmond Ortigues, *Le temps de la parole* (1954), p. 43, commenting on the condemnation of Baius.

In short, unlike the gifts of nature, supernatural gifts are totally out-side any kind of claim. St. Thomas Aquinas explains this perfectly with his usual clarity in an article of the *Summa Theologica* from which I have already quoted a few words:

> Grace, inasmuch as it is given gratuitously, excludes the notion of debt. Now debt can be understood in two ways. First, as arising from merit, which refers to the person who performs the meritorious acts. . . . Second, debt as arising from the condition of nature: if for example one could say that it is a debt to man that he should have reason and the other qualities that pertain to human nature. But in neither way is it called debt in the sense that God is under obligation to the creature: rather it is so insofar as the creature must be subject to God for divine ordination to be fulfilled in it, namely that a given nature should possess given conditions or properties, and that when it performs certain opera-tions, certain consequences should follow.
>
> Natural endowments therefore are void of debt in the first sense, but not in the second sense. Supernatural endowments on the other hand are void of debt in either sense: and therefore they especially deserve the name of grace.[94]

And this is true without qualification, *in every hypothesis.*

We may say again, from another point of view which converges upon the same point, that it is not the supernatural which is explained by nature, at least as something postulated by it: it is, on the contrary, nature which is explained in the eyes of faith by the supernatural, as required for it. "It is the end which is primordial, and which summons up the means."[95] Considered in itself, statistically one might say, my nature or my essence is no more than what it is. There is, let me repeat, no slightest element of the supernatural in it, nor the slightest power to raise itself up to it, nor the smallest principle for laying claim to it. But no more than we can envisage, except in order to represent the thing humanly to ourselves, any real subject existing before being brought into being by the creative act, can we now envisage that nature in its

128

---

[94] *Prima Secundae,* q. 111, art. 1, ad 2um.

[95] Paul Claudel, *Introduction au Livre de Ruth,* 1938, p. 35. One could not say with Schwalm (at least without instantly adding certain corrections): "The universe was first created for itself, then subordinated to the supernatural vocation of humanity; and final-ly, humanity having sinned, the universe was ordered once and for all to the glory of the Redeemer, Christ" (quoted by H. Bouessé, O.P., in *Le Sauveur du Monde,* vol. 1, *La place du Christ dans le plan de Dieu,* p. 127).

concrete reality as existing before having its finality imprinted upon it; and that finality, by God's free will, is a supernatural one. Thus, it is never nature which of itself has any call on the supernatural: it is the supernatural which, so to say, must summon up nature before nature can be in a position to receive it. Even if the supernatural comes first in the order of intention—"it is intended to be godlike before it is to be man"—we cannot therefore conclude that created nature has, in the order of execution, any kind of continuity with the supernatural.[96] In other, and simpler, words, the whole initiative is, and will always be, God's. In everything, God is the first. "Before they call, says the Lord, I will answer them."[97]

129

Nothing in fact could be simpler, and nothing would be simpler to understand and therefore accept, if the whole thing had not gradually been complicated and confused. The greatest doctors in the Christian tradition have never said anything else. They have said it and repeated it, very simply and quite clearly. The explanations we have to supply nowadays are intended as a return to their simplicity. They were able to see in a unified gaze the fullness of God's liberty, without attributing any arbitrariness unworthy of it to his work. The angle of vision is not exactly the same for them all; but their aim is the same none the less, and it leads them all to the same central point. "There is no obligation," writes Père Michel-Ange, a commentator of Duns Scotus, "to picture God as a bad architect unable to conceive in advance the plan of his building. It is certainly built in stages, since that is a necessity with anything that is not infinite, but the toothing-stones are arranged from the first, each in its proper place, to link together the various parts. In creating the human soul destined by nature for a supernatural life, God has given it natural aptitudes for that supernatural life."[98] Now this is

---

[96] One may still say: Nothing could be more false than to maintain that there is "nothing more, after all, in our divine vocation than in the act of creation"; but, on the contrary, it is true to declare that there is nothing less in that act of creation—if we envisage it in God, or in its concrete reality, and not in created nature in so far as that can be separated from its goal—than that divine calling. However, vocation is not the same as realization, even in embryo. Being given finality is not the same as actually possessing (or failing to attain) the end. However ontological, so to say, the effect may be from the first, the call to union imprinted on nature is not yet actual union; it is not even the beginning of it.

[97] Isa. 65:24. Cf. Hoceïn Mansûr Hallaj, Qasïda 1, 2: "I call thee. . . . No, it is thou who callest me to thee! . . ." *Dîvân,* translated and introduced by Louis Massignon (1955 ed., *Documents spirituels,* 10), p. 4.

[98] Père Michel-Ange, "Ossuna et Duns Scot," *Etudes franciscaines* (1910), vol. 1,

not an idea peculiar to Duns Scotus. As Gilson tells us, for St. Augustine "it is because he wills us to be one day with him that God has willed us "to be," for that, in the full metaphysical sense of the phrase, is our only *raison d'être*. . . ."[99] People have sometimes been surprised and even disturbed by St. Augustine's insistence that "hence the image of God [*imago Dei*] does not enter the kingdom of God, unless the impediment of sin hinders it."[100] Or, again, to Julianus of Eclanus: "Why do you not admit the image of God into the kingdom of God, since according to you none has the merit of sin?"[101] But what he first of all thought and said was: "Man is the image of God, because he was made to the resemblance of God."[102] Entry into the kingdom, vision of God, beatitude, dwelling in God, perfect resemblance: in his terms, all are one.[103] Evidently he was far from imposing any kind of obligation, necessity or law upon the Creator.[104]

130

---

p. 426. Note the word "aptitudes," whose meaning must not be forced (any more than that of *"capacitas"*).

[99] *Philosophie et incarnation selon saint Augustin* (Montreal, 1947), p. 44; cf. pp. 47–48. It will be observed that Gilson does not, as some do, deny all metaphysical significance to Augustinism. Cf. *supra,* chapter, 4, pp. 65–66. The same is true of St. Thomas: id., "Sur la problématique thomiste de la vision béatifique," *loc. cit.*

[100] *De peccatorum meritis et remissione,* bk. 1, c. 58 (*PL,* 44, 143).

[101] *Contra Iulianum opus imperfectum,* bk. 2, c. 30 (*PL,* 44, 1154). Other texts in Yves de Montcheuil, "La polémique de saint Augustin contre Julien d'Eclane d'après l'Opus imperfectum," *Recherches de sc. rel.* 44 (1956): 215–18. Cf. *Confessions,* bk. 13, c. 8, n. 9 (*PL,* 32, 848). *De civitate Dei,* bk. 9, c. 2: "[God], with whom alone, in whom alone, and from whom alone the human soul, i.e. rational and intellectual, is happy" (41, 257). *De Trinitate,* bk. 13, c. 9, n. 12: "How much more believable is it that the sons of men by nature should be made the sons of God by the grace of God, and should dwell in God, in whom alone and from whom alone the blessed can be made partakers of his immortality; and in order to persuade us of this, the Son of God was made a partaker of our mortality" (Bibl. aug., 16, p. 300).

[102] *Op. cit.,* bk. 1, c. 63 (*PL,* 44, 1083). Cf. H. Somers, "Image de Dieu et illumination divine," *Augustinus Magister* (1954), vol. 1, p. 457: "In 412 we find the first explicit affirmation that the image belongs to rational human nature. . . . Sin has not destroyed, but only deformed the image in us. This conception was definitively fixed by the Trinitarian speculation of the years 416–18."

[103] For the two goals of vision and of likeness, this way of speaking is based upon St. John. *De Trinitate,* bk. 14, c. 18, n. 24: "The Apostle John says, 'Dearly beloved, we are now the sons of God; and it hath not yet appeared what we shall be. We know, that, when he shall appear, we shall be like to him: because we shall see him as he is' (1 John 3:2). Hence it appears that his full likeness in this image of God will come to be when he will perceive the full vision" (Bibl. aug., 16, pp. 310–12).

[104] *De Trinitate,* bk. 14, c. 8, n. 11 (16, pp. 372–78): before being a participator in God by grace, the soul must be an image of God, which makes it capable of that participation.

Furthermore, St. Augustine was not the first to speak in this way. "When some of the Fathers situate the divine image in the substance of the soul, and resemblance to God in the virtues, we must not take them to mean that the virtues are for them no more than a development of nature and its powers, and not a superior order involving a superior nature: they see the image in the nature we receive as such from the Creator, and the likeness in the spirituality which the Holy Spirit communicates to us as his gift."[105] And in the Latin tradition, after St. Augustine and generally taking a lead from him, many others were to say the same thing. Rupert of Deutz, for instance, at the beginning of the twelfth century: "Further, it was the intention and holy purpose of God and his Word to make man . . . suited to their divinity [*suae divinitatis capacem*]."[106] Similarly William of St. Thierry, in his famous *Epistola ad fratres de monte Dei,* said that it was because God wished to make us "like to him" in "the unity of the spirit" that he created us in his image ". . . in order that we might be like to God, we were created after his image."[107] Similarly St. Bernard: "What is God? . . . The highest beatitude, creating minds to participate in him, . . . opening them to grasp him" [*dilatans ad capiendum*];[108] and again: "Finally, God is charity, and there is nothing in the world [*in rebus*] that can fulfill the creature made in the image of God but God-Charity [*Caritas Deus*], who alone is greater than [the creature]."[109] We find similar ideas in the disciples of Bernard, Isaac of Stella,[110] Aelred of Rievaulx,[111] and so on. Precisely

131

But it is none the less true that it is because he wished it to be a participator that God created it capable of being so by making it an image. Cf. c. 4, n. 6 (1040).

[105] French edition of Scheeben's *Natur und Gnade, Nature et grâce* (Paris, 1957), pp. 186–87.

[106] *De victoria Verbi Dei,* bk. 2, c. 6 (*PL,* 169, 1248 D). Cf. *De Trinitate et operibus eius, In Genesim,* bk. 2, c. 11: "Man has the capacity for divine goodness inasmuch as he is rational [*utpote rationalis*]" (167, 257 A). *De Spiritu Sancto,* bk. 1, c. 11: "He was made in the image of God, because he was made rational; he has not arrived to the likeness of God, because he has not imitated the gift [*donum*] of God" (1581 BC).

[107] *Ep. ad Fratres de Monte Dei,* c. 105.

[108] *De consideratione,* bk. 5, c. 11, n. 24 (*Opera,* ed. J. Leclercq, vol. 3, 1963, p. 486).

[109] *In Cantica,* sermo 18, n. 6 (vol. 2, 1957, p. 107). Cf. *Sermo de conversione ad clericos,* c. 8, n. 15: "Whence this paltriness and wretched debasement, that an outstanding creature that has the capacity for eternal beatitude and for the glory of God on high, inasmuch as it was established by inspiration, stamped with likeness, redeemed by Blood, endowed with faith, adopted in the Spirit, does not find shame in bearing slavery under this corruption of corporeal senses" (*PL,* 182, 843 A).

[110] *Sermo 25* (*PL,* 194, 1772–73). Cf. St. Benedict of Aniane, *Munimenta fidei* (ed. J. Leclercq, *Studia Anselmiana,* 20, p. 37).

[111] *Speculum caritatis,* bk. 1, c. 3 (*PL,* 195, 507 D), etc.

the same kind of bond is affirmed by the scholastics of the golden age, especially by St. Bonaventure who never misses a chance to recall it: "The highest good, for the participation in which the rational creature   132
was made,"[112] and: "Because [the human soul] was made to participate in beatitude . . . , it was made with a capacity for God and thus in its image and likeness,"[113] or again: "Since all creatures were made for God [*propter Deum*] according to the verse: 'The Lord hath made all things for himself' [*propter semetipsum*] (Prov. 16:4), the rational creature alone was made to enjoy God, and to be beatified in him, for it alone is in the likeness."[114]

Thus—and again it is a very simple consideration—the will of God is the first thing here, and therefore God's liberty is total. It is this will which, at every moment of each of our lives, remains first, acts first. His sovereign liberty encloses, surpasses and causes all the bonds of intelligibility that we discover between the creature and its destiny. Nature and the supernatural are thus united, without in any sense being confused. "The end of rational nature is the highest good, which is above nature."[115] The spiritual creature does not find its end in itself, but in God. This is a truth which St. Bonaventure and Alexander of Hales expressed in identical terms, which we find unchanged in Richard of Middleton,[116] Matthew of Aquasparta,[117] and many others, and which   133
St. Thomas Aquinas himself also repeated several times in similar

---

[112] *In 2 Sent.*, dist. 5, dubium 1 (vol. 2, p. 158). *In 3 Sent.*, dist. 1, art. 1, q. 1, ad 4um (vol. 3, p. 11).

[113] *In 2 Sent.*, dist. 18, art. 1, q. 1. Cf. *In 4 Sent.*, dist. 49, art. 1, q. 2: "Since therefore the rational soul was created in the image and likeness of God and was created capable [*capax*] of the most sufficient good, and is not itself sufficient for itself, since it is vain and deficient; therefore I say that it naturally strives for true beatitude" (vol. 4, p. 1003), etc. Toletus takes "capax" in the strongest sense as "disposed," "ordered," "elevated." Cf. A. Arenas Silva, *Gratuidad e Immanencia . . .* , 1963, pp. 28, 36.

[114] *In 2 Sent.*, dist. 19, art. 1, q. 2. Again, dist. 26, q. 4, ad 1um: "The soul . . . was made by reason of beatitude and suited for beatitude." *In 2 Sent.*, dist. 1, p. 2, art. 2, q. 2: "[Every spirit] is immediately ordered to the same end, namely to eternal beatitude" (vol. 2, p. 463, 640–41, 646; cf. p. 398). Cf. Gilson, *Sur la problématique thomiste . . .* , p. 81.

[115] Alexander, *Summa theologica,* secunda pars, n. 510, ad 6um. Bonaventure, *In 2 Sent.,* dist. 29, art. 1, q. 2, ad 4um.

[116] *In 4 Sent.*, dist. 49, art. 1, q. 3: "By the very fact that he was created in the image of God with respect to the soul, [man] has so great a capacity that no good is sufficient to him but the highest good" (E. Hocedez, p. 378).

[117] *Quaestiones disputatae de anima*, q. 11, ad 6um: "With respect to capacity for and participation in glory . . . [rational creatures] all exist equally to the image, and the image is equal, because all are ordered immediately to a single end, namely God in whom all are beatified" (ed. A. J. Gondras, 1961), p. 190.

terms: "Man was made to see God: for this purpose [*ad hoc*] God made him a rational creature, so that he might participate in his likeness, which consists in seeing him" [*in eius visione consistit*][118] or, more briefly, but no less clearly: "The end on account of which a creature is rational is to see God in his essence" [*per essentiam*];[119] "our intellect was made for the purpose of seeing God."[120] What could be simpler, what clearer? It seems to me that the twofold nature of this truth is summed up perfectly in the famous phrase, at once so compact and so complete, which says of the vision of God : "is no part of their nature, but its end [*non est aliquid naturae, sed naturae finis*]."[121]

[118] *De Veritate*, q. 18, art. 1.

[119] *De Veritate*, q. 8, art. 3, obj. 12 (the reply does not contest the principle). Cf. *Tertia*, q. 9, art. 2, ad 3um. *Prima*, q. 12, art. 1; q. 62, art. 4: "To be [for God] and to be happy are the same thing. For to be happy is not the nature of a given creature, but its end." Cf. Giles of Rome, *In 2 Sent.*, dist. 38, q. 1, q. 2 (Venice, 1581, p. 566).

[120] *De Veritate*, q. 10, art. 11, ad 7um.

[121] *Prima*, q. 62, a. 1. Also St. Bonaventure, *In 1 Sent.*, dist. 1, art. 3, q. 2: "Nothing can complete [*finire*] the soul sufficiently but the good toward which it is. This is the highest good that is superior to the soul, and the infinite good that exceeds the powers of the soul" (vol. 1, p. 40). Similarly St. Thomas, *De Malo*, q. 5, art. 1, ad 5um: "The indeterminate reward [*praemium accidentale*] is observed with respect to some created good; but true beatitude is observed only with respect to the uncreated good." Cf. *Compendium theologiae*, c. 144: "But because the final end of the rational creature exceeds the faculty of nature itself. . . ." One can find one echo, among others, of this traditional teaching in the great commentary on Genesis by Valentine Pererius, *In Genesim*, bk. 4 (5th ed., Lyons, 1607, vol. 1, p. 389): "Therefore man was created in the image of God, so that he might be capable of eternity, infinity and divinity in a certain measure [*quodammodo*]: and that there might be no good so great that he would not dare ask it of God and hope to obtain it from him. Truly we can sincerely say to God: Lord, fill with your goods this infinite capacity of our mind and will that you have given us: for if you do not suffer anything to be empty [*vacuum*] in nature, but wish every place to be filled and made up of bodies, how much less are we to believe that you wish some [emptiness] in our souls? You, therefore, who alone can fill our desire with goods, fill our wills, which nothing besides you alone can fill and sate. For just as a dish that is round in shape can be filled on its whole surface only by a object that is similarly round, so also the human soul made in the image of God can be filled and sated only by God, to whom it is similar."

CHAPTER 6

The Christian Paradox
of Man

Once again, this teaching of the theologians of the past still seems to 135
me acceptable. It is something more, I think, than just a "system set
alongside a dogma," as Père Pierre Rousselot said apropos of St.
Thomas.[1] If we abstract certain peculiarities proper to this or that
author—which I have avoided going into—it seems to me too important, too central, too constant, and too clearly formulated, for us to be
able to set it aside without good reason, and I can see no such good
reason. The preceding explanations (and those to come) are intended
simply to complete and to justify their position by stressing an aspect
which has in the past tended to remain implicit, so as to dissipate the
difficulties raised in modern times, and to avoid all the dangers against
which the Church's magisterium has on several occasions warned us.

Having given those explanations, if one goes on to say that there is
no reason actually to imagine for created spiritual nature—our nature,
in other words—any purely natural finality, that is in no sense, as should
by now be abundantly clear, to impair the free and sovereign gratuitousness of the gifts of God. Even if one went on to say that any natural finality has become concretely impossible for that created spirit, that
existing being, it could never be an absolute judgment, but only one
from supposition [*ex suppositione*]. The spirit we speak of in this way will 136
thus always be envisaged in its "historic nature" (if we hold to this
term), in its "instituted nature [*natura instituta*]," or if you prefer, in
Rahner's language, in its "existential" reality.[2] We shall not therefore say

[1] *L'intellectualisme de saint Thomas*[3], p. 182.
[2] In *Orientierung* (Zurich, 1950): 144: "das zentrale und bleibende Existential des

with Père E. Brisbois that "there is naturally in the human will a desire for the vision of God, independent of man's vocation to his supernatural destiny";[3] but rather, with the Augustinian Fulgentius Lafosse: "The innate appetite for the beatific vision is not so natural that it is not at least rooted in the supernatural [*ut non sit supernaturalis saltem radicaliter*], to the extent [*in quantum*] that it is founded upon the elevation of man to a supernatural end."[4] In this way we shall find ourselves once again in accord with those who hold the modern "pure nature" theory, as to their reasons for holding it, but in closer fidelity to the earlier tradition.[5] We shall agree with them fully.

But there is one point upon which we shall continue to differ, at least from some among them—I mean those of whom Père Motte wondered whether one day they would "not apply the notion of nature too univocally to created spirit."[6]

137 For there is nature and nature. If, in contrast with the supernatural order, the being of angels and men as resulting simply from their being created must be called natural, we must allow that their situation, in relation to other natures, is "singular and paradoxical"; for it is the situation "of a spirit which is to become subject and agent of an act of knowledge for which it has no natural equipment, and which is thus to be fulfilled by getting beyond itself."[7] If, then, there is a human nature and an angelic nature, we cannot use the terms *wholly* in the sense in which we speak of animal nature, for instance, or cosmic nature. If

Menschen, wie es wirklich ist." Really, to the extent that this "existential" is conceived as a kind of "medium" or "linking reality," one may object that this is a useless supposition, whereby the problem of the relationship between nature and the supernatural is not resolved, but only set aside; Schillebeeckx explains this in *Revue des sc. philos. et théol.* 48 (1964): 397. See long ago John of Rada, *Controv.*, 13, art. 4 (vol. 4, 1617, p. 423).

[3] "Le désir de voir Dieu et la métaphysique du vouloir selon saint Thomas," *Nouvelle revue théologique* 63 (1936): 1113.

[4] *Augustinus theologus*, vol. 3, p. 184.

[5] Thus I would say with Père Timothée Richard, O.P., *Revue thomiste* (1936): 224: "It is always in relation to the demands of this beatitude which is assigned to us by God, not by nature, that St. Thomas takes his stand." This is how I understand St. Thomas, and how he understood things themselves; with the proviso, however, that in certain circumstances (cf. *infra*), existing nature can be an indication to us of God's will.

[6] *Bulletin thomiste* 4 (1934–36): 590.

[7] Id., ibid., and p. 587. Cf. Schillebeeckx, *Christ the Sacrament* (London, 1963): 1: ". . . the theology of the manuals does not always make a careful distinction between that unique manner of existence which is peculiar to man, and the mode of being, mere objective 'being there,' which is proper to the things of nature."

every created spirit, before being a thinking spirit, is itself "nature,"[8] if, before even being thinking, "it is spiritual nature," then it must also be recognized that, in another sense, spirit is in contrast with "nature." Even in the terminology of the scholastics, and of St. Thomas especially, rational nature [*natura rationalis*] or rational creature [*creatura rationalis*] is not a natural thing [*res naturalis*]. Spiritual beings cannot be confounded with beings known simply as "natural beings": "naturals" [*naturalia*], "natural beings" [*entia naturalia*], "natural things" [*res naturales*], "natural causes" [*causae naturales*], "natural creatures" [*creaturae naturales*], "natural bodies" [*corpora naturalia*], "natural forms" [*formae naturales*]. These "natural beings" are in effect those "which their nature condemns to be no more than what they are. . . . Such beings, so to say, "are existed" (sont existés) more than they exist." The spiritual being, on the other hand, "is not completely defined by its natural form; it transcends it in a certain way. . . . Its nature is not simply to be nature in the sense of finite, determinate, particularized nature."[9] For it is endowed with what St. Augustine calls "mind" [*mens*], or "chief part of the mind" [*principale mentis*], or in St. Paul's phrase, the "spirit of the mind" [*spiritus mentis*].[10] Others use "summit of the mind" [*apex mentis*], or "center   138 of the very mind" [*centrum ipsius animae*], etc. Here is what Harphius says of it:

> It is deeper than the powers [of the soul, *animae*] and excels them, for the powers are united together in the mind [*in mente*] as in their origin; they flow from it as do beams from the orb of the sun, and they flow back into it. And it is that centre in the soul in which the true image of the Trinity shines; and it is so noble, that no name here [on earth] is properly suitable for it, although it manifests itself by many names in circumlocution.[11]

Or again, Bérulle:

---

[8] Cf. *Le Surnaturel,* p. 483: "Paradox of the human mind: created, finite, it is not merely parallel to nature, but is itself nature. Before being a thinking mind, it is spiritual nature."

[9] Joseph de Finance, S.J., *Existence et liberté* (1955), pp. 235 and 8.

[10] *De Trinitate,* bk. 14, c. 16, n. 22 (*PL,* 42, 1052–54); cf. bk. 15, c. 7, n. 11: "It is therefore not the soul, but what excels in the soul, that is called mind" (1065); bk. 14, c. 8, n. 11: "the chief part of the human mind" (1044); bk. 12, c. 7, n. 12: "He was made man in the image of God, where there is no gender, i.e. in the spirit of his mind [*in spiritu mentis suae*]."

[11] *Theologia mystica,* bk. 2, p. 5 (Cologne ed., 1611, pp. 639–40).

. . . There are two sorts of creatures, one spiritual and rational, the other natural. . . . The natural have not so much a likeness as a trace of the Creator imprinted upon them; the spiritual and rational have that likeness, and beyond their natural being . . . they can approach and be united with God.[12]

Hence every spirit, whether in a body or not, enjoys certain privileges which, making him "in the image of" the Creator, make him at the same time superior to the whole order of the universe. This is what another spiritual writer, the Capuchin Constantine of Barbanson, careful of scholastic exactitude, called "the separation of spirit from the completed nature."[13]

There is no point in continuing to stress a distinction as simple and obvious as this, and one which is verified on the most immediately empirical level. It is in no sense, as we see, an invention of modern philosophy. I need hardly say that it has no connection with the Cartesian opposition between the *res cogitans* and the *res extensa*. It expresses a truth which does nothing to compromise the unity of the human being. It was universal in Christian antiquity.[14] It is based upon scripture: Père Festugière has shown this for the idea of the "pneuma,"[15] and Karl Barth could write in his *Church Dogmatics*: ". . . in the OT and NT man is addressed as a natural being also, but still as this distinct natural being, a natural being distinguished by spirit."[16] This is the truth Cassiodorus was summing up when he gave his two definitions of the soul, as *species naturalis* and *spiritalis propriaque substantia*.[17] We find it everywhere, in varying forms, in the works of the great scholastics, especially in St. Bonaventure who distinguishes, among the "naturals" [*naturalia*], the "gross" [*bruta*] from the "rational" [*rationalia*],[18] and St. Thomas who contrasts "natural things" [*res naturales*] with "human things" [*res humanae*], and "naturals" [*naturalia*] or "natural creatures" [*creaturae*

139

---

[12] *Se perdre en Dieu,* unpublished work on the life of Catherine of Genoa, quoted by R. Bellemare, in *Le sens de la créature dans la doctrine de Bérulle* (1959), p. 110.

[13] *Les secrets sentiers de l'amour divin* (1627), ch. 10 (Solesmes ed., 1932, p. 274).

[14] Clement of Alexandria, *Stromata*, bk. 2, c. 19, n. 101, 1: "The domain of nature is plants, seeds, trees and stones"; etc.

[15] "La trichotomie de I Thess. 5:2 et la philosophie grecque," *Recherches de sc. rel.* 20 (1930): 385–415.

[16] Vol. 1, part 1, Eng. trans. *Church Dogmatics* (Edinburgh, 1960), p. 152.

[17] *De anima,* c. 2 (*PL,* 70, 1283 A).

[18] *In 2 Sent.,* dist. 29, a. 1, q. 2, ad 4um; dist. 38, a. 2, q. 1; dist. 7, p. 2, q. 1, etc.

naturales] with "human nature" [*natura humana*],[19] etc. Even when his direct purpose is to establish an analogy rather than to point up a contrast—and we know how he likes to push an analogy as far as possible on certain points—St. Thomas never ceases to presuppose this capital distinction.[20] We see this most clearly in the way in which, having spoken of the laws governing "all ordered natures" [*naturae ordinatae omnes*], he sets apart "the single created rational nature" [*sola natura rationalis creata*],[21] or the way he contrasts Plato and Aristotle with the ancient naturals [*antiqui naturales*].[22] It was Gratry who pointed this out at the end of the last century: "There is this difference between man and all the other inhabitants of this earth, that only man, as St. Thomas Aquinas says, is directly subordinate to the universal and infinite."[23]   140
One might almost say that the ground was being laid for the distinction as long ago as Aristotle, whose famous aphorism "every soul is not nature"[24] referred to the intellectual soul.

It is not, then, a question of denying "the existence of natures, even in the world of spirits":[25] But inevitably, when it comes to spiritual nature, and especially to man who is neither merely a living being, nor a pure spirit, this word "nature" will have two partially different meanings, according to whether it is to be applied to this particular species which we form, among the other species in the universe, or to the

---

[19] *Summa contra Gentiles,* bk. 3, c. 140; c. 69–70: the identification of "natural things" [*res naturales*] and "inferior things" [*res inferiores*]; cf. q. 110. *Prima Secundae,* q. 114, a. 7, ad 3um: distinction between free causes (men) and "natural causes" [*causae naturales*]. *De veritate,* q. 23, a. 1: opposition between "spiritual substances" [*spirituales substantiae*] and "things" [*res*]; etc. *Prima Secundae,* q. 10, a. 1, ad 2um; q. 41, a. 3; q. 110, a. 2, comparing "natural creatures" [*creaturas naturales*] or beings led by God "to the possession of the natural good" with the creatures he leads "to the pursuit of the eternal supernatural"; a. 113, a. 3; q. 114, a. 1.

[20] *De malo,* q. 6, a. 1. *De veritate,* q. 27, a. 2. *De caritate,* a. 9. *In 4 Sent.,* q. 1, a. 1, q. 4.

[21] *Secunda secundae,* q. 2, a. 3. Cf. *Prima Secundae,* q. 26, a. 1. *In Boetium de Trinitate,* q. 4, a. 3; q. 5, a. 1; q. 6, a. 4, ad 5um. *De veritate,* q. 3, a. 2. *In 2 Sent.,* dist. 25, q. 1, a. 1. *Summa contra Gentiles,* bk. 3, c. 147: "Divine providence disposed rational creatures differently from other things, according as they are different from the others in their proper condition of nature."

[22] *Prima,* q. 4, a. 2, et ad 2um.

[23] *Connaissance de Dieu*[2], vol. 2, 1854, p. 292.

[24] *De partibus animalium,* bk. 1, 1, 641 *b*, 9. Cf. *De anima,* bk. 3, 4, 429a, etc. The positive side of Aristotle's teaching is in any case too far removed from the truth that stands out from Christian philosophy for there to be any point in pushing the comparison. Cf. E. Borne, "Pour une doctrine de l'intériorité," *op. cit.,* pp. 17–18.

[25] *Gregorianum* 28 (1947): 393.

nature of spirit in so far as this is something which goes beyond any particular species because it is innately opened to the universal and directly related to God.[26] It was this that St. Augustine was saying when he
noted that man alone, among all the beings in the world, is capable of
beatitude.[27] And it is what St. Thomas was saying on various occasions.
"A natural thing is determinate in its natural being"; on the other hand,
in "rational nature" [*natura rationalis*] there is a certain "superior
appetite" [*appetitus superior*] which takes it out of that narrow determination.[28] The first is "more confined and limited" [*magis coarctata et
limitata*]"; the second "has greater fullness and breadth" [*amplitudinem
et extensionem*].[29] The first sign of that "fullness" and "breadth" proper to
spiritual nature appears in its ability to become, through knowledge,
"all things, as it were" [*quodammodo omnia*]. "Anyone who knew it
deeply would be able to find in it a kind of container for the universality
of things."[30] "The smallest concept, as soon as it has been thought, contains at least the indefinite range of its extension, and through it the
soul "rises above all of nature."[31] This is indeed one of the most striking
aspects of the human paradox: I can "weave into the fabric of my being
the whole universe, of the fabric of which I am naturally a part."[32] It is
this that an ancient writer, Longinus, said when he wrote in his *Treatise
on the Sublime:* "The whole world is not wide enough for the vast grasp
of the human spirit; our thoughts often go further than the skies, and
penetrate beyond the forms which surround and enclose all things."[33]
In other words, as a contemporary, Karl Jaspers, says, thought makes
man "no longer simply one living species among others; he discovers

141

---

[26] The editors of the volume *Serta Albertina*, published in Rome by *Angelicum* (vol. 29,
1944), were right to dedicate it "in honor of our heavenly patron recently chosen by Pope
Pius XII for the researchers of natural things [*rerum naturalium*]." In following the Pope's
own example by speaking thus, they were not only using language current today (cf. the
"natural sciences"), but also that of St. Albert and his era. Among these "res naturales,"
man as such is not included. To realize this needs only a glance at the table of contents:
the study of man figures in it only with a few studies of the body and the blood.

[27] *De diversis quaest.,* 83, q. 5 (Bibl. aug., 10, p. 56).

[28] *De veritate,* q. 25, a. 1.

[29] *Prima,* q. 14, a. 1.

[30] A. D. Sertillanges, *Saint Thomas d'Aquin,* vol. 1, p. 106. Cf. *Prima,* q. 14, a. 2.

[31] Etienne Borne, *op. cit.,* p. 26.

[32] Maurice Nédoncelle, *Existe-t-il une philosophie chrétienne?* (Paris, 1956), p. 95, Eng.
trans. *Is there a Christian Philosophy?* (London, 1960).

[33] C. 29.

himself as something unique, embracing everything, open to everything."[34]

It is this idea, a simple and surely almost incontestable one, which theology must not lose sight of. Rahner has several times shown how important it is for our present subject. Of its very nature, he has written, spirit possesses a "limitless transcendence," which gives the human horizon an "infinite character," and this kind of infinitude is precisely what constitutes the "definition" of man and his "limit."[35] And again, in a study on the relation between nature and grace:

> It might be asked whether the scholastic concept of "nature" as applied to the "nature" of man does not still owe too much to the model of what is less than human (in the train of archaic philosophy with its orientation towards "physics"). What is signified by the "definition," and hence the circumscription, of man's "nature," if he is the essence of transcendence, and hence of the surpassing of limitation? Is it meaningful at all in such a perspective simply to assign to this "nature" an end perfectly defined materially? Not as though the remotest doubt were being thrown here on the fact that man has a nature and that this in itself has an end assigned to it. But these must not and cannot be conceived in such simple terms as the mutual order of a pot and its lid or of a biological organism and its fixed environment. One has only to ask why a supernatural end can be set for man without annulling his nature, and why God cannot do this with the nature of something below man. . . . However universally the formal ontology of nature, end, etc., may extend, these concepts can only be used in the particular matter of each individual grade of being in a highly analogical way. . . .[36]

142

I would basically have only one reservation about this text, a reservation of a purely historical nature: in reality, as we have seen, this

---

[34] Karl Jaspers, *Rechenschaft und Ausblick* (Munich, 1951), French trans. *Bilans et perspectives* (Paris, 1956), p. 159.

[35] *Mission and Grace,* vol. 1 (London, 1963), p. 127.

[36] *Theological Investigations,* vol. 1 (London, 1961), p. 317. My profound estimation for Karl Rahner's theological work and my strong personal affection for him will not be brought into question if I point out that he believed he was disagreeing with me in the study I quote from here, whereas what he was disagreeing with was an article in German which was not merely not by me, but was also for a long time even unknown to me. It would also seem (cf. note 3 on p. 304) that, apart from an article I wrote in 1949, he had read nothing of mine on the subject. I must also make it quite clear that I have never "scorned" the concept of *potentia oboedientialis* (p. 315) except in the very sense in which he himself resolutely rejects it.

"scholastic" concept of nature, which borrows too much from the sub-human, is more the concept of a modern scholasticism; the analogical corrections Rahner wants to make to it were in fact formulated by St. Thomas himself. In his analysis of human nature, moreover, St. Thomas does not stop short at the sign, the universal aptitude for knowledge. He knows, from faith, that beyond this, and more precisely, as all Christian tradition tells us, the human soul has "a centre whence the spiritual faculties grow, a tendency towards all that is and towards God, to whose vision it is just as naturally unable to attain."[37] He knows that while other natural beings bear within them a distant reflection of God, "by way of a trace," only man resembles God "by way of an image,"[38] and that this image, which is "intellectual nature itself"[39] within him, is drawn towards its Model: "It is borne, or was born to be borne, in God."[40] If one recalls these statements of St. Thomas—which are identical with those of St. Bonaventure—one can better understand how true are these words of Gilson: "Thomist nature is not Aristotelian nature."[41]

143

Origen said long ago that our participation in God's image is "our principal substance," in other words, the essential part of our nature.[42] Bérulle was later to echo this common doctrine in his statement that man was not created "to remain within the bounds of nature."[43]

We need not always see such expressions as direct and exact allusions to the supernatural properly so called. Far from it. It is enough first to have recognized that man is not a being enclosed in the narrow circle of his inborn imperfections. In every slightest thing he does,

[37] E. Spies, O.S.B., "Die Philosophie des Gemütes" summarized by H.P., in *Bulletin de théologie ancienne et médiévale* (1938): 2994.

[38] *Prima*, q. 93, a. 6: "So we find in man a likeness to God by way of an image in his mind, but in the other parts of his being by way of a trace." Cf. *Tertia*, q. 4, a. 1, ad 2um; q. 9, a. 2, ad 3um.

[39] *Prima*, q. 93, a. 4: "Since man is said to be in the image of God by reason of his intellectual nature," and ad 1um: "in its principal signification, namely the intellectual nature."

[40] Ibid., a. 8: "The image is found in the soul according as it turns to God, or is born to turn to God." Cf. *In 3 Sent.*, dist 2, q. 1, a. 1, sol. 1, ad 2um.

[41] *Le Philosophe et la Théologie* (1960), p. 60. Cf. Bonaventure, *In 2 Sent.*, prooemium: by sin man lost "the habit, not the appetite, for in this way he lost the similarity, that he nevertheless 'passeth as an image' (Ps. 38:7)" (Quaracchi, vol. 2, p. 5).

[42] *In Ioannem*, bk. 20, n. 22 (Preuschen, p. 355). Cf. Henri Crouzel, S.J., in *Revue d'ascétique et de mystique* (1955), pp. 82–83. See also *Periarchon*, bk. 4, c. 4, n. 9 (Koetschau ed., p. 362).

[43] *Opuscules de piété*, 132, c. 3 (ed. G. Rotureau, p. 389).

whether it be an act of the intellect or the will, whether it be moral or spontaneous, he always "crosses the boundary" and gets beyond the universe. "Man is only man when he surpasses himself, and surpasses brute fact, and that fact would remain unknown to him if he did not, so to say, place himself outside and above it, even if only in order to return within it and establish himself there. It matters not how civilized he is: from the first, in a simple and utterly rudimentary act, the primitive, the child, the cultured man, all, in Aristotle's phrase, dominate, surpass, understand, contain the whole world. Every thought absorbs, so to say, the universality of facts, sets itself free of them, replaces them by its own creation, and is itself, knows itself, develops itself only as it lives 144 that transcendence."[44] "The higher mind exists in the world" [*mens superior existat mundo*].[45] The laws that apply within the cosmos, which therefore completely govern "natural beings," cannot thus be applied without modification to human nature—if we consider in it not merely that which makes it, as we said earlier, "one form with its place in the hierarchy of forms," an animal species of a higher kind, but that "something in [it] which is not the object of experience at all,"[46] that which makes it properly a spirit: that which makes it, in the theologian's definition, "in God's image." Or, to say the same thing in a different way, the *nous* cannot be contained in the framework or formed out of the materials of the *peri psuchēs*.[47]

> An animal species, as long as the centuries have not altered its characteristics, is born, lives and dies according to its own laws, and the role it is given to play in the vast drama of creation is but one role, indefinitely repeated. Our species certainly does not escape this monotonous gravitation. It revolves around an immutable destiny like a planet around the sun. But also like the planet, it is borne along with its sun towards an invisible star. It is not mysterious by its destiny, but by its vocation.[48]

[44] Maurice Blondel, *Dialogues sur la Pensée*, dialogue 8 (Paléonéos), in *Etudes blondéliennes* 3 (1954): 72.

[45] St. Gregory the Great, *Dialogues*, bk. 2, c. 35.

[46] Jules Lachelier, *Oeuvres*, vol. 2, p. 160 (Société de philosophie, 19 November 1908): ". . . and which, though closely united to nature, is nevertheless not a part of it: that is, thought. . . ."

[47] M. D. Chenu, *Introduction à l'étude de saint Thomas d'Aquin* (1950), p. 50.

[48] Georges Bernanos, *Les grands cimetières sous la lune*, p. 85 (abridged Eng. trans. *A Diary of My Times* [London, 1938]). Cf. Etienne Borne, *Passion de la Vérité*, p. 139: "It is impossible to separate in the soul concern for its nature and the restlessness of its vocation."

Will it ever reach that "invisible star"? Is it really called to come to it? Is it even aware that it is that star which is pulling it? In what precisely does its vocation consist? These are all later questions, which we shall have to consider further on. For the moment it is enough to know that there is something in man, a certain capacity for the infinite, which makes it impossible to consider him one of those beings whose whole nature and destiny are inscribed within the cosmos. And it is this that has not been sufficiently taken into account by most of the philosophers and theologians from whom the modern theory of so-called "pure nature" derives. The same mistake can be noted still in some of their heirs (though not all, as we shall see). Hence their habit of working out strictly the fundamental relation of the spiritual creature to God by means of analogies entirely taken from what happens in "nature," in the sense I have just explained. This results in saying—contrary to what all earlier theologians held to be a fundamental and incontestable principle—that every being without exception, whether star, stone, horse, man or even angel, must have its final connatural end, an end proportionate to its nature and therefore of the same order, an end in which its nature might find perfect contentment.[49] But what is thus taken, without any careful examination, to be a basic and universal truth, applies precisely only within "nature" or the cosmos (itself interpreted according to the physics of antiquity, though this aspect of the problem does not concern us here) from which, by a kind of induction, it has been distinguished. When one applies it to the case of the spiritual creature, one is thus in fact doing so only by analogy. And in this case the analogy is not a valid one, for the simple reason that it is a mark of that spiritual creature not to have its destiny circumscribed within the cosmos. Here is what is said by, among many others, Hugh of St. Victor:

> Just as nothing but he can satisfy, likewise we cannot exist outside of him [*usque ad ipsum*]. . . . Therefore we do not establish something else between our God and ourselves, but we make our way for ourselves to him, and for him to us, so that we may be in him and he in us; so that

---

[49] Cf. Edmond Elter, S.J., "De naturali hominis beatitudine ad mentem Scholae antiquioris," *Gregorianum* 9 (1928): 270: "[The fundamental principle for modern authors is:] Every agent tends to an end that is proportionate to him, and as long as he pursues it he rests happily. . . . *The old authors reason differently.* They hold as a fundamental truth in this matter that the human appetite cannot be sated but by an infinite good. No other such good is given but the divine essence, even in itself." The italics are mine.

there is nothing else in which we be beatified besides him, just as there could be nothing by whom we might be created besides him.[50]

"Hugh," comments Paul Vignaux, gives here "the common position in the Middle Ages, according to which the spirit's upward journey stops only at the actual vision of the divine essence. The same God is directly our principle and our end: there can be, outside of him, nothing that will make us eternally happy, just as there could not have been anything, outside him, to create us. . . . For Thomas Aquinas, the theological order was to follow that movement."[51] "The mind, which is capable of God" was Origen's phrase.[52] "Nature, so great and wondrous, capable of the highest nature!" cried St. Augustine.[53] And St. Thomas, too, in "that wonderful digest, the *Compendium Theologiae*":[54] "The final end of the rational creature exceeds the faculty of the nature itself."[55] How can so many "Thomistic" theologians of today miss so clear a statement? Congenitally, the end of the spiritual creature is something that surpasses the powers of his nature or any other created nature; and this because the spiritual creature has a direct relationship with God which results from its origins. Between it and God, as St. Augustine repeated again and again, [there is] "no interposed nature," "no interjected nature."[56] "Nothing falls in between."[57] That is what makes the difference.

On this ground, not thought of in Aristotle's day, our medieval Aristotelians thought exactly like St. Augustine. Without stopping here to consider the old Augustinian tradition,[58] let us listen once again to the

147

[50] *Expositio in Hierarchiam caelestem*, bk. 2 (*PL*, 175, 955 AC).

[51] *Philosophie au moyen âge* (1958), p. 201.

[52] *Periarchon*, bk. 4, n. 36 (*PG*, 11, 412 B; Koetschau, p. 363).

[53] *De Trinitate*, bk. 14, c. 4, n. 6 (Bibl. aug., 16, p. 358).

[54] M. J. Nicolas, O.P., in *La nouvelle Eve*, vol. 2 (1955–56), p. 11, n. 11.

[55] C. 144. Cf. Scotus, *De ordinatione*, prologus, 1: "I grant that God is the natural end of man, but he is not attainable naturally; he is so supernaturally" (*Opera omnia*, 1, 1950, p. 19).

[56] Or again: "with no intervening creature," "with no intervening substance," etc. On this principle of Augustinian mysticism, see my *Catholicisme*[5] (1952), pp. 290–91.

[57] Cf. St. Bonaventure, *De donis Spiritus*, collatio 8, n. 15 (Quaracchi, vol. 5, p. 497), etc.; or St. Thomas, *Secunda Secundae*, q. 2, a. 3, c., et ad 1um.

[58] For instance William of St. Thierry, *Epistola ad Fratres de Monte Dei*, c. 90: "The rational soul [*rationalis animus*] was established by him and for him, so that it be its conversion to him, so that it be its good" (ed. M. M. Davy, p. 132). Cf. *De natura corporis et animae* (*PL*, 180, 717 BC); *De natura et dignitate amoris*, c. 3 (*PL*, 184, 382 B), etc. on man who, made in God's image, is "with the capacity for the fullness of every good."

two great figures of the thirteenth century. St. Thomas Aquinas, Père A. R. Motte tells us, "often used the correspondence between principle and end, between the going out and the return, in order to establish the doctrine of the direct vision of God from the direct creation which he takes as something admitted."[59] Here is how he himself expresses it, in the *De virtutibus in communi:*

> Just as man acquires his first perfection, that is to say his soul, from the action of God, so too does he have immediately from the action of God his final perfection, which is the perfect happiness of man, and he rests in it; this indeed is clear since the natural desire of man cannot rest in anything but God alone. . . . It is fitting therefore, that just as the first perfection of man, which is the rational soul [*anima rationalis*], exceeds the faculty of corporal matter [*materiae corporalis*], so also the final perfection to which man can attain, which is the beatitude of eternal life, exceeds the faculty of the whole human nature. . . .[60]

We find exactly the same teaching in the eighteenth question of the *De veritate:*

> The human mind itself is immediately created by God, and is formed from him immediately as from an exemplar, and for this reason is beatified in him immediately as in an end.[61]

Or, more briefly, in the tenth *Quodlibetum:* "And since the soul has been made by God immediately, it could not be happy unless it sees God immediately."[62] The *Summa theologica* gives the same teaching on several occasions.[63] And if we then turn to St. Bonaventure, we find that he too shows himself just as much an "Augustinian" in this as St.

148

---

[59] "Théodicée et théologie chez saint Thomas d'Aquin," *Revue des sc. phil. et théol.* (1937): 11, n. 2.

[60] A. 10. Cf. *Compendium theologiae,* c. 174, n. 2, distinction between "natural perfections" [*naturales perfectiones*] and "virtues and graces" [*virtutes et gratiae*]; *In Boetium de Trinitate,* q. 3, a. 1, ad 2um: "In the first place with creation God instituted man perfect in the perfection of nature. . . ."

[61] Q. 18, a. 1, ad 7um. Cf. *In 4 Sent.,* dist. 49, q. 2, a. 1.

[62] Q. 8, art. 17.

[63] *Prima,* q. 12, a. 1: ". . . for the final perfection of the rational creature is in that which is its principle of being: any one thing is perfect to the extent that it attains to its principle." Q. 79, a. 4: "But the separate intellect, according to the teaching of our faith, is God himself, who is the creator of the soul and in whom alone the soul is beatified." *Secunda Secundae,* q. 5, a. 2: "According to the true faith God alone is the creator of our souls; in him alone does the beatitude of our soul consist"; etc.

Thomas—so totally is this a common and basic inheritance of Christian thought:[64]

> Since all creatures were made for God, according to the verse: "The Lord hath made all things for himself" (Prov. 16:4), the rational creature alone was made to enjoy [*ad fruendum*] God, and to be beatified in him, for it alone is in his image. Now the other creatures, which only retain the trace [of divinity] [*tenent rationem vestigii*], were made either to manifest the goodness of God, or for the awe [*obsequium*] of the rational creature.[65]

> [The rational creature] was born to be conjoined to God immediately. This [order] is essential to the image, and in this the angel and the soul are considered equal, because the mind of both is formed immediately by the first Truth itself.[66]

> The rational spirit can be neither rewarded nor fulfilled, nor can its capacity be limited, by anything less than God. . . . The soul [is] the image of God, and is born to be carried into God immediately and to be beatified in him. . . .[67]

Hence this different kind of creature has that "unstable ontological constitution" which makes it at once something greater and something less than itself.[68] Hence that kind of dislocation,[69] that mysterious lameness, due not merely to sin, but primarily and more fundamentally

149

[64] Cf. Patrice Robert, O.F.M., "Le problème de la philosophie bonaventurienne," *Laval théologique et philosophique* (1951): 9–13: "When St. Bonaventure sees the vision of God as the satisfaction of all man's aspirations and therefore his perfect happiness, far from stating some special principle peculiar to his own philosophical thought, he is merely recalling the teaching of all the Christian masters on man's final end. St. Thomas Aquinas, not to mention St. Augustine, expresses himself on the matter most definitely, and in terms extraordinarily close to those used by St. Bonaventure."

[65] *In 2 Sent.*, dist. 19, a. 1, q. 2. Cf. dist. 29, a. 1, ad 4um (Quaracchi, vol. 2, pp. 463, 699). D. 16, a. 1, q. 3, ad 6um: "The image universally pursues rational nature, because every rational creature is the image of God" (p. 399). Compare St. Thomas, *Prima*, q. 93, a. 6.

[66] *In 2 Sent.*, dist. 16, a. 2, q. 1. Cf. *In 1 Sent.*, dist. 1, a. 3, q. 2: "Therefore God alone is to be enjoyed. . . . Since the soul is born to perceive the infinite good, which is God, therefore it must rest in him alone and enjoy [*frui*] him alone" (we know what a precise technical meaning this verb "frui" has in the Augustinian tradition). Cf. St. Augustine *De Trinitate*, bk. 1, c. 9, n. 18: "To enjoy the Trinity, in whose image we were made" (*PL*, 42, 832); *Contra Iulianum*, bk. 3, c. 12 (*PL*, 44, 715).

[67] *Breviloquium*, p. 7, c. 7 (Quaracchi, vol. 5, p. 289). *In 2 Sent.*, dist. 18, a. 2, q. 3.

[68] Cf. Paul Ricoeur, *Finitude et culpabilité* (Paris, 1960), vol. 1, p. 22.

[69] One expression of which is the sense of the sublime. Cf. Blondel's analysis in *Vocabulaire de la société française de philosophie*, the word "Sublime."

to being a creature made out of nothing which, astoundingly, touches God. "Like God in its mind" [*Deo mente consimilis*].[70] At once, and inextricably, both "nothing" and "image"; fundamentally nothing, yet none the less substantially image.[71] "Being an image is not accidental to man, but rather substantial."[72] By the fact of being created, man is the "companion in slavery" of all nature; but at the same time, because he is an image—"to the extent that he is in the image of God"[73]—he is "capable of beatific knowledge"[74] and has, as Origen said, "the precept of liberty" implanted deep within him. We can see why Bérulle exclaimed as he did. His lyricism was not misplaced, nor did he exaggerate the teaching of earlier theologians: "There is nothing, there is a miracle . . . , there is a God, there is a nothingness surrounded by God, needing God, able to receive God. . . ."[75]

150   Once again, this does not in any sense mean that spiritual beings have no "nature" or "essence," as some people are too ready to think nowadays.[76] Nor does it mean that their nature is less definitely "structured" than that of other beings whose horizon is circumscribed by the cosmos. It means quite simply that their "nature" is different, and struc-

---

[70] Boethius, *Theological Tractates* (Stewart-Rand ed., 1946), p. 202: "In mind, just like God" [*Deo mente consimilis*]. Cf. *Sainte Trinité et la vie surnaturelle,* by a Carthusian (1948): "That signature of the creating Essence imprinted upon our essence."

[71] Cf. M. D. Chenu, *op. cit.,* p. 4: "The great themes of "traces" [*vestigia*] and "image of God" [*imago Dei*] impregnate even the most scientific of the medieval cosmologies, and were only eliminated by later scholasticism." Gilson, in "L'âme raisonnable chez Albert le Grand," *Archives d'hist doct. et litt. du moyen âge* (1943–45): 69: One has cause to wonder "whether the essence of what Albert says in this matter is not contained in that phrase from the Bible which he quoted, repeated and commented on endlessly . . . : God created man in his image and likeness." The same is true of many others.

[72] St. Bonaventure, *In 2 Sent.,* dist. 16, art. 1, q. 2, 4 (vol. 2, p. 387); q. 3, ad 6um: "The image universally pursues rational nature, because every rational creature is the image of God" (p. 399).

[73] St. Basil, *Traité du Saint-Esprit,* c. 20 (ed. B. Pruche, Sources chrétiennes, 17, p. 205).

[74] St. Thomas, *Tertia,* q. 9, a. 2: "Therefore the rational creature has the capacity for this blessed knowledge, to the extent that it is in the image of God."

[75] *Opuscules de piété,* 114. Cf. Etienne Brulefer, *Super scripta S. Bonaventurae Directorium:* "There are two factors that produce appetite, to wit, suitability [*convenientia*] and want [*indigentia*]; for the rational soul was created in the image and likeness of God and capable of the most sufficient good, and it is not sufficient to itself, since it is vain and deficient, therefore it naturally strives for [*appetit*] true beatitude" (Basle, 1507, fol. 433; quoted by V. Doucet, *loc. cit.,* p. 181).

[76] For the meaning of the word in St. Thomas, see *Prima,* q. 29, a. 1 ad 4um; q. 115, a. 2; *Tertia,* q. 2, a. 1, etc.

tured differently. It has its own laws, which are not those of merely "natural beings." Thus, if we are satisfied to define nature in general as "a well-defined essence, with its proper laws and natural powers," this will apply just as well to the nature of spirits as to that of animals, vegetables or lifeless things. To recognize this is not some kind of reversion to a "pre-Christian idea," nor does it "make the human mind into a thing."[77] But people sometimes go on to add that this nature always and necessarily has "an end corresponding to its powers"; they sometimes suggest that every nature, even spiritual, is "an essence which rests content in the good that is proportionate to it, or pursues that good." These phrases appeared in 1947 in an article in *Gregorianum*[78]—which contrasts completely with the very firmly based assertions of Père Edmond Elter which had appeared a few years earlier in the same review.[79] It is impossible for me to accept such additions. For in fact such is fully the case only with lower natures; it is not true at all of what is most profound in created spirits.[80] "It is most natural for every mind to strive [*appetat*] for the eternal and highest beatitude."[81]

151

Like all his contemporaries, St. Thomas was well aware of the principle invoked by these modern writers. We find it formulated by him in his short work *In Boetium de Trinitate:* "All that is ordered naturally to any end, has some predetermined principles [*praeindita aliqua principia*] by means of which it is able to attain to that end."[82] The only difference is that he put this principle into the mouth of the objector, and was at pains to refute it in the sense in which it was put to him, or to explain it in such a way as to remove the objection. One may be astonished by this, as was the Abbé J. Durantel; one may, like him, try to find "a historical explanation" but one must recognize that "it is a fact."[83]

---

[77] As Maurice Merleau-Ponty said in discussing the ideas of Gabriel Mariel: "La querelle d'existentialisme," *Les temps modernes* (Nov. 1945): 348–58.

[78] "Nature pure et surnaturel" in vol. 2, 1947, pp. 391–92.

[79] Cf. *supra,* p. 110.

[80] Cf. Romano Guardini, *The Last Things* (London, 1954), p. 20: "Man is no longer part of inanimate nature like all the rest, rooted and enclosed in his own nature. His life is proper to himself. Its movement, its growth, are directed from man to God and back from God to man."

[81] Pierre J. Olivi, q. 51 (in *Auer,* p. 49). Richard of Middleton, *In 4 Sent.,* dist. 49, a. 1, q. 6: "All men naturally strive to see God by their intellect" (ibid., p. 54).

[82] *In Boetium de Trinitate,* q. 6, a. 4, obj. 5.

[83] J. Durantel, *Le retour à Dieu dans la philosophie de saint Thomas* (1918), p. 303: "One may be surprised that St. Thomas allowed more to the aspirations of our faculties than to

And for the reasons I have given, I prefer to follow St. Thomas in this rather than a number of modern writers, and to remain faithful to the old principle which the medieval theologians were constantly recalling, in similar if not always identical terms, and which they contrasted with what they called the "error" or the "doubt" or the "silence" of the "ancient philosophers." Duns Scotus expressed this principle by saying that man's end is natural to him if considered in terms of his desire, but supernatural in terms of how it is attained, or by whom it is brought about; in other words, natural or supernatural according as it is thought of as "object of inclination" [*obiectum inclinationis*] or "object of attainment" [*obiectum attingentiae*].[84] In the sixteenth century, in reaction against the doctrines they declared to be a betrayal of Thomist thought, Soto and Toletus were to take it up enthusiastically.[85] They did not then envisage the "pure nature" of the modern schools of thought any more than did St. Thomas himself.[86] But St. Robert Bellarmine, who explicitly put it forward as a possibility, could still speak of "The vision of God, natural with respect to the appetite, but not with respect to perception

152

---

their capabilities; but it is a fact. . . . The question might be clarified by a historical explanation. St. Thomas takes that natural desire for God from John Damascene who also admits an inborn positive knowledge of God which explains the desire. St. Thomas keeps the desire . . . but he considerably weakens the innateness of the knowledge of God: hence perhaps this slight dislocation in his reasoning." Though this remark remains of some interest, I believe that St. John Damascene is not here St. Thomas's only "source," and that the "dislocation" lies in the object itself. For the rest, "there is in the teaching of St. Thomas a more considerable element of natural and innate knowledge and desire of God than is generally recognized" (ibid., p. 362). Cf. *In 2 Sent.*, dist. 3, q. 4, a. 5: "The soul always understands itself and God indeterminately. . . ."

[84] *Ordinatio*, prol. (*Opera omnia*, vol. 1 [1950], pp. 10, 19, 35). Cf. Ephrem Longpré, *La philosophie du Bienheureux Duns Scot* (1924), pp. 184–86. Similarly Gauthier of Bruges, commented on by L. B. Gillon, in *Angelicum* (1949): 124, note (compare St. Thomas, *De veritate*, q. 24, art. 4, ad 1um). Cf. among others B. Mastrius de Meldula, *In 1 Sent.*, disp. 6, q. 2 (2d ed., Venice 1675, vol. 1, p. 382 a).

[85] Soto, *In 4 Sent.*, dist. 49, q. 2, art. 1, etc. Cf. Diego de Deza (d. 1523), *Novae defensiones* (in J. Alfaro, *op. cit.*, p. 241). Toletus also says, *In Primam*, q. 1: "God therefore is the natural end of potency, and the supernatural end of act and operation" (vol. 1, p. 20). Capreolus had spoken in this regard of an "improper natural potency" [*potentia naturalis impropria*]: *Defensiones* . . . , prol., q. 1, art. 5: his position is explained by Père V. Doucet, *loc. cit.*, pp. 187–88.

[86] They are no less definite as to the total gratuitousness of God's gift. Thus Toletus, *In Tertiam*, enarr. 3, q. 23, art. 2: "He beatifies the rational creature by a gratuitous will; and such a beatitude can be said to be exterior to the creature, to the extent that it cannot attain to it by reason of its nature; and it is not due to it by reason of its nature: for beatitude is an inheritance, since it is the riches of God himself." It was this that Baius did not understand.

[*assecutionem*]."[87] However, for my own statement of it I would borrow the words of St. Thomas:

> The rational creature is superior to every creature in its capacity for the highest good through the divine vision and enjoyment [*fruitionem*], although the principles of its own nature are not sufficient to pursue it; rather it requires the assistance of divine grace.[88]
>
> The vision of God itself is essentially the final end of the human soul, and its beatitude. . . .[89] But it is fitting that the created intellect be raised up to so noble a vision by some influence of divine goodness.[90]
>
> Although man is naturally inclined to this end, he cannot pursue it naturally, but only through grace: and this is because of the eminence of this end.[91]
>
> The blessed vision or knowledge is in some way above the nature of the rational soul, namely insofar as it cannot attain it with its own virtue; but in another way it is in accordance with its nature [*secundum naturam ipsius*], namely insofar as it has the capacity for it in accordance with its nature, to the extent that it was made in the image of God.[92]

153

Finally, I will once again add St. Bonaventure's words to those of St. Thomas:

> Since beatitude is nothing but the enjoyment [*fruitio*] of the highest good, and the highest good is above us, none can be made blessed unless he ascends above himself, not by a bodily ascension, but by an ascension of the heart [*cordiali*]. But we cannot be raised above ourselves unless by a superior virtue elevating us.[93]

---

[87] *De gratia primi hominis*, c. 7, in fine. To reject this doctrine, Garrigou-Lagrange thought it reason enough to say that it was the doctrine of "the eighteenth-century Augustinians": *Angelicum* (1931): 49.

[88] *De Malo*, q. 5, a. 1.

[89] *In 4 Sent.*, dist. 49, a. 2.

[90] *Contra Gentiles*, bk. 3, c. 53.

[91] *In Boetium de Trinitate*, q. 6, a. 4, ad 5um. This sentence provides the "argument," so to say, of what is developed throughout book 3 of the *Summa contra Gentiles* (cf. the titles of chapters 50, 52, 53). On St. Thomas's doctrine of man, read the works of Anton C. Pegis, especially *At the Origins of the Thomistic Notion of Man* (New York-London, 1963).

[92] *Tertia*, q. 9, art 2, ad 3um. Similarly Giles of Rome: "Therefore what has intellect and reason is made to attain this end, which is God himself, who is the supernatural good. . . . We cannot attain the supernatural by nature, for it would not then be supernatural" (*Super 2 Sent.*, dist. 22, q. 2, art. 1; Venice, 1488, fol. 328). More briefly, dist. 31, q. 1, art. 1: "The end of the rational creature is the divine vision, which is above nature."

[93] *Itinerarium mentis*, c. 1, n. 1 (vol. 5, p. 296 B).

Eternal beatitude consists in having the highest good; and this is God, a good surpassing out of all proportion all the dignity of human reverence [*obsequii*]. No one at all is worthy of attaining the highest good, since it is altogether beyond all the limits of nature, unless, if God condescends to one, one be raised up above himself.[94]

[94] *Breviloquium,* part 5, c. 1 (vol. 5, p. 252). In a thesis published in 1963, *Dionysius des Kartausers Lehre vom desiderium naturale des Menschen nach der Gottesschau,* Martin Beer notes that I have attributed to St. Thomas the idea of a natural desire for the vision of God. He seems to believe that this is an odd opinion of mine which has been fully refuted. According to him, "a diligent analysis of the texts of St. Thomas on the subject shows that Aquinas must be interpreted" on the contrary "in a negative sense" (pp. 82–83, 189). To do so he has to admit that Denys the Carthusian himself, in order to contradict St. Thomas, began by understanding him in the opposite way (p. 177).

CHAPTER 7

The Paradox Unknown to the Gentiles

Under different forms, and with accentuations varying from one century and school to another, Christian philosophy thus developed the concept of a human nature which is open to receive a supernatural gift. Such a concept was unknown, of course, in ancient philosophy. There is nothing Aristotelian about it—though St. Thomas Aquinas, faithful to his method of conciliation and without any historical scruple,[1] sometimes finds ways to express it in Aristotelian terms. But nor is it Platonic or Plotinian. Though theoretically justifiable by reason, the fact remains that it was wholly shaped and developed in direct dependence on Christian revelation. St. Thomas was well aware of this, and recalled it more than once: "according to the teaching of our faith" [*secundum fidei nostrae documenta*], "but according to the true faith" [*secundum autem veram fidem*], etc.[2] Notwithstanding a groping towards an afterlife or a better life, of which it is hard to discover in each case whether it is more a bodily or a spiritual one, we never do find such a conception expressed by the light of human thinking alone in any organized way. For it involves a whole philosophy of man, presupposing as its basis a certain notion of God which none of the old mythologies, religions, philosophical systems or natural mysticism possessed. For reasoned thought to have arrived at it, there would have been a need not only for belief in a creating God, but also for at least some suggestion of the Charity-God [*Deus caritas*].

For the ancient Greeks—and one may say almost the same of all

---

[1] Cf. *infra*, chapter 8, pp. 153–54
[2] *Prima*, q. 79, a. 4; *Secunda Secundae*, q. 5, a. 2.

thinkers, ancient and modern, other than those whose thinking flows from revelation—every nature must find in itself, or in the rest of the cosmos of which it is an integral part, all that it needs for its completion. Basically, everything has always been perfectly balanced. The apparent imbalance, whether progress or regression, is merely a phenomenon of flux and reflux within a totality that is already complete. The universe is like a snake coiled upon itself: its movement is necessarily eternal, and circular.[3] The well-known Stoic theory of the "Great Year" is only one systematization, following many similar ones, of this extremely widespread view. *Novissima prima:* that is its unchanging principle. One will ultimately gain no more than one had—though perhaps in a different form—from the first, or rather, from all time. One can do no more than regain possession of what one has momentarily—and of course only apparently—lost.

The human soul, for instance, cannot be immortal—nor could it even have the possibility of immortality[4]—unless it be eternal, in other words, properly divine. "Immortal" and "god" are frequently synonymous, and it is the former that is always the stronger term;[5] so much so that gods who are not immortal, like the "gods of the transmigration" in Buddhism, though their situation is temporarily a fortunate one, are in fact wretched beings whose lot is not envied by anyone who hopes for deliverance . . . . "The air that is within us is a fragment of divinity," said Diogenes of Apollonia. "Every spirit is immortal," said Plato, "for whatever moves for ever is immortal,"[6] and Cicero later declared: ". . . the souls of men are divine, and the path back into heaven is open to them when they have left the body."[7] Plotinus, in his turn, was to prove the

[3] Aristotle, *Physics,* bk. 1, 6, 259–63.

[4] I say "even the possibility," for in a sense Christian tradition itself does not allow that the soul is in the fullest sense naturally immortal. Cf. St. John Damascene, summing up the tradition of the first centuries, *De fide orthodoxa,* bk. 2, c. 3 (*PG,* 93, 867). St. Bonaventure gives this account, in *Utrum anima rationalis sit immortalis,* obj. 17: "The Damascene: What begins, comes to an end according to its nature; the soul begins; therefore it comes to an end according to its nature. Answer: to this I say that the soul would end and fall into nothing if it allowed itself to; or that it begins through a natural action and ends through a natural action, for a natural agent cannot be kept [*continere*] in being perpetually: the soul does not begin to be in this way." See P. Glorieux, *Saint Bonaventure, Questions disputées "de caritate," "de novissimis"* (1950), q. 8, pp. 71, 79.

[5] Cf. Cicero, *De natura deorum,* bk. 1, c. 32, n. 90: "The gods therefore have always existed, and were never born, if indeed they are to be eternal."

[6] *Phaedrus.* Cf. *Timaeus,* 90a; Protagoras, 322 a; *Laws,* 3, 3, 701 bc; bk. 10, 99 d.

[7] *De amicitia,* bk. 4, c. 13. Cf. *Tusculans,* bk. 1, c. 23, n. 55; c. 24, n. 56; c. 26, n. 65:

immortality of the soul from its divine character.[8] Aristotle, faithful to this same principle, considered that "whatever has a beginning must have an end."[9] This was generally taken to be the inevitable lot of man. But there are exceptions: "Take courage," say the *Golden Verses,* "for you know that the race of men is divine."[10] "Realize that you are a god": this is the essential message of the *Dream of Scipio;*[11] this, says Macrobius, is the conclusion, the consummation of the whole work.[12] All the Indian sages similarly agree in considering absurd the idea that any being could have had a beginning and not have an end; "they consider it axiomatic that whatever is subject to production must also be subject to destruction."[13] This axiom still remains indisputable in our own time for Ananda K. Coomaraswamy: Hindu writings, he observes, never fall into the error of supposing that a soul which has had a beginning in time could be immortal.[14] Tolstoy, in his last years, also had this idea—borrowed no doubt from India: "If the soul remains alive after death, then it must have also lived before life. Unilateral eternity is meaningless."[15] Anything which has not always existed can only be an ephemeral—or, worse still, a cyclically ephemeral—contrivance. It would be quite impossible for such a being to break out of "the circle of natural fatality." No ambrosia could have any effect upon him.

158

We find this same fundamental conviction throughout the West, among the later disciples of the ancient philosophers. We thus find it, it

"Homer . . . would transfer human [traits] to the gods; I should prefer to transfer divine [traits] to us. . . ." See Tertullian, *De anima,* c. 4 (J. H. Waszink, p. 5).

[8] *Enneads,* 4, 7, Cf. A. J. Festugière, "La composition et l'esprit du *De anima* de Tertullien," *Revue des sciences phil. et théol.* 33 (1959): 143.

[9] *Physics,* bk. 3, 4, 203b. *De partibus animalium,* bk. 1, c. 5. And Sallust the philosopher was to say: "As to the world itself, it must necessarily be imperishable and uncreated. . . . If it does not perish, then it was not created either, for whatever has been created perishes" (*Of gods and the world,* c. 7, note 2).

[10] And the tablet of Petilia: "I am of heavenly lineage."

[11] C. 8, n. 2: "Deum te igitur scito esse," etc. Cf. Epictetus, *Discourses,* bk. 2, 8: "You are a fragment of God; you have within you a part of that God; why then are you unaware of this affinity?" Cf. bk. 1, 3.

[12] "Praesentis Operis consummatio": *In Somnium Scipionis,* bk. 2, c. 12 (F. Eyssenhardt, p. 613). For the neo-Pythagoreans, we share by nature in "the immortal divinity of the sidereal ether": J. Carcopino, *Virgile et le mystère de la quatrième Eclogue* (1930), p. 32.

[13] Alfred Foucher, *La vie du Bouddha,* p. 26.

[14] *The Myths of Hindus and Buddhists* (London, 1913). The author adds that he does not believe that the Christian Gospels have anywhere put forward so unacceptable a doctrine.

[15] Diaries, 21 January, 1910

seems, though in a more moderate form, even in Boethius, who could only believe in the immortality of human souls because he believed in their pre-existence in a cosmos whose permanence reflects the eternity of God.[16] It is not surprising that Christian thinkers, even when far removed from heresy, even when deeply aware of the totally new aspect given to the world by the Gospel, did not, in their essays of theological reflection, immediately overcome patterns of thought which the whole tradition of thinking man imposed upon them. Even less surprising is the doctrine put forward by that neo-Platonism which was influenced by Arab thought and was attacked by St. Thomas Aquinas: according to this doctrine each individual spirit was a divine essence, whose final end was to return to the company and contemplation of the choir of its fellows, the "separated" spirits.

159   The same thing was carried on in the schools that issued from the two great commentators of Aristotle, Alexander and Averroes. Each of these two opposed but closely related groups reasoned from the same principle which they never thought of questioning. One held man to be a properly eternal being, while the other held him to be an individual destined wholly to die—depending upon whether they saw him with Averroes as the one intelligence, or with Alexander as an individual appearing in time.[17] But whatever the arguments of these groups—and each group sought to align itself with Catholic orthodoxy as against the other—they agreed equally in rejecting as meaningless any kind of personal immortality, and thus went counter to scholastics of every shade of opinion.[18] "If the intelligent soul is eternal in the future," declared the Averroist Siger of Brabant in the thirteenth century, "then it is eternal in the past."[19] A faithful echo of classical ideas.

One might take a final example from Marxist materialism in our own day, as interpreted by Friedrich Engels and his disciples: he returns

---

[16] Gilson, *La philosophie au moyen âge* (Paris, 1944), p. 146. Nédoncelle, "Les variations de Boèce sur la personne," *Revue des sciences religieuses* (1955), p. 212. Cf. Remigius of Auxerre, *In Consolationem Boetii:* "Secundum philosophos hoc dicit etc." (P. Courcelle, *Archives d'histoire doctrinale et littéraire du moyen âge* 12 [1959]: 62).

[17] Cf. J. R. Charbonnel, *La pensée italienne au XVIᵉ siècle* (1919), p. 226. Ernest Renan, *Averroès et l'Averroïsme*[2] (1861), pp. 356–57.

[18] Marsilio Ficino, *Opera omnia* (Basle, 1561), vol. 2, p. 1537. Jacob Brücker, *Historia critica philosophiae,* vol. 4, 1 (Leipzig, 1766), p. 62: "Alexander determined that the soul of man is mortal, Averroes that it is immortal, but one [*sed unam tantum*], indeed he asserted that the intellect is something universal. . . ."

[19] *Quaestiones de anima intellectiva,* 5 (P. Mandonnet, vol. 2, p. 159).

to the idea of an eternal matter within which nothing really new is created, and in relation to which all the apparent advances of history are mere surface disturbances which will come and go indefinitely.[20] But we may rest content with recalling, in a very different atmosphere, the various traditions of secret knowledge, occultism and "gnosis"—or rather, as St. Irenaeus called it, pseudo-gnosis. Such traditions kept reappearing; they always declare that the universe as we know it, with its real or apparent multiplicity, is the result of a "fall" or "splintering"; that we are ourselves made up of a mixture of the earthly and the divine; and that for us salvation consists entirely in separating—though the methods for doing so vary—the divine element from the earthly element which is merely an obstructive accretion, in liberating the divine spark which is at present hidden under the ashes, so as to return to the "dignity of our essence" by restoring primal unity. In the words of the *Asclepius:* "Oh, what a marvellous mixture forms the nature of man! He is united to the gods because he has something divine in him which relates him to them; as for the part of his being which makes him earthly, he despises that in himself."[21] One might compare this fragment of a Gnostic poem found at Tourfan:

> Child of the Light and of the gods,
> behold, I am in exile, separated from them.
>
> My enemies fell upon me,
> and carried me off among the dead. . . .
>
> I am a god and born of the gods,
> glittering, resplendent, luminous,
> radiant, perfumed and beautiful,
> but now reduced to suffering.[22]

René Guénon taught the same not so long ago, though his style is rather more metaphysical: "To admit creation *ex nihilo* would be to admit by that very fact the final annihilation of every being born, for

---

[20] Engels, *Dialectics of nature.* "A flash-back from ancient pantheism," considers Etienne Borne, in *Dieu n'est pas mort* (Paris, 1956), p. 83, Eng. trans. *Modern Atheism* (London, 1961), p. 102.

[21] *Asclepius,* 6 (*Corpus hermeticum,* vol. 2, p. 302).

[22] Fragment M 7, quoted by H. C. Puech, in "Gnosis and Time" (1951) in *Man and Time* (London, 1958), p. 70.

what has had a beginning must also have an end, and nothing is more illogical than to speak of immortality in such a hypothesis."[23]

Alone against all these systems, refusing to be talked into either of their two opposing solutions, Christian philosophy opens for man the prospect of a new kind of life, which has been promised to him, and establishes the essential conditions that make it possible. While making heard from century to century "a passionate protest against any deification of the world," whether it be "polytheistic or pantheistic in form,"[24] it upholds in us the God-given hope of an "everlasting life," or a "blessed eternity," in other words, of a divine immortality.[25] It begins by declaring, with a clarity that allows of no misunderstanding: "We have no natural relationship with God"; there are those, says Clement of Alexandria, the first of the great mystical writers of our tradition, "who dare to suggest that we are consubstantial with him; but I do not see how anyone who has once known God could possibly pay heed to them."[26] Origen says the same in no less decisive terms: "Is it not the extreme of impiety to hold that those who adore God in spirit are of the same essence as his unbegotten and blessed nature? What sacrilege and impiety would not follow from speaking thus of God!"[27] And St. Athanasius says: "What relationship is there between the spirit of God and creatures, between him who makes and those who have been made?"[28] And so, with a common accord, think all those who have followed them, just as they themselves follow the Gospel. To claim for ourselves the same substance as God, they all say with St. Augustine, is "to speak sacrilege" [*sacrilegia dicere*]; it is a "perverse opinion" [*perversa opinio*], it is a "great and most plain impiety" [*magna et apertissima*

161

---

[23] Quoted by Lucien Méroz, *René Guénon ou la sagesse initiatique* (1962), p. 217.

[24] Karl Rahner, S.J., *Schriften zur Theologie*, French edition, *Ecrits théologiques*, 1 (1959), p. 23. This, "the fruit of original sin, [is] present always and everywhere, now as well as in other ages."

[25] On this rich idea of divine immortality, or "eternal life": 1 Tim. 6:16; John 17:2-3; Wis. 15:3; such is also the sense of 2 Peter 1:4: "partakers of the divine nature." Cf. the Christmas liturgy, etc. St. Irenaeus, *Adversus Haereses*, bk. 5, c. 21, n. 3: ". . . that man may learn from experience that it is not of himself, but by the gift of God that he receives incorruptibility." Cf. Bouyer, *L'Incarnation . . . dans la théologie de Saint Athanase* (1943), pp. 36–45.

[26] Clement, *Stromata*, bk. 2, c. 16, 74, 1–2.

[27] *In Ioannem 13:25* (Preuschen, p. 249). Cf. *Contra Celsum*, bk. 1, c. 8 (Koetschau, vol. 1, p. 60). *In Ex.*, hom. 6, n. 5 (Baehrens, p. 196).

[28] *First letter to Serapion* (Sources chrétiennes, 15, 1947, pp. 122, 127).

impietas].[29] This admission of our creaturely condition indicates no lack of boldness in them; quite the opposite. But their boldness is something quite different—not presumption, but *fiducia*,[30] not Promethean presumption, but the boldness of hope. It is a total mistake to see in it the revival of "the arrogant teaching from the African [Scipio] to the Emilian in Christian doctrines which present deification as man's final goal."[31] Christians know that "God inhabits an inaccessible light," but there is another phrase which means just as much to them: "Come unto him, and ye shall receive light." To the extent that they humbly believe the first, to the same extent they trust, in the darkness of this world, in the second. It is one and the same faith which makes them certain both that the depths of God are inscrutable to the mind of man, and that they are known to the Spirit of God who wills to communicate himself to man; for "the Word, only Son of the Father, imparts to the saints a kind of kinship with the nature of God the Father and with his own nature by giving them the Spirit."[32] They know therefore that by "reaching the high point of the heart" they will find the God who has made them for himself:

162

> Men will see God to live, made immortal by visions, and coming to God.[33]
>
> They are called inscrutable to man perhaps because he cannot examine them by his own powers. But why could he not, by the gift of the Holy Spirit, if the Lord should deign to bestow this on him? For it is written: God inhabits an inaccessible light; and we nevertheless hear: Come unto him, and ye shall receive the light. This question is resolved as follows, as he is inaccessible to our powers, still we can arrive at him by his gifts.[34]
>
> I estimate that the blueprint [*schema*] of the great Head of family [*Patrisfamilias*] or of the court of majesty appears in those who, climbing

---

[29] *Contra Secundinum manich.*, c. 8 (*PL*, 43, 584).

[30] Cf. Hasso Jaeger, "*parresia* et Fiducia, étude spirituelle des mots," *Studia patristica* 1 (1957): 221–39. Cf. before the Our Father: "We dare to say. . . ." St. Thomas, *In 2 Cor.*, c. 5, lectio 2: "From the appetite of nature arises the fear of death, from the appetite for grace arises boldness [*audacia*]."

[31] Augustin Renaudet, *Humanisme et Renaissance* (1958), p. 47 (in connection with Duns Scotus).

[32] St. Cyril of Alexandria, *In Ioannem*, bk. 10, c. 2 (*In Io.* 15:1); *PG*, 74, 333 CD.

[33] St. Irenaeus, *Adversus Haereses*, bk. 4, c. 20. n. 6 (*PG*, 7, 1036 A).

[34] St. Augustine, *In psalmum 118*, sermo 6, n. 2.

to the high mind [*cor altum*], made more high-minded by a greater liberty of spirit and purity of conscience, are accustomed to greater daring and, wholly restless and curious to penetrate secrets, and to grasp the higher things, and to touch the more perfect things not only of the senses but also of the virtues. . . . Such men therefore dare great things, for they are great and what they dare, they get. . . .[35]

163   In classical antiquity, on the other hand, just as there was no real immortality except for divine natures, so also there was no "returning" to God for any soul that was not already divine in essence. Either, as Pindar perhaps thought when he gave himself up to the influence of mystical movements, "the race of god and of men is the same"; or, "the race of men is one thing, the race of gods another,"[36] in which case to dream of a divine destiny must always be an "upsurge of desire and pride." It could only be a meaningless defiance hurled to heaven, a defiance which Nemesis would always be certain to punish. Thus the sage is the man who works out his reasons and is content to be enclosed within the limits of his nature [*finibus naturae contentus*]," as Cicero says. There is much indeed in the human heart that lends itself to such wisdom. As a Bantu song says:

> Man is below, God is above,
> Oh, oh, each is at home, each in his own house.

And there are several interpretations of a similar saying in the Psalms:

> The heaven is Yahweh's heaven,
>   but the earth he has given to the sons of Adam.[37]

In the days of Homer and Hesiod, the Greeks generally thought the same. Apollo confirms it in the *Iliad*:

---

[35] St. Bernard, *In Cantica sermo,* 32, n. 8 (*PL,* 183, 949 BC and 949–50).

[36] *Nemeans,* 6, 1 (we learn from Clement, *Strom.,* 5, 14, that Pindar was a Pythagorean). The translation is disputed. Aimé Puech translates it, perhaps in order to avoid having to make a choice by stressing the contrast: "There is the race of men, there is the race of gods." The truth is that Pindar says, 5–7: "Mankind is but nothing, and the heaven of bronze where the gods dwell remains immutable." To understand this passage and Pindar's line of thought, see Edouard des Places, S.J., *Syngeneia, la parenté de l'homme avec Dieu d'Homère à la Patristique* (1964), pp. 25–29; and p. 21: "It is wrong, in my opinion, that the sixth Nemean of Pindar has so often been interpreted in a unitary sense."

[37] Ps. 115:16.

> They will never be of one race,
> The gods who are immortal and men
> who tread the earth.

And in the *Odyssey* the soul of Achilles summoned up from Erebos by the sacrifice of Ulysses cries: "Oh do not beautify death to me, my noble Ulysses!" And in the *Iliad*, Glaucos says to Diomedes, when asked about his race before engaging in combat: "As are leaves, so also is the nature of men. The wind spreads the leaves over the earth, and the forest grows and produces new ones, and spring comes. So is the generation of men born and destroyed."[38] One can only be resigned. Any kind of "impatience with limitations" is sheer insanity. Heaven, "dwelling-place of the gods," is "of bronze." "This is the fate which the gods have spun for poor mortals: to live in sorrow, whereas they themselves live exempt from all care."[39] "Fortunate beings," they are jealous; they humble anyone who rises, and will let no one but themselves cherish lofty thoughts.[40] They hold fast to their rank, wishing to preserve intact their privilege and power. For having tried to climb to heaven, the Titans were cast into Tartarus (for the gods are just as jealous among themselves). Prometheus, in his turn, though acting only out of pity for unfortunate humans, was cast out and tormented: "Your unhappiness is a lesson," says Oceanus to him in Aeschylus's tragedy. Aeschylus tells us that each time "ephemeral men" give way to unbounded "fateful and mad thoughts," "Zeus precipitates them from the summit of their proud hopes down to nothingness."[41] Hesiod too says the same thing. Even the first race, though it was a "golden race," was already a race "of perishable men": how much less, then, could there be any question of our seeking, as poor descendants, to rejoin the master of the gods "who rumbles overhead, seated in his lofty palace." Even the heroes, that race

164

---

[38] *Iliad*, 5, 441–42. *Odyssey*, 11, 488. *Iliad*, 6, 146; cf. 17, 25.

[39] *Iliad*, 24, 525–26.

[40] Cf. Herodotus, bk. 1, 32, Solon to Cresus: "The divinity is all jealousy"; 7, 10 (Artabanes to Xerxes) and 3, 40 (Amasis to Polycrates) are similar statements with regard to the ambition of human enterprises but they symbolize the idea of a more fundamental jealousy. Similarly in the poem Gilgamesh, Enkidu, the companion of Gilgamesh, succumbs to the jealous blows of the gods from on high.

[41] *The Suppliants*, 81–98. For a comparison between Greek *hubris* and pride in the Bible, cf. Paul Ricoeur, *Finitude et culpabilité*, vol. 2 (1960), pp. 74–75. Paul Humbert, "Démesure et chute dans l'Ancien Testament" in *Hommage à Wilhelm Vischer* (1960), pp. 63–82.

165   of demi-gods who live in the isles of the blessed, remain for ever far away from the great immortals.[42] If there is any resemblance, any equality, even in a sense any unity, between man and the gods, then it is only in so far as those gods—created by man in his image—share in human miseries and passions, are jealous and quarrel among themselves; it is only in so far as they share in human weakness and mutability, for they, like us, are dominated by the great force, ultra-divine, or supremely divine, impersonal, blind, "without history or location," of Fate. For all of us, men and gods alike, dwellers in heaven and on earth, have only the same borrowed breath of life; all appear bound together by the same Chain of Fate.[43]

Let us learn then, says the wisdom of old, to be resigned to the irremediable. To avoid a cruel disappointment, let us learn systematically to reject any "attempt at metaphysical hope," and let us be content with clinging humbly with all our being to things "as they are." Let us cultivate our own little garden. *Hubris* is the fate most to be feared: we must mistrust any deceiving ambition, for it can only lead to horror and catastrophe.[44] "No mortal," Aeschylus warns us again, "should cherish thoughts above his mortal condition."[45] And Euripides says: "There is no wisdom in dreaming of anything that is not mortal";[46] and when

166   Aphrodite sees Hippolytus "through the green forest, always beside the virgin [Artemis]," she observes in a disapproving and threatening manner that he "has found there society higher than is fitting for a mortal."[47]

---

[42] *Works and Days*, 5, 8 and 109–10. Cf. *Odyssey*, 15, 70: "How bitterly those heroes ruminate upon their fate, so splendid but so short!" André Blanchet, *La littérature et le spirituel*, vol. 3 (1961), p. 22, "Homère perdu et retrouvé."

[43] "Mythology does not furnish a single example of Zeus's violating *moira*" (P. Chantraine, "Le divin et les dieux chez Homère" in *La notion du divin depuis Homère jusqu'à Platon, Entretiens sur l'antiquité classique*, 1 [1952], p. 81). Cf. Gabriel Germain, *Homère* (1961), p. 78: "Zeus . . . directs a force which is not personified, which has no time or place, which we call Fate, and which Homer indicates by the words *moira, asia*, the part assigned to everyone."

[44] Cf. Michel Vinaver, "Les mythes de la Grèce ancienne," 2, *Critique* 95 (1955): 307–11.

[45] *The Persians*, 820. Cf. *Agamemnon*, 764–71.

[46] *The Bacchae*, 395.

[47] Hippolytus, 17–19. It is the *huper anthrōpon phronein* which was condemned by ancient wisdom: Edouard des Places, *Pindare et Platon* (1949), pp. 46, 136. Cf. L. Méridier, "Euripide et l'orphisme," *Bulletin . . . Budé* (January 1928). Claudel, *Jérémie* (ms., p. 9) on pagan philosophies and religions: "When they do not merge the creator into the

Pindar himself, once he no longer believes himself a god from birth, says: "We must lower our eyes to what lies at our feet, and realize what our vocation is in this world; do not aspire, O my soul, to an immortal life." Man, he says elsewhere, is "the dream of a shadow."[48] And Lucretius, in his "philosophic tongue, sad, slow and spondaic":

> . . . Respice item quam nil nos anteacte vetustas
> Temporis aeterni fuerit, quam nascimur ante,
> Hoc igitur speculum nobis natura futuri
> Temporis exponit post mortem denique nostram.[49]

The divine temptation, however, is for ever re-born. Whatever a man may think with his reason, he cannot stop himself having deceptive dreams. Constantly stirred by that "impatience with limitations" which he has in theory disposed of, he continues to "strain, so to say, at the end of his chain," though every effort ends in disappointment. Each time he finds himself thrown back "into his world of dust."[50] It is a wretched experience. All antiquity, giving up a false eternity only to fall back into the closed world of time, bears witness to it. "Ancient thought was not unaware of the religious universe, but was totally unaware, I think, of the sphere of religious expectation, of hope."[51] Christians, too, recognize the existence of a *hubris,* a wrongful excess, and without having to attribute it only to this or that mythical hero unconnected with themselves, can see it in Genesis in "the essence of sin and the chief reason for the deterioration of humanity, which God must draw back with rigorous pedagogy to the realization of its natural limitations";[52]

---

created, we may say that they have no other option than to separate them by an impassable and irremovable gulf."

[48] *Isth.,* 5, 14. *Pythian Odes,* 8, 99; 2, 50–52: "God who touches the eagle in its flight, and meets the dolphin in the sea, knows how to bow down the pride of man."

[49] *De natura rerum,* 1, 3, 972–75: "Look back: what nothingness for us was the old age of everlasting time, before our birth. It is the mirror in which nature shows us the length of time which will come after death." Cf. Chateaubriand, *Essai sur la littérature anglaise,* introduction. Official Marxism has, as we know, canonized Lucretius, though somewhat arbitrarily interpreted.

[50] Gerard of Nerval, Preface to the translation of *Faust* (1828).

[51] Jacques Perret, *Virgile* (1952), p. 157. We shall hardly take as a solution to the problem of man "those proceedings whereby, very easily, but not without due formality, a man, and especially a king, is brought into Olympian society": Jean Bayet, "L'immortalité astrale d'Auguste," *Revue des études latines* 17 (1939): 163.

[52] Paul Humbert, *loc. cit.,* p. 71. Though one may explain the sin of man differently, the thing remains true for the sin of the angels. Cf. St. Augustine, *In psalm. 58,* sermo 2,

but Christians know something more, something which the ancients did not. That the latter lacked hope was primarily because the very idea of a *sursum* and a superabundance, the idea of an order incommensurate with nature, the idea of something radically new, something we might call an "invention in being," the idea of a gift coming gratuitously from above to raise up that needy nature, at once satisfying its longings and transforming it—such an idea remains wholly foreign to all whose minds have not been touched by the light of revelation.

Equally foreign to them, then, must be the idea that goes with it, without which there could only be established the rule of the arbitrary and the meaningless, destructive both of essences and of the laws of reason. For the idea of superabundance presupposes or entails the idea of a certain "power," of a certain innate openness in beings to that superabundance; the idea of the possible gift presupposes or entails the idea of a certain fundamental and interior aptitude for receiving that gift. If God is one day to speak to his creatures in order to bring them to him, then it is certainly necessary for him to have made them in advance as "open and questioning."[53] In other words, it is certainly necessary for there to be a kind of twofold call inscribed by God in the very make-up of these creatures—a call which is as vague and indeterminate in its import as one likes, and which could have remained hidden for ever. This twofold call comes from God's initiative, and it sounds from within the creature as a first natural response. Of course let me say it again, just as he has willed to give himself to men, God could have willed not to do so. Just as he has willed to speak to them, he could have remained silent. Every Christian accepts this; in any case the affirmation that he might have withheld his gift or remained silent is implied by the recognition of the gift and of the word that is heard. Just as he can be constrained by nothing, either from within himself or from outside, in his creation of the world, so nothing can constrain him to give it a supernatural finality.[54] But what we must reflect on is still that creation

168

---

n. 5 (*CCL*, 39, 748–50); and *In psalm. 70*, sermo 2, n. 6: "And whence have I fallen from Thee? When I seek perversely to be like to Thee. . ." (964).

[53] Hans Urs von Balthasar, *Die Gottesfrage des heutigen Menschen* (Vienna-Munich, 1956), French ed. *Dieu et l'homme d'aujourd'hui*, p. 165, Eng. trans. *Science, Religion and Christianity* (London, 1958).

[54] Cf. *supra*, and also my study in *Recherches de science religieuse* 36 (1949): 104: "Had God willed, he could have not given us being, and this being which he has given us, he need not have called to see him"; God "cannot be constrained by anything to give a super-

as it exists, with the unique final end which it has, that creation as effected by God precisely with the object of giving himself to it; that creation as finally illuminated for us by the good news announced to mankind one night at Bethlehem.

Of that fundamental aptitude, that call within nature, that hidden but active reality, the ancients may well have felt some effect, or perhaps rather some expression, some sign. The "magic flight" of certain civilizations of the past has been taken as evidence that they did.[55] But they did not as yet have the means of interpreting correctly what they felt. They knew neither what it was they were looking for, nor how to look. They were quite unable to distinguish the real meaning of "that organic spark of uncertainty, of longing and of discontent which lies at the depths of mankind's inmost being."[56] When they did not succeed in extinguishing it, it obsessed or even deranged them. It could only result in rebellion, followed by a falling back into despair. They could only raise nature too high, or bring it down too low. A fragment of the divine, or the dust of the earth, or a chance and unsteady mixture of the two. Since they could discern in themselves nothing of "truth, wisdom and justice," they could not imagine that they were none the less "capable" in some sense of these divine things, or realize that their greatness consisted precisely in that "capacity." It was not possible for them to say, like St. Bernard, or with the depth of significance he gave the words: "My expression [*verbum*] is neither wisdom nor justice, but it is nevertheless capable of both."[57] Aware of the hazards of their birth, they

169

---

natural finality to my being. . . . I must carefully distinguish and always maintain a double gratuitousness, a double divine gift, and therefore, if one may use such terms, a double divine freedom. There are, as it were, two levels, two floors with no communication from the lower to the higher. There is a double ontological movement, which is doubly unable to be achieved by the creature without that double initiative which calls him into existence, and which then calls him. . . ." By misrepresenting this study, Father Angelo Perego has recently declared, in a symposium published by Mgr. Piolanti, that it not merely deviates from, but is actually a corruption of, Catholic teaching. He seems neither to have read my study properly, nor to know the theological tradition on the subject very well.

[55] Mircea Eliade, "Le symbolisme des ténèbres dans les religions archaïques," *Polarité des symboles, Etudes carmélitaines* 27 (1960): 17.

[56] Paul Claudel, "L'esprit de prophétie" in *J'aime la Bible* (1955), p. 4. This is one application of something tradition never ceases to repeat, which was canonized by the First Vatican Council. Cf., among a hundred others, F. de Vitoria, O.P., commenting on St. Thomas, *Prima*, q. 1, a. 1: "And there is no doubt that without revealed doctrine, the most expert philosopher would inject many errors. . . ."

[57] St. Bernard, *In feria quarta hebd. sanctae*, n. 13 (*PL*, 183, 270 A). *In Cantica sermo,*

could not seriously believe themselves "made for eternity." They could only consider it a ridiculous presumption to link the expectation of a "heavenly generation" with what they knew of "human poverty."[58] There it seemed to them that their only choice lay between an insupportable arrogance and thoughts of utter lowliness, and the best and most far-seeing among them saw both together without ever succeeding in really uniting them. For, as Bérulle explains, "they believed they had enough power over nature to speak as though it were obliged to become perfect, and yet they proposed nothing great, nothing higher than man."[59]

The human inheritance these men of old have left us is a fine one—but it is short. Their religious spirit was often profound, and we should be wrong to scorn their message for us, and not recognize with the Fathers how much "preparation for the gospel" is in it. But ultimately their efforts achieved nothing. St. Thomas Aquinas notes this with deep sympathy on several occasions. They never found the remedy for what Jacques Maritain so aptly calls "the great pagan melancholy." For they never heard the echo in their mortal hearts of that eternal and efficacious invitation to "transcend that premature balance in which science, art and philosophy strive to achieve for us a harmony that is deceptive."[60] For all the profundity of their experience, they could only some-

---

80, n. 2: "The word is truth, is wisdom, is justice. . . . The soul is none of these things. . . . It does, however, have the capacity for them, and strives for them, and hence perhaps [it is] in the image. A noble creature, in the capacity of majesty in fact, in appetite displaying the mark of Rectitude . . ." (*Opera*, ed. J. Leclercq, vol. 2, 1958, p. 278). Cf. St. Thomas, *Prima Secundae*, q. 113, a. 10: "The soul is naturally capable of grace; since, because it has been made in the image of God, it is capable of God by grace, as says Augustine."

[58] William of St. Thierry, *Speculum fidei*: "The things that are eternal and divine appear to be conjoined by some natural affinity to the mind insofar as it is created with a view to eternity [*ad aeternitatem*] so that it is capable of it by intelligence and participates in it by possession [*per fruitionem*]. This is the case to such an extent that even if the mind should dull from vice, it would nevertheless never be deprived of the desire for them [*eorum . . . affectu*] . . ." (*PL*, 180, 386 B). Cf. St. Bernard, *In octava Paschae*, sermo 1, n. 1: "After the Only-begotten of God . . . was in the condition of man, it is not undeservedly that human smallness presumes of celestial generation."

[59] Bérulle, opusc. 133, *Du nouvel homme et de son nouvel oeuvre*, c. 3 (G. Rotureau, p. 397). Cf. St. Augustine, *In psalm. 31*, sermo 2, n. 1: "The human mind [*animus*] was split [*anceps*], wavering between the confession of its weakness and the boldness of presumption, it generally is drawn hither and thither, and it is so driven that there is a precipice for it to fall into on either side" (*CCL*, 38, 224).

[60] Maritain, *La philosophie morale* (1960), p. 102; cf. *Les degrés du savoir* (1932), p. 505, Eng. trans. *The Degrees of Knowledge* (London, 1959), p. 285, on "that nostalgia for higher

times barely sense "obscurely and often through a cloud" the prose of human life.[61] For they did not know of a God, the only being utterly without jealousy, raising up beings out of nothing in time, in order to unite them with his eternity: "calling temporal men, he makes them eternal" [*vocans temporales, faciens aeternos*]. They had as yet no understanding of a being without any past who could none the less be open "to an eternal good"; they had no conception of a finite spirit made to seek the only end worthy of it in the one good totally beyond it.[62] They imagined nothing to compare with that marvellous change which St. Augustine was to sum up so perfectly: "being changeable, they were changed and made partakers of the unchangeable Word" [*mutabiles, commutati, participes facti Verbi incommutabilis*].[63] They withdrew far from the common mass, into meditating upon an illusory eternity, devoting themselves to making "a kind of ghostly analysis of their being in order to work out from it the composition of the star of which it is a ray";[64] or, on the contrary, they felt weighed down with the rest by the burden of time and its perpetual revolving, finding nothing in life that promised anything but old age and death; in neither case did they have any hint in advance of that joyous discovery made by those who follow Christ, who have received the promise of an "incorruptible inheritance," and who therefore can cry with St. Augustine: "There happens in time a new thing that has no end in time."[65] They had no reason to

171

---

contemplation to which so many schools of philosophy bear witness in the vast reaches of human history." Blondel, *Vocabulaire de la société française de philosophie*, art. "Sublime." Cf. St. Thomas, *Summa contra Gentiles*, bk. 3, c. 48, etc.

[61] Cf. Robert Agricola, quoted by A. Bossert, *De R. Agricola* (1865).

[62] William of St. Thierry, *Epistola ad Fratres de Monte Dei*, c. 90: "Nothing is a worthier object of inquiry for the mind or soul [*menti vel animo*] . . . than what alone surpasses the mind itself, which is only God" (ed. M. M. Davy, p. 132).

[63] *Epist.* 140, c. 4, n. 12: "Therefore we who are changeable, once we are changed for the better, are made partakers of the Word, though the Word is unchangeable . . ." (*PL*, 33, 542). In this passage, Augustine contrasts the "false circles" [*falsi circuitus*] with the "straight path" [*rectum iter*], and shows the soul rising from its poverty to be raised to beatitude. Cf. *De Trinitate*, bk. 4, c. 18, n. 24: "Then eternity shall possess our now changed changeability" (Bibl. aug., 15, p. 398). *De civitate Dei*, bk. 12, c. 21, n. 2–4: "But let it not be the case that the words are true [*sed absit ut vera sint*], that threaten us with endless wretchedness. . . . Once these circles have been nullified and defeated, . . . certainly a new liberation comes about. . . . New things can happen. . . . These circles are now driven out!" (Bibl. aug., 35, pp. 222–26).

[64] Hans Urs von Balthasar, *La théologie de l'histoire*, p. 168.

[65] Cf. 1 Peter 1:3-4. *De Civitate Dei*, bk. 12, c. 13, n. 1 (*PL*, 41, 361) etc. In this passage Augustine contrasts the doctrine of the "false circles" [*falsi circuitus*] with that of the

suspect that the "electric wire of the line of death," stretching out before all titanic enterprises, was to break for ever in front of the "path of humility" [*via humilitatis*] begun with the incarnation of the Word of God.[66] If they did not have the vain dream of thinking of themselves as set outside and beyond all these circles of fatality by nature, they could never even dream that one day mankind might give the triumphant cry: "These circles have now been driven off" [*explosi sunt*].[67] They knew neither that they were "created out of nothing," nor that they could one day be "born of God."[68] In short, knowing nothing of the Word made flesh, through whom the miracle takes place, and having never heard the call of his voice, they did not know themselves.[69]

172

To us the good news has been told. "This is the word which by the gospel hath been preached unto us." We have known "him who has set us free from mortality."[70] Whatever generation of Christian history we belong to, we have heard the evidence of those who have seen, heard and touched with their hands the Word of life. We know—and this is

---

"straight path" [*rectum iter*], and shows the soul rising out of its poverty to be raised to beatitude. Cf. St. Thomas, *Summa contra Gentiles*, bk. 3, c. 61: "For the person is a partaker of eternal life through the vision of God."

[66] Cf. Karl Barth, *Römerbrief* [2], p. 230.

[67] *De Civitate Dei*, bk. 12, c. 21, n. 4 (Bibl. aug, 35, p. 226).

[68] John 1:13, 3:5. Cf. 1 Peter 1:23-25: "Being born again not of corruptible seed, but incorruptible, by the word of God who liveth and remaineth for ever, for all flesh is as grass; and all the glory thereof as the flower of grass. The grass is withered, and the flower thereof is fallen away. But the word of the Lord endureth for ever. And this is the word which by the gospel hath been preached unto you." Cf. Irenaeus, *Adv. Haereses*, bk. 3, c. 11, n. 8.

[69] Clement, *Protreptikos*, 1, 2. Once again, the standpoint from which this chapter is looking at things does not make it possible to measure all the distance between the thought of antiquity and the Christian faith, all that was new in the revelation of the Word made flesh. Our view still remains abstract, because we say nothing about deliverance from evil. A page of Paul Claudel, commenting on chapter 35 of Isaiah, casts light on this second aspect: "'The wilderness and the dry land shall be glad, the desert shall rejoice and blossom like the crocus.' Let us pause at these Hebrew lines which still glow in the Latin of St. Jerome. 'It shall blossom abundantly, and rejoice with joy and singing. The glory of Lebanon has been given to it, the majesty of Carmel and Sharon. We are able to see the glory of the Lord, the majesty of our God.' With what tears we may read these lines, crying: It is true! Those despairing regions of ancient poetry, Oedipus, Hecuba, the Fates, all these we have left behind us. And now we have got a bridge to a land of sweetness. *Decor Carmeli et Saron!*" (*Paul Claudel interroge l'Apocalypse* [1952], pp. 68–69, note).

[70] Garnier de Rochefort, *Sermo* 3 (*PL*, 205, 588 B). Cf. Augustine, *In Jo.*, tract. 31, n. 5: "When the fullness of time came, he also came to deliver us from time. For being delivered from time, we shall come to that eternity where there is no time. . . . Therefore we must love him by whom the times were made, so that we may be delivered from time, and fixed in eternity, where there is no more mutability of times . . ." (*CCL*, 36, 296).

knowledge that might well "strike us dumb with amazement"—that God became man in order that man might become God.[71] Our Fathers in the faith say it afresh to each one of us: "Because of you he became temporal, so that you might become eternal"; "He came down that we might go up"; "He became mortal with us, in order that we, with him, might become immortal."[72] He has broken the thread of Fate, he has expanded our horizons and gone before us into an ever new eternity. With St. Leo we repeat: "Therefore the humility of the divinity is our advancement";[73] or with St. Gregory: "While he undertook the shadows of our temporality, he poured in us the light of his eternity";[74] and with Hugh of St. Victor: "Because we were unable to follow him in his majesty, he preceded us in our humility, and from our [sphere] he established a path so that we be able to attain to his [sphere]. . . ."[75] We must thus have a pledge and certain sign of what seems impossible and indeed unimaginable:

> And lest perhaps one should say: it seems impossible for mortals to become immortal, for the corruptible to lack corruption, for mere men to be sons of God, for temporals to possess eternity: from the following verse, which is superior, accept the argument whereby you may trust in the matter of which you doubt: "And the Word was made flesh."[76]

Even today it is just as likely for us to misunderstand what we are. We tend to underestimate the seriousness of these sacred words, and their unfailing newness. At the level of reflection as at that of instinctive

173

174

---

[71] St. Athanasius, *De incarnatione Verbi*, n. 54. St. Augustine, *Sermo* 192, n. 1: "To make those who were men gods, he who was God was made man" (*PL*, 38, 1012); s. 121, n. 5; 185, n. 3; 192, n. 1 (680, 997, 1012) etc. St. Irenaeus, *Adversus Haereses*, bk. 4, c. 20, n. 4 and 5; bk. 5, preface and c. 16, n. 2, etc.

[72] St. Augustine, *In 1 Io.*, tract. 2, n. 10 (*PL*, 35, 1994). *Epist.* 140 (*PL*, 33, 541–42). *Sermo* 166, n. 4 (38, 909). St. Maximus, *Ambigua* (*PG*, 91, 1288 A, 1385 BC), etc. William of St. Thierry, *Speculum fidei*: "Though remaining eternal in himself [*in seipso*], he became man in time, so that we might cross over, through the temporal and the eternal, from temporal things to eternal things" (*PL*, 180, 383 A).

[73] *Sermo* 52, c. 2 (*PL*, 54, 315 A).

[74] *Moralia in Iob*, bk. 29, c. 2, n. 2 (*PL*, 76, 478 B).

[75] *In Eccl.*, hom. 10 (*PL*, 175, 181 BD).

[76] Scotus Erigena, *Homilia in Prologum Ioannis* (*PL*, 122, 295 B). St. Bonaventure, *Itinerarium*, c. 6, n. 4: ". . . the wondrous [*supermirabilem*] union of God and man in the unity of the person of Christ" (*Opera*, Quaracchi, vol. 5, p. 311). Augustine, *In Ioannem*, tract. 2, n. 15: "Do not then marvel, O man, that you are made a son through grace. . . . The Word himself wished to be born of man first. . . . Why then do you marvel, that men are born of God? Bear in mind that God himself was born of men" (*CCL*, 36, 17). John the Carthusian, Epist. 1 (*PL*, 153, 908–9).

reaction, we always find it hard to "realize" all the implications of our faith. "A noble creature in the capacity for majesty":[77] such a description of man seems in fact rather too noble for us. We may even come to find it too demanding. "Man when he was in honor did not understand" [*Homo cum in honore esset, non intellexit*].[78] We find it no easier than the men of antiquity to grasp that "man surpasses man," so we remain enclosed not merely by practical impossibility, or ill will, but on principle "in the circle bounded by human desires."[79] We do not always understand what has been brought into the midst of time and into the nature of temporal beings, so as to transform our *distraction* [*distentio*] into an *intent* [*intentio*],[80] by that "prize of the heavenly calling" [*palma supernae vocationis*] to which we are commanded to tend. Turned inward upon our *human smallness* [*exiguitas humana*], we neither know nor even wish to discover within us the void whose capacity will grow as it becomes filled with the fullness of God.

The Creator's power imprints a movement "deep within his creature, in the heart of the created being, at the moment of its creation";[81] a deep and hidden movement, which is at first different and apparently contradicted by all the surface movements, but which underlies them all.[82] By this movement the spirit, once free of all that holds it back, and as it were "purged of all things," and having completed its novitiate on earth, leaps up to God "with a certain surge which makes it impossible to stop at anything less than that goal which is its creator."[83] The movement is inborn, and therefore spontaneous, with its roots lying deeper than any tendency or commitment of man's free will: a movement not of this or that individual, but of the nature all have in common. The

175

[77] St. Bernard (see *supra*, p. 131).

[78] Ps. 48:13 (Vulgate).

[79] Gérard de Nerval, Preface to the translation of *Faust*.

[80] St. Augustine, *Confessions*, bk. 11, c. 29, n. 39: "I am not preoccupied with what lies before me, but rather am intent on it; it is not with preoccupation [*distentio*] but with purpose [*intentio*] that I pursue the reward of the heavenly calling" (*PL*, 32, 825). See the commentary by J. M. Le Blond, *Les conversions de saint Augustin*, pp. 267–68: "It is thus the supernatural end . . . which in his eyes confers on time its true meaning, which replaces its *distentio* by an *intentio*, and does not merely superimpose one upon the other."

[81] Bérulle, *Oeuvres de piété*, quoted by Jean Dagens in *Le cardinal de Bérulle* (1952), p. 335.

[82] Cf. St. Thomas, *Prima*, q. 60, a. 2: "The will naturally tends to its final end . . . and all other desires are naturally caused by this natural desire. . . ."

[83] Ven. Marie de l'Incarnation, *Lettres de conscience*, 8 (*Ecrits*, ed. P. Jamet, vol. 1, pp. 362–63).

movement of itself achieves nothing, since it indicates no kind of debt or requirement; it remains for ever hidden in its deepest source, and can always be interpreted in quite different terms, as has happened in so many aberrations, so many developments in history which grew out of it. All too often indeed we do not discern it. Revelation gives us the key, but we may not yet know how to use it; or perhaps we may fear to enter that sphere of mystery which it suddenly opens for us: the idea Christianity gives us of what man is may meet several kinds of resistance, some commonplace, some more subtle.

"Man when he was in honor did not understand." But if we can accept it, then we will not try to evade the evidence of those great men in our tradition who have described it. Then, though in no way agreeing with those philosophers who are reluctant even to use such terms as spiritual nature or human nature, we would find no difficulty in recognizing—as Père Joseph de Finance does in interpreting St. Thomas—that the laws of the "dynamism proper to spirit" are not identical with those of the "dynamism of natural forms."[84] There is an essential difference. Whereas the lower creatures which make up the visible cosmos, in which man formerly could think he was completely immersed, "have been created perfect in their condition with no expectation of anything higher," we recognize that human nature "has not been created to remain within the terms of nature,"[85] but is in fact destined "for a state far above its powers."[86] Thus we will unhesitatingly agree with St. Bonaventure when he says: "man is born to be raised above himself."[87] We shall no longer feel obliged to agree with those writers who adopted as a truth of principle the following idea (which St. Thomas put forward as an objection to be refuted): "Nature does not bestow an inclination to something to which all the power of nature is incapable of leading," or this idea: "Natural desire does not extend itself beyond the faculty of nature," or again: "[In man], nothing is natural but that in which he has

176

---

[84] *Etre et agir dans la philosophie de saint Thomas*, pp. 339–40. Cf. O'Mahony, *The Desire for God in the Philosophy of St. Thomas* (1929), pp. 253–54. St. Thomas, *Prima*, q. 14, a. 1; q. 93, a. 4, 6, 8; *Tertia*, q. 4, a. 1, ad 6um; q. 9, a. 2, ad 3um; *De Veritate*, q. 25, a. 1; etc.

[85] Bérulle, *Opuscules de piété*, 132, 3 (Rotureau ed., p. 389).

[86] Ibid., 2 (p. 388). Bérulle continues: "and is capable of being actuated by this new power to which it aspires as to something necessary to it and without which it is defective. . . ." His language is perhaps not always strictly literal.

[87] *In 2 Sent.*, dist. 3, p. 2, a. 3, q. 2 (vol. 2, p. 126).

potency [*potest*] through the mere active principles within him."[88] Nor would we agree with them in taking the paradox to be a contradiction (just as they take for a basic principle what is only in appearance a piece of common sense): "It seems to imply that nature gives the desire for the divine vision, and that it cannot give what is requisite [*requisita*] for such a vision, for instance the light of glory."[89] It is pointless to repeat the old argument drawn from Aristotle, however many new twists one may give it: "If the stars had the capacity to move [*vim progressivam*], nature would have given them the appropriate organs";[90] I would reply, in the same terms as all the great scholastics whom I shall be quoting in the next chapter, that there is nature and nature; that the nature of spirit created by God"s free decision for a supernatural end freely chosen is not comparable in every way either to the nature of material beings, or to the uncreated nature postulated by the ancient philosophers, and that therefore nothing relevant to the case of spirit has been said either by the statement of the old principle, or by the argument about the stars, or by any other arguments of the same kind. "The capacity of the human heart is too great even for the whole world to fill it."[91]

[88] Javelli, *In primum tractatum primae Partis Angelici Doctoris* (Venice, 1595) folio 21, v: "Consequently the philosopher will say, that since desire is for possible things in the absolute, man wishes to know only what he can know through an acting and possible intellect [*per intellectum agentem et possibilem*]."

[89] Cajetan, *In Primam*, q. 12, a. 1, n. 9 and 10. Cf. *De potentia neutra*, q. 2, ad 4um, 3° (*Opuscula*, vol. 3, p. 157). Cf. Cardinal Zigliara's philosophical works, French edition *Oeuvres philosophiques*, vol. 1, "Essai sur les principes du traditionalisme," chapter 3, "Dieu," art. 2, n. 93, p. 117: "Whereas God in his ineffable goodness communicates himself to creatures, giving them being, life and everything by which, through an instinct placed within them, he inclines their nature to seek a determinate end fixed by the eternal wisdom, it is necessary that the benevolent hand of the Lord also put in the hearts of those same creatures the means suitable to reach that end."

[90] Cajetan, ibid., following Aristotle, *De Caelo*, bk. 2: "It does not appear to be true, that the created intellect naturally desires to see God; for nature does not bestow an inclination to something to which the whole power of nature cannot lead; a proof of this is that nature placed the organs for any potency deep within the soul. And in the second book of the *Caelum*. . . ." St. Thomas says the contrary; see for instance *Prima Secundae*, q. 5, a. 5, ad 2um: "The nature of the nobler condition is that which is able to pursue the perfect good, even though it lacks exterior assistance to pursue it. . . ." Cf. Petrus Trigosus, *An in nobis sit naturale desiderium* . . . (Jul. Eymard d'Angers, *Antonianum* [1957]: 5).

[91] St. Robert Bellarmine, *Cantiones de quatuor novissimis*, 4 (*Opera*, vol. 9, p. 448b). Cf. A. R. Motte, O.P., *Bulletin thomiste* 9 (1932): 654: St. Thomas "did indeed distinguish better than anyone between reason and faith, nature and grace, but he none the less perceived in the divine plan a sovereign Unity which we are all too tempted to forget. From

But we must also declare the complementary truth. The recognition that man comes to have of his capacity for God and of the "natural" desire corresponding to it has its necessary context in a recognition of the gratuitousness of the gift which will fulfill it; for like the realization in the conscience of what was before only a hidden possibility, it can but echo the endless wonder of the good news:

> . . . exceeding all joy
> and all desire.[92]

---

the creation of the world to the consummation of the elect in the vision of God, all comes from a single source. Man is made for the beatific vision."

[92] Hymn for the feast of the Holy Name of Jesus. Cf. St. Bernard, *De verbis Isaiae prophetae,* sermo 4, n. 1: "You have the spirit of him who by the abundance of his piety exceeds not only the merits of men, but also their prayers"(*PL,* 183, 351 D); etc.

CHAPTER 8

A Paradox Rejected by Common Sense

179   For the ardent but in fact unfaithful Thomist—which is what Cajetan is here—"reasonable nature is a closed whole within which the active capacities and tendencies are in strict correspondence." "Natural desire does not extend itself beyond the faculty of nature":[1] this is his principle, and it was to become the principle of an entire modern school. Is such a principle really, as has been said, the fruit of a "more philosophically elaborate notion of human nature," a notion which would make it possible to go a step further than St. Thomas, and "delineate more sharply the outlines of a nature without grace"? I should say that it is rather the fruit of a more specialized idea, at once narrower and more specific. It is the effect of a reduced understanding of spirit, as compared with that of St. Thomas and his time, just as it is a descent from the heights which Christian philosophy had once scaled. Cajetan's opusculum, *De potentia neutra,* seems to me to show this most clearly, by his way of reasoning about "the soul" exactly as he does about "matter" and "every other thing":

> Certainly we know the major [premise] that no natural potency is in vain; therefore, if we know the minor [premise] that in matter, or in the soul, or *in every other thing,* there is a natural potency to supernatural act, one should concede, etc.[2]

180   It is to this naturalization of the soul, or the human being, that we must attribute Cajetan's teaching on the *potentia obedientiae.* Not that it

---

[1] *In Primam,* q. 12, a. 1, n. 10.

[2] *De potentia neutra,* q. 2, "Utrum potentia receptiva actuum supernaturalium sit potentia naturalis," ad 4um, 3⁰ (*Opuscula omnia,* Venice, 1612, vol. 3, p. 157).

was he who invented the name, or the thing. But the application he makes of it to the problem of the supernatural end is not that made by St. Thomas. Thus one can say, with Père Martin, O.P., that he brings to the solution of that problem a completely new language: "It seems that this manner of speaking is wholly alien to the teaching of Saint Thomas Aquinas."[3] Someone wrote recently that "it is a complete historical mistake to see this as a malicious 'invention' on his part." In fact no one has ever suggested that it was a malicious invention—or even a pure invention at all. But there is none the less a flagrant deviation from the master in the commentator. It is quite certain that for St. Thomas human nature can be said to be *in potentia obedientiae* to receive sanctifying grace, and that one may speak of it as a miracle, since "universally, every work that can be performed by God alone can be called miraculous."[4] But it must be noted that he only admits these terms, miracle or obediential potency [*potentia obedientialis*], in a generic sense. In fact, as Bernard of Auvergne says, "every creature partakes [*communicant*] in obediential potency [*potentia obedientiae*], because God can do with everything whatever he wants."[5] But having said this, it remains to determine all the specific differences. St. Thomas himself does this both clearly and forcefully. It certainly does not mean that human nature should be conceived first of all as normally endowed with a "purely natural" finality, and only fitted to receive a supernatural finality "beyond nature" [*praeter naturam*] or "against nature" [*contra naturam*], by a definite miraculous intervention. Quite the reverse—for him as for his emulator St. Bonaventure,[6] it is precisely because the ultimate finality of this human nature is supernatural that it can receive sanctifying grace. There is in it not only an "obediential potency" [*potentia obedientiae*], but a certain "natural order" [*ordo naturalis*] to the receiving of that grace, whereas in the case of miracle such "ordo naturalis" does not

181

---

[3] P. Martin, in *Ephemerides theologicae lovanienses* 1 (1924): 352.

[4] *Prima Secundae*, q. 113, a. 10. Cf. *Tertia*, q. 11, art. 1.

[5] Quoted by B. Neumann, *Der Mensch und die himmlische Seligkeit nach der Lehre Gottfrieds von Fontaines* (Limburg, 1958), p. 14, note.

[6] Gillon shows this very clearly for Bonaventure, in "Béatitude et désir de voir Dieu au moyen âge," *Angelicum* 26 (1949): 134, quoting Bonaventure, *De mysterio SS. Trinitatis* (vol. 5, p. 576): "There is here an interesting connection between the 'obediential potency' [*potentia obedientialis*] of the lower creature and the obligation for spirit to submit to the divine light. A simple connection, and not one which allows us to attribute to St. Bonaventure any transposition of the conditions of the 'obediential potency' [*potentia obedientialis*] to the capacity of the soul for grace."

exist.[7] Indeed St. Thomas does not even hesitate to say, so as to indicate the difference from miraculous works performed "beyond the order" [*praeter ordinem*], that the justification of the wicked "is not miraculous of itself" [*de se*], since it is not done "above the natural potency," if it is admitted that "the soul is naturally capable of grace."[8] He considers it a miracle for a man to be given a certain vision of God in this world, but not a miracle in the case of the next world.[9] He even underlines this, on occasion, by making it clear that the obediential potency "cannot be fulfilled" contrary to the natural desire or capacity of the spirit.[10]

St. Thomas also knows, of course, that created grace, the infused virtues and the light of glory—all necessary means for obtaining the end—are not the natural products of human faculties. Many others, whether Thomists or not, know this as well, and it provides a further occasion for using the term *obediential potency*. Duns Scotus, for instance, does so, though he none the less uses in the immediate context such phrases as "God the natural end" [*Deus finis naturalis*], "natural desire" [*desiderium naturale*] and "naturally capable" [*naturaliter capax*].[11] In the order of finality itself, so as to avoid any confusion between the supernatural gift and the mere fulfillment a nature receives from some natural agent, we may join some of the moderns—without in any way departing from the spirit of the past—in specifying that the "passive potentiality" which characterizes human nature in relation to

182

[7] *In 4 Sent.*, dist. 17, q. 1, a. 5, sol. 1: the second of the three conditions for a miracle is that "in the receiving nature there be no natural order for its reception, but only an obediential potency [*potentia obedientialis*] for God." Consequently, if it is a question of a certain effect "that is only from God immediately, and nevertheless in the receiver there is a natural order for receiving that effect by no other means than by itself, it is not miraculous; just as it is clear from the infusion of the rational soul. And likewise for the justification of the impious: because the natural order for the pursuit of the rectitude of justice is in the soul, and it cannot pursue it in any other way than immediately from God; and therefore the justification of the impious is not miraculous. . . ." Cf. *De Veritate*, q. 12, art. 3, ad 18um, on the gift of prophecy.

[8] *Prima Secundae*, q. 113, art. 10. We may here, I think, link St. Thomas with St. Bonaventure, and yet admit with Gillon (*loc. cit.*, p. 142) that "the problem of the vision of God is posed in very different terms for those who uphold Augustinian illumination and those who hold the theory of abstraction."

[9] *In 4 Sent.*, dist. 49, q. 2, art. 7.

[10] *De veritate*, q. 29, art. 3 ad 3um. Cf. S. Dockx, O.P., "Du désir naturel de voir l'essence divine d'après saint Thomas," *Archives de philosophie* (1964): 76. On all this see Gilson, "Sur la problématique thomiste de la vision béatifique" (*loc. cit.*, 1965).

[11] *Ordinatio*, prologus (*Opera omnia*, vol. 1, 1950, p. 58). For other examples, see *Augustinisme et théologie moderne* (Paris, 1965), chapters 6 and 7, Eng. trans. *Augustinianism and Modern Theology* (London: Chapman; New York: Herder & Herder, 1969).

that supernatural gift can be called "specific obediential power"—
"potentia obedientialis specifica hominis"—or "passive obediential
power." But it remains quite clear, from the explanations he has given
us, that for St. Thomas particularly, the simple idea of *obediential potency* conceived not "to express the condition in which God's gift places us
of being able to become children of God,"[12] but to account for the possibility of miracle, is not adequate as a definition of the relationship of
human nature to the supernatural. It does not lay sufficient stress on
"the absolutely special case of spirit."[13]

Now for Cajetan the idea of *obediential potency* is adequate. As Toletus pointed out: "[Cajetan] determined that the potency within us to
see God is *only obediential*."[14] In other words, Cajetan rejects St.
Thomas's principle: "the soul is naturally capable of grace";[15] he reverses
the contrast formulated by St. Thomas, and reduces the case of the
supernatural destiny of created spirit to a particular instance of miracle.
The fundamental reason for this reversal is that he has first reduced
human nature itself to a case merely of one species among others in his
consideration of natural beings. And this double mistake has very grave
consequences.

Already, slightly earlier than Cajetan (1468–1534), Denys the
Carthusian (1402–1471), a more individual and modern writer than he
is usually given credit for being, had expressly limited the desire of spiritual beings to the perfection which suited them "according to the natural dignity, grade, order and capacity of the species proper."[16] Slightly
intoxicated by the neo-Platonic reading provided for him in abundance
by his friend Nicholas of Cusa, he had derived from it the idea that, in

183

---

[12] Cf. Charles Journet, in *Nova et vetera* (1960), pp. 310–11.

[13] Cf. M. J. Le Guillou, O.P., "Surnaturel," *Revue des sciences philos. et théol.* 34 (1950):
233: "I see no disadvantage in speaking of *potentia obedientialis* if one is careful to note
that spirit is an absolutely unique case." L. Charlier, in *Ephem. theol. lovan.* 7 (1930): 20.
H. de Lubac, on St. Thomas, *Compendium theologicae*, c. 104, in *Recherches de Sc. rel.* 35
(1948): 300–305. A certain confusion between the order of grace and that of miracle was
fostered by the incautious analogical extension of this term. Cf. A. Darmet, *Les notions de
raison séminale et de puissance obédientielle chez saint Augustin et saint Thomas* (Belley, 1934).
A. R. Motte, *Bulletin thomiste* 4 (1936): 571. S. Dockx, *loc. cit.*

[14] "Reverendus Toledo in Caietanum, Contradictio prima." This text was published by
F. Stegmueller in *Revue thomiste* 17 B (1934): 360.

[15] *Prima Secundae*, q. 113, art. 10. St. Thomas refers back to Augustine, *De Trinitate*,
bk. 14, c. 8 ("he is his image in the very fact that he is capable of him . . .").

[16] *De puritate et felicitate animae*, art. 55 (*Opera omnia*, vol. 40, p. 431); cf. art. 61
(p. 434).

a hierarchical universe with many levels, every intelligence must naturally have as its last end the contemplation of the intelligence directly above itself. Man's natural end could not therefore be situated in this life at all, but must be to contemplate the lowest of the angelic natures. Only this end could arouse a natural desire in man, for "natural desire tends to the natural end."[17] At least, in this, Denys the Carthusian was fully aware that he was out of tune with the teaching of St. Thomas (and his disciple Giles of Rome).[18] Far from making any secret of it, he set out *ex professo* to refute him, disputing his arguments one by one :

> Saint Thomas strives to prove in many ways . . . that the natural desire of no created mind can rest or be contented, except by the divine substance specifically, as if it is known. . . .
>
> Therefore he [Saint Thomas] supposed that he had to prove. . . .[19]

184   Denys, we can see, "knows how to adapt . . . the traditional data to the needs of his age. . . ."[20] He thus opened the way for Cajetan. The latter's Aristotelianism differed profoundly from the former's neo-Platonism. But both none the less held the same basic position as far as our subject here is concerned, and it was one which is opposed to that held by St. Thomas. Like Denys, Cajetan wanted to see in the human *spirit* no more than the *human* spirit. Like Denys, he turned that spirit back upon itself, enclosing it in "its own species" in the same way as the lower natures: *"such* an intellect, i.e. of man."[21] Like Denys again, therefore, he thought that "if this supernatural order had not been added over and above by God, any intelligence [*intelligentia*] would have a nat-

---

[17] Ibid. And *De lumine christianae theoriae*, bk. 2, art. 56 (*Opera*, vol. 33, p. 454); bk. 1, art. 46–51 (pp. 288–93) etc.; p. 290: "Happiness is due to each according to the quality of its species."

[18] In fact, St. Thomas said such things as this (*Quodl.*, 10, art 17): "Whence we posit the beatitude of the rational creature on this, that it will see God essentially [*per essentiam*]: just as the philosophers, who posited that our souls flow from an acting intelligence, posited the final happiness of man in the accession of our intellect to it." Cf. *In 4 Sent.*, dist. 49, q. 2, art. 1.

[19] *De puritate* . . . , art. 56–61 (vol. 40, pp. 431–34). *De lumine christianae theoriae*, bk. 1, art. 51–52 (vol. 33, pp. 293–94). See however *Summa fidei orthodoxae*, bk. 3, art. 8, n. 1 (vol. 16, p. 343).

[20] G. Dumeige, in *Recherches de sc. rel.* 51 (1963): 311–12.

[21] *In Primam Secundae*, q. 3, a. 7, n. 1: "Just as it is fitting that the final perfection of the intellect as such be true essentially [*per essentiam*]; it suffices, however, that the final perfection of a specific [*talis*] intellect be true specifically [*tale*]."

ural end aside from sin instead of final beatitude."[22] Only, instead of openly refuting St. Thomas like Denys—who is thus a trustworthy witness to the way St. Thomas was understood in the generation immediately preceding Cajetan—Cajetan now claimed to be commenting upon him. It is hardly surprising, then, that he should find himself, as Mgr. G. Philips remarks, "in a great quandary when faced with many of the Angelic Doctor's statements."[23] What is rather more surprising is that so many modern readers of Cajetan do not seem to notice the fact. Yet his commentary on the *Summa Theologica* bears evident traces of it. Thus he admits that to judge by St. Thomas's text it certainly seems "that there is in the soul a natural capacity for grace,"[24] or again, that in places the words used by St. Thomas "are not without ambiguity."[25] One may well regret that, despite that "great quandary," he remained so fixed in his false principle and his false argument that he did not "let himself be shaken."[26]

185

We also see that it is not to Jesuit theology, to Suarez or Molina that we should attribute—as is sometimes done—the authorship of the theory that sees human nature "as a closed and self-sufficient whole."[27] Cajetan is, if not quite the first initiator of it,[28] at least its patron and

[22] *In Primam,* q. 63, a. 3, n. 13: "In this way the philosophers posited these beings to be happy." But St. Thomas precisely did not follow these "philosophers"; as against them he put forward quite a different idea of the human spirit and its destiny.

[23] *Ephem. theol. lov.* (1954): 110, summarizing and commenting on the thesis of Juan Alfaro, S.J., *Lo Natural y lo Sobrenatural, estudio historico desde Santo Tomas hasder Cayetano* (Madrid, 1952). Ibid., p. 111: it is clear from this work that, in the fourteenth and fifteenth centuries, "thinkers of all schools, Thomist, Scotist, nominalist, Augustinian, with but rare exceptions, maintained at once the supernaturalness of the vision, and the existence of a natural desire. The only author of note who heralded Cajetan—and whom Cajetan probably did not know—was Denys the Carthusian."

[24] *In Primam Secundae,* q. 113, a. 10, n. 1: "The first doubt concerns this: The soul is naturally capable of grace. So it seems, according to this teaching, that there is in the soul a natural potency to grace. . . . We said the opposite of this against Scotus in the First Part. . . ."

[25] *Op. cit.,* q. 3, a. 8, n. 1: "are not without ambiguity" [*non ambiguitate carent*] (with regard to the desire to know the first cause in itself). Or again, *In Tertiam,* q. 4, a. 1, n. 6, where Cajetan tries to connect the case of the ability to receive the beatific vision with that of the ability of human nature to be "assumed" by a divine person: "according to the conclusions mentioned here and there."

[26] G. Philips, *loc. cit.,* p. 111.

[27] See, for instance, Karl Eschweiler.

[28] As well as Denys the Carthusian, one may count among their precursors the Spaniard Alfonso Tostat (1400–1455), a prolix writer whose thought was mediocre and

leading authority. It was chiefly he who introduced it into Thomism and, more precisely, actually into the exegesis of St. Thomas himself, thus conferring upon it a kind of usurped authority. Cajetan was followed by Koellin and Javelli, who show signs of being in the same quandary as their master before them, yet they have the same strange assurance. This is not primarily a value-judgment, but a statement of fact upon which it would seem that everyone ought to agree, and which in fact is gradually coming to be accepted: the interpretation by Cajetan and his emulators, which largely determined later Thomism, is far from being wholly faithful to the text on which they are commenting. Without doubt it falsifies the sense.[29]

186   For a long time, there have been good theologians in plenty to point this out. For instance, around the end of the last century, Sestili wrote: "Now Cajetan, though most learned and the foremost interpreter of Saint Thomas, nevertheless in this matter seems patently to depart from Saint Thomas, and is certainly the first to cast doubt on the question."[30] For the rest, whether they agreed with him or not, the major theologians of the sixteenth century made no mistake: they speak of Cajetan far less as an exact interpreter of St. Thomas than as the leading exponent of a new line of thought. Soto, for instance, finds that Cajetan's "gloss" is "tortuous," and that it "destroys the text" of its author.[31] Toletus is equally severe.[32] Not long afterwards, Gregory of Valencia (d. 1604) made no bones about the commentator's infidelity: "Cajetan spoke out of step" [*minime congruenter*].[33] There followed Prudentius, Macedo and many others. Suarez too is well aware that Cajetan's explanation is a modern thesis, the thesis of the "moderniores," though Suarez himself is faithful to the habitual eclecticism which made him

---

without coherence: *In Matthaeum*, c. 22, q. 228; c. 25, q. 648–73 (*Opera*, vol. 11, pp. 133–34; vol. 12, pp. 385, 399).

[29] "It is not merely the proper meaning of the words, but the good sense of St. Thomas himself that is being questioned," wrote Père de Broglie concerning Cajetan in *Rech. de sc. rel.* 14 (1924): 196.

[30] *Op. cit.*, p. 908. Other authors are quoted in chapter 1, *supra*.

[31] "This gloss . . . destroys the text [*destruit textum*]. . . . Cajetan says, . . . but this gloss is tortuous . . . ;" "Nor is the solution of Cajetan valid . . . ;" etc.: *De sacra doctrina, In Primam*, q. 1 (ed. Candido Pozo, S.J., *Archivo teologico Granadino* 21 [1958]: 217–19, nn. 8 and 9).

[32] *In Primam*, q. 1, a. 1, and the text published by Stegmueller (see *supra*, note 14). Cf. *Augustinisme et théologie moderne*, chap. 5, Eng. trans. *Augustinianism and Modern Theology*.

[33] *Commentaria theologica*, vol. 2 (3d ed., Lyons, 1603), col. 99.

"the most deserving man of all the schools of theologians and philosophers,"[34] and he goes on to try to minimize its novelty; he is well aware
that it introduces a new element in considering a certain "third state,"
which its inventors, he tells us, describe as "purely natural."[35] A Spanish
theologian, Juan Alfaro, S.J., has recently taken up the question again;
having first of all determined that Cajetan's own contribution was no
more than a certain extension of the traditional doctrine of the Thomist
school,[36] he is then led to conclude, after a long and painstaking historical enquiry, something quite different. Cajetan, he thinks, gives the
appearance of refuting the arguments of Duns Scotus, but in reality "at
the same time broke from the position consciously defended by the
thomistic theologians"; he "abandons the traditional thesis of the
Thomistic School during the fourteenth and fifteenth centuries regarding the innate appetite to see God."[37]

187

Suarez was not content merely to set out the teaching of Cajetan
and the "moderniores"; unlike Soto and Toletus, he approved of it. Like
Cajetan, and certain moderns, it was apparently only Duns Scotus and
his "innate desire" that he wished to attack. In effect he yielded to the
movement of his age, and abandoned the whole of the old school. Like
the great cardinal's commentary, the *De ultimo fine hominis* of the prince
of Jesuit theologians declares that every "appetite of nature" is neces-

---

[34] Lessius, *De gratia efficaci* (Antwerp, 1610), preface.

[35] *De gratia*, Proleg. 4, c. 1, n. 2: "Cajetan and the modern theologians considered a
third state, which they called purely natural, which, although it did not exist in fact, nevertheless could be thought possible" (ed. Vivès, vol. 7, p. 179). With Cajetan, as with
Suarez, this question of "natura pura" is directly bound up with the concept of man set
out here. Such is not the case with Bellarmine.

[36] In the published pages of his Roman thesis, *Lo natural y lo sobrenatural segun Card.
De Vio Cayetano, Contenido, Fuentes, Originalidad* (Rome, 1950), the author writes: "The
personal contribution of Cajetan in this problem is limited to the achievement of a certain
progress of reduced dimension, within the traditional doctrine of the Thomistic School
and in the direction marked by it. This progress consists only in stating more clearly and
more frequently, and above all in introducing into the whole theology a theory toward
which , in any case, thomistic theology converged necessarily" (pp. 69–70).

[37] *Lo Natural y lo Sobrenatural* . . . (Madrid, 1952), p. 243. There remain some elements of the preceding judgment, though generally more prudent, to be found on p. 412.
Considering this work in the *Revue des sciences philosophiques et théologiques* (1954): 525,
Père Duval wrote, in a praiseworthy desire to make peace: "When Cajetan rejects all natural desire for the beatific vision, he is carrying as far as it will go a point of view shared by
all those who had earlier upheld the possibility of such a desire, that is that such a desire
could not be efficacious." We may note however that St. Thomas and the others did not
state the "possibility," but the actual existence of such a desire. See *supra*, p. 7, note 29.

sarily efficacious in its order, and therefore that such an appetite cannot extend beyond what is possible to the nature which feels it:

> The natural appetite is efficacious in its own order; whence it does not extend beyond what is possible to nature.
>
> Likewise: That which is not possible is not a good in the order of nature: but the appetite tends to the good; therefore the natural appetite tends only to what is good in the natural order.[38]

188

Thus Suarez too believes this to be a first principle, an axiom, a "general conception of the mind" [*communis animi conceptio*], as Boethius puts it. For him, it is without any possible doubt one of those fundamental truths "belonging to the universal patrimony of the human spirit."[39] And he makes no more attempt to prove it than Cajetan. But he draws from it this direct consequence, which was henceforth to be so often repeated: "It is repugnant that an end be supernatural with respect to pursuit [*consecutio*] and natural with respect to appetite, *since the natural appetite is found only in natural potency*. Hence, if the beatitude of heaven is natural with respect to the tendency and intention of the natural appetite, it is natural with respect to any natural perfection."[40]

In speaking thus, we may say that Suarez is stressing "less what properly characterizes the human soul than what it has in common with non-rational natures,"[41] or rather, that he does not see sufficiently well one of the essential points that marks its special characterization. That is why, like Cajetan before him, he refers, with no attempt to justify doing so, to what Aristotle says in the *De caelo* of the movement of the stars: "Nature, in giving them the inclination to a certain motion, gives them the organs for it."[42] That this is relevant seems to him to go with-

---

[38] *De ultimo fine hominis*, dissertatio 18, sectio 2, n. 11 (ed. Vivès, vol. 4, p. 154).

[39] This latter expression, which I use in quite a different context, comes from Père A. d'Alès in *Rech. de sc. rel.* 21, p. 241.

[40] *De gratia*, Proleg. 4, c. 1, n. 8 (Vivès, vol. 7, p. 181).

[41] Blaise Romeyer, S.J., in *Archives de philosophie*, vol. 18, p. 59: "Francis Suarez, like others before him, speaks . . . only of 'obediential capacity.' Scholastics of every school came to do so after him and with him. Did not their Aristotelianism on questions of cosmology and human psychology, however, lead them to lay less stress on what properly characterizes the human soul than on what it has in common with irrational natures? Certainly it made them tend in that direction. . . ." Père Romeyer none the less followed Suarez: cf. *infra*.

[42] *De ultimo fine*, dissert. 16, sectio 2, n. 11 (Vivès, vol. 4, p. 154). Ibid., n. 10 (p. 153): "The innate appetite is infused in the natural potency; but in man there is no potency to supernatural beatitude; therefore there is not such innate appetite." There is the same

out saying; the vital corrections brought to Aristotelianism by St. 189
Thomas are forgotten. He asks again quite candidly: "All other natures
are able to pursue their natural ends by means suitable to their nature:
why then is human nature of a worse condition in this?"[43] Medina reasons like Suarez,[44] as does Báñez, who refers to Cajetan and adopts the
argument drawn from the *De caelo*.[45] John of St. Thomas was soon to
follow, reasoning similarly, not without a certain derivativeness.[46] He
too asks how one can conceive that man could not find satisfaction in
gaining a completely natural end, since all other beings, even inanimate
ones, can: "since, finally, it is granted to any thing, even inanimate?"[47]

Since then the argument has been repeated for three centuries,
never advancing, never establishing its bases. Among the theologians
who adopt it, a certain number at least think and speak of themselves as
strict Thomists, without seeming to notice that they are flatly contradicting St. Thomas. It would be tedious to enumerate them. I need only
mention a few of the most recent, by way of example. There is Canon
Gombault, who asserts that a natural desire to "see" God can only
envisage a wholly natural knowledge of God which provides a natural
happiness.[48] There is Père Garrigou-Lagrange, who writes: "God, the
author of our nature, could not give us the innate natural desire for an
end to which he could not lead us *ut auctor naturae*. The order of agents
would no longer correspond to the order of ends."[49] One could hardly
dictate terms to God with more assurance! There is Père Ambroise
Gardeil, who considers that "to the innate desire there necessarily cor- 190
responds in nature the effective power to realize it, an active power,
making use of appropriate natural means, or at least a passive power,
which requires the correlative active power to make it actual";[50] he

---

appeal to the argument from the *De Caelo* in the author of the marginal note to the text
of Toletus (Stegmueller, *loc. cit.*, p. 363).

[43] *Op. cit.*, dissert. 15, sectio 2, n. 6 (vol. 4, p. 148).

[44] *In Primam Secundae*, q. 3, a. 8 (Venice, 1590), p. 46.

[45] *In Primam Partem*, vol. 1 (Venice, 1587), col. 447–54. Báñez criticizes the formula
used by Scotus and Soto, but his disagreement goes deeper.

[46] This was pointed out by Père Gardeil, *Structure de l'âme et l'expérience mystique*[2]
(1927), vol. 1, p. xix. It is certainly true in this instance.

[47] *Cursus theologicus*, Disp. 12, a. 3, n. 7 and 8 (Solesmes ed., vol. 2, pp. 140–41).

[48] *Le problème apologétique*.

[49] "Le désir naturel du bonheur prouve-t-il l'existence de Dieu?" *Angelicum* (June
1931): 142, note. This would mean the same even if one added the word "innate" to qualify "natural desire."

[50] *Op. cit.*, vol. 1, p. 282. Thus the author thinks he is showing "the disadvantages of
the Scotist position, which makes the supernatural all of a piece with nature."

takes up the induction made by Cajetan and others:

> There is no example of a natural appetite that is not accompanied by the active means to fulfill it. Hunger tends to food, the eye calls for light, but they also possess . . . an organism of means which enables them to take hold of these things. But we do not see that intellectual nature has at its disposal natural energies and instruments that would be capable of taking hold of God. . . .[51]

It is this same principle that is invoked in opposition to the view of Blondel by Père Joseph de Tonquédec in his *Deux études sur "la Pensée"* (1936). For him "a *desire of nature* is essentially proportionate to nature"; it cannot "go towards anything outside the possibilities, the capacities of nature"; in effect, "nature cannot aspire to what would burst its limitations, abolish its proper characteristics, and thus destroy it." Père de Tonquédec considers this as evidence.[52] However, since he wants to interpret not only the evidence but also St. Thomas, he brings in as proof a text from the *De malo* about the sin of Lucifer: according to this text Lucifer did not want to become God's equal, since such a wish would be an impossibility. Such a text, if it proves anything, proves too much: but it does not really bear on our subject at all. What St. Thomas is declaring impossible is not the natural desire to see God, but the ambition to be equal to God; the devil, he says, could not truly want "to be equal to God" because the thing is metaphysically impossible. The discussion in this passage has no bearing on any kind of natural desire, but only on a conscious act of the will, on the nature of one particular disordered will, on a sin. (The text is in fact one of those used, and justifiably so, to show that for St. Thomas normal liberty in the form of peccability is inscribed in the very nature of spirits.) Freely forming a wish to be equal to God is not desiring with natural desire to see God, or as St. Thomas says, naturally desiring beatitude, which consists in seeing God. He thinks this latter so far from impossible in the sense in which the former thing is, that he ends his exposition by saying: "[The devil] sinned by striving . . . for final beatitude, not according to due order, that is, not as it ought to be pursued according to the grace of God."[53] Rather than refer to a text with so little relation to the sub-

191

---

[51] "Le désir naturel de voir Dieu," *Revue thomiste* (1926): 385–86.
[52] *Deux études sur "la Pensée,"* p. 149.
[53] *De Malo*, q. 16, a. 3. Cf. John of Paris, *In 2 Sent.*, q. 26 (J. P. Muller, p. 90).

ject, it would have been preferable to examine at least some of the texts which deal directly with it, of which there are so many in St. Thomas and which are so contrary to the so-called "evidence."

These few examples bring to mind a very temperate observation made half a century ago by Dr. Joseph Sestili, about this very question:

> The doubt [concerning the mind of Saint Thomas] arises from the fact that certain authors, out of a defect of discipline, attempt to remove what is clear by means of uncertainties rather than to explain uncertainties with clear things. And certainly, on this question the teaching of Saint Thomas is considered [*habetur*] to be clear and abundant in his chief works . . . among which are the *Summa theologica* and the *Summa contra Gentiles*. . . . And still they hunt down arguments for explanation in those places where the thesis is not advanced in the same terms, or where the word appears incidentally. This truly is to remove what is clear by means of uncertainties.[54]

Quite recently the argument appeared again, unchanged, under the pen of Père Pedro Descoqs, who gave as his major premise a principle "deriving directly from the principle of sufficient reason."[55] "Desire is natural," he declares, "in so far as the goal to which it aspires is proportionate to nature, in other words, possible to it."[56] One may note, however, that Descoqs makes no reference to St. Thomas whom, as we know, he hardly considers an authority. Père Blaise Romeyer, too, directly invokes only the authority of Suarez in the matter.[57] And finally we must acknowledge a similar discretion in Père Charles Boyer; he is in fact well aware of what St. Thomas says so often of created spirit that does not enjoy the vision of God: "it does not rest" [*non quiescit*]. Thus he does not credit him, at least in the article I quote from here, with

192

[54] "Quod omnis intellectus . . . ," *loc. cit.*, p. 961.

[55] "Autour du mystère de notre élévation surnaturelle," *Nouvelle Revue théologique* (1939): 416–17.

[56] *Le mystère de notre élévation surnaturelle* (Paris, 1938), p. 120.

[57] *Loc. cit.*, pp. 38–39: "The only natural good is that to which I tend by the weight of my nature, as to my last end. And to any good I cannot attain to without grace, I cannot without grace incline with the whole force of my being. That is why Suarez teaches as a doctrine necessary to the understanding of our supernatural end, that it was possible for God to have created man without raising him to a supernatural end." This possibility "for God" is not in question here. On the other hand, by speaking of the "weight of nature" [*pondus naturae*] and removing the problem into that area of the possibilities we recognize for God (in which all Catholic theologians are unanimous), the author returns to precisely the confusions which I am trying to clarify.

that principle he considers universal: "A nature is an essence which *rests content* with the good that is proportionate to it." He merely makes clear that this seems to him not Aristotelianism, but something "reason must admit." This will hardly satisfy all the disciples of St. Thomas. In any case, the discussion will remain open.[58]

"It is rare," Anatole France once said, "for any master to belong to the school he has founded as firmly as his disciples do."[59] Sometimes, indeed, he is not of their school at all. Let us say once more, with Etienne Gilson: "The immutability and fidelity to themselves of which the schools boast are often only apparent."[60] St. Thomas argued on this point quite differently from many of the "Thomists" of today and yesterday—even those who do not refer to Suarez. He never stopped attacking the false principle and the false analogy we have been looking at. He did it as explicitly as it could be done, stressing on every occasion the condition at once paradoxical and privileged of created spirit. The texts I have already quoted are clear enough. There are others equally so whose object is to reject the comparison drawn from the heavenly bodies.[61] And his teaching appears quite clear, even in those texts most inspired by a wish to be conciliatory:

> The nature that can attain perfect good, although it needs help from without in order to attain it, is of a more noble condition than a nature which cannot attain perfect good, but attains some imperfect good, although it need no help from without in order to attain it, as the Philosopher says (*De Caelo* ii. 12). Thus he is better disposed to health who can attain perfect health, albeit by means of medicine, than he who can attain but imperfect health, without the help of medicine. And therefore the rational creature, which can attain the perfect good of happiness, but needs the Divine assistance for the purpose, is more perfect

193

---

[58] In *Gregorianum* 28 (1947): 300–301. Cf. *supra*, chapter 4. Among the theologians who hold the modern thesis, some recognize quite clearly, like Denys the Carthusian, that they are contradicting St. Thomas. Thus Arriaga, for instance, in 1643, in his *Disputationes in Primam Partem*, vol. 1 (Antwerp): *De visione Dei*, disp. 4, n. 1: "[The argument] that seems to have been that of Thomas is taken from universal appetite. . . . This line of reasoning, however, is in no way convincing. And thus finally Cajetan confesses. . . . Secondly, it is proven by Thomas. . . . I answer . . ." (pp. 65–66).

[59] *La Vie littéraire*, vol. 3, p. 320.

[60] *Le philosophe et la théologie* (1960), p. 121.

[61] Thus *De substantiis separatis*, c. 2. Or, as against those who speak of an action of the heavenly bodies upon our minds, this recalling of the general principle: "Intellect exceeds all bodies in the order of nature" (*Summa contra Gentiles*, bk. 3, c. 4).

than the irrational creature, which is not capable of attaining this good, but attains some imperfect good by its natural powers.[62]

One may admire St. Thomas's cleverness in undermining the analogy of the stars which attracted many people at the time, and which was later to attract Cajetan and his followers, by borrowing a principle from that same second book of the *De caelo* from which the analogy actually came. Thus he manages to use the philosopher to refute him, without appearing to attack him. He quotes him, as usual, just at the moment when he diverges basically from his doctrine, and by means of an ingenious comparison he succeeds in introducing the special case whose originality he is affirming under the guise of a general law.[63] The greatness of scholasticism was that it calmly overturned the old formulas while making the least possible change in their elegant outward appearance.[64] St. Thomas excelled at this.[65] No one was better at practicing this method, proceeding from a "sovereign indifference to history," which consisted not merely in "saving" the philosopher as far as he could,[66] but in "placing his most personal creations" under his patronage, in "metamorphosing the doctrine he is commenting on by filling it with new meaning,"[67] in "shading the differences of doctrine to bring to

194

---

[62] *Prima Secundae*, q. 5, a. 5, ad 2um. Cf. *Rev. Toledo in Caietanum,* Contradictio prima: "In many instances we see the natural appetite, but the act is wanting. . . . One truly would have to wonder at this, and therefore reject it, if the act toward which the natural potency and the genuine propensity exist were impossible. Further, God himself is always ready and prompt to bring assistance. For indeed what we can do with friends, we seem to be able to do by ourselves, says Aristotle" (Stegmueller, p. 363).

[63] Cf. the trenchant remarks of Gilson, *L'esprit de la philosophie médiévale* (Paris, 1932), vol. 1, p. 244, Eng. trans. *The Spirit of Medieval Philosophy* (London, 1936), p. 243. And *supra,* p. 108.

[64] Cf. Maurice Nédoncelle, *Existe-t-il une philosophie chrétienne?* (Paris, 1956), p. 68, Eng. trans. *Is there a Christian Philosophy?* (London, 1960).

[65] St. Bonaventure is sometimes less hesitant to criticize Aristotle openly. Thus *In Hexaemeron,* collatio 6 (Quaracchi, vol. 5, pp. 360–61), *De donis Spiritus sancti,* coll. 8, n. 16 (5, 497), *In 2 Sent.* (2, 17 and 23), though his attitude is often similar to that of St. Thomas.

[66] Thus, *In 4 Sent.,* dist. 49, q. 1, a. 1, q. 4, solutio, having disagreed quite sharply with Aristotle ("this position does not seem to be rational"), St. Thomas ends by leaving the door slightly open to save him: "I do not deny, however, that there may be some participation in beatitude in this life . . . , and concerning this happiness the Philosopher, in the *Ethics,* sets another life, which is after this life, neither affirming nor denying being [*ens*]."

[67] Etienne Gilson, *Le Thomisme*[4], pp. 117, 139. Also his "Cajetan et l'humanisme théologique," *Archives d'histoire doctrinale et littéraire du moyen âge* (1956): 130, 135. Cf. *Le philosophe et la théologie* (1960), p. 164: "Such a metamorphosis [of the God of Aristotle

light a factitious harmony,"[68] to such an extent that many of those who
came after him have been deceived by it.

"It is as summary to describe St. Thomas as an Aristotelian as to
describe the Cistercian mystic as a Ciceronian."[69] St. Thomas bases his
concept of man on solid natural foundations which he owes in large
195   measure to Aristotle. This is indisputable. He situates the human soul
in its rightful place in the hierarchy of forms, making it a principle of
unity like the other forms of nature. But "his own conception of the
human soul as an intellectual substance capable of subsisting without
the body" is a far cry from Aristotle.[70] With his theory of the "human
composite" he is none the less also, in essentials, heir to the Augustinian doctrine of the spirit (*mens*), as Père Ambroise Gardeil has recently
most opportunely reminded us, though he does not indicate all that is
involved in the fact.[71] He was certainly not the prisoner of any more or
less naturalist system of thought, whether Aristotelian or neo-Platonist.
On this fundamental point he spoke like the Augustinians of the previous century, who said: "Only the rational creature is so made that it is
not its own good, but he by whom it was made is; it is then a great dignity, that no good but the highest should be sufficient for it. . . ."[72] He
speaks like the theologians of the preceding generation: "The intellect is
so noble that it has an action so noble and an object so noble that it be
above itself."[73] He also shows that he is in perfect agreement with the

into the Christian God] goes far beyond what one can call, however freely one uses the
term, 'a few modifications.'" R. A. Gauthier notes that on the subject of beatitude "it
seems that St. Thomas did not recognize the extent" of the break with Aristotle "which
originated in the depths of his Christian consciousness; in any case, he did not denounce
the philosopher's error, and only corrected it without seeming to touch upon it at all"
("Trois commentaires 'averroïstes' sur l'Ethique à Nicomaque," *Archives d'hist. doct. et litt.
du moyen âge* [1948]: 252). Stanislas Breton, *Saint Thomas d'Aquin* (1965), p. 19: "Creative incomprehension is the gift proper to genius."

[68] G. Théry, O.P., *David de Dinant* (1925), p. 90. See also Georges Ducoin, S.J.,
"Saint Thomas commentateur d'Aristote," *Recherches de philosophie* 1 (1955): 85–107.

[69] M. D. Chenu, *Introduction à l'étude de saint Thomas d'Aquin* (1950), pp. 26–27.

[70] Gilson, "Cajetan et l'humanisme théologique," *loc. cit.,* p. 130. For another example of St. Thomas' conciliatory explanations without doctrinal compromise, see *Prima
Secundae,* q. 111, a. 1, on the hierarchical principle in Denys.

[71] *Op. cit.,* vol. 1, p. xxix. On the need for a more effective return to this teaching, see
Noël, translation of Tauler, especially vol. 8, p. 316.

[72] Hugh of St. Victor, bk. 1, tit. 7, *De dignitate et libertate rationalis creaturae* (PL, 177,
482–83). The text adds: "and likewise the great freedom that it cannot be compelled to its
own good."

[73] Alexander of Hales, *Summa theologica,* n. 510 (vol. 2, p. 748), reply to the 10th
objection.

originators of the Franciscan school, whose line of thought could be summed up in the unceasingly repeated axiom: "The greater the creature, the more it needs God" [*quo maior creatura, eo amplius eget Deo*];[74] or: "There is a greater dignity in the intellectual nature that it be ordered to a perfection greater than what it can attain by its own powers."[75] Of course, making first of all less use of the physical analogy than did the Thomist school, these theologians were naturally less likely to fall into the comparison we have noted. But none of this applies to St. Thomas himself: he was far indeed from taking for identity or parallelism what was really only analogy, really an unlikeness rather than a likeness.[76] To the objection of the "philosophers," as formulated soon afterwards by Duns Scotus: "This vilifies nature, that it cannot pursue its perfection by its natural powers [*naturalibus*]," we may say that he had already given in substance the same reply as Scotus: "In this, nature is more dignified." He had already shown, as Scotus does, that in fact it is a mark of superiority for that nature to have such a "passive capacity" for a perfection which no created nature could achieve by its own "active causality." And like Scotus too, if the objection were raised of the principle from the *De caelo:* "since nature is less deficient towards better things" [*minus deficiat in melioribus*], he would reply firmly: "what is adduced is not to the point" [*illud quod adducitur non est ad propositum*].[77]

196

Thus it is in perfect fidelity to the teaching of the leaders of both great schools—of whom Cajetan betrayed the first while appearing to make use of him to refute the second—that Soto could write, of the desire for the vision of God:

[74] Ossuna, etc. Cf. the articles by Père Michel-Ange, *Ossuna et Duns Scot, Etudes franciscaines,* 1910.

[75] B. Mastrius of Meldula, *In primum librum Sententiarum,* disp. 6, q. 2 (Venice, 2d ed., 1675, vol. 1, p. 383).

[76] See, for instance, *Prima Secundae,* q. 41, a. 3: "There is a natural love; we may also speak of desire and hope as being even in natural things devoid of knowledge" [*Est amor quidam naturalis, et desiderium, et spes potest quodammodo dici etiam in rebus naturalibus cognitione carentibus*]. We also see from this that the analogy worked both ways for him.

[77] Duns Scotus, *De ordinatione,* Prologue, q. 1, n. 26: ". . . In this, nature is more dignified than if the supreme [happiness] possible to it were placed in it naturally; nor is it any wonder, that there be in a certain nature a passive capacity to perfection greater than its active causality extends" (*Opera omnia,* vol. 1, Rome, 1950, p. 47). Cf. *Lectura . . .* (vol. 16, 1960, p. 16). *Reportata,* q. 3, n. 7: "And I am not here vilifying the superior nature; rather I am dignifying it. . . ." Cf. Paul Vignaux, "Humanisme et théologie chez Jean Duns Scot" in *La France franciscaine, Recherches de théologie, philosophie, histoire* (1936), pp. 223–24.

Cajetan says that Saint Thomas is speaking of man with the knowledge of faith. . . . But Saint Thomas is speaking of man absolutely, and mentions man in his natural powers, and he says of him that he has a natural desire to see God.

But the argument is this: Aristotle, de Caelo 50 and 59, says that if nature had given to the stars an inclination to motion, it would have given them the potency and the instruments. . . . Therefore, if nature has not given us the instruments by means of which we might arrive to beatitude, it is a sign that he did not give us a natural inclination toward it either. To this I answer that in this God dignifies our nature more, because he gave us the supernatural potency to pursue [beatitude].[78]

197

And we have an equally faithful witness later in Gregory of Valencia:

This is the argument of the excellence and dignity of human nature: that it is not sufficient for it unto the highest beatitude, because it could naturally and without divine assistance pursue it.[79]

With St. Thomas as with Duns Scotus, thus summed up by Soto and Gregory of Valencia, and with the unanimous tradition of the great period of theology—which has not been wholly without exponents in recent centuries—let us say it again: "In this, man is magnified, in this he is dignified, in this he surpasses every creature."[80] With all of them, and for the same fundamental reasons, we too must reject the principle and the analogy which, from their original place among the objections to be refuted,[81] have gradually worked their way in modern times into the body of doctrine. We shall not say, then, with Cajetan, as though speaking of different species within a single genus governed by the same laws: "in matter, or in the soul, or in any other thing." We shall not agree with him in determining the laws of spirit according to the laws of the stars. We shall reply that though Aristotle may well have been right

---

[78] *De sacra doctrina in Primam*, q. 1 (C. Pozo, *Archivo teologico granadino* 21 [1958]: 218, 223).

[79] *Commentaria theologica*, vol. 2, *In Primam Secundae*, disp. 1, q. 5, punctum 5 (3d ed., Lyon, 1603, col. 117 C). Cf. vol. 1, col. 1219–29.

[80] Cf. St. Thomas, *De malo*, q. 5, art. 3; *Summa contra Gentiles*, bk. 3, c. 147, etc. Petrus Trigosus (*loc. cit.*, p. 12). See my own *Le drame de l'humanisme athée* (Paris, 1963), pp. 15–20.

[81] It was thus for Scotus as for St. Thomas or St. Bonaventure. In *loc. cit.*, p. 1, n. 7 (vol. 1, p. 5), Scotus proposes the objection: "To every passive natural potency corresponds a certain active natural [potency], otherwise the passive potency in nature would seem ineffectual [*frustra*], if it could be reduced to action by nothing in nature." For the answer see ibid., n. 74ff. (vol. 1, pp. 45ff.).

about the stars, the analogy could not in any circumstances apply to men.[82] We shall not be misled by an apparent induction which is really begging the question. We shall take exception to any arguments based on so deceptive a method. We shall realize too that by presenting his thought on the matter in the form of a commentary on the *Summa,* Cajetan was really, as Gilson has said, producing a *Corruptorium sancti Thomae,* "the most effective," alas, "ever written."[83] We shall give our support instead to those who, during recent centuries, have spoken against the analogy drawn from the *De caelo,* such men as the famous Cardinal Brancati de Lauria (1612–1693), a religious, "one of the most learned theologians of his time":

> Now potency to beatitude is not ineffectual [*frustratoria*] since man can pursue it by the assistance of God. Indeed nature gave [man] passive and active potency toward it, but not proximate [potency] nor proximate dispositions, because pure nature cannot give these. God therefore, operating in the natural order, gave intellect to nature, and also a will inclined to the vision and possession [*fruitio*] of him; he did not give it in this order the other requisites to see and possess him, but rather in

---

[82] Cajetan, *De potentia neutra,* q. 2, ad 4um, 3⁰. Cf. ibid., ad 1um: ". . . whether potencies found in natural things in which supernatural acts are received are naturally inclined toward them." Cf. Henri Rondet, S.J., "Le problème de la nature pure au XVIᵉ siècle," *loc. cit.,* p. 492, on Cajetan, *In Primam,* q. 1, nn. 9–10: "Here Cajetan reads his master with the same *a priori* approach as he used for St. Augustine. . . . He should have discussed the pages where St. Thomas shows us that the greatness of the rational creature is precisely his unceasing dependence upon God, and the fact of having to expect from another the end for which he was made. But Cajetan has told us earlier that the obediential potency [*potentia obedientialis*] is the aptitude of a thing [*aptitudo rei*] to do what God wills of it. . . ."

[83] "Cajetan et l'humanisme théologique," *Archives d'histoire doctrinale et littéraire du moyen âge* 22 (1956): 133–36. I would not of course qualify the whole of Cajetan's commentary thus.

On the essential point we are dealing with here, agreement would now seem to be general. See *supra,* chapter 1. Cf. Juan Alfaro, S.J., *Lo Natural y la Sobrenatural, estudio desde Santo Tomas haster Cayetano* (1952), p. 243. More recently, Mgr. A. Piolanti, in *Divinitas* 1 (1957): 95: "Di fronte all' imperversare del luteranesimo, che mescolava natura e sovrannatura, il Gaetano insistette sulla divisione e separazione dei due ordini in modo da negare alla sola natura qualunque desiderio naturale delle divina visione. Nel Commentario alla Summa egli ha dato al problema del soprannaturale una impostazione forzata; ha accentuato eccessivamente la distanza ricorrente tra natura e grazia." The author forgets however that Cajetan's commentary *In Primam Partem* was finished on 2 May, 1507, well before the appearance of "luteranesimo." On the other hand, to agree with St. Thomas in admitting a more organic link between nature and grace is not to admit any lesser "distanza" between them in themselves; quite the reverse in fact.

199   another order, ever raising human nature to another state and to the
number of the citizens of the heavenly Commonwealth [*caelestis Reipub-licae*]; and with a view to this state he cooperates with [nature] for the
attainment of beatitude, bestowing the light of glory and the habit of
charity, and making himself present to it in the fashion of an object [*per
modum obiecti*]: And so it is clear, that this inclination is not ineffectual
[*frustra*].[84]

We are thus reminded, by way of a warning against a dangerous tendency in the other direction, of the line of thought that was common to
all the great masters of scholasticism because common to the whole of
the tradition they were nourished by.

"The comparison fails [*non est similis ratio*]," pronounced St. Thomas:

> Irrational creatures are not ordered to an end higher than that which is
> proportionate to their natural powers: consequently the comparison
> fails.[85]

And again, quoting and rejecting the argument drawn from the *De
caelo:*

> The rational creature, which can attain the perfect good of beatitude,
> but needs divine assistance for the purpose, is more perfect that the irra-
> tional creature, which is not capable of attaining this good, but attains
> some imperfect good by its natural powers.[86]

Those who, after too cursory a reading of St. Thomas, have mistaken
the objection here for the reply—and many have done this quite
recently—have done so in the name of the "pure Aristotelianism" which
St. Thomas is supposed to have professed. But their erroneous reading
is the result of a more fundamental and twofold error: on the one hand,

---

[84] Laurentius Brancatus de Laurea, *Commentaria in quatuor Libros Sententiarum,* Disput. 15, *De appetitu beatitudinis,* art. 6, n. 137 (Rome, 1665), vol. 4, p. 339.

[85] *Prima Secundae,* q. 91, a. 4, ad 3um. The objection was this: "Human nature is more
sufficient than irrational creatures. But irrational creatures do not have any divine law
beyond the natural inclination given to them. Therefore the rational creature is far the
lesser. . . ." There is the same rejection of the analogy, in regard to the peccability of spirit,
in *De veritate,* q. 24, a. 7, ad 5um. Cf. *In 2 Sent.,* dist. 23, q. 1, art. 1, ad 2um: "There is no
comparison between the corporeal and the spiritual creature."

[86] *Prima Secundae,* q. 5, a. 5 (Whether Man Can Attain Happiness by His Natural
Powers), ad 2um. Cf. the objection: "Since man is more noble than irrational creatures, it
seems that he must be more sufficient than they. But irrational creatures can attain their
end by their natural powers. Much more therefore can man attain beatitude by his natural powers."

what they take for pure Aristotelianism is in fact more of a "Wolffian rationalism," and on the other—which is what concerns us here—they fail to recognize the profound originality of Thomist thought, which involves the contribution of "the Christian experience of the human soul with the capacity for God [*capax Dei*]."[87]

200

"I answer that it is not the same [*non est simile*]," said St. Bonaventure, similarly:

> The objection is that in all creatures, if they are distant from the end to which they are ordered, is given the virtue by which they may attain that end; just as is clear in fire, which when it is down can be carried up by its lightness; therefore, either free will was more wretched among the other creatures, or, if other creatures naturally have the potency to come to their end, it seems far more vigorous [*fortius*], because in this instance man would have potency [*posset*] through the virtue of nature before the state of wretchedness.
>
> To this objection, that other creatures can attain the end to which they are by the virtue of their nature, I answer that it is not the same thing; for the end of the rational creature is the highest good, which is above all nature. But the end of other creatures is a created good, which is within the confines of nature [*terminos naturae*]. Therefore the rational creature has a greater need of the gift of grace to be able to attain its end than do other creatures.[88]

This was the teaching expounded by Eudes Rigaud:

> Any other inferior creature has the virtue of attaining that for which it is, for it is not above it, since it is pure nature; not so man. . . .

---

[87] This is made clear by Père Louis B. Geiger, O.P., in "S. Thomas et la métaphysique d'Aristote" in *Aristote et saint Thomas* (Louvain, 1957), pp. 175–220, especially p. 217. Cf. André Hayen, S.J., in *Teoresi* (1954): 127. The same readers might also have been deceived by certain phrases in which St. Thomas speaks only of an elicited desire: this in regard to hope (*De spe*, q. 1, ad 8um), or charity (*In 3 Sent.*, dist. 27, q. 2, a. 2, ad 4um). In explaining St. Thomas one may, *mutatis mutandis*, apply what he himself says about the relationship between the natural world and the world of faith to the relationship between spirit and the material world. He borrows concepts and theories from the material world which, it must be realized, are only similes. Cf. *In Boetium De Trinitate*, q. 2, a. 3: "[In sacred philosophy we can make use of] the second, to make known through some similes that are to be made."

[88] *In 2 Sent.*, dist. 29, a. 1, q. 2 (Quaracchi, vol. 2, pp. 698–99). The fact that the objector speaks first of all of free will and not of nature in general makes no difference to the body of the objection, nor, therefore, to the answer. The expression "I respond, that it is not the same" is frequent in Bonaventure's works.

201   Nor for this reason was man inferior to the other creatures, for beyond that which he was by nature, he was also a rational creature. . . .

To strive for beatitude is of greater nobility than to have potency [*posse*] for any natural act, or to have potency to attain any natural object. . . .[89]

Such too was the teaching of the *Summa* of Alexander of Hales,[90] and such was to be that of Peter Olivi,[91] and of Matthew of Aquasparta who, still replying to the same objection, wrote: "Nor does it detract from the nobility of nature, that it does not by its virtue have potency from this; nay rather it is a witness to its nobility, that it is ordered to so noble an end . . .";[92] it was also the teaching of Duns Scotus, with his peremptory: "This is not to the point."[93]

Could there be a clearer, more definite condemnation in advance of the excesses of the modern idea, so pregnant with consequences? Can anyone genuinely believe that to turn the objection into the answer was really only a way of taking the answer to the objection "as far as it would go"? Can such a reversal possibly be termed merely a development, a kind of nuance added to the teaching of the past? Is it not, on the contrary, quite clear that there emerges from these texts of St. Thomas and St. Bonaventure, and similar texts, a certain concept of man which is certainly more paradoxical—there seems no way round that word—but also more harmonious and loftier than the one which later came to hold sway? The principle that human nature—and ultimately every other spiritual nature—cannot have a real desire, a truly ontological desire, for any but the end which it is capable of giving itself or which it can require as of right by forces at its own level: this principle, treated by so

202   many modern scholastics as a first principle, is simply, as Père Guy de

---

[89] *Quaestiones de gratia et libero arbitrio*, ed. P. Pergamo, *Studi Francescani* 7–8 (1935–36): 97–98. Cf. Lorenzo M. Berardini, O.F.M.Conv., *La nozione del soprannaturale nell'antica Scuola Francescana* (Rome, 1943), pp. 91–92.

[90] *Summa of Alexander*, no. 510 (Quaracchi, vol. 2, pp. 744, 747).

[91] *In 2 Sent.*, q. 56 (*Bibl. Franciscana medii aevi*, vol. 5, 1924, p. 301): "Both according to the Faith and according to right reason, it is established that every rational nature is essentially such that its proper and final end cannot be attained through created nature, but only through a supernatural agent. . . ." Olivi adds: "And nevertheless it would be heretical and erroneous to say that every rational nature essentially and naturally demands such a perfection and end, hence and for this reason natural to it. . . ."

[92] *De gratia*, q. 5 (p. 114).

[93] *De ordinatione*, prol., a. 1, n. 26 (*Opera omnia*, vol. 1, Rome, 1950, p. 47).

Broglie says, a "false piece of evidence."[94] "A truth of simple common sense and complete satisfaction," says one of its protagonists, Père Pedro Descoqs,[95] who supposes that he is thereby giving it authority. That indeed is precisely what it is: the fruit of that kind of dormant common sense which shuts the door to all truth, the fruit of that superficial "common sense" which rejects any paradox on the grounds of its being "incoherent" and a "misuse of words,"[96] and the fruit of that cheap "common sense" which is forever watering down Christianity, but which Christianity knocks sideways whenever it is taken seriously, either in thought or in life:

> Whenever a theory is established, and seems to give a certain satisfaction to common sense, yet pushes the human mind no further forward, then Christianity appears as the divine *stimulus,* and by its loftiest and most inaccessible dogmas overturns the artificial balance of a stultified "wisdom," to set reason to work to pursue itself. Not only does it shake it up, but by the dogmas I spoke of it provides it with a motive to return to itself, a means of reflecting upon and analyzing its own principles.[97]

It is not only rational speculation that profits in this way from that divine *stimulus* which any "common sense" philosophy would want to avoid: theological reflection also needs just that same stimulation if it is to remain worthy of the faith it aims to work out, to avoid the temptation towards facility and towards the constant slipping back into "common sense."

Furthermore, this "truth of simple common sense" is, as we have seen, contrary to the thought of all the great masters of scholasticism. St. Thomas, as we know, was perfectly well aware of this general principle so misused by modern "common sense": "Natural desire cannot be unless it can naturally be had for a thing."[98] But this makes it all the more important to note that he does not invoke it as a universal principle, and that he refuses to apply it automatically to the case of created

203

---

[94] As long ago as 1924, *Rech. de sc. rel.* 14, pp. 228–29, etc. Similarly L. Veuthey, *De naturali desiderio . . .* , *Miscellanea Franciscana* 39 (1939): 215.

[95] "Autour du mystère de notre élévation surnaturelle," *Nouvelle revue théologique* (1939): 416–17.

[96] Cf. D. Palmieri, *Tractatus de ordine supernaturali*[2] (1910), p. 155: "The parts of this system are incoherent, and there is misuse of words."

[97] Frédéric Morin, *Dictionnaire de philosophie et de théologie scolastiques,* vol. 1, col. 63–64 (Migne, *Encyclop. théol.,* vol. 21, 1856).

[98] *In 3 Sent.,* dist. 27, q. 2, a. 2, ad 4um.

spirit in relation to its last end.[99] It is not therefore to this particular Thomist principle that our "truth of simple common sense" leads us. Ontologically it can better be compared, *mutatis mutandis,* to the principle posed as an abstraction by Karl Marx in the last century. Man, say our new theologians, our "common sense" theologians, only desires the end he can attain.[100] "Nature in accordance with itself does not have an inclination unless it is within the limits of nature."[101] Man, says Marx similarly, never sets himself any problems he cannot resolve.[102] St. Gregory the Great, on the other hand, said: "If the soul were not so great, it would never put such questions; and if it were not so small, it would resolve at least the questions it puts."[103] And St. Leo the Great "This is the vigor of great minds . . . here fix desire, where it cannot cast its sight."[104] Thus, whether with being or with knowing, there is always the same human paradox, that fundamental paradox which forces us to recognize its parallel in the Christian paradox. This is the basis of that "humanism" which Paul Vignaux calls "medieval humanism,"[105] and which we can simply call Christian humanism, though it is something

204

[99] In the passage quoted, it is only question of an objective and particular desire, following upon a love of friendship. In other cases it is question of a desire that is not only effective, but efficient, or, as St. Thomas himself says (see supra, chapter 5), "sufficient." Thus *De Spe,* q. 1, a. 8; *Prima Secundae,* q. 62, a. 3; *De virtutibus in communi,* a. 10.

[100] Cf. Javelli, O.P., *In primum tractatum Primae Partis:* "From his knowledge of the effect of the first cause, namely eternal motion, [the pure philosopher] desires to know the first cause; and nevertheless it does not follow that he desires to know its essence, since he does not possess the faculty to attain to such a state" (fol. 21 v). This is reasoning that is not to be found in St. Thomas. However one can see that it could grow out of his text. Cf. my own *Sur les chemins de Dieu* (1956), pp. 169–73, Eng. trans. *The Discovery of God* (London, 1960), chapter 6.

[101] *In Contra Gentiles* (Sestili, vol. 1, 1897, p. 41).

[102] For him, as Etienne Borne says in *Passion de la Vérité* (1962), p. 169, "history is an atheist providence which provides humanity only with difficulties it can then abolish."

[103] St. Gregory, *Moralia in Iob,* bk. 8, c. 32, n. 54: "[Our mind] seeks to know what it is not equipped to answer to itself, and in its ignorance it falls short of what it seeks prudently [*sub eo ignara deficit, quid prudenter requirit*]. Considering itself at once broad and narrow, it does not know which alternative is true, because if it were not broad, it would at least discover exactly what it seeks" (*PL,* 75, 835 BC). Cf. J. B. Metz, in *Archives de philosophie* 24 (1961): 267, on "the spiritual destiny of man, who always has more questions in his head than he can answer for himself."

[104] *In Ascensione,* sermo 2, c. 1 (*PL,* 54, 397). Cf. E. Thurneysen, on the great critical questions which bring our whole humanity into question, those great questions of the beyond (*Dostoevsky,* London, 1964).

[105] *La philosophie au moyen âge,* pp. 132–33, Eng. trans. *Philosophy in the Middle Ages* (New York, 1959).

far more profound than what is usually meant by the term. Just as the "baskets" of the Buddhist scriptures, according to the Mahayana, "have no lids," so the human mind "has no ceiling,"[106] and if it is ever to find rest and joy in fulfillment, it can only be on condition—as St. Gregory again assures us[107]—of passing, by the grace of a higher power, beyond itself.

To sum up, in order to gain a coherent and simple picture of our subject, the intelligence must free itself of two errors of imagination: thinking of God in the same way as man, and thinking of man in the same way as a "natural being." What we may have begun by taking as essential preconditions for thought about this problem of man's supernatural end are no more than preconditions of imagination, approximations suggested by common sense, clumsy analogies, which must one by one (though in different ways) be ruthlessly criticized. Then, if the criticism appears justified, we must resolutely enter that "negative phase" I spoke of. We certainly shall not find a wholly satisfying position. Such positions, in regard either to basic human problems or to the essential requirements for understanding the faith, do not exist. Therefore this can only be the start of a reflection which, though firmly based and with a definite direction, is none the less destined never to come to any final conclusion. The human mind is so made—and it would be a lack of humility to dispute it—that though it can criticize its own representations (once it has become aware of them), it cannot replace them so easily with others. With methodical study it can discover just what is inadequate about those representations: Indeed it is in this activity, this act of identifying its own weakness, that its greatness is most apparent—for it is only in being judged that its weakness can be seen. But, on the other hand, the intellect will never produce the perfect formula which will bring its quest to an end. To do so would be to quit its human condition. That is why it may appear to us at some moments that this kind of work of critical reflection is something negative. It seems, at the least, to be compromising, by a series of over-subtle moves, the truth which we felt certain we possessed completely, though our spontaneous expression of it may admittedly have been clumsy. Beneath all the

205

---

[106] Cf. Henry Duméry, *La philosophie de l'Action* (1948), p. 172.

[107] *Moralia in Iob*, bk. 20, c. 27, n. 56: "Truly it attains the coolness of true happiness [*laetitiae viriditatem*] when, raised up by the grace of contemplation, it crosses itself over" (*PL*, 76, 171 B).

anthropomorphism, in all the concepts so largely assisted by imagination, at least it contained a certain truth. It held it *in tuto*. Are we quite certain that the truth itself is not now being brought into doubt?

Such is the objection—or rather the instinctive, unreasoning fear—which any real attempt at reflection always arouses. Such, we may say, is the temptation which is always there to stop the intellect from its work. The life of the mind cannot be conceived without an element of constant seeking: "As long as we live, we necessarily must always seek."[108] As with the life of the body, it cannot help giving rise to "restlessness." This is so even in the firmest declaration of faith. The proclamation of every dogma is like the lifting of every seal in the Apocalypse: "it is a kind of unleashing of problems on to mankind."[109] St. Thomas says of the believer: "the motion of his thinking remains restless in him,"[110] and indeed he himself gave the example "of a dialectic so active, of such a wind of indefinite discussion, that he learnt, as it has been said, to pose as many problems as he solved."[111] Only the activity of God is without movement—if one can express it thus.[112] And, conversely, only death is "wholly restful." Our intellect therefore doubts itself. In that seeking which is always "restlessness," and in that restlessness which is for ever an inner "dispute," it is afraid of finding itself divided within, of no longer recognizing itself, of finding itself drawn incessantly into a spiral of problems.[113] It is afraid of inducing vertigo in itself.

206

---

[108] Hugh of St. Victor, *De sacramentis*, bk. 2, P. 14, c. 9 (*PL*, 176, 570). Cf. St. Augustine, *De Trinitate*, bk. 15, c. 2, n. 2: "Faith seeks, intellect finds . . . and in turn the intellect still seeks him whom it found" (Bibl. august., 16, p. 422); *In Psalmum 118*, sermo 3, n. 1: "Thus this question is resolved so that a more difficult other one might arise" (*CCL*, 40, p. 1671); etc.

[109] *Paul Claudel interroge l'Apocalypse* (1952), p. 19, note. And Christian revelation appears "throughout history, as the great stimulus, and not the implacable yoke and hard servitude of reason" (Frédéric Morin, *Dictionnaire de philosophie et de théologie scolastiques*, vol. 1, avertissement: Migne, *3rd. Encyclop. théol.*, vol. 21, 1856, p. 10).

[110] *De veritate*, q. 14, a. 1, ad 5um. Similarly, *Secunda secundae*, q. 2, a. 1: the "cogitatio fidei" which gives birth to "theology" is not cut short but carried on by it.

[111] Louis Foucher, *La philosophie catholique au XIXᵉ siècle* (1955), p. 268.

[112] Cf. Scotus Erigena, *De divisione naturae*, bk. 1, c. 12: "I say that God is not moved outside of himself, but by himself, in himself, unto himself. . . . For he is not in himself properly said to be at rest or moved. These two statements seem to be opposite to each other: but true reason forbids opposites to be thought of or understood in him" (*PL*, 122, 453 A).

[113] Cf. the excellent commentary by Hugh of St. Victor, *In Eccl.*, hom. 17, on: *and he handed the world over to their disputes*. "His dispute itself afflicts [man]. Deservedly, for dis-

That there exist such uncontrolled reflections, such spiralling "restlessness," is only too clear. But what is not so clear is that in the present case the fear is unfounded. For we are dealing with an "understanding of faith," which must always presuppose at its base, as a first and permanent condition, the gift of faith itself. We are dealing with a search which is constantly guided by that faith. With such a guide it cannot take a false turning. It never tries to get beyond it. Furthermore, with inborn modesty it never seeks to possess it more securely. Faith has its own light, which can be far brighter in the intellect of a simple believer 207 than in that of the finest theologian. The effort of "understanding" cannot be directed to anything but a better reflective realization of the gift of faith—something not only of value in itself, but fulfilling a need in this. For both reasons such an effort is fully justified. But, let me say again, it develops wholly within that gift, and at every stage will be measured closely against it in its results.

Some people do not feel the need to make such an effort. Yet they often have an equal need, at the level upon which their natural thinking generally takes place, to give themselves a certain coherent view of dogma, a view more systematized than is the teaching of the Church, to make that teaching more assimilable to them and prevent possible errors. In short, they have just as much need for a certain theology. Hence there is a permanent usefulness in theories formed from concepts which belong to the common pattern of thought, and which are based upon representations that are not criticized too rigorously. Denys the Carthusian characterized such theories very well by saying that they appear "to include lesser difficulty and wonder, and to be effective for the satisfaction of the people."[114] Their intellectual worth may not be great. Yet to accept them, to give them a place while discerning their limitations, is not pure pragmatism, for they are useful not merely for this or that reason, but for the preservation of a truth. Though limited, their truth value is far from non-existent. Simply to reject them would result in error. At the beginning of this study I mentioned a case in point, referring to the so-called theory of *scientia media:* this remains a

pute always means restlessness and controversy. . . . And this restlessness is itself a great dispute that man has in his instability, so that he does not feel it, since he is divided and alienated so that he is not one whole. Consider now the great dispute that man works on earth. It is multiple, and drawn out, and excessively complex; with the result that it cannot easily come to an end until man himself receives his end . . ." (*PL*, 175, 237 CD).

[114] *Opera omnia*, vol. 26, p. 642.

necessary support for those who need to conceive the relationship
between grace and human freedom in an organized system, and who
cannot otherwise manage to preserve the idea of freedom adequately.[115] A similar example can be found in that other theory which
improves on St. Anselm by creating a conflict in God's mind between
justice and mercy; and there are many others.

208

Theories of this kind, though standing on apparently firm ground,
are not always without danger. Though their very mediocrity protects
them from any risk of rampant heterodoxy, they can none the less, by
producing too facile a solution, blur the paradox of faith. In any case,
no study that is really scrupulous about truth, as theology should aim to
be, could ever rest content with them. It is not that it wants to do away
with them: on the contrary, in a backward sweep it returns to their presuppositions, to look at them critically, and purge them of whatever is
over- imaginative and still unworthy of their divine object. This does not
produce any kind of mental wavering. Theology, in remaining subject to
that divine object as it is authentically put before it, is never without
solid roots or precise guide-lines. It is firmly orientated. Its "restlessness," according to the pattern of the human condition and the life of
faith, is healthy. Nor can it, in the nature of things, ever arrive at any
other theory that is final, complete and totally satisfying, for such a ter-
mination belongs neither to earth nor heaven. The whole of tradition
tells us this: it is one of the forms of the fruitfulness of the mystery that
it gives birth in man's mind to a movement which can never end. To be
afraid of it is a failure of faith. The believing intellect fearlessly gives
itself to this work, in a trusting humility, well aware that, far from ever
bringing into doubt the truth of the mystery which it first recognizes
and then permanently holds to, it tends only to show it more profoundly
and more wonderfully. "Far more wonderfully, and far more profoundly" [*longe mirabilius, longeque secretius*].[116]

---

[115] Père Auguste Valensin has justified this type of thinking intellectually by pushing
it to its extreme point, in a paragraph in his small work *Autour de ma Foi* (1948), pp.
114–16. Let us note, however, that such theories, though serving to maintain the truth
under examination, generally by that very fact compromise a complementary truth, which
it is often equally important to preserve. We know well enough what was the weakness of
Molinism. I have tried to show how the modern theory of "pure nature," with its notion of
natural beatitude and all that goes with it, fatally sacrificed other elements.
[116] St. Augustine, *Confessions*, bk. 11, c. 31, n. 41 (Bibl. august., 14, p. 342).

CHAPTER 9

The Paradox
Overcome in Faith

This mystery of the supernatural, which is the mystery of our divine   209
destiny, appears rather like the framework within which all the other
mysteries of revelation have their place. It can be envisaged under many
aspects; it poses many problems to the mind. The original scholasticism
was devoted chiefly to elucidating what follows from the fact that a created and therefore finite intelligence is called to see God directly, as he
is in himself. "No created substance can, by its own power, attain to
seeing God in his essence."[1] To see God "face to face," to know him "as
he knows himself," and thus to enter with him into a sharing of life and
of love—how is this possible? Later, especially since the sixteenth century, a different problem came to demand more attention. If it is true
that this vision of God "per essentiam" is none the less our destiny, it is
therefore the supreme good to which, in one way or another, "the desire
of our nature" tends: how then can it be wholly gratuitous? There is a
second paradox connected with the first. We are creatures, and have
been given the promise that we shall see God. The desire to see him is
in us, it constitutes us, and yet it comes to us as a completely free gift.
Such paradoxes should not surprise us, for they arise in every mystery;
they are the hallmark of a truth that is beyond our depth. "Faith
embraces several truths which appear to contradict one another." It "is
always a harmony of two opposing truths."   210

"There are," said Pascal, "many truths, both of faith and of morals,
which seem contradictory, and yet fit together in a wonderful order."
Heretics, "being unable to reconcile two opposing truths, and believing

[1] St. Thomas, *Summa contra Gentiles,* bk. 3, c. 52.

that to admit one involves excluding the other, therefore accept one and reject the other, and think that we are simply doing the reverse."[2] In saying this, he was not merely developing a theme familiar to the writers of Port Royal. He was expressing a conviction traditionally held by the Church in every age. Even in the second and third centuries, the orthodox opponents of Marcion put it forward. Tertullian, writing to refute Praxeas, declared of the dogma of the Trinity: "Not understanding that the unity of God does not exclude organization (economy), simple minds are afraid of the word."[3] Much later, in the fourteenth century, the great theologian of Greek orthodoxy, Gregory Palamas, in a dialogue on the communicability and incommunicability of God and the things of God, makes his mouthpiece Theophanes say:

> As you see, O Theotimes, the most venerable theologians—Athanasius, Basil, Gregory of Nyssa, John Chrysostom, Maximus—teach us two things. First they tell us that the divine essence is incommunicable, then, that it is in some way communicable; they tell us that we participate in the nature of God, and that we do not participate in it at all. We must therefore hold both assertions, and set them together as the rule of the true faith. Those who accept one in order to attack the other must be considered impious and foolish. In reality, they hold neither; they contradict one another, or contradict themselves. Yet the saints have told them that this doctrine of contradiction is the mark of narrow minds, whereas for the intelligent man who meditates honestly upon the things of God, all things unite in harmony.[4]

It is precisely the same law which Bossuet was later to state in his *Histoire des variations:*

> Whenever two truths which seem opposed must be brought into harmony, as in the mystery of the Trinity and that of the incarnation, being equal and being inferior, and in the sacrament of the Eucharist being present and being figured, there naturally develops a kind of language which appears confused, at least as long as one has not, so to say, the key of the Church and the total comprehension of the total mystery.[5]

It has often been pointed out, too, that the various forms of Protestantism were often religions of antithesis: authority or freedom? Bible or Church? and so on. The fullness of Catholicism always presents a

211

---

[2] *Pensées.*
[3] *Adversus Praxeam,* c. 2 and 3.
[4] *Theophanes* (PG, 150, 932 D).
[5] Bk. 4, c. 32 (*Oeuvres,* Lachat ed., 14, 1863, p. 166).

character of synthesis. It is only that it is not an immediate synthesis, nor one that is humanly achieved. It is not possessed by the light of reason: it is first of all believed in the darkness of faith. One begins, as Bossuet says again, by holding "the two ends of the chain." A synthesis indeed; but for our natural intellect, it is a synthesis of paradox before being one of enlightenment.

The same must be said of each individual mystery, whether in its relations with other mysteries, or its equally necessary harmony with the truths of the intellectual order. Love is the free gift above all others—and yet Christianity makes it a commandment: what problems that gives rise to! The Lord says in Zechariah: "Return to me . . . and I will return to you"—an excellent argument for Pelagianism. But we read in Lamentations: "Make us return to you, O Lord, and we shall return"—which seems a good argument for precisely the opposite heresy.[6] The Church however does not choose: she keeps both texts, and quotes them together in her Councils.[7] Similarly, if the Word is begotten, how can he be eternal? If he depends on the Father, how can he be his equal? Two unanswerable points for the Arians. But before going into the arguments, Hilary of Poitiers replies that it is better to trust the word of God than the reasonings of human subtlety. The eternal birth of the Word in the bosom of the Father, and his sonship which makes him at once equal and subject to him, are to him mysteries of faith for which it is not surprising that we do not possess any ready-made key in our reason.[8] Having meditated at length on the union of grace and freedom, and having given explanations which we today still find most illuminating, St. Augustine could none the less write, realizing the difficulties that never cease to arise: "This question . . . is as difficult to settle as when free will is defended, then the grace of God seems denied, but when the grace of God is asserted, then free will is deemed to be cast aside";[9] and what theologian, however convinced of his system, cannot make the same admission? A century ago Scheeben noted, as we all must, "two teachings in the Church which appear to be contradictory, and have nevertheless both been held firmly by her."[10]

212

[6] Zech. 1:3; Lam. 5:21.

[7] Cf. Council of Trent, Session 6, c. 5.

[8] St. Hilary, *De Trinitate*, bk. 11, c. 12; bk. 12, c. 18 and cc. 26–31. Cf. P. Smulders, *La doctrine trinitaire de saint Hilaire de Poitiers* (Rome, 1946), pp. 173, 178–80.

[9] *De gratia Christi*, c. 47, n. 52.

[10] French edition of *Natur und Gnade, Nature et grâce* (1957), p. 48.

We find a similar statement in Origen. This was in regard to a different problem, and one which does not really trouble us now. God, he said to himself, must be a creator and omnipotent from all eternity, and yet one cannot admit that any creature is co-eternal with God. Since the point is not important here, neither is the solution; but what is of interest to us is the universal relevance of the comment which this apparent contradiction inspired in Origen to the conflict that takes place in the mind: "Since therefore there is a battle between human thought [*cogitatio*] and intellect [*intellectus*], with the most valid reasons rushing to the mind on either side and fighting each other, and tormenting the sense of the contemplator each on its own side . . ."— always, after every attempt and every flash of understanding, "once again human intelligence is dulled in this. . . ."[11] Saint Augustine also puts forward similar ideas about the same problem in the *De Trinitate*.[12]

213 William of St. Thierry, that subtle psychologist of the faith, also noted the "hesitations of thought" [*haesitationes cogitationum*] which must always accompany the "thoughts of faith" [*fidei cogitationes*]; but he went on at once to reassure the faithful soul who undergoes them, urging that they be not mistaken for a different kind of doubt or anxiety which results from a certain "dishonest rationality" [*rationalitas improba*] that takes up an aggressive attitude with regard to faith.[13]

Once again, do not such statements express what is the experience of every theologian worthy of the name, indeed of every believer, as he reflects upon the mystery?

Obviously not every case is the same. It can happen sometimes that dogma, by forcing the mind to find out the truth about itself, delivers it from many irrational illusions and prejudices. It can also happen that the effect of revelation on human experience indirectly results in the formation of fresh concepts which lead to the gradual disappearance of the contradictions which were a problem at first. But though these explanations may well play a part, they are not enough to account for

---

[11] *De principiis*, bk. 1, c. 4, n. 4 (Koetschau ed., pp. 66–67).

[12] *De Trinitate*, bk. 1, c. 4, n. 3: "Consequently it is difficult to contemplate and to know fully the substance of God that makes changeable things with no change in itself, and creates temporal things with no temporal motion of itself; therefore the purgation of our mind is necessary, and being not yet endowed with it we are nourished by faith and are led along certain easier paths so that we may become fit and capable [*apti et habiles*] of grasping it" (*PL*, 42, 821).

[13] *Speculum fidei* (*PL*, 180, 388 D, and 378 AB; cf. 381 B).

the most important cases—not fully, at any rate. The only adequate answer must be found in the very idea of what mystery is.

This idea of mystery is perfectly acceptable to reason once one has admitted the idea of a personal and transcendent God. The truth we receive from him about himself must exceed our grasp, simply because of its superior intelligibility: understood [*intellecta*], it can never be grasped [*comprehensa*]. The distinction is elementary, and accepted by Descartes as well as St. Augustine and the scholastics. How could one possibly agree with Malebranche that "the Word unreservedly communicated all that he possesses as Word and eternal Wisdom whenever we question him with serious attention"?[14] Or at least, how could one believe that a finite intellect could be capable of receiving such a communication in its entirety? Revealed truth, then, is a mystery for us; in other words it presents that character of lofty synthesis whose final link must remain impenetrably obscure to us.[15] It will for ever resist all our efforts to unify it fully. This is baffling to a philosophy of pure rationality but not to a philosophy which recognizes in the human mind both that potential absolute that makes it declare the truth, and that abyss of darkness in which it remains by the fact of being both created and bodily. "Either . . . or," says rationality, believing that it can get to the bottom of everything, because it makes itself the yardstick, and thinks that its own limits are the limits of being itself. It accuses Christian thinking of "a kind of hunger for what is absurd and contradictory"; thinking that what is incomprehensible must therefore be unintelligible, it considers the doctrine of mystery to be a "sophism," an unwarranted overstepping of the bounds of common sense and reason.[16] The idea of the Trinity,

214

[14] Cf. Fénelon, *Réfutation du système du P. Malebranche*, c. 19 (Paris ed., vol. 2, 1849, p. 115). It was this rationalist tendency that Léon Brunschvicg found attractive in Malebranche. Cf. my own *Sur les chemins de Dieu* (Paris, 1956), ch. 5, Eng. trans. *The Discovery of God* (London, 1960), chapter 5.

[15] A similar position, philosophically generalized, is to be found in Etienne Borne, *Passion de la Vérité* (1962), p. 249: "The characteristic of faith is to believe . . . in the mysterious and real convergence of two truths. And that convergence does not take place by means of some compromise which takes away everything positive from each and leads it diplomatically to make concessions to the other; the unifying duty of the mind is to accept from each all that is clear-cut and uncompromising, and take them together, opposed and united, for it is absolutely true that from man's point of view, the tension between truths is the truth above all others."

[16] See D. Hume, *The Natural History of Religion* (quoted in Thomas Huxley, *Hume* [London, 1880]). And how many others have there been since him!

for instance, or even the idea of an infinite personal God is, from its point of view, a square circle. Throughout it finds "wilful contradiction, systematic absurdity, logical errors," and so on. Or, because St. Thomas along with all Catholic tradition professes that God is present everywhere in his creation, it accuses him of "implicit pantheism." Limited and enclosed, this philosophy of rationality is a philosophy of the dilemma and the univocal statement. "Contradiction is not distasteful enough to you," wrote Renouvier to Secrétan, of problems concerned not with revelation itself, but with the very being of God.[17] His correspondent, he thought, was leaving behind the honest thinking of the philosopher to enter upon the arbitrary ways of theologians who "try to lift thought above its proper conditions and look for truth outside the laws of understanding, outside consciousness altogether."[18] The objection is reminiscent of certain theologians of our own day, who hasten to speak of contradiction as soon as they hear phrases that seem even slightly paradoxical;[19] in so doing they reject any truth that surprises them, without perceiving that to be really logical they should be rejecting numerous other incontestable truths, both of faith and reason, which only fail to surprise them because they are so used to them.

But Secrétan replied to his friend: "You think too little of synthesis. . . . The contradictions whose terms are necessary certainly add up to a lacuna in what we know or what it is possible for us to know. . . . The contradictions which we really cannot resolve mark the boundaries of our understanding."[20] And, returning to the charge some years later: "You can keep reproaching me for bringing together the irreconcilable . . . ; I in turn reproach you with mutilating the human mind."[21] He was in fact making his own formulation of a doctrine which was perhaps

---

[17] Letter from Renouvier, 13 April, 1869 (*Correspondance de Renouvier et de Secrétan*, p. 22).

[18] *Histoire et solution des problèmes metaphysiques* (1901), p. 10. Cf. *Le Personnalisme* (1903), pp. 53–54: "The concept of personality is a single one," and therefore God, being personal, is like man a finite being with a body . . . ; pp. 183–84.

[19] Cf. *Gregorianum* (1947): 394; Philip J. Donnelly, in *Theological Studies* (1950): 399, etc. On the other hand, Père Bouessé, O.P., says in *Théologie et sacerdoce* (1938), p. 64: "Natural, non-efficacious desire. This is a paradox which brings reason to a dead end and dissipates the Gospel message."

[20] Letters from Secrétan, 15 July, 1869, and 26 April, 1873 (*Correspondance* . . . , pp. 24, 93).

[21] 11 December, 1875 (p. 127). Cf. Marcel Méry, *La critique du christianisme chez Renouvier*, 2 vols., 1952.

most forcefully and paradoxically expressed by Nicholas of Cusa: "I know from experience how necessary it is to enter the darkness, to admit the coexistence of contraries which exceed my power of under-standing, to look for truth where there seems only to be impossibil-ity. . . . The place, O my God, where we can see you unveiled is surrounded by the coming together of things contradictory; it is the wall of the Paradise where you dwell, and we can only enter it by conquering reason, which stands guard at the gate.[22]

216

Charles Secrétan and Nicholas of Cusa were partly right. They were right to recall to the human intellect that it too is a creature. They were right to reject, as does St. Thomas, "that intransigent conceptualism which sometimes seems to want to submit even the mind of God him-self to its laws."[23] But they are, both of them, too quick to admit that the *contradictio* that appears at first must always remain completely irreconcilable for us. They did not perhaps place sufficient trust in that "superior reason" [*ratio superior*], spoken of by St. Thomas and St. Augustine, which makes possible—though in a still distant way, and more by intuition than actual intelligence—a first "contemplation of things eternal."[24] For although we cannot yet penetrate "the wall of Par-adise," we are not condemned, even leaving mystical experience aside, to keep what the scholastics called the "mode of understanding possible to us" [*modus intelligendi nobis possibilis*], for ever at its lowest possible level. "There is certainly a middle term between pure reasoned affirma-tion of a fact and the positive perception of the 'how' of it."[25] The jour-ney need not always be a direct one. A defeat forced upon reason may, in some cases, mean a widening, or as Richard of St. Victor says, a dilat-

217

---

[22] Cf. *De visione Dei*: "Your great apostle Paul, who has been taken beyond the walls of coincidence into paradise where and only where you, who are the gate of delights, can be seen by revelation" (*Opera*, 1, 1514, fol. 108a). See also, for instance, Letter 5, to Gaspard Aindorffer, Abbot of Tegernsee (M. de Gandillac, *Oeuvres choisies de Nicolas de Cues*, p. 366). In his letter to Renouvier of 13 April, 1869, Secrétan makes explicit reference to the teaching of Nicholas of Cusa (*Correspondance. . . .*, p. 25).

[23] Etienne Gilson, *L'Etre et l'Essence* (1948), p. 160. Cf. St. Thomas, *In 2 Sent.*, d. 3, q. 1, a. 2; and d. 39, q. 3, a. 1.

[24] St. Thomas, *De veritate*, q. 10, a. 6 and 7, commenting on St. Augustine, *De Trini-tate*, bk. 12, c. 4: "What Augustine says here must be referred to the higher reason which inheres in the contemplation of eternal things" (6, ad 6um); "The words of Augustine must be referred to precognition . . ." (ad 3um); "In some way, all knowledge was origi-nally imparted to us in the light of the acting intellect."

[25] Joseph de Finance, S.J., *Existence et liberté*, p. 159.

ing of it.[26] For there is a flexibility in reason, as the history of doctrine shows, and when it abandons the narrow rules of too human a rationality and appears to be overwhelmed by the weight of mystery, something analogous to a conversion takes place within it, a kind of rebirth, an entry into a new world.[27]

To give a present-day example, it is surely this that Paul VI is referring to in the encyclical *Ecclesiam suam* when he speaks of "the many paradoxes which severely test the thinking of those concerned with ecclesiology," and calls on them to see beyond them and resolve them "in the experience, illuminated by doctrine, of the living reality of the Church itself."[28]

On the other hand, as we have seen, while our knowledge is and cannot help being defective, it has at least that wonderful power that exalts it at the very moment of having to admit defeat: namely the power of self-criticism. It is never enclosed, never wholly bounded by its objective concepts. It can stand back, as it were, and judge them. The results of such scrutiny may well be negative, but even so they are enough to remove the scandal of contradiction by enabling the mind to affirm the existence of an ultimate harmony even when it cannot see it. But they will never add up to a positive solution so clear that the mind has no more to do than repose in it. Père Sertillanges explains this very well, in relation to human action—which we know to be free although it depends wholly upon God. Once we have grasped, he tells us, that "God is the origin, the transcendent origin"—which we in fact understand without really understanding it, understanding only that it could not be otherwise—"no objection remains, and the co-possibility of the relative and the absolute is intact." Only, he adds immediately, "do not conclude from this that I am claiming it as established. To *establish* positively the co-possibility of the relative and the absolute, one would have to define them both; and one of them is indefinable. . . . As long as God remains inaccessible in himself the meeting-point of his being with ours and his action with ours must remain no less inaccessible."[29]

[26] *Beniamin minor,* c. 82: "The capacity of human sense surrenders to that to which it is divinely inspired, and unless it leaves the narrows of human reasoning, it does not expand the scope [*sinus*] of its intelligence to receive the mystery [*arcanum*] of divine inspiration" (*PL,* 196, 58 B).

[27] Leo XIII, the encyclical *Aeterni Patris:* "When the Saviour's grace has re-established and increased the natural faculties of the human mind. . . ."

[28] *Ecclesiam suam,* 6 August, 1964, n. 40.

[29] St. Thomas d'Aquin, vol. 1, 3d ed., 1922, pp. 266–67. Another example: there is

218

When it is between two truths of faith that the ultimate harmony cannot be seen, to choose one and reject the other then becomes heresy properly so called. We have a series of classic examples of this in the great trinitarian and christological heresies, which are extreme and obvious cases. But even within the limits of orthodoxy, any theology too concerned to find clear-cut harmonies and explanations with no loose ends will always be in danger of upsetting the balance of the dogmatic synthesis by lightening the weight of one or other of the two apparently contradictory propositions. This is true of those systems which try to make the divine Trinity in unity more amenable to the understanding by minimizing to the utmost the category of "relation" which enables us to think of the persons, by speaking of the "extreme poverty" of their personal being and by describing the three divine persons in consequence as being "as little distinct from one another as possible": the divine persons, one notes, are wholly relative to one another, and in the scale of categories relation is the *"ens minutissimum."*[30] It is true too of those other systems which, the better to safeguard Christ's divinity, so minimize the consequences of his incarnation that his human reality is compromised.[31] The modalist or unitarian tendency, the monophysite or docetist tendency, are, as are their opposites, the result of an over-eagerness to reconcile the contrasting elements of the mystery.[32] They are the consequence of wanting to be easily satisfied, of seeking a success which would dispense one from seeking further. They are the consequence of a theology of pure rationality[33] refusing to transcend itself and thus becoming a kind of contradiction. But it is only from this formal point of view that we are concerned with them here.

219

---

such a thing as rational credibility, and yet there is no "natural faith"; it is this problem which has underlain nearly all the research and discussion about the act of faith for over fifty years. Cf. Roger Aubert, *Le problème de l'acte de foi.*

[30] Once again, how much more penetrating is Bérulle: "In this world, this category of relation is one of the least, *tenuissimae entitatis,* and in the world of grace it is one of the most powerful and important. . . . This follows from the fact that, in the Trinity, of which grace is the image, we find relations which are constitutive and the origins of the divine persons. Quoted by H. Brémond, *Histoire littéraire . . . ,* vol. 3, p. 83.

[31] Karl Rahner's theological reflections on the incarnation in *Schriften zur Theologie* 3 (Einsiedeln, 1956), pp. 47–60, French trans. *Écrits théologiques* 3 (1963), pp. 81–101.

[32] It is hard, however, as we must recognize, to escape it completely. Absolutely perfect balance is usually superficial, and may even be no more than verbal. Hence the ever open possibility, but also the frequent injustice of charges about unorthodox tendencies.

[33] Cf. Maurice Blondel, quoted in Frédéric Lefèvre, *L'itinéraire philosophique de Maurice Blondel* (1928), p. 183: "Animus all too often becomes the important thing, to such a point that Malebranche took it for the very Word of God. . . ."

How different from this avid seeking and this over-hasty arrival is the spirit of St. Thomas Aquinas, who made his own these counsels and statements of St. Hilary:

> Make your start, continue, persevere. I know that you will not reach the goal, but I shall rejoice at your progress. For he who devoutly treads an endless road, though he reach no conclusion, will profit by his exertions. But do not bring yourself to this secret, and do not immerse yourself in the mystery of endless [*interminabilis*] truth, presuming to grasp the height of understanding; but understand that these are incomprehensible things.[34]

In a certain number of other cases, only one of the two opposing truths is a dogma proper, although both together form a kind of indivisible Christian inheritance. Here the temptation is greater, in order to gain the desired peace of mind cheaply, to eliminate or at least water down, blur or neglect the apparently contradictory truth. This seems to me precisely what has happened, in regard to the supernatural, with the second problem I have just indicated. Theologians have come up against an apparent opposition between two elements which are equally stressed by the tradition concerning the supernatural destiny offered to man: on the one hand the fact that it is fundamental; on the other the fact that it is a totally free gift. Longing for a clear solution on the immediate level of understanding, they have allowed themselves to be guided uncritically by analogies drawn from social relationships, or even from the material universe. Now any reconciliation at this level involves some sacrifice. There could be no question of sacrificing the gratuitousness, since it was a positive dogma; therefore it was the fundamental character of grace that had to a greater or lesser extent to be dropped. The result has been the speculation about "pure nature"—in a quite different sense from that given it by the scholastics of old, as we have seen—a speculation ever more pervasive and widespread. And, where there has not been great care, this has even led to a certain compromising of the gratuitousness. It should have been realized, as Dr. J. Sestili so opportunely pointed out, that this "apparent conflict" between two truths of different orders was normal.[35] Reflection should have led to a

220

---

[34] *Summa contra Gentiles*, bk. 1, c. 8, quoting Hilary, *De Trinitate*, bk. 2, n. 10. Père Chenu, *op. cit.*, p. 253, invites us to consider this text as "a personal confidence" from St. Thomas.

[35] "Quod omnis intellectus . . . ," *loc. cit.*, pp. 955–56: "Hence comes the apparent battle in the union of these orders of truth; namely, in connecting capacity, possibility,

reaction against man's natural disposition "to deny anything he cannot understand."[36] These theologians had largely forgotten one of the first principles of traditional philosophy: that, whatever rationalist philosophers may say in their wish to limit us within the narrow bounds of their immanence,[37] understanding is not the whole measure of human reason;[38] that "metaphysical reason" triumphs only by breaking free of the "processes of abstract understanding";[39] and that such understanding "remains subject to the spirit."[40] Once again, this is a lesson that could have been learnt from St. Thomas Aquinas.[41]

     221

"Metaphysics," says one contemporary philosopher, "is not a build-up of concepts by which we try to make our paradoxes less obvious; it is the experience we have of them in all the situations of our personal and collective history."[42] This certainly involves some abdication of the intel-

---

natural appetite, with the insufficiency of nature and the negation of the exigency to see God. . . . Or should perhaps this truth be denied because the manner of the union does not yet appear evident?"

[36] Pascal, *De l'esprit géométrique*.

[37] Cf. Léon Brunschvicg, *De la vraie et de la fausse conversion* (1951), p. 89: "that supposed reason which, claiming that it transcends understanding, only uses the instrument of conceptual dialectic for extra-philosophical ends."

[38] Joseph Maréchal, S.J., in *Revue des questions scientifiques* 74 (1913): 633.

[39] Aimé Forest, *Du consentement à l'être* (1930), p. 97: the "attitude of consent" is obtained "against the habits and perhaps against the requirements of thinking that sets out to define and fix": it is "a kind of victory of metaphysical reason over the processes of abstract understanding." Cf. the theologian quoted by Henri Bremond, in *Prière et Poésie*, p. 6, note: one must not resign oneself to "allowing the ends of intelligence and wisdom to be confiscated by the votaries of understanding and rational science."

[40] Cf. M. D. Chenu, *op. cit.*, commenting on the Thomistic distinction between *intellectus* and *ratio*. Gabriel Marcel, *Le mystère de l'être*, vol. 2, 1951, p. 113, Eng. trans. *The Mystery of Being*, vol. 2, "Faith and Reality" (London, 1951), p. 112: "We can use the word [obscurity] in this connection only as opposed to a superficial clarity which is that of the understanding." I cannot share the illusion of Léon Brunschvicg when he proudly writes: "Since philosophy crossed the threshold of the intelligence . . ." (*op. cit.*, p. 253).

[41] Cf. *De veritate*, q. 15, a. 1, etc. *Secunda Secundae*, q. 49, a. 5, ad 2um: "The certitude of reason is from the intellect [*ex intellectu*], but the necessity of reason is from the defect of nature [*ex defectu intellectus*]." *In Boetium de Trinitate*, q. 6, art. 1, ad 3um, on "proceeding rationally" [*rationaliter procedere*] and "proceeding intellectually" [*intellectualiter procedere*]; though man is characterized by the former, it must not be forgotten that "the limit [*terminus*] of the whole human consideration is very much the intellectual consideration," etc. The distinction between *ratio* and *intellectus* corresponds analogically in St. Thomas to the distinction between "understanding" and "reason." Cf. Pierre Rousselot, *L'intellectualisme de saint Thomas* (Paris, 1924), Eng. trans. *The Intellectualism of St. Thomas* (London, 1935). Etienne Gilson has several times in recent years drawn attention to this sadly neglected book. See too Balthasar, *La gloire et la croix*, vol. 1, especially pp. 323–81.

[42] Merleau-Ponty, *Sens et non-sens*, p. 191.

ligence, if it means a refusal to step outside the sphere of our most immediate experience to seek a solution to the problems which that experience poses. It is in any case certainly true that theology is not, or ought not to be, a buildup of concepts by which the believer tries to make the divine mystery less mysterious, and in some cases to eliminate it altogether. To reject this idea of theology does not mean that we think of it as something less ambitious, but quite the reverse: it is by rejecting this idea that we lift it above human banality.

222   Because of a lack of sufficient awareness—and also perhaps of a sufficient real knowledge of tradition[43]—a problem which should have provided a stimulus to thought has been turned into a stumbling-block. People took hasty flight to what seemed the "safest" position, and felt that they thereby possessed dogmatic truth in peace. But by this oversimple method of preserving the gratuitousness of the supernatural order, they were, to put it mildly, lessening its meaning. They were making it not merely an "accident" in the scholastic sense—which is understandable—but something completely accidental in the ordinary sense, and therefore, one must admit, something superficial. They were dooming themselves to see it as merely a kind of superstructure. It followed inevitably that man could not only have managed quite well without it, but that even now he could with impunity disregard it. It was deprived of any hold on human thinking or human existence. Christian thought was thus bounded by a narrow circle, in a quiet backwater of the intellectual universe, where it could only waste away. By the good offices of some of its own exponents, who were aiming to preserve its transcendence, it became merely an "exile."[44]

The price is heavy, but has the longed-for peace at least been gained by it? Far from it. Any repose of mind gained so easily can only be artificial. It does not express that harmony which can result only from overcoming opposition. Reason which has been suppressed will have its revenge all too soon by declaring that in such conditions the supernatural as presented to it, as forced upon it, is merely an illusion. In a hun-

---

[43] V. Doucet, *loc. cit.*, p. 202: "Because of the decadence of scholastic philosophy, [which is] the necessary concomitant of the ignorance of the old Scholastics, the doctrine on the innate appetite to true beatitude has progressively been abandoned."

[44] M. D. Chenu, *Introduction à l'étude de Saint Thomas d'Aquin*, p. 6: "To see a major theologian born and at work, in a century when theologians and theology were not cut off from the world, its conditions, its perspectives, its techniques, and its culture, is a marvellous spectacle, and a lesson for those who see later theology exiled and vainly jealous of its rights."

dred ways it takes up again the cry of Siger of Brabant: "Let us discuss
nothing of God's miracles for us, when we are discussing natural things   223
in natural terms!—Let no reason be given for miracles!"[45] Some theologians may choose paradoxically to take up this same cry, though with
the opposite intention, their aim being to protect the faith by isolating
it completely. They may choose to blind themselves to the consequences of the premises they have themselves put forward: "a philosophy apart" and "a theology apart" are in strict correlation, both in
history[46] and in logic. "It seems," Jacques Maritain has said, "that in the
time of William of Vair and of Charron, and later of Descartes, it was as
though thinkers who were still Christian had thought up a purely natural man whose duty was to philosophize, and upon whom was superim-
posed a man with the theological virtues and a duty to merit heaven."[47]
As Père L. Malevez has rightly diagnosed, here lies one of the deepest
roots of all that is negative in modern secularization.[48] Who would seriously undertake to prove that the responsibility for this attitude, and
the more ambitious and more negative one that so soon followed it, can
be laid at the door of philosophers alone?

Faith, too, could not be slow to protest against a system which muti-
lates the inheritance of tradition. All tradition, in effect—taking the
word in its widest sense—passing from St. Irenaeus, by way of St.
Augustine and St. Thomas and St. Bonaventure, without distinction of
school, presents us with the two affirmations at once, not in opposition
but as a totality: man cannot live except by the vision of God—and that
vision of God depends totally on God's good pleasure. One has no right
to weaken either, even in order to grasp the other more firmly. After a
long eclipse, people have finally come to realize this. They have also   224
heard in a thousand forms the objection provoked by a dualist theology:
it is that which for several decades has given rise to a number of theories

---

[45] Siger, *De anima intellectiva*, c. 3; and the first commentary on the *Physics* (F. van
Steenberghen, *Siger de Brabant*, pp. 683 and 679). Cf. Gilson, *Dante et la philosophie*, pp.
311–15, Eng. trans. *Dante the Philosopher* (London, 1948), pp. 311–16. The modern
attempts to free Siger from the taint of Averroism, though very erudite, seem to me to
have failed.

[46] It is hard to determine historically which of the two comes first. The best solution is
to go back to Descartes. One will not, I think, be wrong in attributing to Paduan philosophy a very strong influence upon the new theological orientation.

[47] "La notion de philosophie chrétienne," *Bulletin de la Société française de philosophie*
(session of 21 March, 1921): 62.

[48] L. Malevez, "L'esprit et le désir de voir Dieu," *Nouvelle revue théologique* (1947): 28.

which set out to make room once more for that "natural desire" which
the early writers spoke of. Their very diversity is an indication of the difficulty they find themselves in. It is equally an indication of a definite
advance both in original thinking and in a return to theological tradition.

But all too often there remains the same timidity,[49] the same impa-
tient anxiety to eliminate every paradox from the human situation and
arrive at a positive and clearly understandable result; so much so that
this "natural desire" to see God which they have been trying to re-establish is twisted almost at once into a vague "wish," a wholly Platonic
"prayer" quite inadequate for the work it should be doing. St. Thomas
Aquinas conceived of a desire which, though not efficacious, was none
the less "radical,"[50] absolute, and in no sense "conditional."[51] His teaching about the situation of the damned further shows clearly how completely he dissociated the two ideas—efficacious and absolute—in his
thinking.[52] Yet among the very people who were most anxious to return
to the sources, there were many who soon came to envisage no more
than some kind of "velleity" totally contrary both to the language and
teaching of St. Thomas: for though he knew the word *velleitas* well, and
used it in other cases, he never makes use of it in the many texts concerned with this particular question.[53] And here again the same can be
said of St. Bonaventure, to whom an "appetite of velleity" [*appetitus
velleitatis*] was an "appetite for impossible things" [*appetitus impossibilium*].[54] Similarly, having referred to the well-known Thomist principle:
"The desire of nature cannot be vain" [*desiderium naturae nequit esse*

225

---

[49] This is true, it seems to me, even in the article quoted, p. 24: "[People affirm simul-
taneously] that the desire for God is non-efficacious and unconditional: but these two
attributes are in fact mutually exclusive." However, on p. 31, referring to still other problems (grace and liberty, the will of Christ), the author shows that he wants to avoid the
over-narrow point of view he seems to have adopted at first.

[50] "Radical impulsion," says J. Maréchal, *Le point de départ . . .* , vol. 5, p. 315.

[51] Père Motte has shown this in *Bulletin thomiste*, vol. 4, pp. 581–82. The texts dealing
with "antecedent intentions" which Père Garrigou-Lagrange quotes against him (*Revue
thomiste* 19 [1936]: 208–11) are not relevant.

[52] Capreolus, *In 4 Sent.*, dist. 49, art. 3: the damned "strive for beatitude not only by a
conditional appetite, but by an absolute appetite" (*Defensiones theologicae D. Thomae*, vol.
7, 1908, pp. 181–82). See *infra*, chapter 10, pp. 193–94.

[53] Thus *Prima Secundae*, q. 13, art. 5, ad 1um; *In 2 Sent.*, dist. 33, q. 2, art. 2, ad 2um,
on the subject of a "will for impossible things" [*voluntas impossibilium*].

[54] *In 2 Sent.*, dist. 7, P. 1, art. 1, q. 2, ad 7um: "Appetite of velleity [*appetitus velleitatis*]
which is for impossible things [*appetitus impossibilium*]." Cf. *infra*, chapter 12.

inane], they water it down as far as possible and then, recoiling from its "serene daring,"[55] try to relegate all "its effects to the sphere of pure possibilities, leaving out of account all those texts which clearly assert the opposite.[56] There is also the heroic, but to my mind more irrational, solution of consciously sacrificing a whole section of the traditional texts—even some of the most definite and clear—on the grounds that they cannot all be reconciled. This is what Père Jacques de Blic did, for instance, when he spoke of a "twofold teaching of St. Thomas," and set aside the texts which seemed to him "apologetic" in character, retaining only those in which the vision of God appeared to him as placed "above all natural desire."[57] There are certain others who still do this, in the belief that it would be vain to try to reconcile two series of statements which seem to them contradictory.

This, it seems to me, is to be too easily discouraged, and over-fearful. 226 I am convinced that Thomist teaching on this point is essentially coherent, and I do not even see any need to reconcile the texts by "recalling that [this] teaching is primarily a synthesis, a harmonizing of somewhat diverse tendencies," as Abbé J. Durantel recently declared.[58] St. Bonaventure's comment on St. Augustine seems to apply rather well to St. Thomas here: "One must not believe that so great a man contradicts himself, especially in matters in which he does not retract."[59] It is one thing to fail to see how to reconcile two things, and quite another to suppose that St. Thomas himself was unable to do so. It is quite true

[55] Cf. Georges Van Riet, in *Revue philosophique de Louvain* 62 (1964): 370–71.

[56] Cf. *Summa contra Gentiles*, bk. 2, c. 55. *Prima*, q. 75, a. 6 (dealing with immortality). *De Malo*, q. 5, art. 1, ad 1um. *In 4 Sent.*, dist. 49, q. 1, sol. 4. The argument St. Thomas bases upon this principle "leads not merely to the possibility of intuitive vision, but to its existence" (J. de Blic, *Mélanges de science religieuse* [1947]: 97). Similarly Edgar De Bruyne, *Saint Thomas d'Aquin* (1928), p. 97. Dom M. Cappuyns, *loc. cit.*, p. 121. S. Dockx, *loc. cit.*, pp. 86–90, etc. One will however note with Fr. Anthony Finili, *Natural Desire*, p. 9: "Natural desire for God is a step in the argument, not the initial assumption." Compare Bonaventure, *In 1 Sent.*, dist. 8, P. 1, art. 2, q. 2 (vol. 1, p. 161).

[57] *Mélanges de science religieuse* (1947), p. 97. It is this position which led the author to think himself forced to "recognize the undeniable material fact that St. Thomas gives a double teaching on the question of angelic peccability" (*loc. cit.* [1944], p. 278). As I think I have shown, that teaching is in fact quite coherent, and such is also the opinion of Père André Hayen, "Théologie de l'amour divin et métaphysique de l'acte d'être," *Teoresi* 9 (1954): 87–88.

[58] *Op cit.*, p. 362.

[59] *In 2 Sent.*, dist. 4 (Quaracchi, vol. 2, p. 140). Or St. Jerome's remark about Origen, *Apologia adversus Rufinum*, bk. 2, c. 13: "Origen is no fool [*fatuus*], and I know it: he cannot say contradictory things" (*PL*, 23, 456).

that there are two series of texts in St. Thomas, but when they appear to contradict each other—which they do, even verbally—it is because they are concerned with two different orders: the first series is concerned with, for instance, the order of necessary connections, the second with that of free will; the first speaks of natural appetite, the second of an elicited act of desire; and so on. As for the two essential statements which people cannot see how to reconcile, for St. Thomas as for the other authors, their apparent contradiction is primarily the effect of the object itself, whose contrasting elements it is impossible for our gaze to unify fully:

> In the association [*conjunctio*] of these terms [sc. man and God] it is no wonder if the intellect of those who seek and introduce inconsistencies [*inconvenientia*] finds no rest: the chain of association cannot appear perfect from any side, and this from the internal meaning of the terms. The discussion involves the determination of form [*habitudo*] between finite and infinite, between nature and that on which [nature] totally depends and is altogether on the order of the unsurpassable.[60]

These reflections are given by Dr. Sestili in reply to the objection that, if one must admit the existence of a natural desire to see God, "the greatest disorder would follow in the intelligent nature." He takes them up again with increasing insistence, in terms which it may be useful to read again now:

> Questions of this type cannot be settled by taking up the concepts as they are found in the terms of inclination and end of the same specific or generic nature; here [*heic*] indeed the relative end [*finis*] or terminus is the divine nature, which exists above and beyond all genus and species, and consequently these concepts, though they are true, are nevertheless analogic and not univocal. . . .
>
> Hence comes the apparent battle in the union of these orders of truth; namely, in connecting capacity, possibility, natural appetite, with the insufficiency of nature and the negation of the exigency to see God: for in ascending to God, the attempt of joining the degree of nature with unsurpassable divine being fails; likewise in descending from the fullness and perfection of being: joining its degree with the insufficiency of nature fails. But the distinct truth of these orders is intrinsically evident. What then? Or should perhaps this truth be denied because the manner

227

---

[60] J. Sestili, *De possibilitate desiderioque primae causae substantiam videndi* (as an appendix to the edition of the Commentaries of Sylvester of Ferrara on the *Summa contra Gentiles*, vol. 3 [Rome, 1900]), p. 950.

of the union does not yet appear evident? Not at all. That would be to cut the knot of science that cannot be fully loosed.[61]

The conclusion Dr. Sestili draws here is the same as my own. Whether it be in the historical study of the theologians of the past— those he calls the "doctors of the ancient knowledge" [*doctores antiquae sapientiae*][62]—or in one's own original theological work, it is surely better, if one cannot yet see the way to a solution, to "hold both ends of the chain."

But there is more that one can do, as I think I have made clear. Though one cannot reduce everything to the clarity of a simple vision free of all mystery, one can at least advance dialectically to the harmony which lies beyond the apparent opposition. And this will be easier if, taking the notion of God's transcendence with total seriousness, we stop seeing the call to the supernatural and the offer of grace in a chronological series, as though the second is governed by the first: as though God were bound by his own call once uttered, and could not then recall his offer. The offer of grace expresses, in the sphere of moral liberty, the same act of divine loving kindness that the call to the supernatural expresses in the ontological sphere. Thus there is nothing in the former to diminish beforehand in any way the gratuitousness of the latter. Neither is exterior to the other, and therefore neither comes before the other. There is always the same unique sovereign initiative at work in both, and the only difference lies in relation to us, because we are at once nature and liberty, an ontological tendency and a spiritual will.

228

Those however who have decided that it is necessary to posit first of all a certain "purely natural" human order in which that call is not heard, go on to admit, not realizing that by doing so they are destroying the essential of what they want to save, that in the actual, historical and concrete order, this call places God under an obligation in our regard by actually giving us a right—leaving aside the intervening problem of sin—to demand that he give us grace, and eventually, if we are faithful, the light of glory. Thus, not content with having imagined an order of things in which our relationship with the Creator might have been ruled solely by the laws of commutative justice, they seem to imagine those same laws as being the basis for the order we actually have, since God

[61] *Op. cit.*, pp. 955–57.
[62] *Op. cit.*, p. 941.

has made the decision to "raise us up."[63] Surely, for all they may say of gratuitousness, this in fact does away with it completely. Surely, too, it abolishes hope, or at least makes it relate only to our present sinful state—for anyone who thinks a thing is his due does not hope, but simply demands.[64] Surely this, as Fénelon said of a similar situation,[65] "is to destroy God's freedom in giving out his graces, [to make] the greatest of all graces merely a debt, and [to confuse] the order of nature with the supernatural order."[66]

229

[63] Cf. E. Brisbois, "Le désir de voir Dieu et la métaphysique du vouloir selon saint Thomas," *Nouvelle revue théologique* 63 (1936): 1103–4: "Just as it was impossible for the will naturally to desire the absolute perfect good as its last end, so it is necessary that, once called to that perfection, it should be ordered to it as to the final good which it necessarily demands, just as in the natural order it demands its natural last end to which it is naturally ordered. There must then be, in the nature that is called to supernatural beatitude, a new subjective disposition, a new demand, prior to any deliberate exercise of the will, prior even to faith and sanctifying grace." It may be that this is merely an unfortunate choice of words; but it is surely significant that the word "demand" is so readily accepted, despite the fact that the idea of demand is what he is intending to get rid of. And even in authors who do not use the word, the idea seems to be admitted.

[64] Cf. St. Hilary, *Tractatus in psalmum 15*: "Preserve me, Lord, for I have hoped in you. He who asks for his due has no hope; now if anything is due to me, I claim it by law" (*PL*, 9, 893).

[65] Fénelon, *Troisième lettre en réponse . . . celle de Mgr l'Évêque de Meaux*: "Is it chimerical . . . to say, with the Catechism of the Council of Trent, that God could have bound us to serve his glory without giving us any reward?" (vol. 2, p. 664). *Première lettre à M. de Chartres* (vol. 3, p. 129; *Oeuvres*, Paris ed.). Here Fénelon is criticizing the teaching of Bossuet. I am not concerned here to see whether he is justified in so doing or not; I simply think that, without canonizing his own teaching in any way, we can apply it here. Nor, I must repeat, am I indicating heresy in the theologians whose theories I am examining, for we are dealing here only with the adequacy of explanations which relate to affirmations that we all hold unconditionally to be true.

[66] Early in this century, Johannes Wehrlé wrote one day to his friend Maurice Blondel, with regard to a polemical pamphlet by Mgr. Turinaz which had just appeared (and which I have not succeeded in finding): "Read with care the final paragraph on page 59, which considers the hypothesis that Christianity might not exist. One might well conclude from it that, given our present condition, God would have failed in a duty of strict justice in not giving it to us. Now this is not simply applying a certain method of immanence to the subject; it is, arising from the same principle and going further, a statement that God is giving us in the supernatural something owed to us, and that if he did not give it, be would be simply unjust. In his condemnation of us he goes ten times further than we do, and finds in our immanence not the power to *recognize* the free gift we are in fact given, but the claim to require *as a right* a gift that is necessary for us and obligatory for God." Cf. *supra*, p. 52.

CHAPTER 10

A Finality
That Has No End

Let me here declare my debt towards a number of contemporary Thomists who have done a great deal since the turn of the century to set us free of the complications in which modern scholasticism had become embroiled. The thinking they have done, based on historical investigation, has made possible a return to the great tradition which was fairly widely forgotten or distorted during an earlier period. Not only have they made it possible, but they have in part effected it. They deserve their own historical study, to recount in detail the gradual rediscovery of the most classic theses of Christian anthropology together with their adaptation to new situations, and to try to set out the often dramatic conflicts which that rediscovery and adaptation produced. 231

The work might include a prologue: especially worthy of mention are several names of those who helped to pave the way, especially that of Gratry in France, whose work has been rightly recalled by Père Victorin Doucet, O.F.M.,[1] Canon Louis Foucher[2] and Albert Milet. Around the middle of the nineteenth century, while Rosmini was working towards a better interpretation of the relationship between the natural and supernatural orders, an interpretation which depended too heavily on his general theory of knowledge,[3] Gratry was explicitly renewing links with   232

---

[1] "De naturali seu innato supernaturalis beatitudinis desiderio iuxta Theologos a saeculo XIII usque ad XX," *Antonianum* 4 (1929): 202–3.

[2] *La philosophie catholique en France au XIXᵉ siècle avant la renaissance thomiste et son rapport avec elle, 1800–1880* (1955), pp. 197–236.

[3] In several of his works, especially his introduction to St. John's Gospel (published posthumously, 1882). Certain of Rosmini's propositions which were censured in 1882 dealt with the beatific vision.

Thomist thought in his treatise *De la Connaissance de Dieu.* Though his efforts remained unsatisfactory, being based upon insufficient scholarship, they proceeded from a fundamentally true and profound intuition, and were dedicated to the service of an "inspired philosophy" whose importance is not perhaps sufficiently recognized. "As soon as a spirit knows that there is a God," said Gratry, "it wants to see God, as St. Thomas constantly affirms":

> Now that desire, a negative desire I agree, a desire through deprivation and regret, however indirect, blind and non-efficacious it may be in itself, is still enough to show that our intellect, since it has that regret, will only find total rest and perfection in the higher light which the vision of God will give it. But whether that desire is, in man, either essentially natural or simply inborn, resulting of necessity from the nature of rational intelligence itself, as almost the whole school thinks, or whether it is merely a kind of extra impulse from God; whether it results from the fact of creation, or derives from God's will to raise every intellect to the intuitive vision, and is thus what St. Thomas calls "the natural order directed towards the supernatural end": and whether that extra impulse must, in its turn, be called natural or supernatural, does not matter. Since in any case that impulse from God is interwoven with reason, reason as it is given to us, it must follow that reason—right reason—can demonstrate the possibility of the supernatural light, the intuitive vision, and prove its necessity, if spirit is to attain to its final perfection and achieve perfect rest.[4]

But at that very moment when dissertations on the "supernatural order"[5] were beginning to proliferate, this was only one isolated voice. Gratry made a point of quoting the clearest statements from St. Thomas's two *Summas,* phrased, as he said, with "a kind of geometric precision"; he made a point of refuting Baius, and also of explaining the bull *Auctorem fidei* condemning the Synod of Pistoia; he was careful to distinguish in man two kinds of possible perfection gained by supernatural assistance, and to make clear that he need not have been given the gift which raises him "to his final perfection, that is his supernatural end, which consists in seeing God's essence"; in an excess of precaution he even added, at the end of the second edition of his work, a long scholarly note based on information given him by his theologian friend,

233

[4] 1853; vol. 2, 2d ed., 1854, pp. 358–59. See also pp. 290–312.
[5] Gratry himself uses the term, *loc. cit.,* p. 279.

Abbé Gillet.[6] But the ignorance of traditional theology was so profound at that time, even in the self-styled "traditionalist" school, that he was censured in 1857 by Rohrbacher, the author of a history of the Catholic Church,[7] and had almost no following.

Nearer to our time, and incomparably more complete and important, is the work of Maurice Blondel, starting with the famous thesis *L'Action* (1893). Certainly in *L'Action* "the Thomist notion of the *desiderium naturale videndi Deum* is never mentioned." It has not always been sufficiently recognized that the dialectic is set in motion not by the magnetism of the vision, but the original movement of will towards it, and that "the conclusion of that dialectic is neither the necessity nor even the possibility of the beatific vision, but the duty of man to want what God wills." The actual difficulty which the young Blondel came up against was quite unrelated to the problem St. Thomas had to solve. His perspective therefore is quite different. What he is essentially concerned with in *L'Action* is "the behavior man must pursue during this life, not the beatitude he may long for in the next." Père Henri Bouillard, who points out these differences, indicates still another, more important one, which was to remain even when Blondel in his later works made an attempt to return in some sense to the point of view of the school philosophers:

> In St. Thomas, indeed, the natural desire to see God seems to envisage its end directly, like all natural appetites, without being crossed by any inward contradiction. In Blondel, on the other hand, the will for the infinite, or need of the supernatural, is directed to substituting in us the divine will for our own will; it cannot therefore envisage its end except by way of accepting a kind of death. St. Thomas shows that our will can only be satisfied by God himself giving himself to us. Blondel adds, actually as part of the dialectic whereby he establishes a similar conclusion that man can only be open to that divine action by way of a passive purification, a constant mortification. . . . He does not merely show that our action calls for something more than it is possible for us to achieve alone; the admission he finally makes is that "the natural order is not enough for our nature, yet it nevertheless rejects the supernatural. . . ." That is why the "need of the supernatural" revealed in the dialectic of

234

---

[6] "Vicar General of Blois, later appointed by Pius IX as one of the theologians involved in the preparatory work for the Vatican Council" (A. Largent, "Gratry," *Dict. de théol. cath.*, vol. 6, col. 1760).

[7] Vol. 5, 1857, p. 556, where, however, the problem is not really dealt with.

L'Action is of a different kind from the "natural desire to see God" expressed in the *Summa theologica* or the *Summa contra Gentiles.*[8]

These comments are sufficient to show both the uselessness of certain over-zealous attempts to establish harmonies, and the falsity of certain lines of criticism which flow at bottom from a misunderstanding of the real question at issue. It is none the less true that, by the discussion it gave rise to, and even more by the trains of reflection it started in other perceptive minds, Blondel's work made an important contribution to returning our attention to the theological tradition about our supernatural end, and especially to Thomist teaching on the point.

However, as generally happens, the mass of neo-Thomists, whether before or after Blondel, rediscovered not so much St. Thomas himself as the later forms of Thomism. It was the effect of a similar law which made archaeologists, writers and artists, when rediscovering the middle ages, in fact rediscover primarily the fifteenth and even sixteenth centuries. Fifty years after Gratry, and a few years after Blondel's entry upon the scene, Dr. Sestili published, in the form of an introduction to an edition of Sylvester of Ferrara's commentary on the *Contra Gentiles,* the epoch-making statement: "For every intellect naturally desires the vision of the divine substance."[9] In it he declared that he wanted to "iso-235   late the teaching of St. Thomas from among the obscure or adulterated interpretations which had accumulated around it in the course of time, as the golden age of scholasticism was left behind." In other words, everything remained to be done. But though Sestili's dissertation had a certain *succès d'estime* it did little to shake the dualist certainties which still held the field.[10] It was somewhat later that the school I have spoken of began, with the work of two eminent scholars; one, Père Pierre Rousselot, died while still young, killed in 1915 during the First World War, and the second, Père Joseph Maréchal, died at the beginning of the

[8] *Blondel et le christianisme* (1961), pp. 130–31.

[9] (Rome, 1900), p. 907: ". . . they did not dare a temeritous illustration of the mind of Aquinas, since in this matter he shines by himself with the brightest of lights; but rather with the desire in their hearts of sifting the splendid and distinguished teaching of Thomas from obscure and impure interpretations, which [had arisen] through the progress of time since the golden age of the ever receding scholastics, . . . they sifted around it." Cf. *supra,* chapter 9, pp. 181–83. See also the same author's *In Summam Theologicam S. Thomae Aquinatis,* Prima pars, q. 12, a. 1.

[10] In any case, it was by no means totally faithful to St. Thomas. Cf. V. Doucet, in *Antonianum* 4 (1939): 204, where it is still greeted as "pulcherrimum opus."

Second. Rousselot's thesis, *L'Intellectualisme de saint Thomas* (1908), and later Maréchal's volumes, *Le Point de départ de la métaphysique,* published between 1922 and 1926, though they contain questionable elements, remain major works which mark a genuine beginning. Rousselot's thesis was, says Gilson, "the first in date of the attempts, of which there have been many since, to find a Thomist answer to the problems of our time, not by adapting the doctrine in any distorting sense, but in an effort to restore its true principles in their purity of meaning"; and Gilson adds that "on re-reading that fine book, after so many years," he was struck by its "perspicacity."[11] As for Maréchal's books, they originated in "a kind of intuition" which, around the same time, was suggesting to the young professor at Louvain "that only the formal element in the old scholasticism had been examined, and that it still remained to show, in contrast to this, the dynamic principles which gave rise to the tremendous syntheses of the middle ages."[12] As a result of the stimulus given by these two Jesuits, it is true today—even truer than when Victorin Doucet used the phrase in 1929—to speak "of a new era that has begun with a return to the ancient scholastic teaching."[13]

236

Both theses provoked a storm of disagreement. Both made their authors a host of fervent disciples. Many other works took their inspiration from them. On the precise point we are dealing with in this work, the position which they hold or indicate still, as I have said, seems to me rather too timid, and based on inadequate historical research. It has also remained perhaps over-dependent on conceptions or points of view that are too modern. On the other hand, they are by way of being works of philosophy (or the history of philosophy). A study undertaken from a theological standpoint and on a wider basis might lead more directly to more complete results. So at least it seems to me. But their work is an intellectually more modest one. For myself, thanks to a direct and lengthy examination of the texts, and with the help of the numerous

[11] "La possibilité philosophique de la philosophie chrétienne," *Revue des sc. relig.* 32 (1958): 188, note.

[12] Albert Milet, "Les 'Cahiers' du Père Maréchal, sources doctrinales et influences subies," *Revue néoscolastique de philosophie* 43 (1955): 232. On Maréchal's connection with Blondel and Rousselot: ibid., pp. 241–51. The author notes the influence of Gratry, read in 1899 (pp. 236–37). It is also worth consulting the three volumes of *Correspondance* between Maurice Blondel and Auguste Valensin (Paris, 1957–65), and *Auguste Valensin, textes et documents inédits* (1961). The fourth volume only appeared posthumously in 1947.

[13] *Loc. cit.,* p. 208.

190 The Mystery of the Supernatural

detailed studies published in the last fifty years, in my search for this same return to tradition on which all their effort seems to me to converge, I have always had the sense, not of counteracting that effort in any way, but of helping it to achieve its goal.

It must be admitted that there is a certain failure of method in some of the works of this school. They are quite sound in their exegesis at the outset, when it is a matter of establishing the position of the older writers, and especially of St. Thomas, in regard to the desire to see God and the unity of their final concept of beatitude. But they tend to become vaguer, or further from the texts,[14] and sometimes more arbitrary, more caught up in irreconcilable hypotheses, when they then try to define the limits of that desire, to clarify its precise correlative end, and ultimately to reintroduce a further dualism by some new idea of natural beatitude. That they assign great importance to the Thomist axiom, "the desire of nature cannot be in vain" [*desiderium naturae nequit esse inane*], seems to me excellent, but the interpretation they give of it is only half true.[15] As much as—perhaps more than—any theological scruple, these timidities and reticences seem to me to be, at least in some cases, the result of philosophical prejudices not yet totally removed: I have explained these in the preceding chapters. Sometimes too the problem has been studied less for itself than in view of problems of a different kind, and people have tried to discover an intellectual dynamism which will form an adequate basis for the absolute validity of our knowledge, rather than directly to consider and analyze the desire of spirit: a perfectly legitimate undertaking, but one which narrows the perspective considerably. "The Absolute has set its mark upon the basic orientation of our intellect"; "the natural impulse of our intellectual faculties directs them towards the immediate intuition of absolute Being," although that intuition "is beyond the powers and outside the requirements of any finite intelligence left to its natural resources alone": this is what Maréchal demonstrated;[16] but one might add—and he would certainly not dis-

237

---

[14] Cf., in relation to the important articles by Guy de Broglie, the opinion of one informed critic, Père Henri Rondet, in *Recherches de sc. rel.* 35 (1948): 521: "Historically speaking, it is hard to agree with his conclusions." Or at least, with all his conclusions; for these articles did much in their day to illuminate the question. See also Doucet, *loc. cit.*, pp. 205–6.

[15] See *supra*, chapter 9, pp. 180–81. Maréchal concluded not only to a "negatively possible" supernatural destiny, but to "the absolute (positive) possibility of that beatitude" (*Le point de départ de la métaphysique*, cahier 5, Bruges-Paris, 1949, p. 421).

[16] *A propos du sentiment de présence* (1909), p. 68.

agree—that "the need for the absolute is something considerably beyond the plane of knowledge."[17] By limiting oneself in the question of the "desire to see God" to "too merely speculative a theory,"[18] is one not all too likely to raise further difficulties, and compromise the fully supernatural quality of God's gift, at the same time as depriving oneself of the support of many texts?[19]

238

Finally, when, we compare the major representatives of this school with one another, we do not always succeed in finding a sufficiently definite body of teaching to be able to judge it with precision.

If we remember first what they agree about, we shall in fact be recalling where it is that we agree with them. They all speak of a certain "positive openness" to the supernatural, an openness which is something different from, and far more than, any mere "non-repugnance." Thus all recognize that the problem of the supernatural is unique, and not simply another form of the problem of the miraculous. They all proclaim with St. Thomas, using as he does very Augustinian phraseology:[20] "Nothing can *quiet* the finite desire of the intellect"; "The natural desire of substances separated from God *does not rest* in the natural cog-

---

[17] Jacques Leclercq, *Le philosophie morale de saint Thomas devant la pensée contemporaine* (1955), p. 287. Cf. my own *Sur les chemins de Dieu* (1956), chapter 6, Eng. trans. *The Discovery of God* (London, 1960), chapter 6. Maréchal, *Le point de départ*, vol. 5, p. 421: ". . . we deduce legitimately from the basic disposition of our faculties. . . ."

[18] Maurice Blondel, *Exigences philosophiques du christianisme* (1950), p. 224; cf. pp. 225–32. Earlier, Testis (= Blondel) wrote of Rousselot in "La Semaine sociale de Bordeaux et le Monophorisme," taken from the *Annales de philosophie chrétienne* (1910): 68–69: "The supernatural does not consist solely in a vision or an intuition, however speculative, however possessive of being; it also, and above all, consists in a marvellous relationship of love, in the deific adoption which in a sense turns the metaphysical order upside down, though without destroying it, the relationship that must come into being between Creator and creature in order that the creature, a slave, be brought into the inner life of the Trinity as a son. One might have an infinite wish to know the infinite fully without ever desiring, without ever suspecting this 'inebriation,' this 'madness,' which is of a different order altogether from intellection. . . ." It would take too long to draw out all that is implied in texts of this kind, of which there are many in Blondel's works. They deal with such a variety of points as to go far beyond the preliminary problem which is all we are concerned with in this book.

[19] A critical note on this subject is also presented by Jacques Maritain, *Quatre Essais sur l'esprit dans sa condition charnelle* (1939), pp. 139–40, and 162; *Neuf leçons sur les notions premières de la philosophie morale* (1951), pp. 89–108. See also my own "Sur le chapitre XIV du *Proslogion*," *Spicilegium Beccense* 1 (1959): 295–312.

[20] Apart from the well-known "until it rests in you" [*donec requiescat in te*] at the beginning of the *Confessions*, and the "you are always at rest, for you are yourself the rest" at the end, see the passage in *De Genesi ad litteram*, bk. 4, c. 18, n. 34 (*PL*, 34, 309).

nition they have, rather it is more aroused [*incitatur magis*] to seeing the divine substance";[21] or again, expressing the same principle the other way round: "The intellectual creature does not attain its final end, except when its natural desire *is quieted.*"[22] They all say with him, not only of "separated substances" properly so called, but of all created spirit and especially of man: "The beatitude of man is the ultimate good of man, in which his desire *is quieted.* . . . For this desire *will not be quieted* until it attains to the first cause, which is God, that is to the divine essence itself."[23] And again, they all say with the early Thomists: "When we say that beatitude is the final end, we mean final in the sense that it quiets the intellective appetite most fully, and once it possesses it, seeks nothing more";[24] and indeed with later, and less strictly Thomist writers: "in the possession of anything besides God, man does not rest [*non quiescit*] naturally."[25] In this, they are faithful not only to their master St. Thomas but, in essentials at least, to the thought (in some ways so different) of St. Anselm,[26] as well as to that of the whole early scholastic tradition, whether Thomist or Scotist.[27] And it is in this that they diverge from the dualism which had become generally accepted by their own day.

[21] *Summa contra Gentiles,* bk. 3, c. 50; quoted by J. Maréchal, *Le point de départ de la métaphysique,* vol. 5 (1926), p. 311. Cf. c. 48: "The more someone understands the more the desire of understanding increases in him; this is natural to all"; and c. 40, on the knowledge of faith: "Natural desire is quieted through happiness, since it is the final end. Knowledge does not quiet the desire of faith, but inflames it further."

[22] *Summa contra Gentiles,* bk. 3, c. 62.

[23] *Expositio in Matthaeum evangelistam,* c. 5. Cf. the anonymous *Quaestio* on the beatific vision (Toulouse, ms. 737, fol. 164), quoted by Gillon, *loc. cit.,* p. 118, note 2: "It seems that the soul has been imperfectly endowed unless it attain the knowledge of God without mediation. Indeed the soul, by reason of its intellective part, is capable of the highest truth. If therefore it cannot attain the highest truth unless by some mediating creature, that which adheres to it immediately is a creature. But then it would not rest simply; for there is no rest but that in which rest is simple and perfect, which only is in God, not in nature. For the creature, by the very fact that it is a creature, always leads into something else, that is to say, the Creator."

[24] Hervé de Nédellec, *De beatitudine,* q. 1 (unpublished work, quoted by Juan Alfaro, S.J., *op. cit.,* p. 223).

[23] Toletus, *In Primam,* enar. 1, q. 1, art. 1 (Rome 1869, vol. 1, p. 20).

[26] *Monologium,* c. 70 (*PL,* 158, 216 CD).

[27] Thus Duns Scotus, *Opus oxon.,* IV, dist. 1, q. 6, n. 5: "It is impossible for potency to be perfectly quieted except in what is best, in which the essence of its object [*ratio objecti sui*] is saved. But the whole being [*totum ens*] is an object by reason [*sub ratione*] of good will, and by reason of true intellect. Therefore the intellect and the will are quieted only when their object is in the height of its perfection. But in no finite thing can it be in its highest perfection. Therefore, only in the Infinite." John Tinctor (Alfaro, pp. 235–36), etc.

But where the difficulties arise with them all is in their attempts to   240
give a positive explanation of that *non quiescit.*

These attempts certainly vary a great deal. Sometimes, for instance, the natural desire to see God is described as "an attraction not in itself conditioned"; an attraction which, if not satisfied, "torments" the spirit, and in its vehemence[28] may even "torture" it. Sometimes—even for the same theologian—that same desire is no more than a mere "supererogatory wish"; it is no more than a "mild Platonic attraction" felt for "the infinite," no more than the vague desire for "a blessing one would like to receive." Sometimes, remembering St. Thomas's *incitatur magis,* one of them explains most pertinently that "to have an idea of God is in no sense to possess God"; he will then show that "the development of our knowledge, far from providing us with an inferior substitute to replace the beatific vision, and thus give an illusory satisfaction to the hunger felt by our nature, must necessarily result in increasing that desire," and thus of "torturing" us even more. Sometimes, on the other hand—and again it is the same writer speaking, a few pages further on—we are comfortingly reassured by being told: "One does not really see why the principle of all or nothing should be the last word of wisdom," and it is pointed out—which is certainly incontestable—that God need not provide for our pleasure "the highest satisfactions it is capable of"; which takes us rather far from the position towards which we seemed to be moving, a position defined by one mystical writer in these terms: "God made the soul in his image and likeness in order to give himself to it, knowing that anything he would give it apart from himself would be as nothing for it."[29]

It follows that there is the same uncertainty in the actual words used   241
for the desire and its characteristics. Sometimes, for instance, "desire" [*desiderium*], "appetite" [*appetitus*], and "intention" [*intentio*] are taken as synonymous;[30] then, arbitrarily setting aside any absolute desire as

[28] Cf. Bérulle text quoted *supra*, p. 58: "the powerful weight of that inclination."

[29] Eckhartian sermon for St. John the Evangelist, in Noel, *Oeuvres de Tauler*, vol. 4, p. 497. And Tauler himself, *Sermon* 36, n. 4: "The soul bears within it a spark, a depth, whose thirst even God, who can do everything, cannot quench except by giving it himself. Were he to give it the spirit of all the forms of all that he has created in heaven and on earth, even that would not satisfy the soul nor quench its longing. That thirst is in it of its nature. That is the depth, the desire, which stifles these corrupt, worldly men. . . ."

[30] In *Divus Thomas* (Piacenza), 39, 1936, A. Raineri points out rightly that "desiderium" is not "intentio," and that the categories of efficacious and non-efficacious do not apply to "desiderium" as such. Cf. Capreolus, *Defensiones theologicae D. Thomae* 7 (1908),

synonymous with efficacious intention and definite movement of will, we are presented with the natural desire to see God as "purely in the nature of a velleity," and even as the mere velleity for "one good" among others: it thus becomes hard to understand how this velleity-desire can then be distinguished from that vague "complacency" [*complacentia*] which Suarez[31] and Báñez[32] admitted in our nature under the precise title of "velleity" [*velleitas*] and "conditioned desire" [*desiderium conditionatum*], or "simple and inefficacious affect" [*simplex et inefficax affectus*], or "imperfect appetite of some simple complacency" [*appetitus imperfectus et simplicis cuiusdam complacentiae*]. But in view of this it is hard to understand their reason for proclaiming that they are returning to St. Thomas as against the corruptions of Suarez. Nor can one see any sense in so many passionate controversies between adversaries who are basically so much in agreement that they end by using even the same words. Nor can one possibly understand how it was possible to come so close to Suarez's teaching and then describe his principle as "false evidence." Sometimes, on the other hand, the word "velleity," which seems to sum up the doctrine completely, is rejected as quite inaccurate, since, as they rightly say, it is a question of a desire which though "nonexigent" is "rooted in nature," and therefore "essential";[33] thus the older terminology is restored, though not all of the early scholastic doctrine. Sometimes it is admitted unequivocally that the "elicited desire" spoken of at first is the sign of a deeper and more universal appetite, an appetite of a different kind, which is the true "desire of nature." Sometimes, on the

242

---

pp. 181–82 (*In Sent.*, dist. 49, q. 3): the damned "strive for beatitude not only by a conditional appetite, but by the absolute appetite": is their desire then not efficacious?

[31] *De ultimo fine hominis*, disp. 16, sectio 3, n. 7: "Although man, situated in pure nature, might conceive some conditioned desire of this vision, nevertheless, if he lived prudently, he would not be disquieted, but would be content with his natural lot; just as in the same way [*illo modo*] man would be able to strive to understand without intellectual progress [*sine discursu*], and this striving nevertheless would neither solicit nor trouble the soul; for he would know being [*esse*] in respect of a fact quite alien to human nature, and for this reason not necessary being. As a result, an elicited affect of this kind might arise properly from the innate appetite toward the appetite's concern. And so it is manifestly clear about other velleities that they are concerned with impossibilities. . ." (ed. Vivès, vol. 4, p. 156). *De divina substantia eiusque attributis*, bk. 2, a. 7, n. 11 (vol. 1, p. 66). Cf. Leibniz, *Théodicée*, 404: velleities are "a very imperfect kind of conditional acts of the will."

[32] *In Primam*, q. 12, art. 1 (1584 ed., p. 447). *In Primam Secundae*, q. 3, art. 8 (vol. 1, 1942, pp. 122–23, 127).

[33] Thus Père Philippe de la Trinité, "Du péché de Satan et de la destinée de l'esprit d'après saint Thomas d'Aquin" in *Satan, Etudes carmélitaines* (1948), p. 66.

other hand, the idea of an "innate appetite" seems to be used to deny the ontological nature of the desire, so that the term "elicited appetite" no longer means any more than a certain desire which may spontaneously arise in the consciousness in response to certain effects—in other words, the terminology of the past is being abandoned twice over at the very moment when a return to literal fidelity is being claimed. For the appetite, which is set aside by being classed as "innate," is the very same as what the older theologians called "natural appetite."[34] As for the so-called "elicited" appetite, as explained, it is quite foreign to these same theologians, who rightly spoke only of "elicited acts." "Inclination is not a natural appetite, a certain elicited act; but it is just like the first perfection," says Duns Scotus;[35] and St. Thomas, for whom elicited acts are acts of the will, sees in the natural appetite the desire of intellectual nature itself, so much so that "every *intellect* naturally desires the vision of divine substance."[36] This, however, has not prevented a recent author from setting out to give us St. Thomas's teaching "on the elicited appetite."[37]

243

It is all a fine muddle, as we can see. It reaches a peak of confusion in certain odd inconsistencies; for instance we find one interpreter of St. Thomas beginning by strongly maintaining the idea of an "unconditional" desire, which turns out, however, to be no more in his eyes than a simple "velleity," whereas another interpreter proceeding in a similar but in some ways opposite manner begins by rejecting "velleity" as too weak, later defends the idea of a still conditional—indeed "humbly conditional"—desire, and finally brings the two terms together by speaking from then on of a "conditioned velleity-desire."[38] It is easy to see the

[34] Cf. Victor Doucet, *loc. cit.*, p. 169: "One should keep in mind that this appetite which we call today 'innate' was simply called natural appetite among the ancient theologians."

[35] *In 2 Sent.*, dist. 6, q. 2, n. 10 (*Opera omnia*, Vivès, vol. 12, p. 355).

[36] *Summa contra Gentiles*, bk. 3, c. 57; cf. c. 50: "desiderium intellectus," etc. Cf. Durand of Saint-Pourçain (d. 1334), *In 4 Sent.*, dist. 49, q. 8, n. 7: "Know that, as far as concerns our purpose, the appetite is twofold, namely natural and elective. . . . The act of the natural appetite is not some elicited act . . . ; but the act of the elective appetite (as I mean it here) is not the natural inclination alone, but is a certain elicited act that is called willing [*velle*]. . ." (*In Sent.* [Paris, 1550], fol. 362 r). Similarly Peter of la Palu (d. 1342) who so often disagreed with Durandus: *In Sent.* (Venice, 1493, fol. 236 v).

[37] Enrico di S. Teresa, "Il desiderio naturale della visione di Dio," *Ephemerides carmeliticae* 1 (1947): 83: "Dottrina generale di S. Tommaso sull'appetito naturale e l'appetito elicito."

[38] Mgr. Pietro Parente puts it far better, *Enciclopedia cattolica*, vol. 4, 1950, col. 1482:

intention governing the choice of such formulas. But if the older theologians did not take so much trouble in the matter, it was because they had far less difficulty over the gratuitousness of the supernatural gifts. Epithets like "conditional" or "conditioned," nouns like "velleity," and even more the note of humility (or, as Suarez put it, of "prudence") which is linked with them, can only be applied to acts which are free, conscious, personal, and moral. It is not possible to see how these words could be applied to a desire "of nature," still less to an appetite, which is often described (as it is by St. Thomas) as the appetite of the intellect as such. Such a form of "appetite" does not fall into the categories of submission or non-submission, of humility or pride.[39] Here again, St. Thomas and Duns Scotus are agreed. For the former, every intellect tends towards the vision of God, and its desire cannot be satisfied until it attains to it: "This desire does not rest unless it attains the highest hinge [*cardo*] and maker."[40] And for the latter, who is the more explicit on the point:

244

> Natural will is not of itself [*de se*] immoderate, but only inclines [*inclinat*] by way of nature, and in this there is no immoderation, for it inclines as it accepts to be inclined [*inclinari*], and nothing else is in its power; but in the power of the will, as it is free, in producing an act there is only "being inclined" [*est tantum inclinari*], or less.[41]

Macedo, linking together the two theologians in his usual way, sums this up as follows: "Appetite is not act, and it deeply lacks freedom."[42] And Toletus says the same thing in other terms when he establishes the difference between natural and elicited appetite to explain how the damned continue to desire God *absolute* by the first, but desire him in a wrong way, *immoderate,* by the second.[43]

"In the order of intention this desire is absolute and efficacious, but in the order of execution it remains inefficacious and conditioned to supernatural aid."

[39] The same thing will be noted in regard to Père Blaise Romeyer, for whom our natural capacity to be raised up to the order of vision is "a docile appetite for the personal Love of God" (*Archives de philosophie,* 18, p. 58).

[40] *Summa contra Gentiles,* bk. 3, c. 50, etc. Cf. E. Brisbois, *Nouv. revue théol.* 63 (1936): 1092.

[41] *In 2 Sent.,* dist. 6, q. 2, n. 10 (vol. 12, p. 355). Cf. *In 4 Sent.,* dist. 49, q. 9, n. 3: "Si tollis hunc appetitum, tollis naturam" (vol. 21, p. 319).

[42] *Collationes . . . ,* vol. 1, p. 16. Earlier, John of Rada, *Controversia* 13: by natural appetite, "neque meremur, neque demeremur" (vol. 4, p. 426).

[43] *In Primam Secundae* (in A. Arenas, *op. cit.,* p. 14). See also Peter of la Palu, *In 4 Sent.,* dist. 49, q. 7 (Venice, 1493, fol. 237 v); quoted by Doucet, pp. 186–87.

On the other hand, what difference can one thenceforward see between the concept of the "humbly conditional or conditioned desire" in which this line of thought finally results, and the "conditional and non-efficacious desire" of Père Garrigou-Lagrange, to give one example,[44] from whose thinking it was originally planned to diverge in order to return to a more authentic Thomism? Or what difference is there between this and the "velleity-desire" or "dream" of Père de Tonquédec,[45] who also belongs to a very different school? What difference is there between all these writers and Suarez? Yet all of them reject Suarez in so many words and proclaim their fidelity to St. Thomas alone. And all fall equally under the criticism which Père Motte made of some among them in the name of Thomism: "'Conditional' is no more justified [than 'non-efficacious'], for the desire to see God is directed towards an unlimited good; it is an absolute desire."[46] If there is one thing that is quite certain, and easily verifiable, it is that, as we have already said, St. Thomas was well aware of the concept of "velleity," and it was for him a "conditioned will" [*voluntas conditionata*][47] or an "incomplete will" [*voluntas incompleta*],[48] or an "imperfect will" [*voluntas imperfecta*],[49] since it is a "will of the impossible" [*voluntas de impossibili*], or "will for impossible things" [*voluntas impossibilium*][50]—on this partic-

245

[44] *Revue thomiste* 19 (1936): 208.

[45] *Op. cit.*, p. 161.

[46] *Bulletin thomiste*, 4, pp. 581–82.

[47] *In 4 Sent.*, dist. 14, q. 1, a. 1, 6, ad 3um: "Although the complete act of the will [*voluntas completa*] is not in respect of the impossible, a certain velleity is, i.e. the conditioned will; indeed the velleity that something had been the case if it were possible." Cf. dist. 17, q. 2, a. 1, 1, ad 3um; dist. 43, q. 1, a. 4, 1, ad 2um; *In 3 Sent.*, dist. 27, q. 2, a. 1, ad 4um, etc.

[48] *Prima Secundae*, q. 13, a. 5, ad 1um: "The complete act of the will is only in respect of what is possible and good for him that wills; but the incomplete act of the will is in respect of the impossible, and by some it is called velleity, because, to wit, one would will [*vellet*] such a thing, if it were possible." *Prima*, q. 19, a. 6, ad 1um: "It can be said . . . that a just judge simply wills a murderer to be hanged; but in a qualified manner he would will him to, to wit, inasmuch as he is a man; such a qualified will may be called velleity, rather than an absolute will. . . ." *Tertia*, q. 21, a. 4; Suppl, q. 79, a. 1.

[49] *De malo*, q. 16, a. 3, ad 9um: "What is called the will for impossible things [*voluntas impossibilium*] is not a perfect will tending to something to be pursued, for no man tends to what he reckons to be impossible . . . rather it is a certain imperfect will, called velleity, for someone would wish [*vellet*] for that which he reckons to be impossible, but under this condition: if it were possible. . . ."

[50] See also *In 2 Sent.*, dist. 33, q. 2, art. 2, ad 2um: "[That will] that is for impossible things, which must be called velleity rather than will. . . ."

ular point Suarez agrees with him.[51] And it is no less certain that St. Thomas, like St. Bonaventure[52] and unlike Suarez, never uses it of the desire to see God. Thus we find in the true Thomist tradition both terms, conditional desire and velleity, continuing side by side, and both equally excluded from all the passages dealing with "natural desire."[53]

246   These hesitations and uncertainties which mar some of the writings of the new school must not blind us to the great positive good in it. But they involve one consequence which we must consider. They do become naturally communicated to the idea which these writers are seeking to formulate of a "beatitude" at once natural and transcendent. St. Thomas, although he envisaged it only indirectly in connection with the knowledge which "separated substances" can have of God, certainly knew of such a concept from the teachings of Arabic peripatetics and neo-Platonists,[54] but it had no place in his own thought. In the course of the long argument worked out in the third book of the *Summa contra Gentiles,* a single chapter is considered sufficient to refute it.[55] In fact, it simply envisages two beatitudes: that of this world and that of our "heavenly homeland" [*patria*]; that of the "philosopher" and that of the "saints." It has even been said that when it comes to nature, Saint Thomas adopts the wisdom of Aristotle quite happily, and gives beatitude a profoundly terrestrial horizon.[56] Without any intervening hypothesis, he constantly contrasts the perfect felicity the Gospel promises us "after this life" with a certain "final happiness of man that can be had in this life."[57] Furthermore, the concept in question is

---

[51] *Loc. cit.*: "that it be manifestly clear concerning other velleities that they are concerned with impossibilities."

[52] *In 2 Sent.,* dist. 7, p. 1, art. 1, q. 2, ad 7um; "The appetite of velleity which is for impossible things."

[53] Thomas of Strasbourg, *In 4 Sent.,* dist. 49, q. 3: "A thing can strive for something, or desire it, in three ways. . . . The third way is by conditional desire; for instance, whenever man strives [*appetit*], if it were possible, that he would fain fly . . ." (*In Sent.,* Venice, 1564, p. 196 r). Durandus of Saint-Pourçain, *In 4 Sent.,* dist. 49, q. 8, n. 18: "a conditioned willing [*velle*] or some velleity." Capreolus, *Opera,* vol. 6, p. 171; and p. 180: "velleity, or conditional appetite," etc.

[54] Cf. *In 4 Sent.,* dist. 49, q. 2, art. 1; *Quodl.,* 19, art. 17; *Summa contra Gentiles,* bk. 3, c. 41–45.

[55] *Summa contra Gentiles,* bk. 3, c. 50.

[56] M. Nédoncelle, *Existe-t-il une philosophie chrétienne?* (Paris, 1956), p. 42, Eng. trans. *Is There a Christian Philosophy?* (London, 1960).

[57] *Super librum de causis expositio* (ed. Saffrey, 1954), pp. 1–2. For other texts see my article "Duplex hominis beatitudo," *Recherches de science religieuse* 35 (1948): 290–99.

absent not only from St. Thomas's own thought, but also from that of his contemporaries.[58] Yet in the new scholasticism it becomes indispensable, and the kind of beatitude it indicates must be considered as definitive. But in what does it consist? Here again, opinions vary. 247

Does natural beatitude mean contentment in a natural end truly attained and possessed, which can give the being a completely stable and positive satisfaction, "without restlessness," though never cloying?[59] Can one therefore consider it as a genuine final end for human nature? Or must one take rather more seriously St. Thomas's "it rests not" [*non quiescit*]? Should one not accept the comment about it given in the seventeenth century by the Jesuit Julius Caesar Recupitus: "The abstractive knowledge of God is disquieting [*inquietativa*], and the more it is perfect, the more it is disquieting."[60] In this last case, then, must it not be concluded that, apart from the vision of God, man, remaining inevitably unfulfilled, has no real *end* in the true sense? Left to nature alone, in other words remaining for ever "imperfectus," he would be condemned never to know more than a "kind of anxious joy," which would consist in "always poetizing reality by dreaming," and "expanding possession by desire," while continuing to call upon "an indifferent and silent heaven."

Such is the explanation arrived at by one of the finest representatives of the new Thomist school whose merits I have indicated. It is certainly more logical, and closer to St. Thomas himself, than the earlier one, because in rejecting the idea of a closed and static natural happiness it rejects more completely all dualism properly so called. This explanation makes the only destiny possible to spiritual beings that are 248

---

[58] As another witness to the earlier doctrine, we may also quote Godfrey of Fontaines, *Quaestiones disputatae*, q. 3: "Man . . . is ordered to a twofold perfect life, or to a twofold happiness: natural, to wit with respect to human citizenship, and supernatural, with respect to heavenly citizenship;" and q. 2: "There are some things that order man to his supernatural end, to wit to the contemplation of God in his essence, which is had in heaven; there are other things that order man to his natural end, to wit to his earthly preservation [*civiliter conservandum*] and to the contemplation that can be had in this life" (B. Neumann, *op. cit.* [1958], p. 17).

[59] Thus Pallavicini, *In Primam Secundae*, disp. 2, q. 2, a. 5, n. 4: "not yet satisfied," and yet "without restlessness."

[60] *De veritate*, bk. 6, q. 1. There is also a good explanation in Macedo, *Collationes*, 2 (1673), pp. 398, 399: "If a final end of natural beatitude only should be proposed to the rational nature, it would rest in it not at all. . . . The will remains restless, and will not be gladdened [*beabitur*]. . . . And [man] would be tortured more than he would enjoy. . . ." Cf. Savonarola, *Triumphus crucis*, bk. 1, c. 13, bk. 2, c. 4.

not "raised up," not in fact called to the beatific vision, to be a kind of
endless pursuit by a "radical inclination" of their "highest and inaccessible limit."[61] Aware of the insurmountable difficulties raised by the modern notions of a "natural end" and a "natural happiness," whether seen
as something ultimately cloying or not, a certain number of theologians
are today following this line of thought which was first opened by
Joseph Maréchal. Though contributing their own detailed explanations,
they all recognize as he did, and without the reservations we noted in
the others, that in line with the argument of the *Summa contra Gentiles*[62]
the vision of God face to face is the only genuinely final end for any created spirit, since it is the only end which can totally satisfy its desires.
Thus, for Père Philippe de la Trinité, "a spiritual nature that is not historically orientated to the beatific vision would still not be a static
nature, directed to no end," for there is for all spiritual natures "only one
unique, supernatural final end, and no possible alternative happiness."[63] For Père Le Guillou, interpreting St. Thomas, natural happiness, though "a thing of nature" [*aliquid naturae*], could not possibly be
called "the end of nature"; "it is clear that perfect possession of God is
the final end of created spirit, whether angel or man, the end *simpliciter*"
and therefore, "apart from being effectively called to that vision, man
would remain in a sense in a state of incompleteness."[64]

The critical value of such a solution, or rather perhaps of such a line
of thought, is undeniable. But to elude the obvious difficulties in this
way results in later coming up against another less obvious one. That
249   eternal incompleteness, which keeps desire alive, and which suggests a
never-ending advance towards the good which will never be totally possessed, is somewhat reminiscent of St. Gregory of Nyssa's famous definition of God as "he who is sought."[65] But note that if we are to be able

[61] Cf. Joseph Maréchal, S.J., *Etudes sur la psychologie des mystiques*, vol. 1, 2d ed.,
p. 237, from whom all these expressions come.

[62] *Summa contra Gentiles*, bk. 3, c. 50, 57, 59, etc.

[63] *Loc. cit.*, p. 82.

[64] "Surnaturel," *Revue des sc. philos. et théol.* 34 (1950): 234. In his interesting work,
Man's Last End (Saint Louis—London, 1949), Fr. Joseph Buckley, S.M., seems at first to
follow this same line of thought: "Man has no determinate, concrete last end in the natural order" (p. 164; cf. p. 232). But that statement means for him simply, in the natural
psychological order, "a multitude of partial goods, with God as first cause thereof attained
only after the manner of partial good" (p. 232).

[65] *In Cant. Cant.*, hom. 6; and *In Eccles.*, hom. 7, n. 6: ". . . the finding of whom is
always to seek him; for it is one thing to seek and another to find: but the proceeds of

to speak of real dynamism and real advance, we must take it that the further forward one goes towards an inaccessible goal, the closer one in fact gets to it. As long as this is so, the idea put forward here can claim to constitute an original solution, different in kind from those which envisage a certain "state" of natural happiness, and more satisfying than any of them. As long as this is so, then this idea can grant for "uncalled" spiritual beings a certain delight in their development, rather than the agony which must be the lot of a being whose endless pursuit, spurred on by an ever more vehement desire, never really gets anywhere at all.

But is it in fact so? Is the asymptotic image it suggests not an illusion? Is it not, like all other concepts of indefinite advance, deceptive?[66] Real advance, effective movement forward, with the delight it brings, presupposes at least the beginnings of possession. Such is certainly what is meant by St. Gregory of Nyssa and the other Fathers: "When man has reached perfection [*consummaverit*], then he begins":

> Once the soul, striving for the heights, has begun to share, in so far as it can, in the divine benefits, then once more the Word draws it as though it were still at the start of its ascent. . . . Once again he says: "Arise" to one who has already arisen, and "Come" to one who has already come. In truth, to rise at all, one must rise for ever, and for those who run towards the Lord, there will always be a great distance to cover. When he says "Arise and come," the Word demands that one constantly arise, and never cease to run forward, and every time he gives the grace of a greater advance.[67]

250

The same thing is understood in the explanation which St. John of the Cross gives in *The Living Flame:*

> It seems that the more the soul desires God, the more it possesses him, the more delight and joy it feels. Thus the angels, whose desire is fulfilled, rejoice in possessing God; they never cease to have their desires satisfied, and are never the least wearied, and being unwearied, they never cease to desire. . . .[68]

---

seeking is the seeking itself" (*PG*, 44, 892–93, and 720 C), etc. As we know, the same theme was dear to St. Augustine, St. Bernard, and many others.

[66] Cf. Nicholas Berdyaev, *Essai d'autobiographie spirituelle,* French trans. p. 376. "An infinite progress is an absurdity."

[67] St. Gregory of Nyssa, *In Cant. Cant.,* hom. 5 (*PG*, 44, 873–76). For other texts see my own *Sur les chemins de Dieu,* pp. 191, 201, 334–37; and von Balthasar, *Présence et Pensée* (Paris, 1942), pp. 69–76.

[68] *The Living Flame of Love,* 3, 22 (Silverio, 4, p. 60). Cf. St. Francis de Sales, *Treatise*

And it is in this sense too that we can understand what Nicholas of Cusa says in his small book *De visione Dei:*

> The more I comprehend that you are incomprehensible, O my God, the more I attain to you, because I attain better the object of my desire. . . . The eternal principle which has given birth to my desire leads it to an unending, infinite end. . . . The end of the intellect is simply to penetrate all things while not penetrating them. It is satisfied neither by the intelligible which it knows, nor by what it does not know; it is satisfied only by him whom it knows to be so intelligible that he can never be totally understood.[69]

But in the hypothesis I have just been discussing this is not the case. Père Yves de Montcheuil seems to have seen the difference very clearly when he wrote of the first philosophy of René Le Senne:

> If the end is inaccessible and must always elude our grasp, then one cannot say that one grows nearer to it with every unification one achieves. And if it is the attractiveness of the end which draws us, the desire to bring about that harmonious union of persons, then the realization that it is infinitely beyond us must stop short the movement of the spirit. . . . For on the way, we already taste the end through hope. If there were no longer an end, there would be no more way, for what makes it a journey is not that it moves away from its starting-point, but that it draws nearer to its point of arrival.[70]

251

It was a similar argument that led Félix Ravaisson, in his well-known *Rapport,* to set aside, and rightly, the popular musings of Jean Reynaud: "One may wonder," he wrote, "whether to treat heaven as J. Reynaud does, by making it almost identical with earth, is not in fact to abolish it; whether to do away with the journey is not in fact to do away with the goal; whether to take away absolute perfection is not also to take away the whole idea of perfection. . . ."[71] There is something in this movement towards nothing, envisaged by some theologians as the destiny of man left to his nature, that is rather reminiscent of "that unhappy tower

---

on the Love of God, bk. 3, chapter 15: "The spirits of the blessed are overwhelmed by two wonders: one for the infinite beauty they contemplate, and the other for the depth and infinity they have yet to see in that same beauty. Dear Lord, how wonderful is what they see! but dear Lord, how far more so is what they do not see!" etc. (Fr. ed. p. 313).

[69] Chapter 16.

[70] "Une philosophie du devoir," *Mélanges théologiques,* pp. 238–39.

[71] *La philosophie en France au XIXᵉ siècle⁴* (1895), p. 50.

that rose storey by storey, and yet never touched even the edge of the sky."[72] There are other images which come to mind too—Penelope's tapestry, or the stone of Sisyphus. The hypotheses of Le Senne and Jean Reynaud were not, of course, exactly the same as those we are examining here—the differences are obvious; yet the central point of the argument brought against them by Père de Montcheuil and Félix Ravaisson seems to me to apply perfectly to them. "An indefinite advance which never reaches the boundary is simply a journey across the relative with no absolute, a time with no eternity, and ultimately is merely the idea of movement rather than the reality."[73]

If it were absolutely necessary—though the attentive reader will have grasped by now that I do not think it so—to try to imagine the essential activity of a created spirit to whom God did not will to give any access to his own joy, I would prefer to borrow a simile from Pseudo-Denys, though without claiming to be creating any coherent hypothesis, or to be doing more than illustrate the situation of created being in regard to God. In the third chapter of *On the divine names* Denys speaks of intellects performing "without principle and without end . . . their incessant revolution" around being.[74] Père Ambroise Gardeil, inspired by this chapter, wrote a fine description of the movement of the contemplative soul, already attracted by the vision of God, but still bound by the last bonds of earthly life. "Its regard remains desperately fixed in expectation." It moves "without moving away from the divine centre which holds its heart." At last there arrives the moment when he whom it has contemplated without yet possessing him opens that centre, "breaking the circle of its circular movement."[75] The expectation in which this soul has waited is hope, for it knows God's promise. But by transposing the image of Denys and of Père Gardeil, one can apply it differently. One can imagine a being—a spirit like our own—bearing deep within its nature a similar attraction, but unconsciously. That being would not know itself. God, who will never give himself to it, has not revealed to it what lies in its own depths. But that attraction, despite being unknown to it, would be none the less real. It would underlie everything it did. It would therefore be not properly speaking a

252

---

[72] Victor Poucel.

[73] Jules Monchanin, *De l'esthétique à la mystique* (1955), p. 44.

[74] *De div. nom.*, c. 3, nn. 8–9.

[75] A. Gardeil, *La structure de l'âme et l'expérience mystique*[2] (1927), vol. 2, p. 265.

particular appetite or desire, but the soul of all its desires. The motive power of such a desire, constantly exercised, would be a substantial activity of such a being, dominating and governing all the others, without ever itself being objectified, because it would be for ever moving around God, though without knowing it: "for it unknowingly is circling around God."[76]

But, as we know from Christ, "universal gyration is not the ultimate reality."[77]

253   To return to the hypothesis discussed in this chapter, not only does it not of itself provide a fully satisfactory solution, but neither does it seem in harmony with the explanations St. Thomas gives in a number of places, notably in the third book of the *Summa contra Gentiles:*

> The closer a body that tends to its own place by a natural appetite approaches its end, the more vigorously and quickly it is moved. . . . Since, then, it tends more vehemently towards something later than it does earlier, it is not moved to infinity, but rather tends to something determined. We find this is the desire for knowledge, etc. Any intellectual substance therefore has a final beatitude and happiness: to know God.[78]

In the *De anima* St. Thomas says that nothing is moved to infinity [*in infinitum*]; the idea of continuing to become without ever reaching any conclusion is not attractive; there must of necessity be some ultimate goal when one will finally be wholly in act. Otherwise the journey can only be one of despair. The spirit which never reaches the goal, the vision of God, has failed to achieve its destiny.[79]

Nor does the new hypothesis seem any more in harmony with the ideas of St. Bonaventure, who says quite unequivocally:

> Some authors have said that God is never immediately seen, neither on earth nor in heaven. . . .

---

[76] Scotus Erigena.

[77] I have borrowed the expression from André Préau.

[78] Bk. 3, c. 25; and again, ibid.: "To leave into infinity is not in the appetite of nature, for the desire of nature would be frustrated since it is not possible for it to cross over into infinity." The object here is not exactly the same, but the reasoning is of a similar pattern.

[79] *De anima,* q. 16, ad 3um. The principle stated in the objection is assumed in the answer. See also *De malo,* q. 5, a. 1, obj. 1 and resp. Cf. Aelred of Rievaulx, *Speculum caritatis,* bk. 1, c. 21: "Each individual thing is restless for its order; once ordered, it is at rest"; c. 22: "It does not lose the appetite for beatitude, and as long as it labors in an unhappy circle, it never rests" (*PL,* 195, 524 C, 526 A).

But this position is heretical and condemned, and deservedly, for it is contrary both to reason, since the soul cannot rest perfectly until it sees God in himself [*in se ipso*], and to Holy Scripture, for it is said (1 Cor 13:12): "Then I shall know even as I am known," and (1 John 3:2): "We shall see him as he is."[80]

The note of "heresy," of course, attaches only to the opinion Bonaventure is directly criticizing, the one I spoke of in chapter three. And the argument from scripture is only against that, too. But the argument from reason, adumbrated by St. Bonaventure, and spelled out by St. Thomas, applies to every hypothesis. Once again, Gilson expounds the thinking common to both great doctors, in his work *The Spirit of Medieval Philosophy:*   254

> Even when it is proved that he who desires will never by his own powers attain the whole end of desire even if he has no reason to hope for any help that could make him capable of it, the desire experienced remains there, not in the least extinguished, but rather exasperated into anguish by the very sense of its own impotence. This anguish St. Thomas knew; and Alexander of Aphrodisias knew it, and Averroes, and Aristotle: "In this it is sufficiently clear how great an anguish their famous geniuses suffered";[81] for this is the anguish of the human intellect itself which has in itself the power to become all things, and, grasping the existence of Being from the starting point of sense, would become *that;* and cannot.
>
> Here, and only here, the familiar formula St. Thomas so often repeats in connection with this question attains its full meaning: "it is impossible for natural desire to be vain."[82]

This dynamism which is gradually being introduced into the modern idea of natural beatitude, and saving it from rigidity, is thus, as I have suggested, an indication of a welcome move towards a return to more traditional theology. But it is a beginning that will not complete itself; it must be followed up. If it stops where it is, no more will have been done than to add one further stroke to that naturalizing of the earlier doctrine which is all that is really involved in the idea of natural beatitude as a final and transcendent end. For, let me say it again, it is *within* the one

---

[80] Cf. *supra,* chapter 3, p. 44.

[81] *Summa contra Gentiles,* bk. 3, c. 48. It continues: ". . . and we shall be freed from these anxieties, if we posit, according to the foregoing proofs, that man can attain to true happiness after this life, since the soul of man is immortal."

[82] *The Spirit of Medieval Philosophy* (London, 1936), p. 260.

and only beatitude, within the joy of God, that an advance used to be seen in the past, and not merely an advance, but as St. Bernard went so far as to say, following the Fathers, a desire, a seeking: "And the happy finding does not by any means strike out [*extundit*] holy desire, but stretches it out [*extendit*]. Is the consummation of joy the destruction of desire? Oil is greater than it, for it is greater than the flame; so in this case too. Gladness will be filled; but there will be no end of desire, nor, for the same reason, of seeking."[83]

255 But whatever may be the case as regards these last points, or the internal divergences we have noted, the writings of the Thomist school in which they appear lean very heavily, in putting their doctrine before us, on an interpretation of the axiom so beloved of St. Thomas: "Natural desire cannot be vain"—an interpretation which I have, I think, shown to be incorrect.[84] Therefore, happy as I am to agree with these writings, or rather perhaps to follow them, in the working out of the first part of their thesis, I would be most hesitant to go along with them to the end, since my own plan is to begin by a full return to the thought of St. Thomas and his contemporaries on this subject. Though I would not claim to have succeeded completely, I hope that, thanks to their help, we have come somewhat closer to this thought. Without denying what I owe to the masters who taught me, I think that their historical analysis remained incomplete, and that had they had a better understanding of the theological perspectives of the past, the inner coherence of their own synthesis would have been better assured.

---

[83] *In Cant.*, sermo 84, n. 1 (*Opera*, ed. J. Leclercq, vol. 2, 1958, p. 303). The same may be said, *mutatis mutandis,* of the following statements of Leibniz, *Principes de la nature et de la grâce fondés en raison,* n. 18 (*in fine*): "Thus our happiness will never consist, nor ought it to consist, in a full enjoyment in which there would he nothing further to desire, and which would thus make our minds dull; but rather in a perpetual advance to new joys and new perfections."

[84] Cf. *Le Surnaturel,* pp. 467–71. My interpretation was that earlier given by Gilson, as is clear from the text I have just quoted; also, it would seem, that of G. Van Riet. Father S. Dockx, as we saw earlier, has recently taken it up again and established it on a firm footing. For other names see *supra,* chapter 9, pp. 181–82.

CHAPTER 11

The Unknown Desire

If there is one thing that the foregoing analyses have made clearer than any other, it is that while it may be quite legitimate to argue from completely abstract hypotheses, it ultimately neither explains nor justifies anything. It is not in the order of pure possibilities that our essential problems will be solved. It remains indispensable in any hypothesis to be quite clear about this question of gratuitousness within the order that actually exists. To this fact we must keep returning. By tending in a different direction, that part of modern western theology which we have had to criticize—not for what it says, but for what it does not say—is grasping at shadows rather than the reality. The explanations I have given have undoubtedly shown this.

But there remains one objection still to be considered. However "natural," however real it may be, the desire for the vision of God is in no case what determines God's actually giving that vision. God is not governed by our desire. The relationship between the two things must in fact be the opposite one: it is the free will of the giver which awakens the desire. This is incontestable. There can be no question of anything being due to the creature. But, one may perhaps say, it remains true none the less that once such a desire exists in the creature it becomes the sign, not merely of a possible gift from God, but of a certain gift. It is the evidence of a promise, inscribed and recognized in the being's very self. Is one not then right to conclude from the existence of that desire to the effective reality of the gift? St. Thomas certainly seems to reason in this way. But if so, then man is surely arriving by the use of his natural reason alone at the knowledge that he is made for the vision of

God, which seems to make the effective supernatural become the object of natural knowledge.

It is clear that this fresh objection is not concerned with the gratuitousness of the divine offer, but rather with the mysterious nature of the dogma from which we learn of the offer's existence. One may perhaps recall the discussion which sprang up not long ago about the "mystery of our supernatural elevation."[1] Père Guy de Broglie had been accused of rationalizing the mystery because he wished to demonstrate by reason the natural desire to see God. He had no difficulty in refuting the accusation. He showed that he was quite right in thinking that natural reason can recognize in us a "radical aptitude for supernatural happiness"; in fact, in his theory this power of reason was not the ability to know either the essence of such happiness or the fact that we were actually called to enjoy it. There was, therefore, no cause "to show so much suspicion" of a thesis so limited in scope, as though it "unfolded some unheard of secret."[2] It was quite wrong to cut short the discussion by appealing to the nineteenth-century condemnation of Frohschammer, or indeed to any other decision of the magisterium. The suspicion would, however, be well founded, and possibly even necessary, if we were to combine the thesis I have been defending with the one supported by de Broglie. For this would mean declaring that natural reason has the power to reveal to us that we are in fact called to the vision of God. But is the desire for the beatific vision really, in its full nature and force, able to be known by reason alone?[3] This I do not believe.[4]

259   Remembering always what St. Thomas himself says, ". . . those things

[1] *Nouvelle revue théologique* (1937, 1938, 1939). Pedro Descoqs, *Le mystère de notre élévation surnaturelle* (1938).

[2] A. R. Motte, O.P., *Bulletin thomiste* 4, p. 579.

[3] One may say with Père de Broglie, *Recherches de science religieuse* 15 (1925): 19: "Who then would be so rash as to hold that the *idea*—like you I say the *idea*—of the beatific vision cannot be conceived by our natural powers?" But one may say further, and I think it important to make this clear here, that it is a far from univocal idea.

[4] As the result of some strange carelessness, someone has written (*Gregorianum* 28 [1947]: 382): "Père de L. declares—and it is, we may say, the major thesis of his book—that the existence of this desire [to see God] enables us to be certain that we are in fact elevated to the supernatural order"; and again (p. 384): "The author's thought seems to be this: the desire to see God . . . proves strictly that we are called to the beatifying vision. . . . In short, we have an absolute desire for the beatifying vision, which enables us to be certain that we have been created for that end." There could be no reference to support these assertions. In my book which appeared in 1946 (p. 489, note 1), I made it clear that I avoided examining this point of doctrine which is "argued among theologians."

that are expected above reason in the final end of men,"[5] I want to remain firmly within theology. I am not trying to establish a philosophical thesis, but to study a dogmatic statement and all that it implies. I do not say that the knowledge gained by reason of a natural desire, outside any context of faith, "proves strictly that we are called to the beatific vision," and that therefore we can naturally attain "the certainty that we have been created for that end"; on the contrary, I say that the knowledge that is revealed to us of that calling, which makes us certain of that end, leads us to recognize within ourselves the existence and nature of that desire.[6]

People frequently reason as though all the mystery were on God's side, and there was nothing in man that eludes the grasp of common experience or natural reasoning. Our whole nature should, in theory at least, be comprehensible to us, and we have the key to understanding all its manifestations. But this is somewhat illusory. I do not think that anyone who really thought about it could maintain anything so clear-cut.

"Man himself is very deep" [*valde profundus est ipse homo*]." "Man is a mystery. He is so in his very essence, in his nature. Not because the infinite fullness of the mystery which touches him is actually in himself, for it is strictly inexhaustible, but because he is fundamentally a *pour-soi* purely in reference to that fullness. When we have said everything the mind can take in, everything definable that is to be said about ourselves, we have as yet said nothing, unless we have included in every statement the fact of our reference to the incomprehensible God; and that reference, and therefore our nature itself in the most fundamental sense, is not really understood at all unless we freely allow ourselves to be caught up by that incomprehensible God. No one must think that we can understand man otherwise than by grasping him in his movement towards the blessed obscurity of God."[7] This teaching, recalled recently by Karl Rahner, was one beloved of the Fathers of the Church, both Latin and Greek. In its wider interpretation, as in its origins, it is not specifically Christian, but it acquires a specific character in relation to the doctrine of revelation.

Man, the Fathers tell us, is "in the image of God," not merely

260

---

[5] *Summa contra Gentiles*, bk. 4, c. 1; *Tertia*, q. 1, art. 3.
[6] See *supra*, especially chapter 7.
[7] *Schriften zur Theologie* 3 (Einsiedeln, 1956), pp. 47–60 (theological reflections on the incarnation), French trans. *Ecrits théologiques* 3 (Paris, 1963), pp. 81–101.

because of his intellect, his free will, his immortality, not even because of the power he has received to rule over nature: beyond and above all this, he is so ultimately because there is something incomprehensible in his depths.[8] "Who has known the mind of the Lord?" asks St. Paul.[9] "For my part," adds St. Gregory of Nyssa, "I also ask: Who has known his own mind? Those who think themselves capable of grasping the nature of God would do well to consider whether they have looked into themselves. . . . Our mind bears the imprint of the incomprehensible nature through the mystery that it is to itself"; "if the nature of the image could be grasped, then it would be an image no longer."[10] And similarly St. Ephraim: "Who then can enter into himself and understand himself?"[11] And St. Zeno of Verona: "In no way can the substance of nature be grasped by human operations. No one knows it save him who made it. . . . The image of God is necessarily incomprehensible and invisible."[12] And St. Maximus the Confessor: the rational creature does not naturally know its own roots, "those deep and strong roots" which support it; furthermore, in the opening which grace operates in its being, it understands that it cannot understand itself.[13] And St. Augustine in his *Confessions:* "Although no man knows the things of a man, save the spirit of man which is in him, yet there is something of man which the inner spirit of man itself does not know."[14] So great and wonderful is man's nature![15] So great is the "deep" that answers to the deep of God himself![16]

261

---

[8] To give one reference among many, St. Augustine, *De symbolo,* 1, 2 (*PL,* 40, 628). For a commentary on this and other similar texts, see Gilson, *The Spirit of Medieval Philosophy* (London, 1936), pp. 219ff. Karl Rahner says the same thing: "We have perceived the very depths of our being when we have become as incomprehensible as God himself is." See also Bossuet, *Instruction sur les états d'oraison,* second treatise, chapter 26 (ed. E. Levesque, 1897, p. 68).

[9] Rom 11:34.

[10] *De hominis opificio,* c. 11 (*PG,* 34, 156 B).

[11] In Edmund Beck, O.S.B., "Die Theologie des hl. Ephraem," *Studia anselmiana,* 21, p. 98.

[12] Bk. 2, tract. 19 (*PL,* 11, 455–56 and 456 B).

[13] *Ambigua* (*PG,* 91, 1188 C); *Quaest. ad Thalassium,* 56 (*PG,* 90, 584 AB) etc. Cf. von Balthasar, *Liturgie cosmique* (Paris, 1947), p. 102.

[14] Bk 10, c. 5, n. 7 (*PL,* 32, 782). Cf. *De anima et eius origine,* bk. 4, n. 8: "We cannot grasp ourselves"; and n. 10: "And see, it is more sought than comprehended" (*PL,* 44, 529, 530).

[15] *De Trinitate,* bk. 14, c. 4, n. 6: "Nature, so great and wondrous" (*Bibl. august.,* 16, p. 358).

[16] Gerhoh of Reichersberg, *In Psalmum 41,* v. 8: "Deep calleth on deep. Since our

Following the Fathers and the writers of the twelfth century, the early scholastics gave frequent explicit approval to this view. The position of Duns Scotus is an interesting one to note. He explains it in an important text, the "Controversy between philosophers and theologians as to the necessity for revealed doctrine" with which he begins his great work, the *De ordinatione*. According to the "philosophers," he says, there is no such thing as supernatural perfection. To every passive power of nature there corresponds in nature an active principle, and there is therefore no need to imagine any superior order in which man might need to be given revelation. But in arguing thus, by natural reason alone, the "philosophers" can only err, or remain in doubt, "about the end in particular." To all the arguments and repetitions, but one answer is needed: 262

> They accept that our nature, or our intellective potency, is naturally knowable to us; this is false, under the very and specific rule [*ratio*] under which it is ordered to such an end, is completely capable of grace, and has God as the most perfect object. In fact, our soul is not known to us, nor is our nature in its present condition, except under some general rule that is beyond the reach of the senses [*abstrahibili a sensibus*]. . . .

Man needs revelation, then, in order to know distinctly what is his last end:

> If it is objected against this that man in the state of established nature can know his own nature, and therefore also the end of his nature. . . , I answer. . . : It would require to say that the knowledge of established man is such that it is different from other [knowledge]. But at least in respect to the wayfaring man in his present condition, it is called supernatural knowledge, because it exceeds its natural faculty; I say that it is natural according to the state of fallen nature.[17]

Duns Scotus speaks here only of man in his present condition, "pro statu isto"—an expression he often uses. It is only of such a man that

___
nature, and above all the substance of the rational soul which is profoundly incomprehensible to itself according to the physical reason [*physicam rationem*] and is like the deep, calls on the substance and knowledge of God in himself [*in se*], which likewise is an even greater deep, since the essence of the Divinity is incomprehensible to every creature, even though it is graspable [*capabilis*] by the rational creature" (*PL,* 193, 1516 AB).

[17] *De ordinatione*, prol., Pars 1, "De necessitate doctrinae revelatae" (*Opera omnia,* vol. 1, 1950, pp. 17, 21). On these "philosophers" see Gilson, *Jean Duns Scot* (1952), pp. 12–17.

the "philosophers" speak; it is only in connection with him that the need for revelation is queried. Elsewhere he concedes, though without subjecting the matter to any critical argument, that in a less imperfect state, natural reason might have been able to know more. Here, in writing to refute those who rejected the faith, he wisely limits the field of discussion: "at least in his present condition" [*saltem pro statu isto*]. And this is all I wish to quote from him here. Without entering into the windings of the long, subtle, and complicated dissertation which takes up the whole first part of this Prologue, I would merely indicate that in his view the reasons brought against "the opinion of the philosophers" about our final end could only have been discovered after the event; they presuppose that we have first been enlightened by supernatural revelation, and therefore, in reality, "these are but theological persuasions, from beliefs to belief [*ex creditis ad creditum*]."[18]

263   The tradition was to be carried on in the sixteenth century by such major theologians as Soto and Toletus. In his treatise *De natura et gratia,* Soto speaks of "that light to which we have no access, where both our end and the goal of our actions are hidden."[19] In his commentary on the *Summa theologica,* Toletus declares—as usual in opposition to Cajetan: "If man knew his nature perfectly, he would know that his end is the vision of God"; he does not, any more than St. Thomas, restrict this statement, or this supposition, to the hypothesis of a so-called "elevated" nature; but he also says, correspondingly, that it is not surprising that the nature of our soul cannot be wholly known to us, since it is spiritual and very close to that of the angels.[20]

[18] Ibid., p. 9. Cf. *In 4 Sent.,* dist. 49, q. 8 (ed. Vivès, vol. 21, p. 305). See also John of Rada, *Controversiae theologicae inter S. Thomam et Scotum,* pars 1, Venice, 1604, pp. 17–19; pars 4, 1617, pp. 407–11. Francis of Meyronnes (d. 1325), observes de Gandillac, is not faithful to Scotus, "if it is true that he thinks man can know naturally that eternal happiness is his true end." Fliche and Martin, *Histoire de l'Eglise,* vol. 13 (1951), p. 367, note 3.

[19] Bk. 1, c. 4: "The knowledge of that inaccessible light, where our end, and the goal of our actions, are hidden . . ." (p. 10). What a contrast with Cajetan's assurance: "The response of Scotus, who says that the soul according to this reason is unknown, does not fully settle the issue. The essential knowledge [*cognitio quidditativa*] of something leaves nothing of its nature unknown: for it contains formally or virtually the whole knowledge [*notitiam*] of it" (*De potentia neutra,* q. 2, ad 4um, 2°). Soto did not let these trenchant phrases intimidate him.

[20] *In Primam Secundae,* q. 3, a. 8: "If man knew his own nature perfectly, he would know that his final end is the divine vision." Cf. J. M. H. Ledesma, S.J., *Doctrina Toleti de appetitu naturali visionis beatificae . . .* (1949), p. 22. *In Primam Partem,* q. 1, a. 1, q. 2

This, as we know, is also the constant position of the Augustinian school connected with Giles of Rome. Some of its members express the matter with particular clarity. Thus Gerard of Sienna (d. 1336):

> The rational creature is so good that there is nothing by which it may be happy but God alone. . . . This nature that is capable of God cannot be ordered to be quieted by enjoyment [*fruitione*] in anything below God; the rational creature is of this kind; therefore, etc. The major [premise] is evident because potency, which is capable of a greater good, is never quieted in a lesser good. . . . This reasoning in respect to the minor proposition proceeds from beliefs.[21]

264

It is really this same teaching, though in less strictly metaphysical language, that St. Francis of Sales is trying to give to Théotime in his *Treatise on the love of God:*

> We have a natural inclination towards the sovereign Good, in consequence of which our heart has a certain inward hastening and a constant restlessness, without being able to be appeased in any way, nor to stop showing that its full satisfaction and lasting content are lacking. But when our sacred faith has represented to our mind the beautiful object of its natural inclination, then, Théotime, what comfort, what joy, what a thrill there is throughout our soul which then, as though completely overwhelmed at the spectacle of such glorious beauty, cries lovingly: "O how beautiful thou art, O my Beloved, O how beautiful thou art!"
>
> The human heart tends to God by its natural inclination without properly knowing who he is; but when it finds him at the fount of faith, and sees him so good, so beautiful, so gentle and so kind to all, and so disposed to give himself as sovereign good to all who want him, then, what joys and holy movements there are in the mind, to be united for ever to that supremely lovable goodness! I have at last found, says the soul thus moved, I have found what I longed for. . . .
>
> We sometimes feel certain joys which seem to come quite unexpectedly, with no apparent cause, and which are often the forerunners of some greater joy. . . . Then, when that joy arrives, our hearts receive it with open arms, and recalling the delight they had felt without realizing

---

(Rome, 1869, vol. 1, p. 20): "The nature of our soul cannot be known in this way by natural knowledge; and this is no wonder, since it is spiritual, having great closeness with the angels." "But Cajetan believes that the nature of man can fully be known aside from his knowledge, for such a capacity is not natural but obediential" (p. 18). Cf. *Augustinisme et théologie moderne,* pp. 177–78.

[21] *In 1 Sent.,* dist. 1, q. 2 (in J. Alfaro, *op. cit.,* p. 380).

its cause, they then know that it was a kind of forerunner of the happiness that has now arrived. Thus, my dear Théotime, our heart has for so long inclined to its sovereign good, it did not know to what that inclination tended; but as soon as faith has shown it, then it sees that this was what its soul sought, what its mind looked for and its inclination gazed at. . . .[22]

"And I myself do not fully grasp all that I am." "We do not know all that we are, nor are we exactly what we know. Light and life, word and experience, are not united."[23] This consideration of a sensitive philosopher applies primarily to the very depths of the soul. "There is," says another philosopher, "in man's pre-comprehension of himself, a wealth of meaning which thought can never equal."[24] Certain depths of our nature can be opened only by the shock of revelation.[25] Then, with a new clarity, deep calls upon deep. By revealing himself to us, Bérulle used to say, God "has revealed us to ourselves."[26] Every light cast on God is at the same time reflected back on to man. Thus, just as the Buddhist believes he can understand in a single intuition both pain and its remedy, the origin of evil and the way to deliverance from it, so by perceiving something of the holiness and love of God we become aware of our own sinfulness.[27] Commenting on Isaiah, Origen says that the prophet began to see his wretchedness at the moment of beginning to glimpse the glory of God.[28] William of St. Thierry says the same thing in

[22] Bk. 2, ch. 15 (*Oeuvres*, vol. 4, 1894, pp. 136–38).

[23] Jacques Paliard. For the idea that man is the being with a mystery in his heart that is larger than himself, see Balthasar, *Prayer* (London, 1961).

[24] Paul Ricoeur, *Finitude et culpabilité*, vol. 1 (1960), p. 26.

[25] Cf. my own *Catholicisme*[4] (1947), pp. 294–97. R Bultmann has said that in every way revelation gives to the believer, through the gospel, a decisive light on profane existence, which is not visible to philosophy.

[26] St. Augustine said something similar in the *Confessions*, bk. 10, c. 2 and 3: "And from you, O Lord, for whose eyes the depths of man's conscience are naked. . . . For what is it for man to hear from you of himself, but to know himself . . . ?" (Bibl. august., 12, pp. 142, 144).

[27] Yves de Montcheuil, *Leçons sur le Christ*, p. 123. Cf. Gabriel Marcel, *Journal métaphysique*, 3: "One might say that what we are immediately aware of is not, is not yet sin. . . . It seems to me that the realization of my sin only enters my awareness in so far as I become awake to the infinite love with which I am loved" (in *Fontaine*, April 1946, pp. 594, 600). Paul Claudel says something similar: "What do we know of God's will, when the only way we can know of it is by going against it?"

[28] *In Isaiam*, hom. 4, n. 2 (on Isa. 6:4): "Before you see the vision, do you not confess yourself to be wretched, O Isaiah? No, says he: as long as he sees Oziah, and it does not come into my sense that I am wretched; for I begin to know that I am wretched when I

a more general way: "Never is the mode of human imperfection better grasped than by the light of the countenance of God in the mirror of divine vision,"[29] and Marie de l'Incarnation says: "The purity of his spirit shows us the impurity of ours."[30] Similarly, it is by the promise given us of seeing God face to face that we really learn to recognize our "desire."

Of course the two cases are not completely parallel. In the first case we are dealing with a wholly religious reality; and furthermore, the correspondence is direct and is established totally by way of contrast. In the second, a reflection of a metaphysical kind arrives at what the revealed object implies: beginning with a fact, the promise that we shall see God face to face as a free gift, a promise that is part of the Christian revelation, one examines how this can be possible, and by its light one interprets observations or inductions whose precise bearing could not previously be recognized. It remains that the desire of the mind, which does not fall within the scope of empirical psychology, is not deduced from purely rational premises either. The "natural inclination to the sovereign good" of which Francis of Sales spoke was only translated into consciousness first under the aspect of a desire for happiness in general, a desire which might not merely mistake its object, but even pursue quite worthless objects: it was this same distinction that fascinated Bonaventure, the distinction between the "knowledge of beatitude in general" and the "knowledge of beatitude in particular," the former being "inborn," the latter given to us by faith.[31] It was a distinction gen-

267

---

see the vision, my king Oziah the leper dying, and I say: woe is me! Now even I begin to confess to the Lord and to say of myself: woe is me! just as Isaiah says: woe is me! . . ." (p. 260). Cf. Severus of Antioch, *Homily 115* on the appearance of God: "Oh, how immense is the height of God's goodness to us! It is through that, indeed, I also realize the magnitude of our sin. . . ."

[29] *Epistola ad Fratres de Monte Dei*, c. 3 (ed. M. M. Davy, p. 148). Cf. *In Cantica:* "More swiftly is he sent back into the house of his poverty . . . , knowing to some extent what he lacks" (*PL*, 180, 526 AC).

[30] *Ecrits* (ed. Dom Jamet), vol. 4, p. 246. Cf. Edmond Ortigues, *Le temps de la Parole* (1954), p. 55: "The true knowledge of sin cannot be had by simply turning us back in upon ourselves, but is discovered only by returning from oneself to the Word of God." Cf. Bossuet, *Histoire des Variations*, bk. 1, n. 17, on the subject of our sins which we do not always know: "Man will always be a great enigma to himself, and his own mind will always be the subject of an eternal and impenetrable question to him" (ed. Lachat, vol. 14, p. 31). This is not true only in a moral sense.

[31] *In 2 Sent.*, dist. 38, dubium 1: "The knowledge of beatitude is twofold: in general and in particular. Knowledge of beatitude in general is innate to everyone; but knowledge in particular, that is, of where beatitude should be placed, we have by the habit of faith in

erally held in scholasticism.[32] Similarly, the movement of the intellect, never satisfied with the knowledge it has, constantly rising from cause to cause, can be interpreted as a sign of the spirit's desire—and as we know, this was a consideration particularly dear to the mind of St. Thomas.[33] But in order to interpret that sign so well, to discern so clearly in it the desire to see the first cause in his very essence, it was surely necessary for St. Thomas to be at least "orientated" by his faith. It must at least, as Père Roland Gosselin points out, be that faith which gives him "complete certainty" in his interpretation.[34] For the actual desire, though it certainly exists in every man, being inherent in his nature, is not in him *personaliter,* as the early writers say: it is only in him *simpliciter* or *naturaliter.*[35] Or, if one admits that it is not entirely unknown, because of its spiritual character, it may be said that, like the soul, it is the object of a knowledge that is called "habitual," "built into the soul itself" as Bonaventure put it, or as he also says, the object of a knowledge "arising from a sense of need,"[36] but not of any "actual" and positive knowledge.[37]

268

some manner, and in some way it is expected to be had through conformity to God [*deiformitas*] by grace. . . ." Cf. dist. 22, dub. 3.

[32] Thus Matthew of Aquasparta, *Quaestiones de gratia,* q. 2: "Man . . . can be beatified in no created good, nor can his appetite be ended by any created good, but he is ordered to beatitude and to a certain end, which wholly exceeds both reason and the virtue of nature and its faculty" (Doucet ed., p. 47). And earlier, William of Auvergne, *De Universo,* bk. 2, 1, c. 9, on what he calls that "state of glory" [*status gloriae*]: "This state is not known in our world as yet, save through faith and revelation" (*Opera omnia* [Paris, 1674], vol. 1, p. 817 A). Cf. St. Thomas, *In 4 Sent.,* dist. 49, a. 1, ad 1um; *De Veritate,* q. 22, a. 7; *Prima Secundae,* q. 5, a. 8.

[33] Cf. my own *Sur les chemins de Dieu,* chapter 6, Eng. trans. *The Discovery of God,* chapter 6.

[34] "Béatitude et désir naturel," in *Revue des sciences philosophiques et théologiques* (1929): 200: "The prime conviction which gives direction to his analysis and gives him complete certainty is his faith in the word of God. . . . Faith in the beatific vision must be considered as exercising a positive and decisive influence on the argument itself!

[35] Hugh of St. Cher, *In Sent.;* and anon., *In Sent.,* quoted by Père Gillon, *Angelicum* (1949), pp. 17–19.

[36] *In 4 Sent.,* dist. 49, p. 1, q. 2, ad 1–3.

[37] The desire itself growing, according to St. Bonaventure, from the "habitual" knowledge of God which is in the depths of the rational soul made in his image: *Quaestiones de Trinitate,* q. 3 (Quaracchi, vol. 5, p. 49); q. 1, fund. 7: "If such an appetite cannot exist without some knowledge [*notitia*], it is necessary that the knowledge, by which it is known that the highest good or God exists, be planted in the soul itself" (p. 46). But St. Thomas, as we know, is even more sober on the point. Cf. some comments in L. B. Gillon, O.P., "Béatitude et désir de voir Dieu au moyen âge, 2," *Angelicum* 26 (1949): 127–33.

Such a desire then takes nothing from the character of the marvellous and "incredible"[38] newness of the revelation in Christ of our final end; it makes that end no less utterly "ineffable." Here we can agree with Cajetan: "This end is hidden from us, because it is the supernatural end of our soul."[39] This is what I have tried to show in an earlier chapter. But for us, unlike Cajetan, it is not the absence of any desire that is the reason for that ignorance: rather it is the depth of our desire. I would rather say, with Père Rousselot: "That which, were there no divine offer, would merely be a seeking for something in impenetrable darkness, can, thanks to the light of faith, be expressed in a clear series of syllogisms."[40] "What do you know," asked Meister Eckhart, "of the possibilities God has given human nature? Those who have written of the soul's capacity have not gone beyond the point to which their natural reason takes them; they have never got to the bottom; and many things must be hidden from them, must remain unknown."[41] The bride only knows herself when she answers the bridegroom's invitation.[42] Bérulle was right in saying that the movement "imprinted by the power of the Creator deep within his creature," that movement that is "natural to the soul, is hidden from it in this life, just as the soul is hidden from itself. . . . It sees neither its being, nor what is at the depths of its being";[43] it is "Jesus Christ who reveals within us someone whom we do not know," it is Christ "who speaks our soul to us."[44] Thus the mysterious nature of the dogma remains unimpaired. It remains "the King's secret":

269

> Although God is the final end in consequence, and the first in the intention of the natural appetite, nevertheless it is not fitting that it be first in the knowledge of the human mind, which is ordered to the end; rather [it is fitting that it be first] in the knowledge of the ordainer: just as is the case with other things that tend to their own end by natural appetite.

[38] St. Augustine, *In psalm. 109*, n. 2 (*CCL*, 40, 1602). And nothing short of faith in the incarnation can enable us to believe in that "ineffable immortality" promised to us (1603). See *supra*, chapter 7.

[39] *In Primam*, q. 1, a. 1, n. 7 (fol. 1 v). Cf. Javelli, *Expositio in Primum tractatum Primae Partis*, q. 1, a. 1 (fol. 1 r).

[40] *Op. cit.*, p. 188.

[41] *On eternal birth*. See also the text of Bérulle quoted supra, pp. 74–75.

[42] Cf. Paul Claudel, "L'Ecriture sainte" in *J'aime la Bible* (1955), p. 56: "He will instruct her and teach her who she is, for she does not know. . . ."

[43] *Opuscules de piété*, 27 (ed. G. Rotureau, 1943, p. 134).

[44] Mgr. Blanchet, *Conférences de Notre Dame*, 1957, first conference, p. 8. Cf. Balthasar, *Die Gottesfrage des heutigen Menschen*, French trans. *Dieu et l'homme aujourd'hui*, p. 149, Eng. trans. *Science, Religion and Christianity*.

Nevertheless it is known from the beginning and is directed in some
generality, according as the soul strives to well-being and well living,
which exist only when God has [the soul].[45]

It is hardly surprising then that beatitude—the only beatitude—
"transcends all rational investigation." St. Thomas himself, starting from
his principle that a desire of nature can never be in vain, knows that he
can only arrive at a sure conclusion because he is reasoning within
faith.[46] Like St. Bonaventure whom we have quoted, he knows that the
"desire bestowed" [*desiderium inditum*] or "innate" is not of itself explicit
and conscious, since he sets out to make it explicit by showing that its
end can only be the vision of God; and he also knows that in the conscious desire for happiness, God is at first desired only implicitly.[47] There
is much truth in what Cajetan and Báñez say, though each in his own
270 way draws conclusions that go too far: "The divine Thomas proceeds as a
theologian, although he uses natural reasons as aids [*quasi ancillis*]."[48]
This appears particularly true in the *Summa contra Gentiles* which is, in
the eyes of one of its recent commentators, Anton C. Pegis, "a theological work profoundly mingled with a theological enterprise and no less
visibly governed by a precise theological plan."[49] In fact one entire chapter of the second book is devoted to distinguishing the "philosopher's"
point of view from that of the "theologian."[50] It is, then, as a theologian
(like Duns Scotus) that St. Thomas sets out to develop a complete and
loftily philosophical apologetic (if I may be forgiven the term). In his
own special way, he imitates the "saints"—of whom he says elsewhere in
a different context: "The reasons employed by holy men to prove things
that are of faith are not demonstrations; they are persuasive arguments
showing that what is proposed to our faith is not impossible."[51]

---

[45] St. Thomas, *In Boetium de Trinitate*, q. 1, a. 3, ad 4um.

[46] Cf. *In 3 Sent.*, dist. 27, q. 2, a. 2: "But because a certain happiness is promised
us. . . ." *In 4 Sent.*, dist. 49, q. 2, a. 1: "Just as, by reason of faith, we posit that the final end
of human life is the vision of God . . ."; etc. Cf. *In 1 Sent.*, prol., q. 1, a. 1, ad 3um.

[47] Cf. *In 2 Cor.*, c. 5, lectio 2: "Therefore the rational creature is not moved by nature
to desire this [=to enjoy heavenly glory and to see God in his essence], but by God himself, who makes us for this . . ." (ed. Vivès, vol. 21, p. 94).

[48] Báñez, *In Primam Secundae* (*Commentarios ineditos . . .*, ed. V. Beltràn de Heredia,
vol. 1, 1942, p. 81).

[49] "Qu'est-ce que la *Summa contra Gentiles?*" in *L'Homme devant Dieu*, vol. 2 (1964),
p. 172.

[50] C. 4: "Because the philosopher looks at creatures in one way, the theologian in
another."

[51] *Secunda Secundae*, q. 1, a. 5, ad 2um.

These reasons may be just reasons of convenience or not even that when it comes to truths of pure faith, such as the incarnation or the Trinity, the truths which St. Thomas reserves for the fourth and final book of the *Summa contra Gentiles*. But he sees the problem of beatitude as being an intermediate stage. There he does proceed by way of rational demonstration; this however is only secondary: the demonstration moves into "the area of investigation of reason within faith";[52] and on the other hand "a rational demonstration, however convincing to reason, always falls short when the truth which it is by way of demonstrating is a mystery of faith." Therefore it is only when the intrinsic possibility of the vision of God has "once been admitted by faith" that "the argument based on the impossibility for natural desire to be vain comes to apply to that truth of faith, so that to deny that possibility would not merely be to contradict a truth of faith, but would actually go counter to reason."[53]

271

This explanation of Père Dockx, which harmonizes with the general interpretation of the *Summa contra Gentiles* given by Anton C. Pegis, seems to provide us with the means of reconciling opinions which diverge from each other by each stressing one part of the text, or one aspect of Thomist teaching. That teaching is certainly complex, and I would hardly claim here to define it fully, but only to point out that St. Thomas did see the problem we are concerned with in this chapter. Even if reason can "suspect the existence" of that beatitude, it "cannot suspect its nature. Thus, as soon as they wished to speak about it, "the philosophers were grossly and inevitably mistaken."[54] These wonders which God intends for us at the end of time are "above reason," just as they are above anything we have any right to.[55] "Natural forces are not enough either to conceive them, or to desire them":[56]

---

[52] Pegis, *loc. cit.*, p. 176.

[53] S. Dockx, O..P., "Du désir naturel de voir l'essence divine d'après saint Thomas," in *Archives de philosophie* (1964), pp. 94, 95.

[54] R. A. Gauthier, O.P., *loc. cit.*, p. 263, commenting on *In 2 Sent.*, dist. 18, q. 2, a. 2; dist. 19, q. 1, a. 1.

[55] *Summa contra Gentiles*, bk. 4, c. 1, in fine: "The things which, being above reason, are looked for in the final end of man. . . ." Cf. *Tertia*, q. 1, a. 3: "For what springs from the will of God alone, beyond any debt to creatures, can only come to our knowledge insofar as it is given in Holy Scripture, through which the divine will comes to our knowledge." Cf. Peter Trigosus, *loc. cit.*, p. 9: "Therefore there remained hidden in us from the beginning a natural inclination. . . ."

[56] *De Veritate*, q. 14, a. 2: "The good of man exceeding the proportion of human nature is another thing, because natural powers are not sufficient to obtain, think about or desire it."

Now eternal life is a good exceeding the proportion of created nature, since it exceeds its knowledge and desire.[57]

That is the first reason why we need divine revelation and divine grace. But furthermore, even when the natural desire for the vision of God—which we must remember is not the same as an elicited desire— has been recognized, defined and analyzed, its end is still only known "aliquo modo."[58] No more than we can ever desire it truly "sufficiently," can we conceive it in any adequate way. Even in the light it gets from God, and at whatever phase one looks at of its intellectual or spiritual life, the believing and hoping soul is ultimately left "facing an intrinsically impenetrable mystery,"[59] "what no eye has seen, nor ear heard, nor has the heart of man conceived."[60] We may recall comments of St. Bernard, St. Thomas Aquinas and St. Robert Bellarmine on these words of St. Paul's:

> Ineffable words to be sure; even though he does not give me something to hear, still he gives me something to desire, and let it be pleasing to get a whiff [odorare] of what it is not granted to hear.[61]

> No one can see glory but he who is in glory; there remains both the desire and the intellect of those who are not in it; this indeed is the manna left us and the new name written on the stone, which no one who receives it knows.[62]

[57] *Prima Secundae*, q. 114, a. 2. Cf. William of St. Thierry, *Speculum fidei:* "And although nature has an appetite for these [eternal goods] by virtue of grace creating, still it only distinguishes [*dignoscit*] them perfectly by virtue of grace illuminating, and only takes hold of them if God grants it" (*PL*, 180, 386 C).

[58] St. Bonaventure, quoted above.

[59] A. R. Motte, in *Bulletin thomiste*, vol. 4, p. 579.

[60] 1 Cor 2:6–9. St. Thomas, *Prima Secundae*, q. 62, a. 3. Cf. the commentary by Georges Didier, S.J., *Désintéressement du chrétien* (1956), pp. 46–47. St. Augustine, *In Ioannem*, tract. 1, n. 4.

[61] *In Cant.*, s. 67, n. 7 (*Opera*, ed. J. Leclercq, vol. 2, p. 193). William of St. Thierry, *Epist. ad Fratres de Monte Dei*, bk. 3, c. 1, on the heavenly beatitude [*beatitudo caelestis*]: "It is so great, so unknowable, that no eye has seen it, no ear has heard it, nor has it come into the heart of man" (*PL*, 184, 354). See also John Tinctor (d. 1469), *Lectura in Primam S. Thomae* (in J. Alfaro, *op. cit.*, p. 236).

[62] *Quodl.* 8, q. 7, a. 16. Cf. *Summa contra Gentiles*, bk. 4, c. 54: "Man could be led to this because, in his ignorance of the dignity of his nature, he adhered to things existing beneath God as to an end" (hence the fittingness of the incarnation). While rejecting the thesis of Duns Scotus (which was in fact that of all the early writers), Cajetan was aware that he agreed with him about man's natural ignorance of his true end. *In Primam*, q. 1, a. 7: "Concerning this part, note that Scotus . . . disagrees neither in the conclusion nor in the reasoning; but in the reason for which this end is hidden from us naturally. . . ."

The vision of God, in which eternal life properly consists, is not only a supernatural thing, but exceeds even every created nature, so that it can be neither known, nor grasped, nor understood unless God himself reveals it: The eye hath not seen, etc.[63]

---

[63] *De justificatione,* bk. 5, c. 12 (*Opera,* vol. 6, 1873, p. 368).

CHAPTER 12

The Call of Love

273   It is not a question of something new in every respect, something for which there has been no preparation, no previous awareness. None of our mysteries is of this kind: if it were so, these mysteries would be utterly artificial, lacking ontological depth, or it would mean that we ourselves lived in some very different world. Only those who are theory-mad, who pay more attention to their own ideas than to the facts through which God's plan appears, could imagine such a thing. There is too much evidence, throughout human history, of man's universal desire—now more, now less clearly formulated—for God. But in itself that desire remains none the less hidden "in the ontological depths,"[1] and only the Christian revelation makes it possible to interpret either its indications or its meaning correctly. It is revelation which brings a final judgment to bear on all this human evidence: it condemns its *hubris,* estimates its deviations and brings to light its core of truth. Desire to see God, desire to be united with God, desire to be God: we find all these, or similar phrases, outside Christianity and independent of it. But how equivocal they all are! For instance we can certainly see the mystical aspirations of which history gives us so many examples—some

274   curious, some magnificent—that bear witness to that destiny for which God has made us, but we can only do so by projecting upon them the light of our faith. Taken literally in themselves, especially when it comes to the theories commenting on them and systematizing them, we should be equally justified in condemning them as the absolute antithe-

---

[1] Once again, I am borrowing a phrase from Père Joseph de Finance, *op. cit.,* commenting on St. Thomas. As we have just seen, this position was held even more definitely by Scotus.

sis of Christian salvation. Similarly, people have quite legitimately quoted the famous passage from the *Nicomachean Ethics* in which Aristotle, finding human happiness too limited to be satisfying, speaks of "that greater than human life" which we must try to attain; this has, not unjustifiably, been recognized "as a stepping-stone to the supernatural"; but, since to Aristotle "it is the act of rational contemplation which constitutes that divine life in man, an act which begins and ends in ourselves," it would be equally justifiable to condemn it "as pure philosophy's permanent claim to the supreme place, however high that might be."[2]

In such cases there is at least ambiguity. What might quite rightly seem, after the event, and allowing for some fundamental changes, as having been a "preparation for the Gospel," is also, and in fact primarily, an obstacle to it. The idea of God, upon which all else depends, has not been inserted once and for all in the human mind like a "rational monolith,"[3] and I think it is hardly enough to say that this idea "as praised by the Greeks has been renewed by Christianity," if by this it is meant that Christianity had only to complete it without any need to alter it in any way, or to contradict anything in it.[4] It can certainly be said that by supernatural revelation a superior order of truth came to be added to the truths of natural reason, but that is only true, at most, at an abstract level, and in reality things are not quite so simple. It is good to speak of God, remarked Newman, but it is a word that contains an entire theology, and one must make clear of what God one is speaking.[5]

275

[2] Blondel, *Lettre sur les exigences . . .* (1896), p. 49 (*Premiers écrits*, vol. 2, 1956, p. 56). Cf. St. Thomas, *Summa contra Gentiles*, bk. 1, c. 5; bk. 3, c. 48; *Super librum de causis expositio* (ed. Saffrey, 1954, pp. 1–2).

[3] Blondel, *La Pensée*, vol. 2 (1934), p. 527. Cf. St. Thomas, *Prima*, q. 13, a. 10. Giles of Viterbo: "But the fount of dissension is the lack of consensus about the meaning of the word God" (quoted by Eugenio Massa, "Egidio da Viterbo, la metodologia del sapere" in *Pensée humaniste et tradition chrétienne aux XVe et XVIe siècles* [1950], p. 196).

[4] Cf. A. D. Sertillanges, in *Revue thomiste* (1904): 382: "The idea of God . . . was renewed by Christianity. Yes indeed, but it was, from the strictly philosophical point of view, by *completing* Greek philosophy rather than by *contradicting* it. It was in the second place by adding the religious point of view, which was essentially a *practical* one, to the results of speculation"; and on p. 383, on "Christian philosophy": "supposing that there is one, and that it is anything other than Greek philosophy brought to its conclusion." Père Sertillanges was later to modify his thought in what seems to me a more satisfactory sense.

[5] *The Idea of a University* (1852). Cf. M. Nédoncelle, *La philosophie religieuse de Newman*, p. 277.

Without denigrating the value of any anticipation, or belittling in particular, as too many people do today, the marvellous work of the man whom St. Augustine hailed as "the father of theology,"[6] and that of his most original disciple who produced the notion of "pure act," one may nevertheless have a stronger sense of the newness of Christianity. For in truth "the Christian God is incomparable."[7] And we must not forget that the "eternal life" promised by Christ consists in the vision of that God, the "one true God."[8] Coming to complete and transform our idea of God and, though we still use the same words, to transform our idea of the vision of God,[9] revelation cannot help at the same time transforming and completing our idea of man and his desire, and ultimately, at least if we consent to it, of the desire itself. Thus we realize that we must wait "for life in the other world to possess the only true good which can attract him whose thoughts are the thoughts of God," and not "the happiness desired by him who thinks of selfish satisfaction as a good; for God does not think selfish satisfaction a good."[10] We are led, therefore, to the pure notion of *agape*. Revelation then forces us to "break out of the categories of our natural intelligence,"[11] and the upheaval this brings about, though not changing the unchanging laws of reason, results in the formation of certain new categories, some of which may well appear completely natural to the philosophy of the future. In short, "it is the Christian faith which, by setting the notion of the infinite being and our relationship with him at the center of the whole revealed idea of God, makes us understand our nature, our des-

276

---

[6] Cf. *De civitate Dei*, bk. 8, c. 4 (*PL*, 41, 227–28). Plato, *Resp.*, bk. 2, 379 a.

[7] Nédoncelle, *Existe-t-il une philosophie chrétienne?* p. 23, Eng. trans. *Is There a Christian Philosophy?* (London, 1960). The New Testament message "is that God loves us: overwhelming news which bursts with an intensity and joy quite different from the pale goodwill of a philosophic divinity. Nothing in the ancient world, nothing since then in the modern world, comes near it. It is surprising only that historians could query the fact and even attempt comparisons. The Christian God is incomparable. He bursts into the human consciousness as something totally new—unless we confuse the few fluting tones heard in the preceding centuries with that crashing, overwhelming symphony which sounded suddenly in human ears for all the ages to come."

[8] John 17:3.

[9] For Origen and Plotinus, for instance, the word is the same. "Beatific vision" vocabulary depends both upon scripture and upon Greek philosophy (cf. Plato, *Phaedrus*, 247 c and 251 b: "blessed vision." Cf. Blondel, *La Pensée*, vol. 2, p. 409: "The supreme life of thought is not the same thing as a 'pure vision.'"

[10] Yves de Montcheuil, S.J.

[11] *La Sainte Trinité et la vie surnaturelle*, by a Carthusian (1948), p. 33.

tiny, the nature of the material world, of morality, and of the history of mankind."[12]

Thus when we find St. Augustine (following Origen[13]) telling us that the Platonic philosophers had a shadowy view of heaven, in other words that they were able to conceive the vision of God as being man's true end, and were deceived only as to the road, the means of reaching that end—in other words the mediation of the incarnate Word[14]—must we accuse him of attributing the knowledge of a supernatural mystery to natural reason? Must we complain that, by a transposition no historian would have made, he has overgenerously attributed to those authors some of the ideas he held by faith? Must we deny his right to read the *Enneads* as a Christian? No; we must instead consider the concrete situation the Church was in in his time, and also the apostolic intention behind his reflections.[15] We can only marvel at the assimilative power of Christian life as manifest in his attitude, and conclude with Mgr. Régis Jolivet that by means of Augustine's comments on Plato "it was not Augustine who became a neo-Platonist, but Plato who became a Christian."[16] We must furthermore take cognizance of all the reservations implied in the marked contrast established in so firm a statement as this (even as to the choice of the first term of the contrast): "If there is a middle path between one who is advancing and that to which he is advancing, there is hope of getting there; if, however, it is wanting or unknown where one should pass, what help is it to know whither to go?"[17] and again: "What does having a true understanding of the unchangeable good profit one who does not have the means to be freed

277

[12] Louis Foucher, *La philosophie catholique en France au XIXe siècle* (1955), p. 222, summing up Gratry's ideas. Cf. Claudel, *L'Épée et le Miroir* (Paris, 1939), p. 256: "The lance held by Longinus went further than the heart of Christ. It opened God, it passed to the very center of the Trinity."

[13] Origen, *Contra Celsum*, bk. 7, c. 44.

[14] *Sermo* 141, n. 1: "They did not discover by which road one arrives to so great, ineffable and beatific a possession." *Confessions*, bk. 7, c. 9, nn. 13–15; c. 21, n. 27: "It is one thing to see the homeland of peace from the treetops and not to find the path to it and to make attempts by the road . . . , and it is another to keep to the path leading thither provided by the turnpike of the heavenly emperor."

[15] *De vera religione*, c. 4, n. 7: "If those men could have spent their lives with us . . . , with a few changed words and sentences they would become Christians, just as many Platonists of recent times and ours have."

[16] *Le problème du mal d'après saint Augustin* (Paris, 1936), p. 136.

[17] *De Civitate Dei*, bk. 11, c. 2 (Bibl. august., 35, p. 36).

from evil?"[18] In short, here as elsewhere, we can see the truth of Etienne Borne's observation: "Christian Platonism is a historical fact; but this demanded of St. Augustine a confrontation and a combat like that between Jacob and the angel, from which one of the protagonists, philosophy, emerged limping and bearing the traces of its lucky defeat."[19]

We can, then, readily admit that it was more important to Augustine to denounce "Platonist presumption" than the intellectual insufficiency of its analyses; it mattered more to him to bring believers to Christ by "conversion of heart,"[20] to follow the humble Christ in humility here below, than to speculate profoundly upon the different fashions of conceiving the vision of the supreme good. But we can and must admit also that, had he analyzed his own thought more reflectively, he would certainly have reached the conclusion that seems so clear to us: that knowledge of man's final end achieved by Platonists (or others) was and could be only a faint analogy of what Christians have had revealed to them. He would have been the first to recognize that the knowledge of the way affects the knowledge of the goal, and that one cannot therefore be wrong about the one without also being wrong about the other. He would have had no need to seek beyond his own principles in order to understand that the "life of happiness" a man might seek to provide for himself must be different in kind from that which he discovers as a promise and begs as a gift.[21] He would have welcomed the nuance, or perhaps correction, discreetly introduced by one of his disciples who spoke of the "pilgrim love from afar" [*peregrinus amor de longe*] on the part of the best among the sages of old.[22] He himself, after all, spoke forcefully of a *humility of God* [*humilitas Dei*] which must be the model for the indispensable *humility of man* [*humilitas hominis*]. He loved to define the knowledge of the true God by means of the experience of charity—something quite foreign, as he knew, to his "philosophers," especially Plotinus.

278

---

[18] *In Ioannem*, tract. 98, n. 7 (*PL*, 35, 1884). Cf. *De vera religione*, c. 4, n. 7 (Bibl. august., 8, p. 34).

[19] *Passion de la Vérité* (1962), p. 63.

[20] Cf. J. M. Le Blond, *Les conversions de saint Augustin* (Paris, 1950), pp. 131–60.

[21] *Epist.* 155, n. 2: "They wished in some way to forge a blessed life for themselves, and they thought it was to be achieved rather than obtained, although there is no giver but God" (*PL*, 33, 667). Cf. Gilson, *Introduction à l'étude de saint Augustin*[2] (1943), pp. 141–46, 309, Eng. trans. *The Christian Philosophy of St. Augustine* (London, 1961).

[22] Hugh of St. Victor, *In Ecclesiasten*, hom. 16 (*PL*, 175, 231 B).

You think of the essence of God? You are thinking of his quality? Whatever you have imagined, he is not; whatever you have grasped by thinking, he is not. But so that you may get something as a foretaste: God is charity; the Charity that we love. . . .[23]

He says too that the wonder of the beatific vision is that we shall see in it him who sees us: "to see the seer" [*videntem videre*]. What we are promised, he says, is the vision of God living and seeing: "The vision of God, who lives and who sees, is promised us!"[24]

Seeing face to face,[25] speaking mouth to mouth,[26] being in the presence of the bridegroom,[27] drinking the life of beatitude from its fount:[28] all this is certainly far from Plato. At the end of the ascent to which he calls us, Plato shows us "beauty itself, illuminated, pure, unmixed,"[29] perfect beauty; but that perfect beauty is not complete beauty. That vision which he promises us is as nothing beside Christ's promise: "I will manifest myself to him,"[30] or beside those tremendous words we read in St. Paul: "Then I shall understand fully, even as I have been fully understood."[31] "We need to be a bit disenchanted from Plato," says one of his most faithful admirers[32]—from Plato and so many other fine minds, from Aristotle on, though Aristotle's thought marked an advance upon that of his master. For him the supreme principle is no longer the objec-

279

---

[23] Cf. *De Trinitate*, bk. 8, c. 8, n. 12 (Bibl. august., pp. 64–66). St. Bernard, *De consideratione*, bk. 5, c. 14, n. 30 (*Opera*, ed. Leclercq, vol. 3, p. 492). William of St. Thierry, *De natura et dignitate amoris*: "Ipsa caritas est oculus quo videtur Deus" (*PL*, 184, 390).

[24] *Sermo 69* (*de verbis Domini*, 10), c. 2, n. 3 (*PL*, 38, 441). Cf. Gregory of Nyssa, *De oratione dominica*, 2 (*PG*, 44, 1137 AB).

[25] *De Trinitate*, bk. 1, c. 13, n. 31 (Bibl. august., 15, 1955, p. 178). On this Pauline phrase see Dom Jacques Dupont, *Gnosis*, pp. 114, 118, 146.

[26] *De Genesi ad litteram*, bk. 12, c. 26, n. 54 (*PL*, 34, 476).

[27] *In epistolam Ioannis*, tract.: "I shall, she said, show myself to him. Let us desire and let us love, let us blaze if we are brides. The bridegroom is absent, let us hold up, he whom we desire will come."

[28] *De Genesi ad litteram.*, ibid.: "There the blessed Life is drunk at its Source." Cf. St. John Damascene, *De fide orthodoxa*, bk. 4, in fine (*PG*, 94, 1228 A). St. Gregory the Great, *In evangelia*, bk. 2, hom. 37, n. 1 (*PL*, 76, 1275 AC). Ps. 35:10: "For with thee is the fountain of life; and in thy light we shall see light."

[29] *Symposium*, 29. Cf. Etienne Borne, "Pour une doctrine de l'intériorité," in *Intériorité et vie spirituelle* (1954), pp. 14–16.

[30] John 14:21, quoted by St. Thomas, *Summa contra Gentiles*, bk. 3, c. 52.

[31] 1 Cor 13:12. Cf. Gal 4:9.

[32] Auguste Valensin, S.J., *Regards sur quelques penseurs* (1955), "Platon," chapter 8, p. 161.

tified idea, but a living mind, the supreme intelligence, and also the supreme intelligible, "thought of thought": "We call God," he says, "an eternal and perfect living being";[33] but that eternal and perfect living being is eternally unaware of us imperfect beings; no movement of love makes him turn even a glance towards us, and therefore, in return, "only a madman would say that he loved Zeus."[34] But since the time of Plato and Aristotle, "a light has shone in our sky,"[35] and all is new. The Platonist *epistrophe* has been succeeded by the Christian *metanoia,* something very different and far more fundamental.[36] The "beatific vision" is no longer the contemplation of a spectacle, but an intimate participation in the vision the Son has of the Father in the bosom of the Trinity.[37] Revelation, by making us know in his Son the God of love, the personal and trinitarian God, the creating and saving God, the God "who was made man to make us God," has changed everything.

Here we are faced with a whole new series of considerations and problems which, as I said at the beginning, it is impossible to deal with in the limits of this study. But I would like, in conclusion, to recall once again that revelation of love—not merely of the love of God, but of God who is love.

"God is simply the Lord. There is therefore nothing existing outside him which could result in anything approaching a 'destiny' imposed on him. He is also master of himself, and there is therefore no 'movement of being' within him which he is inwardly constrained to obey. God is absolutely free. . . . But he loves truly and really."[38] The ocean of being is the ocean of liberty. But (and this is not a "but" of modification) he is also the ocean of love. He is love, and it is by believing in love along with St. John the apostle that we gain some genuine understanding of

---

[33] *Metaphysics,* bk. 7, 1072 b.

[34] *Ethics,* 2, 11, 1208 b.

[35] Clement of Alexandria, *Protreptikos,* 11, 114, 1.

[36] Cf. Paul Aubin, S.J., *Le problème de la "conversion," étude sur un terme commun à l'hellénisme et au christianisme des trois premiers siècles* (1963).

[37] Cf. Ambrose Autpert, *In Apocalypsin,* bk. 10: "The Only-Begotten Son of God and mediator of God and man among men Christ Jesus sees the Father just as he is seen by the Father" (*Maxima Bibliotheca Patrum,* vol. 13, 649 A).

[38] Romano Guardini, "Le sérieux de l'amour divin," in *Dieu Vivant,* chapter 2, Eng. trans. *The Living God* (London, 1957). Cf. von Balthasar, *Liturgie cosmique* (Paris, 1947), p. 192, commenting on St. Maximus, on "that ultimate point of being where being and love coincide fully in liberty." See also his *Glaubhaft ist nur Liebe* (1963); Eng. trans. *Love Alone* (New York: Herder & Herder, 1968).

the divine liberty: "All the ends of the earth were in his hands, because they could not have existed from eternity but in his power: so once the key of love was opened by his hand, creatures came forth."[39] The relationship between man and God can never be conceived as being fundamentally governed by any natural law, or any necessity of any kind, interior or exterior. In the gift of himself that God wills to make, everything is explained—in so far as it *can* be explained[40]—by love, everything, hence including the consequent "desire" in our nature, in whatever way we understand that desire. For this reason, it is not very satisfactory to describe it as a *natural* desire, though "natural" seems the only term to use if we are to distinguish it from anything artificial or superficial, while at the same time avoiding any confusion with what is properly and positively supernatural. It might be useful to observe further that even the word "desire" or "appetite"—like "vision," "beatitude," and so many other terms used in religious and theological language[41]—must not be used without great care and precision. It has been traditional in theology for too long to be rejected without grave disadvantages, and too obviously human not to be spontaneously used here; but it is too heavily dependent on the ancient concept of "eros" and the theories of ancient physics not to give rise to certain misunderstandings. In this book I have tried, while giving such explanations as have seemed indispensable along the lines of the most authoritative theologians, primarily to stress the major permanent elements of the tradition itself, and to keep close to it both in language and teaching; I have therefore continually followed the authors I have quoted in speak-

281

282

[39] St. Thomas, *In 2 Sent.*, prologue.

[40] As Jules Lequier puts it: "In understanding that liberty is incomprehensible, you have understood all that can be understood about it" (*Oeuvres complètes*, 1952, p. 410).

[41] "Vision": see *supra*, p. 294, note 9. As for beatitude, as understood in Catholic theology, it is certainly something different from the simple "happiness" of current speech. It is true none the less that the doctors of the Church, and especially Augustine, could not in treating of it reject at the start the very ancient statement of the problem they had inherited from earlier thinkers: "Is man made for happiness? and in what does happiness consist?" There is undoubtedly something essential and therefore eternal in this way of putting the problem, and it would be going too far to reject, as some people seem to wish to, any kind of eudaemonism. However a certain amount of thinking remains to be done in order to highlight the double transformation: of ancient conceptions into the Christian conception, and of natural desire into disinterested love. "The supernatural vocation to grace infinitely surpasses the natural vocation to happiness, and fulfills it without destroying it" (Etienne Borne, "Du bonheur à la béatitude," *Revue de philosophie* [1935]: 450).

ing both of "desire" and of "nature."[42] Let us at least say that, if one is
not to weaken its meaning, it is important to remember that such a
"desire," even before the transformation which it must undergo in order
to attain its goal, is different in kind from all the desires of our common
experience. "Deny your desires," said St. John of the Cross, "and you
shall find what your heart desires."

It is equally important to get rid of any idea of a God who, though
free in theory, is basically morally determined by the perfection of a certain possible universe to create that universe. God is not subject to the
"reason of the best" as to any "determining reason."[43] His mind is not a
kind of reservoir in which all the combinations of the possible preexist,
as it were, before the real and "claim existence in proportion to their
perfections," competing among themselves until the one which is best
triumphs over all the rest.[44] This notion of modern rationalism, as sys-
283   tematized in the theories of Leibniz and Wolff,[45] turns creation into
something "like an analytical deduction."[46] It places in God, and somehow above him, a whole complex of objective essences forcing themselves upon his attention; while powerless of themselves to pass into the

---

[42] And the two terms are in strict correlation. Anselmian Augustinianism might perhaps offer a basis for a series of other explanations. Cf. St. Anselm, *Monologion*, c. 68:
"Therefore nothing was more patently made for this than the rational creature, as it loves
the highest essence above all, just as it is the highest good, nay rather as it loves nothing
but [the highest essence] or because of it. . . ."

[43] It is the first principle of Leibniz's "sufficient reason," the true principle of the
"determining reason," without which "nothing ever happens": *Theodicy*, I, 44; *Monadology*,
32; etc. And one may query "whether Leibniz does not completely transform [the idea of
what is objectively possible] in order to preserve its name. . . . In the ordinary sense of the
word, it was impossible that anything in the world should be other than it is, since the
actual choice of this world has in fact eternal reasons, and could not be different from
what it has been" (A. Lalande, *Vocabulaire de la Société française de philosophie*, on the
word "Possible"). The same criticism was made by Bayle, in *Réponse à un provincial*, ch.
165: "Thus he could only do what he did. Thus what has not happened or will never happen is strictly impossible." see also Fénelon's *Réfutation du système du P. Malebranche*,
chapter 6. On the other hand, cf. the distinctions made by Bonaventure, *In 1 Sent.*, dist.
44, art. 1, q. 1: "Whether God could have made a better world with respect to the substance of the constituent parts."

[44] Leibniz, *Principes de la nature et de la grâce fondés en raison*, n. 10; *Monadology*, n. 54
(Robinet ed., 1954, pp. 49, 103).

[45] Cf. Gilson, *L'être et l'essence* (Paris, 1948), pp. 182–83: according to Wolff it is not
absurd that God should depend upon himself, for that does not in any way impair his
freedom (*Theologia naturalis*, I, 339), etc.

[46] Gilson, *op. cit.*, p. 181.

actuality of real being, those essences weigh upon the Creator's decision at least "with a force of suggestion or a deductive attraction which
might well be called irresistible." One may note that Leibniz's God does
not, strictly speaking, abdicate "his independence when he pronounces
according to reason," since he is "himself sovereign reason";[47] none the
less, in this system, "if God chooses a given world because it is the best,
it is because that world has intrinsically more reason to exist; God's
choice is absorbed into the perfection of the thing that must exist
because it contains in itself all the reasons for existing."[48] But, however
reasonable the form it takes, such an idea must be demolished. God is
in no way governed by "prototypes." There is no idea within him prior to
his Word. He has no other "form," no other "reason for things" than
that Word, that unique Word, begotten by him. "From you is your likeness, the form of all."[49] The multiplicity of ideas is but the Logos
alone."[50] Though simply as exegesis Augustine's interpretation of the
first verses of John's Gospel may be doubtful, it none the less contains a
profound truth; it is still Platonist, but a Platonism transformed—as
Origen's was[51]—by the revelation of Christ. In the Word all is "reason";
all the "intelligible world" is concentrated in him—but the Word proceeds from the Father and lives in the bosom of the Father, "consubstantial" with him. When we say that God creates all things by his Word,
what we mean is that only God creates: "not only being, but also
essence itself is said to have been created." We must say it, and we can
do so without overstepping the bounds of reason precisely because we
believe that the Word is in God, and that the Word is God. "Behold how
God is truthful: not by participating in, but by generating truth"; this
was said not by Descartes, but St. Augustine.[52] Nor was it Descartes,
but St. Thomas who said: "Before having being, essence itself is noth-

284

[47] Jacques Jalabert, *Le Dieu de Leibniz* (1960), p. 221.
[48] M. Gueroult, *Les principes des indiscernables et de continuité chez Leibniz,* lecture given 1 March, 1962.
[49] St. Augustine, *Confessions,* bk. 12, n. 38 (Bibl. august., 14, p. 410). Cf. *De Trinitate,* bk. 4, c. 1, n. 3 (Bibl. august., 15, p. 342); *De diversis quaestionibus,* q. 46 (Bibl. august., pp. 122–28, 726–27, a note by G. Bardy, *Les idées dans la Pensée divine*).
[50] St. Maximus the Confessor, *Ambigua* (PG, 91, 1081 C).
[51] For whom "the world of Ideas is absorbed into the unity of Christ. Their multiplic-ity is transformed into a wealth of aspects (*ennai, epinoiai*)" (von Balthasar, *Parole et Mys-tère,* p. 122, note 26).
[52] *In Ioannem,* tract. 39, n. 8 (*CCL,* 36, 349).

ing, except perhaps in the intellect of the creator where it is not a creature, but the creating essence."[53]

In other words, there are no eternal essences endowed with some
kind of "essential existence" until, by the creative act, they pass into
"actual existence." In God there is only God:

> Nothing in God but God
> No cause but He
> Who creates causality.
>
> Nil in Deo praeter Deum:
> Nulla causa praeter eum
> Qui creat causalia.[54]

To represent what might have been is a device indispensable and well-
founded, and therefore doubly legitimate, to help us realize both the
intelligibility of the world and the freedom in which it was created. But
if it is taken too seriously, it can defeat its end and become a kind of
"myth,"[55] than which nothing could be more contrary to Christian phi-

285   losophy. For such philosophy will no more allow the slightest moral
necessity to influence God's action than it will any metaphysical necessity:[56] "It is impossible for God to act out of natural necessity [or even]
out of some moral necessity."[57] It will always refuse to postulate any
kind of "forces preexisting before the divine will."[58] It will always—
which is really saying the same thing—refuse to assign any form of
cause to the divine will: the cause of willing in God is "his own will."[59]

[53] St. Thomas, *De Potentia*, q. 3, art. 5: "Whether there could exist something that has
not been created by God," ad 2um.

[54] Adam of St. Victor (?), *Hymn for the feast of the Trinity*, Poitiers breviary (J. M. Neale,
Sequentiae ex missalibus [1952], p. 64). St. Bernard, *De consideratione*, bk. 5, c. 7, n. 15:
"There is therefore nothing in God but God" (*Opera*, ed. J. Leclercq, vol. 3, p. 479; *contra*
Gilbert of la Porrée).

[55] Jules Lachelier, *Vocabulaire de la soc. fr. de phil.*, art "Origine." Cf. Jean Trouillard,
"Le Cosmos du Pseudo-Denys," *Revue de théol. et de phil.* (1955), p. 55: ". . . without one
having to suppose in God a heaven of possibilities and norms logically anterior to the
creative act as would have to be the case with ourselves."

[56] See J. Maréchal, *Le point de départ de la métaphysique*, vol. 5 (1926), p. 178. As
against this, Leibniz, *La cause de Dieu . . .*, n. 21: liberty "excludes metaphysical necessity
. . . ; but it does not exclude moral necessity. . . ."

[57] St. Thomas, *De Potentia*, q. 1, art 5.

[58] Blondel, *La philosophie et l'esprit chrétien*, p. 45.

[59] St. Thomas, *Prima*, q. 19, art. 5; or *Summa contra Gentiles*, bk. 1, c. 87: his "cause of

"Whatever has appeared done by the Word visibly in time, was in existence before all time in the will of the Word creating:"[60] If we go on to divide being into possible and necessary being, we must not forget that these very distinctions draw their origin "from the divine will itself."[61] "All necessity and impossibility is subject to his Will."[62]

But if we are to remain completely faithful to this spirit of Christian philosophy, there is another pitfall to be avoided. Just as we must exclude the notion of a will moved by a "sufficient reason," so we must also exclude that of a good which is of its nature diffused as the rays of the sun are diffused, as one Platonist tradition has it,[63] or as "the sun of the knowledge of the Buddha illuminates the whole dharma-dhatu."[64] "The good that diffuses itself" [*Bonum diffusivum sui*]: this axiom, related to the Platonist adage concerning the good which is above all desire,[65] seems only to have been formulated late in the Latin middle ages—when it was constantly quoted as being authoritative. It can be understood in various ways. Pseudo-Denys did not apparently "suspect the difficulties" that such an idea "might present to Christian thought."[66] St. Thomas had no more scruple than many others in making use of the now classic metaphor,[67] just as St. Augustine saw nothing

286

---

willing" [*causa volendi*] is "his willing himself" [*ipsum suum velle*]; one must also remember "that one cannot posit any process of understanding [*discursus*] in the will of God." Cf. *De Potentia*, q. 3, art. 15, ad 14um. St. Anselm, *Cur Deus homo*, bk. 2, c. 17 and c. 5.

[60] Ambrose Autpert, *In Apocalypsin*, bk. 2 (*loc. cit.*, vol. 13, p. 469 F). Scotus Erigena, *De divisione naturae*, bk. 2, c. 2, 21; bk. 3, c. 9 (*PL*, 122, col. 529, 561–62, 642).

[61] St. Thomas, *In Perihermen.*, 1, 14: "But there are differences of being [*entis*] possible and necessary, and therefore necessity and contingency in things take their origin in the very will of God . . . , just as from the first cause, which transcends the order of necessity and contingency."

[62] St. Anselm, *Meditatio* 11: "Just as no necessity or impossibility precedes his willing or not willing [*velle aut nolle*], likewise his creating or not creating. . . ."

[63] Plato, *Republic*, bk. 6, 517 b. Plotinus, *Enneads*, I, 6, 9.

[64] *Avatamska*. Cf. Paul Demiéville, *Le concile de Lhasa*, vol. 1 (1952), p. 95, note 1.

[65] *Timaeus*, 29 c.

[66] Joseph de Finance, S.J., *Existence et liberté*, p. 19. Denys, *De divinis nominibus*, c. 4, n. 1, 4. Cf. V. Lossky, *Théologie négative et connaissance de Dieu chez Maître Eckhart* (1960), p. 63, note 90: "The formula *bonum est diffusivum sui*, which the theologians of the Latin middle ages quote as an authority taken from Denys, does not belong to the author of Denys' work. It does however sum up fairly satisfactorily one aspect of Denys' thought: good by his essence, God pours out the rays of his goodness like the sun which gives light by the very fact of existing. . . . This in no way implies that Denys holds any automatism in creation. . . ."

[67] *In 2 Sent.*, prologue. On the creative expansion of the good according to the school of Chartres: J. M. Parent, *La doctrine de la création dans l'École de Chartres* (1938), pp.

wrong in using the metaphor of the sun to describe the illumination of
men by Christ, "the light of the world";[68] but he could when necessary
recall that it was no more than a metaphor, that it illustrated only one
aspect of the truth[69]—although it might in fact be a most useful comparison in demolishing the opposite, imaginative view whereby the
ideas of divine liberty, the supernatural and grace were bound up with a
notion of narrowness, particularism or arbitrariness.[70]

    One must, *a fortiori*, be careful to correct—if not wholly to avoid—
the neo-Platonist metaphors of flux, of gushing, of "effluence," of ema-
nation, of soaking into things. God is not, as one might think from
some Platonist expressions also taken up by Denys, a generosity pour-
ing himself out;[71] it is at best inadequate to see him simply as that "fundamental generosity" which must mean, for the Absolute, simply the
fact of being essentially communicable;[72] or that kind of generosity
which is no more than a de-sacralized charity. Those who, in order to
avoid "contingentist theories" which might tend to anthropomorphism,

287

59–68. On the axiom, *bonum diffusivum sui,* and its implications for St. Thomas: T. A.
Audet, "Approches historiques de la Summa Theologiae" in *Etudes d'histoire littéraire et
doctrinale,* Institute of Medieval Studies, Montreal, 17 (1962), pp. 9–29. St. Augustine
made similar use of Platonist formulas about creation. Cf. Jean Baptiste Du Roy, in
Recherches augustiniennes 2 (1962): 443, note 114.

    [68] *In Ioannem,* tract. 34, nn. 2–4 (*CCL,* 36, pp. 311–13).

    [69] *De Potentia,* q. 3, a. 15, ad 1um: "The simile of Dionysius is intelligible as far as con-
cerns the universality of diffusion . . . , but it is not intelligible as far as concerns the depri-
vation of will." *Prima,* q. 19, a. 4, ad 1um; q. 24, a. 4, ad 1um. *De veritate,* q. 10, a. 7, ad
10um: ". . . just as is manifest of the sunbeam, by which all things in the lower sphere are
caused and renewed; and to this extent it is comparable to divine goodness which causes
all things, as says Dionysius." *In de divinis nominibus,* c. 14, lectio 1. Cf. J. Durantel, *Saint
Thomas et le Pseudo-Denys,* p. 138. Similar remarks could be made on the subject of the
"*agathothētos hyperbolē*" which, according to St. John Damascene, moves God to make
himself shared: *De fide orthodoxa,* bk. 2, c. 2 (*PG,* 94, 846).

    [70] Cf. Ruysbroeck, *The Adornment of the Spiritual Marriage,* bk. 2, c. 66: "Divine grace
is to God what rays are to the sun."

    [71] Pseudo-Denys, *De divinis nominibus,* c. 1, 3: "He is . . . the generous fount of all
life. . . ." St. Bonaventure, *Itinerarium mentis in Deum,* c. 6: "The highest good therefore,
most highly diffuses itself. . . . The instantaneous [*ex tempore*] diffusion in the creature
cannot but be centered in a point with respect to the immensity of eternal goodness." St.
Ignatius Loyola, *Spiritual Exercises,* the contemplation *ad amorem:* All beings flow from
God "as rays flow from the sun, as waters flow from the spring" (no. 237); and *Story of a
Pilgrim,* n. 29: "One day he pictured in his mind the way in which God had created the
world; he seemed to see something white, with rays coming out of it, and God sending
out light from it."

    [72] Joseph de Finance, *Existence et liberté,* p. 175.

accept rather too readily Platonist or Plotinian theories as if despairing in advance of purifying any personalist theory by the laws of analogy, are in danger of steering from Charybdis on to Scylla.[73] No theory will dispense with the need for correction by analogy. It is very true however, as Jean Trouillard reminds us, that anthropomorphic representations of choice, indifference and contingency "do not overlap with those of gift, grace and gratuitousness."[74] Nor is it a matter of carrying them over bodily, as it were, into God. But these notions of gift, of grace, of gratuitousness, as they come to us from the Christian faith, do not seem to me to be identifiable with the ideas we find in the ancient philosophies either, at least without modification. I would not, for instance, be too eager to speak of God as a wave flowing over us, or a light glowing. Nor would I say with Simone Weil that "God loves . . . as an emerald is green."[75] We must recognize that such language is ambiguous to say the least. God's goodness—"goodness, that supremely august word!"[76]—is a "willed goodness," a goodness which is also benignity. God is love in person, love which freely, and not because of any law or inner determination, creates the being to whom he wills to give himself, and gives himself freely. "Not that neutral *bonum,* but that living flame of charity: *Bonus.*"[77] "That brilliance, by which God is seen face to face, is not of nature, but of condescension and grace."[78]

288

---

[73] Cf. Louis Millet, *Le symbolisme dans la philosophie de Lachelier* (1959), p. 191.

[74] *La procession plotinienne* (1955), p. 79.

[75] *La connaissance surnaturelle,* p. 77: "God loves, not as I love, but as an emerald is green. He is 'I love.' And I too, if I were in the state of perfection, would love as an emerald is green." It seems to me however that here it is simply that the language does not do justice to the thought.

[76] St. Maximus, commentary on the *De divinis nominibus,* 13 (*PG,* 4, 413 C).

[77] Blondel, in *L'itinéraire philosophique de Maurice Blondel,* by Frédéric Lefèvre (1928), p. 238. St. Augustine, *Confessions,* bk. 13, c. 2: "For of the plenitude of your goodness your creature subsists." Cf. Victor Goldschmidt, *La religion de Platon,* pp. 55–56: "The 'goodness' exempt from all envy of the Demiurge must not be interpreted at its face value as goodwill, nor *a fortiori* as an outpouring of love. It is the goodness of a good workman, so to say: the pleasure in work well done. But it can happen that that work does good to the matter which is its object and the universe which results from it. Every good workman always has in view the good of what he is making or tending (*Republic,* I, 342 c). But in that too, the idea of good will is secondary: the doctor is working for the good of the patient, but it is not necessarily out of love that he is doing so. . . ." It may be added that the Demiurge of the *Timaeus* still leaves us in the anthropomorphism of myth.

[78] St. Bonaventure, *In 2 Sent.,* dist. 3, p. 2, art. 3. St. Augustine, *De Genesi ad litteram,* bk. 1, n. 11: "In God there is the highest, holy and just goodness; and in fact love coming into its works not from indigence but from beneficence." Cf. St. Thomas, *De Potentia,*

289   Our God is "a living God, ever new, ever in the state of being an explosion and a source, subject to no necessity arising out of that creation which he brought from nothing, a God for ever inventing the heaven in which he dwells, and whose next move we can never foresee."[79] He is "a God who surpasses the capacity of any desire."[80] He is a God of whom it would be blasphemy and madness to suppose that any demand of any order whatsoever could be forced upon him, in whatever hypothetical situation one may mentally place oneself, or whatever concrete situation one may imagine creatures to be in. A God of whom one can, and indeed must always say that he need not have given himself, and could still not give himself to his creatures. "Nothing, then, limits the sovereign independence of God who gives himself."[81] It was Anselm—the doctor who developed most fully in Christian thinking the structuring of intelligible connections and the use of necessary reasons—who said: "His will operates only in him. No necessity precedes his will."[82]

Let us say it once more in conclusion: God could have refused to give himself to his creatures, just as he could have, and has, given himself. The gratuitousness of the supernatural order is true individually and totally. It is gratuitous in itself. It is gratuitous as far as each one of us is concerned. It is gratuitous in regard to what we see as preceding it, whether in time or in logic. Further—and this is what some of the explanations I have contested seem to me not to make clear—its gratuitousness remains always complete. It remains gratuitous in every hypothesis. It is for ever new. It remains gratuitous at every stage of

290   preparation for the gift, and at every stage of the giving of it. No "dis-

---

q. 3, art. 15, ad 14um, of which Père L. B. Geiger rightly says: "The strict technicality of his terms is more eloquent to those who read them aright, than the most inflamed outbursts" (*La Participation . . .*[2], p. 102, note).

[79] Claudel, in *Correspondant* (September 1921), p. 802.

[80] Ruysbroeck, *The Adornment of the Spiritual Marriage*, vol. 2, c. 53, p. 157.

[81] *Le Surnaturel*, p. 494.

[82] *Cur Deus homo*, bk. 2, c. 17: "No necessity or impossibility precedes his willing or not willing [*velle aut nolle*]. . . . Know that all that he himself willed existed from necessity . . ." (Sources chrétiennes, 91, pp. 426–36). Cf. *De veritate*, c. 10: "All things are indebted to him; but the highest truth itself owes nothing to anything; and what is, is for no other reason than why it is." Compare Augustine, *De Genesi ad litteram*, bk. 6, c. 15, n. 26: ". . . his will is the necessity of things" (*PL*, 34, 350). St. Francis of Sales was to say of all divine calls: "God is himself obliged by himself, urged and provoked to do this by the stirrings of his infinite goodness and mercy" (*Entretiens spirituels*, 18, Annecy ed., p. 388).

position" in creatures can ever, in any way, bind the Creator.[83] And here we may happily record the substantial agreement not only between St. Augustine and St. Thomas, and other early writers, but also between St. Thomas and his commentators, from Cajetan onwards, as well as the theologians of our own day, however they may differ in their attempts to explain *how* the supernatural gift can never become part of our nature,[84] how supernatural beatitude can never become for us, in any situation, whether real or even conceivable, a goal that is "necessary and due."[85] But also, as Malevez wrote not long ago at the conclusion of a study which I particularly value for its penetration and good will, "the stage of pure nature is infallibly surpassed by the fullness of creative love."[86] "Out of the great love with which he loved us. . . ."[87]

> Why do we break out into so many sermons on this topic in vain, and multiply so many eloquent speeches to no avail and chatter into so great a crowd of words?

More than one reader may wonder about this, as he glances through this book. Certainly the author has wondered about it quite often. The quotation is from a medieval disciple of St. Augustine and St. Thomas[88] who was questioning himself one day about this very subject.

291

The answer is to be found in the nature of our intellect: we cannot receive divine revelation without at once starting to ask questions, one leading on to another. We can only try to answer them. But in our necessarily groping explanations, however far we seem to go, we know that we can never arrive at the *terra incognita* itself. These are only the detours by which we try to come back to that simpler and richer fact which first sent us farther on our journey. I hope that amid so many detours we have not lost sight of the central truth which it has been my whole purpose to illuminate. My eyes have remained constantly fixed upon that "outline of the summit"[89] traced for us in Scripture:

---

[83] Eudes Rigaud, *Quaestiones disputatae de gratia:* "And disposition in the creature in no way compels the creator himself" (Dhont, *op. cit.,* p. 178; cf. p. 176).

[84] Cf. Cajetan, *In Secundum Secundae,* q. 23, art 2, n. 4: "Charity is such an accidental form that it can be connatural with no made, or makeable, creature, but only with the divine substance."

[85] Cf. J. de Finance, *Etre et agir dans la philosophie de saint Thomas,* p. 343.

[86] "L'esprit et le désir de voir Dieu," *loc. cit.,* p. 31.

[87] Eph 2:4. Cf. von Balthasar, *Prayer* (London, 1961), French trans. *La prière contemplative,* p. 136: "Nothing is as free as love; and apart from love there is no liberty."

[88] Giles of Rome, *In 2 Sent.,* dist. 32, q. 2, art. 1 (Venice, 1581), p. 466.

[89] Gustave Martelet, S.J., "Sur le motif de l'Incarnation" in *Problèmes actuels de christologie* (1965), p. 79.

Blessed be the God and Father of our Lord Jesus Christ, who . . . chose us in him . . . that we should be holy and blameless before him. He destined us in love to be his sons through Jesus Christ, according to the purpose of his will, to the praise of his glorious grace which he freely bestowed on us in the beloved.[90]

[90] Eph 1:3–6. Cf. the wonderful first chapter of Richard of St. Victor's *Liber exceptionum* (Châtillon ed., 1958, p. 104): "God, the highest good and immutable good, knowing that his beatitude can be communicated and wholly diminished, made the rational creature in order to make it a partaker of his beatitude. . . ." Von Balthasar, *Phénoménologie de la verité* (Fr. trans., 1952, p. 260): "Since love is the decisive reality, the seraphim cover their face with their wings, for the mystery of eternal love is such in its inner essence that its night, in the excess of its light, can only be glorified in adoration."

Index

OF RELATED INTEREST

Karl Rahner
THE TRINITY
A ground-breaking treatment of the doctrine of the Trinity.
0-8245-1627-3; $18.95 paperback

Johann Adam Möhler
SYMBOLISM:
EXPOSITION OF THE DOCTRINAL DIFFERENCES BETWEEN CATHOLICS AND PROTESTANTS AS EVIDENCED BY THEIR SYMBOLICAL WRITINGS
The magnum opus of one of the fathers of modern Catholic theology.
0-8245-1665-6; $29.95 paperback

Karl Adam
THE SPIRIT OF CATHOLICISM
A brilliant and widely influential reflection on the fundamental nature of the Catholic faith and the Catholic Church.
0-8245-1718-0; $19.95 paperback

Yves Congar
I BELIEVE IN THE HOLY SPIRIT
Congar's magisterial treatise on the Holy Spirit, now available in a single volume.
0-8245-1696-6; $29.95 paperback

At your bookstore, or to order directly from the publisher, please send check or money order (including $3.00 for the first book plus $1.00 for each additional book) to:

THE CROSSROAD PUBLISHING COMPANY
370 LEXINGTON AVENUE, NEW YORK, NY 10017

We hope you enjoyed The Mystery of the Supernatural. *Thank you for reading it.*

crossroad
herder